CW01184852

ERASMUS'S
LIFE of ORIGEN

ERASMUS'S
LIFE *of* ORIGEN

A New Annotated Translation of
the Prefaces to Erasmus of Rotterdam's
Edition of Origen's Writings (1536)

TRANSLATED WITH COMMENTARY BY
THOMAS P. SCHECK

Foreword by Richard L. DeMolen

The Catholic University of America Press
Washington, D.C.

Copyright © 2016
The Catholic University of America Press
All rights reserved
The paper used in this publication meets the minimum requirements of
American National Standards for Information Science—Permanence
of Paper for Printed Library Materials, ANSI Z39.48-1984.
∞

Cataloging-in-Publication Data available from the Library of Congress
ISBN 978-0-8132-2801-3

To Fr. David Robinson, SJ, of Ave Maria University

CONTENTS

Abbreviations   ix

Foreword by Richard L. DeMolen   xi

Author's Preface   xv

Introduction   xxix

1. Erasmus's Program for Theological Renewal   1

2. Introduction to Origen   43

3. Origen's Legacy in the Catholic Exegetical Tradition   71

4. Erasmus's Reception of Origen   99

5. Erasmus's Prefaces   138

Appendix: Sixteenth-Century Assessments of Erasmus   187

Selected Bibliography   217

Index   227

ABBREVIATIONS

ACW	Ancient Christian Writers
ANF	Ante-Nicene Fathers
ASD	Opera omnia Desiderii Erasmi Roterodami
CE	Contemporaries of Erasmus
CSEL	Corpus Scriptorum Ecclesiasticorum Latinorum
CT	Concilium Tridentinum, Diariorum, Actorum, Epistularum, Tractatuum nova collectio
CW	The Complete Works of St. Thomas More
CWE	Collected Works of Erasmus
DCB	A Dictionary of Christian Biography
DS	Compendium of Creeds, Definitions, and Declarations on Matters of Faith and Morals (Denzinger)
EEC	Encyclopedia of the Early Church
FOTC	Fathers of the Church
GCS	Die griechischen christlichen Schriftsteller der ersten drei Jahrhunderte
HE	Historia Ecclesiastica (Eusebius)
JECS	Journal of Early Christian Studies

ABBREVIATIONS

JTS	Journal of Theological Studies
LB	Desiderii Erasmi Roterodami Opera Omnia
LCC	Library of Christian Classics
LW	Luther's Works
NPNF1	Nicene and Post-Nicene Fathers: First Series
NPNF2	Nicene and Post-Nicene Fathers: Second Series
PG	Patrologiae Cursus Completus: Series Graeca
PL	Patrologiae Cursus Completus: Series Latina
SC	Sources chrétiennes
WA	Luthers Werke

FOREWORD

At long last Thomas P. Scheck offers us a lucid presentation of two priest-scholars who lived thirteen hundred years apart and strove to promote orthodoxy and to combat heresy with courage and persuasion. The third-century Origen of Alexandria served as a role model for the sixteenth-century Erasmus of Rotterdam. In their pursuit of truth they focused attention on sacred scripture and sacred tradition.

Erasmus's *Life of Origen* (1536) underscores the heroic virtues of this Church Father. He opines that Origen was a saint who is worthy of emulation, even though both contemporary and subsequent critics have accused him of maintaining unorthodox positions. Again and again, Erasmus insisted that Origen was an outstanding exegete and teacher of classical literature, who interpreted sacred scripture tentatively rather than authoritatively. In the face of hostile criticism, Erasmus admired Origen's steadfast humility. He was above all a life-giving homilist, catechist, and apologist in the early church. He so impressed Erasmus that the prince of humanists adopted a reform program that placed the imitation of Christ at its center. Despite Origen's accomplishments, his works were vigorously condemned by the Fifth Ecumenical Council in 553. As a result only a fraction of his writings has survived the onslaught.

Furthermore Dr. Scheck points out that Origen's critics in the sixteenth century were equally vituperative. Leading Catholics such as Noël Béda and Jacob Latomus as well as such Protestant spokesmen as Martin Luther and Philipp Melanchthon accused him of promoting "poisonous doctrine." In contrast, Erasmus maintained that church doctrines before the Council of Nicaea (325) were mercurial in nature. Their very fluidity led to both praise and blame in subsequent generations. He argued that several canonized Church

Fathers, including Athanasius, Augustine, Basil the Great, John Chrysostom, Cyprian, Irenaeus, and Jerome, had promoted positions that would later be regarded as unorthodox in the 1520s and 1530s. On the other hand, the twentieth-century French cardinal and theologian Henri de Lubac concluded in 1964 that Origen was an obedient child of the church because his intentions counted for something in the midst of his forthrightness. Erasmus's two-volume edition of Origen's writings was the last of his published works. It appeared posthumously in September 1536, two months after his death. His prefaces manifest a laudatory appreciation of Origen, hailing him as an "outstanding doctor of the Catholic Church."

Origen of Alexandria was a diocesan priest who had been ordained in Palestine by the local bishops so that he could preach officially in the name of the church. He was distinguished for his learning and eloquence—speaking in a conversational manner and applying scriptural passages (both old and new) to the lives of his listeners. Origen lived well before religious orders of men were formed. By the time of the sixteenth century, there were four major groups of religious life in the church. The oldest of the religious orders in the west were the canons regular of Augustine, who were founded in the fifth century, and consisted of various offshoots—all of whom followed the rule of Augustine, which promoted a life of love, community service, and obedience. Erasmus was a member of this order since his adolescence and remained as such throughout his life. He was ordained to the priesthood in 1492. As I have demonstrated elsewhere, Erasmus received papal permission to live outside the houses of this order and to wear a modified form of the canon's white habit under that of the black soutane of a secular priest.

Following the establishment of the canons regular, orders of monks appeared, following the rule of Benedict which was composed in the sixth century. The rule of Benedict is distinct from that of Anthony of Egypt, who is regarded as the founder of eastern monasticism in the fourth century. The third group of religious orders was the mendicant friars who emerged in the thirteenth century. They included Franciscans, Dominicans, Carmelites, and Augustinian Hermits (to whom belonged Martin Luther). These four orders of friars developed their distinctive rules and religious garb. The fourth religious order were clerics regular, among whom are found the Theatines, the Barnabites, the Somaschi, and so forth. Technically, the Society of Jesus (or Jesuits) is part of the clerics regular. Erasmus was therefore never a monk in the formal sense, since he followed the rule of Augustine. He guarded his independence and devoted his genius to scriptural studies and scholarly editions of the Church Fathers. He saw these efforts as the means to combat the teachings of Protestant divines.

In the appendix, Dr. Scheck quotes Bishop Friedrich Nausea (1490–1552) of Vienna, who lauded Erasmus as the most brilliant ornament of the Catholic church and expressed his hope that Erasmus would soon belong to the number of canonized saints. I believe that this was also the intention of the author of this *tour de force*. I highly recommend Dr. Scheck's groundbreaking contribution to patristic and Reformation studies. I am also convinced that it will ruffle the feathers of some readers who have distanced themselves from these two remarkable men, because they misunderstand what John Henry Cardinal Newman calls "the development of Christian Doctrine" in 1845. Newman opines: "The great Origen after his many labors died in peace; his immediate pupils were Saints and rulers in the Church; he has the praise of St. Athanasius, St. Basil, and St. Gregory Nazianzen." What more can Origen expect from mortal men than to have the praises of holy men throughout the centuries?

Richard L. DeMolen
Founder of the Erasmus of Rotterdam Society (1980)
Editor-in-chief of *The Erasmus of Rotterdam Society Yearbook* (1981–93)

AUTHOR'S PREFACE

Erasmus of Rotterdam (1466–1536) has been a greatly misunderstood figure in the history of Catholic theology. That at least is the opinion of the French theologian and cardinal, Henri de Lubac (1896–1991), who in his memoir summarized the aims of a section of his *magnum opus*—*Medieval Exegesis, Part IV*—in which he had surveyed Renaissance humanism by saying:

> I tried to show through a number of topical examples, as I had already done in lesser proportions for Erasmus ... that even the most serious historians of humanism and the Renaissance, for the reasons I stated, were not able really to understand the great Christian humanists. But there are certain currents of opinion in the intellectual world that it would be illusory to hope to turn around.[1]

One who admires Renaissance humanism might despair upon reading the last sentence. It seems that certain prejudices against Erasmus and other Renaissance humanists are so deeply engrained in the academic and religious culture that they appear impossible to challenge. However, in a footnote to this passage, de Lubac offers a ray of hope: "Yet, through his long thesis on the *Ratio verae theologiae* of Erasmus, Father Georges Chantraine seems to have won the game, at least with respect to some." The work in question is G. Chantraine's *Mystère et Philosophie du Christ selon Erasmus* (Gembloux: Duculot, 1971), which I will engage in the course of this book.[2] It is encouraging to hear de Lubac say that Chaintraine's defense of Erasmus has won out in

---

1. Henri de Lubac, *At the Service of the Church: Henri de Lubac Reflects on the Circumstances that Occasioned His Writings*, trans. Anne E. Englund (San Francisco, Calif.: Ignatius, 1993), 139.

2. De Lubac wrote a preface for this work: *Theology in History, Part One: The Light of Christ. Part Two: Disputed Questions and Resistance to Nazism*, trans. A. E. Nash (San Francisco, Calif.: Ignatius, 1996), 44–48.

France, "at least with respect to some." From what I can tell, its impact in this country is still minimal.

The gist of de Lubac's observation is that many Catholic historians in the late nineteenth and early twentieth century have portrayed the Renaissance humanists in a false light. It is not difficult to illustrate the kinds of prejudices de Lubac is speaking of. Joseph Sauer in his 1917 *Catholic Encyclopedia* article on "Desiderius Erasmus" depicts Erasmus as a cold-blooded, poisonous, subversive, religiously indifferent, rationalistic, paganizing, and, above all, egotistical scholar. According to Sauer, Erasmus's inborn vanity increased over time almost to the point of becoming a disease. In exegesis, Sauer says, Erasmus favored a cold rationalism and treated the biblical narratives like pagan myths. Erasmus's "philosophy of Christ" was allegedly a purely natural ethical ideal guided by human sagacity (without any reference to Jesus Christ). Erasmus allegedly taught that the interpretation of scripture should be left to the individual's private judgment (implying that Erasmus rejected all dogma and repudiated the magisterium of the Catholic church). The straw man, or rather, the demon depicted in this essay is Erasmus the proto-modernist, Erasmus the free-thinking Protestant liberal, Erasmus the Voltairean skeptic and mocker of religion.

A similar hatred of Erasmus is exhibited by the German church historian Joseph Lortz, whose influence in twentieth-century ecclesiastical historiography was enormous. I acknowledge that Lortz was profoundly learned and strikingly more tolerant than preceding generations of Catholic historians of the Reformation. But the toleration and respect he showed to Luther dried up when it came to assessing Erasmus fairly. For according to Lortz, Erasmus was "the antithesis of the Christian."[3] Indeed, he was "profoundly unchristian. He is adogmatic. He has no more concept of dogma as an exact statement of Christian teaching than did the men of the Enlightenment or modern liberal Protestants."[4] No one who has read Erasmus's *Explanation of the Creed* could possibly agree with Lortz. In that work Erasmus surpasses the dogmatism even of the *Roman Catechism*, especially in the section on Christology.[5] But it seems unlikely that Lortz ever read Erasmus's *Catechism*. Biased portraits like these, based on ignorance, show clearly that such scholars have

---

3. *The Reformation: A Problem for Today*, trans. John C. Dwyer, SJ (Westminster, Md.: The Newman Press, 1964), 71.

4. Ibid.

5. The Catechism in question is Erasmus's *Explanation of the Creed* (1533). It is found in English translation in Desiderius Erasmus, *Spiritualia and Pastoralia*, ed. John W. O'Malley, *Collected Works of Erasmus* 70 (Toronto: University of Toronto Press, 1998) [hereafter "CWE"].

not formed their judgments by the careful study of Erasmus's writings, but have simply cobbled together pieces of slander based on hearsay and "headlines" that had been recorded by previous writers.[6] During his own lifetime Erasmus defended himself against one rabid attack from a Catholic scholar named Alberto Pio in these words: "From all this it is clear what it means not to read what you are criticizing, what it means to put together a dangerous slander from the notecards of your employees, what it means to weave together a patchwork accusation from small fragments broken off from here and there."[7] At the end of chapter 1, I show that Yves Congar's damning criticisms of Erasmus repeat accusations that were actually refuted by Erasmus himself in his controversy with Alberto Pio and in his reply to the Paris theologians. The charge of vanity and egotism is particularly offensive, since people who knew Erasmus and lived with him, such as Thomas More and Beatus Rhenanus, said that he was a very humble person, to the point of being self-effacing and overly compliant.[8]

Many devout Catholics I have encountered have been influenced by these sorts of prejudices and regard Erasmus with suspicion. Some express shock that any genuinely Catholic scholar could admire him. I am referring not merely to lay Catholics, but to seminary-trained priests and to scholars with doctorates even from Roman universities. When I inquire into the specific reasons for their suspicions and the particular works of Erasmus that have caused offense, often I find that Erasmus's critics are not actually familiar with his works (let alone with his patristic editions). Rather, there are eerie reminiscences from a high school religion class, a seminary or Western Civilization course, that Erasmus was an aloof rationalist and a religious skeptic. There are vague rumors about Erasmus's mockery of certain abuses that existed in the church of his day, his jokes about weird scholastic terminology and frivolous questions, his wisecrack (spoken in response to Luther's defamation of the Catholic church), that he (Erasmus) would continue to "put up" with the Catholic church, and the Catholic church would have to

---

6. Lortz's attacks on Erasmus have been coherently silenced by C. J. De Vogel, "Erasmus and His Attitude towards Church Dogma," in J. Coppens, ed., *Scrinium Erasmianum*, 2 vols. (Leiden: Brill, 1969), 2:101–32. For very interesting studies of Lortz's own Christian faith, see M. B. Lukens, "Joseph Lortz and a Catholic Accomodation with National Socialism," in *Betrayal: German Churches and the Holocaust*, ed. R. P. Ericksen and S. Heschel (Minneapolis, Minn.: Fortress, 1999), 149–68; R. Krieg, *Catholic Theologians in Nazi Germany* (New York: Continuum, 2004), chap. 3.

7. *Controversy with Alberto Pio* (CWE 84:283).

8. For more on Beatus Rhenanus and his *Life of Erasmus*, see the important article by K. Enenkel, "Beatus Rhenanus' Second Vita Erasmi (1540)," in *The Reception of Erasmus in the Early Modern Period*, ed. K. Enenkel (Leiden: Brill, 2013), 25–40.

keep "putting up" with him.[9] Moreover there is the cloudy memory that a pope, once upon a time, completely condemned his writings by placing them on the Index of Prohibited Books. This last point is true, and I will discuss it in the appendix; but for now I will say that these same devout Catholics tend to forget that a pope once condemned the writings of Thomas Aquinas, and that Dante's name stood directly above Erasmus's on the Index, along with all vernacular translations of the Bible.[10] To fall afoul with a pope, or to have one's writings placed on an Index does not necessarily imperil one's orthodoxy, as I will also discuss in the appendix.[11]

In his defense of Erasmus against some of his modern detractors, de Lubac called attention to Erasmus's remarkable production in the field of patristic studies. Between 1516 and 1536 Erasmus edited at least twelve complete editions of the writings of the Greek and Latin Church Fathers: Jerome (1516),

---

9. The source is *Hyperaspistes* I (CWE 76:117): "As for seeming, as you say, to sail between Scylla and Charybdis, I have nothing to answer unless you declare which church you call Scylla and which Charybdis. From the Catholic Church I have never departed. I have never had the least inclination to enlist in your church—so little, in fact, that, though I have been very unlucky in many other ways, in one respect I consider myself lucky indeed, namely that I have steadfastly kept my distance from your league. I know that in the church which you call papistical there are many with whom I am not pleased, but I see such persons also in your church. But it is easier to put up with evils to which you are accustomed. Therefore I will put up with this church until I see a better one, and it will have to put up with me until I become better. And surely a person does not sail infelicitously if he holds a middle course between two evils." For a sound interpretation of this passage that debunks Renaudet's grotesque distortion of Erasmus's intentions, see Louis Bouyer, *Erasmus and His Times*, trans. Francis X. Murphy (London: Newman Press, 1959), 146.

10. See G. A. McCool, *The Neo-Thomists* (Milwaukee, Wis.: Marquette University Press, 2003), 7.

11. I also am becoming more and more convinced that many people derive their assessment of Erasmus's character and beliefs simply from staring too long at Hans Holbein's famous portrait of him sitting at his writer's desk, with pursed lips, clothed in robes of velvety softness. Fr. Stanley Jaki, for example, claims that Dürer's and Holbein's paintings "give him away as one who tries to hide something." This leads Jaki to conclude that Erasmus secretly must have been an atheist. See Stanley Jaki's introduction to Christopher Hollis, *Erasmus* (Pinckney, Mich.: American Council on Economics and Society, 1997), vii. In a similar way J. Huizinga and J. Lortz both spoke of the "velvet softness" of Erasmus's character, apparently reflecting on his overcoat. Yet there was nothing soft about Erasmus's life, which was hard and characterized by chronic physical suffering and self-sacrifice. He endured the agony of kidney stones for most of his life and endured these horrendously painful sufferings repeatedly with fortitude and steadfast faith in God's goodness. He slept little, ate in moderation, and worked extremely hard until the very end of his life. Moreover, if a man's character and religious thought is to be assessed from a painting, rather than from his writings, what shall we conclude about Thomas More's character from Holbein's painting of him? It displays a man wearing even softer clothing, with a silkier sheen. Yet More is not usually depicted in effeminate terms.

Cyprian (1520), Arnobius (1522), Hilary (1523), John Chrysostom (1525), Irenaeus (1526), Athanasius (1527), Ambrose (1527), Faustus of Riez (1528), Augustine (1529), Gregory Nazianzen (1531), Basil (1532), and Origen (1536).[12] De Lubac said that a person "would have to be blind not to see that nothing was less affected, nothing more sincere than Erasmus's enthusiasm for the Fathers. He loves to love them; he literally lives with them."[13] Who are these blind persons to whom de Lubac is alluding? To me it seems sad to reflect that de Lubac would even feel compelled to have to defend Erasmus against the charge of insincerity. Who would be so uncharitable and judgmental as to claim that Erasmus's incredible scholarly production in publishing the writings of the Church Fathers in excellent editions during the last twenty years of his life was carried out with insincere and base motives? Yet this indeed has been Erasmus's fate. A number of scholars, Catholic and not, being unable to deny Erasmus's staggering productivity, have condemned his motives.[14] De Lubac, in contrast, adorned his study with a portrait of Erasmus.[15] He found precisely in Erasmus's devotion to the Church Fathers, and his unceasing exertions to make their writings available to the church, proof of his sincerity, orthodoxy, and constancy.[16] So do I.

I am not certain how much benefit came to the Catholic church from the writings of Erasmus's Catholic critics, such as Martin Dorp, Edward Lee, John Batmanson, Noël Béda, Jacob Latomus, Jerome Aleander, and Alber-

12. For a the brief discussion of each of Erasmus's patristic editions, see Jan den Boeft, "Erasmus and the Church Fathers," in *The Reception of the Church Fathers in the West: From the Carolingians to the Maurists*, ed. I. Backus, 2 vols. (Leiden: Brill, 1997), 2:537-72.

13. "Il faut s'aveugler pour ne pas le voir: rien n'est moins apprêté, rien n'est plus sincère que l'enthousiasme d'Érasme pour les Pères. Il les aime d'amour, il vit littéralement avec eux." *Exégèse Médiévale: Les Quatre Sens de L'Ecriture* (Paris: Aubier, 1964), 2:463.

14. In the sixteenth century, Cardinal Jerome Aleander was probably the most prominent curial accuser of Erasmus's motives. He endeavored throughout much of his ecclesiastical career to see Erasmus burned at the stake. The modern ecclesiastical historian Joseph Lortz was a great admirer of Aleander. After acknowledging that the popes, as well as Thomas More, John Fisher, and many others, all supported and defended Erasmus, Lortz writes of Aleander with dramatic flair: "There was only one man on the Catholic side who in some measure recognized in time the danger embodied by Erasmus. This was the papal nuncio, Aleander, himself a humanist of some standing." Joseph Lortz, *The Reformation in Germany*, trans. Ronald Walls, 2 vols. (New York: Herder and Herder, 1968), 1:155. It seems strange that Lortz would prefer Aleander's judgment of Erasmus to that of Thomas More, and that he would describe Aleander as "a humanist of some standing." To my knowledge Aleander did not publish any works of his own.

15. Cf. R. Voderholzer, *Meet Henri De Lubac*, trans. Michael J. Miller (San Francisco, Calif.: Ignatius, 2008), 102.

16. *Exégèse Médiévale*, 2:427.

to Pio.[17] But it seems quite certain to me that very great advantage came to the Catholic church in the sixteenth century from Erasmus's editions of the Church Fathers. It is noteworthy that the books and articles that paint Erasmus's character in the worst colors tend to downplay or simply ignore his patristic editions, as if they simply did not exist. Yet they were clearly one of the focal points of his scholarly work during the last twenty years of his life on earth.[18] To me such neglect would be equivalent to writing a biography of Neil Armstrong and leaving out the part about the lunar landing; or of Jerome, and failing to mention his commentaries on the prophets. De Lubac never found the time to write the book on Erasmus that he had intended.[19] Had he written such a book, doubtless it would have given great attention to Erasmus's patristic scholarship.

In addition to receiving inspiration from Henri de Lubac's scholarly appreciation of Erasmus, and his readiness to challenge some of the reigning paradigms in the academic culture, the particular work that has provided the model for the present translation is: Desiderius Erasmus, *Patristic Scholarship: The Edition of St Jerome*, edited, translated, and annotated by James F. Brady and John C. Olin.[20] In 1995 I corresponded with Dr. Olin, a Catholic historian at Fordham University, because I had read some of his translations and shared his enthusiasm for Erasmus. I asked him innocently enough why, in his opinion, Erasmus had been so roughly treated by so many Catholics, especially during the four hundred years between the Council of Trent and the modern period. To me it seemed that Catholics should take pride in this scholar and son of their church, who was so learned and productive in his ecclesiastical scholarship. Indeed, the more I learned about Erasmus and his times, as the full scope of his writings became increasingly accessible in English through the *Collected Works of Erasmus* translation project, the more I felt that Erasmus was perhaps the most learned and reliable Catholic exegete, apologist, catechist, and theologian in the pre-Tridentine Catholic church of the sixteenth century. Olin replied to this query in a hand-written missive:

Your comment was well made. It is hard to understand. The explanation lies in the fact that he was caught in the middle of the great Protestant-Catholic division which

17. Of this group Marten Dorp revoked his criticisms of Erasmus's scriptural studies and became Erasmus's open supporter. His colleagues at Louvain retaliated by denying him the renewal of his certification to teach theology. Dorp lost his income for one year as a result.

18. In "Erasmus and the Church Fathers," J. den Boeft says that it is curious that Erasmus's lifelong preoccupation with the Church Fathers "is almost absent from the pages of Huizinga's justly famous monograph" (538).

19. See his comment in *At the Service of the Church*, 141.

20. CWE 61.

remained a very polarized state of affairs until quite recently. A better understanding of him and his work came only with a more ecumenical outlook in general. His letters to Leo X were only delivered to John XXIII, as someone has remarked.[21]

I believe there is a lot of truth in Olin's analysis, especially in the idea that the Second Vatican Council (1962–65), summoned by Pope John XXIII, has created an intellectual atmosphere within Catholicism that is much better equipped than previous generations to receive Erasmus's reform ideas sympathetically. One very obvious example is Vatican II's explicit support for the use of vernacular translations of scripture by Catholic laity.[22] Erasmus had been one of the strongest Catholic proponents for vernacular Bibles in the sixteenth century and had famously appealed for this in the *Paraclesis* of his 1516 New Testament. Yet he was virulently attacked for his views during this lifetime by the theologians of the Sorbonne, Alberto Pio, and others.[23] The bishops of the Council of Trent vigorously debated this question.[24] Regrettably (in my opinion), they ultimately decided to support the position of Erasmus's critics, that the availability of vernacular Bibles does more harm than good.[25] However, the magisterium at Vatican II has now officially changed its mind about this disciplinary matter, and so Erasmus, though he lost the battle, has won the war.

Another example of the way Erasmus anticipated the Second Vatican Council is in the *Decree on Priestly Formation* 5, where the bishops of the Coun-

---

21. See my "In Memoriam John C. Olin (7 October 1915–6 June 2000)," *Erasmus of Rotterdam Society Yearbook* 21 (2001): 90–93.

22. See *Dei verbum*: "Easy access to sacred Scripture should be provided for all the Christian faithful. That is why the Church from the very beginning accepted as her own that very ancient Greek translation of the Old Testament which is named after seventy men" (no. 22). This text can be found in Heinrich Denzinger, *Compendium of Creeds, Definitions, and Declarations on Matters of Faith and Morals*, ed. Peter Hünermann, R. Fastiggi, and Anne Englund Nash, 43rd ed. (San Francisco, Calif.: Ignatius, 2010), 4229 [hereafter "DS"].

23. In his *Controversy with Alberto Pio*, Erasmus writes: "I have long ago given a clear indication of my opinion about making the Bible available to the common people, so let the cabbage so often reheated not make the reader sick. As to your statement that pearls should not be cast before swine, and that what is holy must not be given to dogs, you have a low opinion of the Christian people if you consider they deserve to be compared with pigs and dogs. Surely Christ saw fit to reveal his mysteries without discrimination to the simple and uneducated, and yet lately we have begun to hear that the masses should be barred altogether from the reading of the Bible" (CWE 84:97)

24. See R. McNally, "The Council of Trent and Vernacular Bibles," *Theological Studies* 27 (1966): 204–27.

25. See Rule IV of the "Ten Rules Concerning Prohibited Books Drawn Up by the Fathers Chosen by the Council of Trent and Approved by Pope Pius," in *The Canons and Decrees of the Council of Trent*, trans. H. J. Schroeder (Charlotte, N.C.: Tan Books, 1941), 279.

cil directed that before seminarians take up properly ecclesiastical sacred studies, they should be equipped with the humanistic and scientific training that enables young people to undertake higher education in general. In addition they should acquire a command of Latin as well as a "suitable knowledge of the languages of sacred Scripture."[26] Moreover, the same document describes the study of sacred scripture as "the soul of all theology."[27] It adds that the eastern and western Church Fathers should be taught, as well as Thomas Aquinas.[28] Such a program of theological studies, with its humanistic, linguistic, and scriptural focus, but without exclusion of scholasticism (Aquinas), resembles Erasmus's proposals, as I will show more clearly in the first chapter of this book.

Without making any reference to Erasmus, Joseph Ratzinger seems to confirm Olin's insight about the significance of the Second Vatican Council when he describes the theology that made the Second Vatican Council possible and shaped it as "a theology and a piety that is constructed on the basis of Holy Scripture, the Fathers of the Church, and the great liturgical heritage of the whole Church. At the Council this theology succeeded in nourishing faith not only on the thinking of the last hundred years but on the great stream of the whole tradition in order to make it richer and more alive, simpler and more open."[29] *Mutatis mutandis*, this synopsis of the meaning of Vatican II strikes me as very similar to Erasmus's vision for church reform and renewal in the sixteenth century. L. Halkin agrees that the Second Vatican Council was "an Erasmian Council if there ever was such a thing."[30]

I begin this book with these references to de Lubac and Olin partly as a tribute to these scholars, who along with Louis Bouyer, Georges Chantraine, and Richard L. DeMolen were among the pioneers in the Catholic project of rehabilitating Erasmus in the twentieth century. In fact Olin encouraged me personally to endeavor in my scholarship to demonstrate the link between Erasmus and the Church Fathers, and in this work I am attempting to do so. Also by these references I wish to assure my readers that I will indeed discuss

26. J. Gallagher, ed. and trans., *The Documents of Vatican II* (New York: America Press, 1966), 449.

27. Ibid., 451.   28. Ibid., 452.

29. See his "Epilog: Zehn Jahre nach Konzilsbegin—wo stehen wir?," in his *Dogma und Verkündigung* (München: Erich Wewel Verlag, 1973), 439. This text is translated by J. Komonchak as "Thomism and the Second Vatican Council," in his *Continuity and Plurality: Essays in Honor of Gerald A. McCool, S.J.* (Fairfield, Conn.: Sacred Heart University Press, 1998), 53–73.

30. *Erasmus: A Critical Biography*, trans. John Tonkin (Oxford: Blackwell, 1993), 295; citing G. Chantraine, "Théologie et vie spirituelle chez Érasme," *Nouvelle revue théologique* 91 (1969): 808–10.

the matter of Erasmus's controversial Catholic reputation. I will do so briefly in what follows in this preface, and in more detail in the appendix of this book. Because I have challenged a number of popular caricatures of Erasmus and of the Council of Trent (which is often depicted as the Catholic church's official repudiation of Erasmian humanism), I feel obligated to clarify and support my opinions in some measure. I shall do so in spite of the fact that Erasmus's own legacy in the Catholic church is not the sole concern of this volume.

It remains my firm belief that Erasmus was always fundamentally Catholic and in fact became more consciously and overtly Catholic after his open breach with Martin Luther in 1524. I say "open breach" not in the sense that Erasmus had ever been in alliance with Luther, but Erasmus had initially strongly disapproved of how many of Luther's Catholic opponents were handling the case, and he publicly distanced himself from them. Many of Luther's initial Catholic critics were also opponents of Renaissance humanism. They had attacked Erasmus (and other humanists) before they attacked Luther, and they blamed Luther's revolt on the humanist movement. Erasmus himself, however, personally had been suspicious of Luther's ambitious and proud spirit from the very beginning of his first contact with him. In any case once Luther's schismatic intentions became clearer to him, Erasmus expressed regret about the severity of some of the things he himself had written earlier in criticism of the Catholic church. He insisted that these things had been written without any malicious intent and of course they were written when the church was in a tranquil state.[31] To these points I would add on Erasmus's behalf that many of these controversial things were written at the instigation and with the endorsement of Thomas More. Erasmus admitted many times that he was unable to foresee what use the first Protestants would make of his satirical criticisms of abuses then current in the church, namely to make these things a pretext for their schisms. In light of the new situation brought

---

31. For instance, Erasmus writes to Pope Adrian VI on December 22, 1522: "In my day I have written with some freedom, for this was then encouraged by the peaceful state of things, and I never suspected the rise of times like these. But now—now that I see Christendom brought into great peril, we must above all be on the lookout and allow absolutely no scope to individual feelings. I have no desire to be a prophet of evil; but I see more peril threatening than I could wish, and more than many men perceive. May Christ turn it all to a happy outcome!" (CWE 9, ep. 1329). Similarly, in his *Controversy with Albert Pio* (1529), Erasmus wrote: "In addition, while I confess that I have done and written certain things that I would not have been about to do or write had I been able to divine that this epoch was going to dawn, I also affirm that my soul always recoiled from a zeal for revolution and from inciting to insurrection, as it recoils even now, and I hope never to repent this attitude" (CWE 84:20).

about by the Protestant revolts, Erasmus changed the tone of his writings, but without abandoning his fundamental convictions about the critical need for internal and external church reform. L. Bouyer assesses this correctly:

> Long before the Lutheran Reformation, Erasmus had reached the conclusion that one of the main evils from which the Church was suffering was the general prevalence of a superstitious religiosity that was wholly exterior to and in profound ignorance of the true interior life. On the other hand, when the heretical Reformation did break out, he energetically maintained that it would never have succeeded had it not been able to use this state of affairs as a pretext.[32]

Erasmus's popular reputation as a religiously indifferent and weak character, as a satirist and mocker of the Catholic church, rather than as its good shepherd, bold defender, and apologist against Protestant innovations, which is how the popes of this lifetime assessed him, is based almost entirely on two factors: (1) a misreading of the intentions of his early satire, *Praise of Folly* (1509) where, from the home of Thomas More, Erasmus humorously and without malice ridiculed and satirized abuses, not institutions; and (2) ignorance of Erasmus's later anti-Protestant writings (those written 1523–36). The latter factor has been caused at least in part by their lack of availability in modern language translations until quite recently. In spite of the fact that Thomas More wrote a defense of Erasmus's *Praise of Folly*, the misinterpretation of this one satire has ruined Erasmus's reputation among many pious Catholics today, some of whom are not aware that Thomas More acclaimed this particular work of Erasmus.[33] Sauer, for example, in the article cited above, says that *Praise of Folly* was not intended as healing medicine but as a deadly poison. This assessment directly contradicts the claims Erasmus makes about the work in the preface and in his letter to Martin Dorp in which he explains his intentions in *Praise of Folly*.[34] It also contradicts Thomas More's assessment of the work. Those who adopt this negative conception of Erasmus's character

---

32. *Erasmus and His Times*, 192.

33. In my judgment the best modern discussions of Erasmus's intentions in *Praise of Folly* are Halkin, *Erasmus: A Critical Biography*, 74–89, and J. McConica, *Erasmus* (New York: Oxford University Press, 1991), 81–99. More's defense is found in *The Complete Works of St. Thomas More*, vol. 15, *In Defense of Humanism: Letter to Martin Dorp, Letter to the University of Oxford, Letter to Edward Lee, Letter to a Monk, with a New Text and Translation of Historia Richardi Tertii*, ed. Daniel Kinney (New Haven, Conn.: Yale University Press, 1986), 107 [hereafter "CW"]. More says that the admirers of *Folly* came from the most learned, not from the common crowd. Only the learned understand the book. This is why those two or three theologians got angry: "On the basis of what others told them, they thought she said more than she did, while perhaps if they themselves understood what was actually said they would not feel provoked."

34. Cf. CWE 3, ep. 337.

and motives presume that he was being disingenuous and that Thomas More was deceived about him. To maintain this assessment they are compelled to overlook all that Erasmus wrote after his break with Luther, in addition to misinterpreting what he wrote before his break with Luther.[35]

Time, I believe, is now very much on Erasmus's side, since the full scope of his writings is now becoming accessible to English readers and is no longer buried in his extremely difficult classical Latin. Modern writers will no longer be able to get away with what Sauer and his troupe got away with. Many of the older caricatures of Erasmus's alleged "modernism" and "anti-dogmatism" have no future whatsoever. They have already been completely discredited in academic circles, though they are dying a hard and slow death at the popular level. The chief problem is that Erasmus's satire of specific *abuses* then current are illegitimately generalized into being global attacks on the *institutions* of the church. Thus, for example, Erasmus criticized religious pilgrimages undertaken with worldly and superstitious motives, and prayers invoking the saints made with essentially pagan and sinful attitudes. These legitimate pastoral concerns are distorted into the claim that Erasmus attacked without qualification the proper use of religious pilgrimages and the Catholic custom of invoking the intercession of the saints.[36] In reality Erasmus's firmly defended these practices against Protestant attacks.[37] Likewise Erasmus's concern that *some* scholastic (medieval) theologians, including Aquinas and Scotus, went to excessive lengths in using Aristotelian philosophy in their theological commentaries is frequently converted into the *global* assertion that "Erasmus had

---

35. Another example of a modern scholar who simply lacks the literary and theological sensibilities to assess *Praise of Folly* fairly is J. J. Mangan, *Life, Character & Influence of Desiderius Erasmus of Rotterdam: Derived from a Study of His Works and Correspondence*, 2 vols. (New York: Macmillan, 1927). He claims (1:290–325, 2:347–49) that *Praise of Folly* was intended solely to blacken and defame all monks and theologians as well as the institution of monasticism. But Mangan posits that later in his life, in 1533, Erasmus allegedly "recanted" his earlier position and wrote for monasticism "the greatest panegyric within the memory of man," when he published one of the works of Haymo on the Psalms, dedicated to John Emsted, dated Freiburg, February 28, 1533. Mangan is correct in commending Erasmus's panegyric to good monks in the 1533 preface, but he badly misunderstands Erasmus's criticism of bad monks in *Praise of Folly*. Bouyer says that the literary genre of Erasmus's most famous book has been understood by very few Catholic scholars: "One thing is certain, and it is all that concerns us here, namely, that the *Praise of Folly* must be allowed the same latitude that all competent historians today grant to More's *Utopia*. In works like *Utopia* and *Folly*, the most literal interpretations are the most fallacious" (*Erasmus and His Times*, 102).

36. Even in the latest volume in the *Collected Works of Erasmus* series (CWE 78:457n271), the editors erroneously state that in *Praise of Folly* Erasmus "denounced traditional beliefs and practices." Rather, he denounced abuses associated with traditional beliefs and practices and defended the proper use of such things.

37. See Erasmus's work, *On Prayer* (CWE 70).

nothing but disdain for scholastic theology," or that Erasmus denied that the divine Logos was operative during in the Christian medieval era.[38] In reality, Erasmus greatly admired Thomas Aquinas as the greatest of the medieval theologians, and he essentially adopted the substance of Aquinas's theology as his own. Erasmus viewed his own scholarly contributions as aimed at helping the contemporary practitioners of scholastic theology, at least those who displayed any degree of openness to the Renaissance, to flourish more authentically in their chosen field of study (scholastic theology), which happened not to be Erasmus's chosen field of study, which was New Testament studies and patristics. I think it is noteworthy that in his *Hyperaspistes* II Erasmus wrote a very learned vindication of the orthodoxy of scholastic speculation on the operation of divine grace and human freedom, submitting his defense to the judgment of the Catholic church. This is the very scholastic speculation that Martin Luther had unjustly and ignorantly accused of being Pelagian.[39] Yet what modern person is even aware that Erasmus defended scholasticism in this manner? I believe that future research will confirm that Erasmus's later works, such as *Hyperaspistes* I and II, his *Explanation of the Creed* and work *On Prayer*, as well as his other anti-Protestant works, provided dogmatic guidance to the theologians of the Council of Trent. To my knowledge no one has attempted to prove this up to now.

Similarly, Erasmus's ridicule of contentious monks, greedy priests, popes addicted to luxury, or of idolatrous and superstitious attitudes then current among lay Catholics are often twisted into the allegation that he undermined the Catholic *institutions* of monasticism, priesthood, papacy, and the sacramental system. Protestant ideas are thus unjustly projected onto Erasmus. But no one has the right to distort Erasmus's views in this manner. As C. J. De Vogel aptly writes: "It is never the Sacraments that are disparaged by Erasmus—but (quite rightly) his indignation goes out to those who, after receiving the Sacrament, e.g. Communion, just go on living as if nothing were due to Christ anymore."[40] Is someone who rebukes the man who attends Mass but lives selfishly and ignores the misfortunes of his neighbor attacking the church's sacraments or defending them? Is someone who censures immoral and avaricious priests

---

38. This is the claim of A. Auer, *Die vollkommene Frömmigkeit*, 137, cited with approval by Louis Dupré, *Passage to Modernity: An Essay in the Hermeneutics of Nature and Culture* (New Haven, Conn.: Yale University Press, 1993), 199.

39. Cf. CWE 77. Parts of the Luther/Erasmus debate may also be accessed in Clarence H. Miller, ed., *Erasmus and Luther: The Battle over Free Will*, trans. Clarence H. Miller and Peter Macardle (Indianapolis, Ind.: Hackett, 2012).

40. "Erasmus and Church Dogma," 123–24.

undermining the priesthood, or protecting it from sacrilege? Is someone a friend or enemy of the papacy, who is brave enough, as Erasmus was in *Praise of Folly*, to censure the worldly war-mongering popes of the Renaissance for their addiction to luxury, greed, immorality, and war?[41]

Thomas More was one of the first to see the injustice in these sorts of popular distortions of Erasmus's intentions. In his *Letter to Martin Dorp*, More pointed out that Dorp had unjustly construed Erasmus's criticism of *some* theologians as directed against *all* theologians *everywhere*.[42] More's letter was effective in bringing about Dorp's conversion from being Erasmus's severe critic into his firm supporter, at great professional cost to Dorp himself.[43] I hope that the present book may contribute to this same sort of effect among some Catholic readers. I find it very significant that the only two canonized saints of the first half of the sixteenth century who personally knew Erasmus, namely Thomas More and John Fisher, shared his opinions, agreed with his assessment of the decadence of many clergy of this period, and wholeheartedly adopted his vision for theological renewal.[44] Moreover they were

---

41. Unlike Dante, Erasmus never names the popes he rebukes.

42. See Thomas More, *In Defense of Humanism: Letter to Martin Dorp, Letter to the University of Oxford, Letter to Edward Lee, Letter to a Monk, with a New Text and Translation of Historia Richardi Tertii*, in CW 15:39.

43. See the article on Dorp in P. Bietenholz and T. Deutscher, eds., *Contemporaries of Erasmus: A Biographical Register of the Renaissance and Reformation*, 3 vols. (Toronto: University of Toronto Press, 1986) [hereafter "CE"]. In *Erasmus and His Catholic Critics*, 2 vols. (Nieuwkoop: De Graaf, 1989), Erika Rummel writes: "More's arguments were persuasive, but the *coup de grâce* was his proof that Dorp's own writings could be interpreted as irreverent, if read by a mean-spirited critic. In the dedicatory epistle accompanying his edition of [future Pope] Adrian's *Quaestiones quodlibeticae* Dorp had explained that he was 'interrupting his serious studies' to undertake the task at hand. Did this mean that editing Adrian's works was not a serious business?" (1:9).

44. For instance, consider John Fisher's assessment of the moral quality of the prelates of the Catholic church of Rome from his work *Against Velenus*: "Perhaps someone will say, 'Nowhere else is the life of Christians more contrary to Christ than in Rome, and that indeed among the very prelates of the Church, whose manner of living rather is diametrically at variance with the life of Christ. For Christ was the lover of poverty; they fly poverty so much that they are zealous for nothing more than the accumulation of riches. Christ spurned the glory of this world; there is nothing they do not suffer or do for the attainment of glory. Finally Christ afflicted Himself with frequent fasts and ceaseless prayers; they neither fast nor pray but are wholly given over to luxury and lusts. These same persons, moreover, are to all who lead a sincere and Christian life a very great scandal, namely, as men whose morals are so divorced from the teaching of Christ that through them Christ's name is blasphemed in the whole world.' These things perhaps are an adversary's objections against our stand. But these very things confirm our argument. For since we behold the sees of all other Apostles now to be occupied everywhere by infidels and this see alone which was Peter's continues under Christian rule yet which has deserved destruction with all the others

his unqualified defenders and forthright opponents of his sixteenth-century Catholic critics. This is the elephant in the room of Erasmus's modern Catholic despisers. Why do they remain silent about More and Fisher's support for Erasmus, or try to explain it away in a ridiculous manner?[45] I give significant emphasis to the views of these two saints in the pages that follow, both in the first chapter and in the appendix, since the church has officially judged them to be models of sanctity and orthodoxy. In many respects it appears to me that the validity and orthodoxy of Erasmus's assessments and proposals stand or fall with More and Fisher, since they lived under the same religious conditions, substantially agreed with him, supported him, and wrote in his defense. To condemn Erasmus outright is to condemn them.

I shall conclude this preface by saying something that doubtless will be received as a piece of folly by many, but it is spoken with complete sincerity. The Catholic church required eight hundred years to recognize Jerome of Stridon as one of its "Four Great Doctors of the Latin Church." He was declared a doctor in eighth century, which was ratified in the thirteenth. It took the church over six hundred and fifty years to canonize "Albert the Great," teacher of Thomas Aquinas. Thomas More and John Fisher themselves, both of whom died as martyrs, were raised to the altar exactly four hundred years after their bloody deaths in 1535 at the hands of King Henry VIII. Why could it not take five or six hundred years for the Catholic church to recognize the sanctity and dogmatic reliability of Erasmus of Rotterdam? As I said, I believe that time is now on Erasmus's side, thanks to the *Collected Works of Erasmus* project. The full scope of his writings will soon be entirely accessible, and I believe that the result of this will be that one day the church will recognize the holiness and orthodoxy of this beloved son (if she can only make room for his humor, which, God knows, we all need!).

---

because of its unspeakable crimes and vices, what else can we think but that Christ is most true to His word, who in spite of being aroused by their many and great injuries still keeps His promises even to His fiercest enemies? The faith preached by Peter in Rome has not failed heretofore, and there still remains the true succession in the Church whose rise comes from Peter and whose rock and steadfast foundation, as it were, Christ made Peter." Quoted by Edward Surtz, *The Works and Days of John Fisher* (Cambridge, Mass.: Harvard University Press, 1967), 75. I am not aware of any passage in Erasmus that compares with this in the severity of its judgment of Roman prelates.

45. For instance, Joseph Lortz says of Thomas More's acclaim for Erasmus's *Praise of Folly*: "It was one of the most characteristic qualities of Thomas More that he never interfered in the affairs of others and refrained from saying anything that would harm a friendship unless it involved a vital matter of conscience" (*Reformation: A Problem for Today*, 69). It seems clear to me that Lortz has never turned one page of More's *Letter to Dorp*.

INTRODUCTION

The thesis of this book is that Erasmus's lifelong exertions in advancing biblical and patristic scholarship demonstrate the sincerity, vitality, and orthodoxy of his program for the renewal of Catholic theology in the first half of the sixteenth century. My pièce de résistance, so to speak, is found in chapter 5, where I provide the first English translation of the prefaces to Erasmus of Rotterdam's edition of Origen's writings.[1] Included in this material is Erasmus's *Life of Origen*, a biographical portrait of Origen of Alexandria (185–254) in which Erasmus sets forth Origen's virtues for emulation and asks censorious critics of Origen to consider the life he lived before they harshly judge and condemn him. Erasmus regarded Origen not only as a wonderful homilist, but indeed as an "outstanding doctor of the Church," a "chosen instrument" protected by divine providence to bring great advantage to the Catholic church. Indeed Origen was a man to whom the Catholic church owes a great debt, especially for his contribution to the exegetical tradition. Erasmus's *Life of Jerome* has been called his "Biographical Masterpiece."[2] I hope that one day his *Life of Origen* may possess a similar honor. The prefaces to Erasmus's edition of Origen comprise about fifteen folio columns of Latin text and are found in the standard edition of Erasmus's Latin works.[3] The edition of Origen's writings was the final work of Erasmus, his "torso," as

---

1. Basel: Froben, 1536.

2. J. Macguire, "Erasmus's Biographical Masterpiece: *Hieronymi Stridonensis Vita*," *Renaissance Quarterly* 26 (1973): 273.

3. Jean Leclerc, *Desiderii Erasmi Roterodami Opera Omnia* (Leiden: 1703–6; reprinted in New York: Hildesheim, 1961–62), 10 vols. [hereafter "LB"], 8:425–40. They have not yet appeared in the modern critical edition of Erasmus's writings: *Opera omnia Desiderii Erasmi Roterodami* (Amsterdam: North Holland Publishing, 1969–) [hereafter "ASD"].

they say, or unfinished work. He was laboring on the edition when he died in Basel on July 11/12, 1536, completing a lifetime that was devoted to the advancement of both secular and sacred learning. The Origen edition was the last of his (at least) twelve published editions of the writings of the Greek and Latin Church Fathers and was published posthumously. I am pleased to say that here is found the only modern language translation of this final written work of Erasmus of Rotterdam.

My aim in the first four chapters is to help prepare the educated but non-specialist general reader to understand and appreciate Erasmus's edition of Origen by providing context and background to the edition. In the first chapter I introduce the main principles of Erasmus's program for the renewal of Catholic theology in the sixteenth century to those who are not familiar with them. This subject continues to be poorly understood when it is discussed or alluded to in scholarly literature. The texts plainly show that Erasmus did not repudiate scholasticism in an unqualified sense, though he did make some serious criticisms of scholasticism. Erasmus sought to see contemporary scholastic theologians practice greater restraint in respect to their method of speculative questions and to see the current scholastic curriculum supplemented and aided by biblical and patristic studies, so that scholastically inclined theologians might flourish more authentically.

In the latter part of the first chapter, I discuss Catholic opposition that arose to Erasmus at the Universities of Louvain and Paris in response to his proposals. The central issue of that debate was whether the study of scripture (in its original languages) and the writings of the Church Fathers should be permitted to supplement current theological studies, or whether scripture and the Fathers should be read solely through the prism of the scholastic authorities, who were to be the theological mainstay. Though Erasmus may have lost the battle at the Universities of Louvain and Paris, Erasmian theological reform was warmly embraced in Catholic universities in England, Austria, and Poland during the pre-Reformation period, precisely when it was being opposed in some places on the continent. Moreover, a number of language institutes were established throughout Europe which implemented the main principles of Erasmian humanism.

I further show something that modern scholarship has scarcely noticed, that the first Protestants, Luther and Melanchthon, framed their religious revolution explicitly as a critique of certain aspects of Erasmus's theological program. In particular they repudiated the primacy Erasmus attributed to the ancient Greek and Latin theologians, which did not cohere well with the Protestant *sola scriptura* principle according to which Luther and Melanchthon, not the Church Fathers, bore supreme interpretive authority. This hardly lends support to the popular anti-Erasmus slur invented by some monks of his own day and repeated by many thereafter: "Erasmus laid the egg that Luther hatched." The truth, as Erasmus himself pointed out, is that Erasmus laid a hen's egg, whereas Luther hatched a chick of an entirely different species.[4] No one, in fact, has ever proven that Erasmus agreed with any of Luther's condemned doctrines.

I conclude this chapter with a brief critique of two influential modern Catholic scholars who were dismissive of Erasmus, the church historian Hubert Jedin and the Dominican systematic theologian Yves Congar. Both men plainly agreed with the monks cited above, that Erasmus planted the seeds that sprouted into the Protestant Reformation and even the "Enlightenment." I reply that it is one thing flippantly to condemn Erasmus as "un-catholic" and "un-dogmatic," while it is another thing to demonstrate to the public that one is familiar with the content of Erasmus's writings and his actual positions. Clearly Jedin and Congar have rejected an Erasmus who never existed in history, but who was conjured up by their imaginations.

In the second chapter, I briefly introduce the modern reader to the life and writings of Origen of Alexandria. My assumption is that many readers of this book will require a basic introduction to this church writer. As one of my students said, "Catholics know about St. Jerome, but they don't know about Origen." Although there are numerous good books available on Origen today, it seems essential to provide at least some background on him, since otherwise the reader will not be able to evaluate Erasmus's praise and criticism of Origen and his assessments of Origen's works. In this essay I describe some of the basic principles of Origen's Christian exegesis of scripture, which was a focal point of Erasmus's appreciation of Origen. Yet Erasmus also criticized the excesses of Origen's allegorical method. For this material I admit to being indebted to the Origen studies of a number of modern scholars, especially to Henri de Lubac, whose magnanimous reception of Origen, it seems to

---

4. Cf. his letter to Johannes Caesarius on December 16, 1524: "I 'laid the egg, and Luther hatched it.' An astounding statement by those Minorites of yours, which should earn them a fine big cowl of porridge! The egg I laid was a hen's egg, and Luther has hatched a chick of a very, very different feather. I am not surprised that those pot-bellies should be the source of such remarks, but it astonishes me that you agree with them. And yet you yourself could be the best witness to my constant disapproval of Luther's virulence, afraid as I was that the thing would end in rioting and bloodshed" (CWE 10, ep. 1528).

me, was largely anticipated by Erasmus and is now prevalent in post-Vatican II Catholic theology, though unfortunately not in the field of Catholic exegesis.[5] It appears that the full harvest of de Lubac's magisterial appreciation of Origen has not yet been reaped in the field of Catholic biblical studies.[6]

Chapter 3 offers an overview of Origen's theological and exegetical legacy in the western church, a legacy that was made possible largely because a substantial selection of his writings had been translated from Greek into Latin by Jerome (347–419/20) and Rufinus of Aquileia (345–411). In spite of the condemnation of "Origenism" at the fifth ecumenical council of 553 AD, Origen became an important teacher of the Catholic church in the west by means of the Latin translations of his writings that had been carried out by Rufinus and Jerome. Origen's great influence in the west is one of the assured results of de Lubac's studies in his work *Medieval Exegesis*. Above all in this chapter I focus on the influence of Origen upon Jerome, the Church Father whom Erasmus revered the most, and whom the Catholic church has always regarded as its greatest exegete of scripture.[7] It is simply impossible to dispute that Jerome's exegesis, both of the Old Testament and of the New, is deeply imbued with Origen's thought. This shows that Origen's influence goes far beyond the question of the specific use of his surviving writings, since many of his works that are not extant also shaped Christian exegesis in profound ways.

Also in this chapter I discuss the pre-Erasmus printed editions of Origen's writings of the late fifteenth and early sixteenth century. In this section, with permission from the University of Notre Dame Press, I reuse and update my research first published in a section of my book, *Origen and the History of Justification*.[8] To the present day, scholars continue to promote what I regard as the mistaken idea that Origen was virtually unknown in the west until Erasmus (or Pico della Mirandola) came along and began promoting his writings in the late fifteenth or early sixteenth century. Without wishing to deny the importance of the printing press in spreading the knowledge of Origen's (and others') writings more widely, I do not see how this popular narrative can be maintained in the wake of the research of Henri de Lubac.

---

5. See D. Farkasfalvy, *Inspiration and Interpretation: A Theological Introduction to Sacred Scripture* (Washington, D.C.: The Catholic University of America Press, 2010), 120–39.

6. There are signs of hope. L. T. Johnson and W. S. Kurz show an appreciation of Origen in their *The Future of Catholic Biblical Scholarship* (Grand Rapids, Mich.: Eerdmans, 2002), 64–90.

7. At the Council of Trent, Jerome was recognized as "the greatest doctor in explaining the Sacred Scriptures." Pope Benedict XV's encyclical *Spiritus Paraclitus* (1920) is devoted to Jerome.

8. Thomas Scheck, *Origen and the History of Justification: The Legacy of Origen's Commentary on Romans* (Notre Dame, Ind.: University of Notre Dame Press, 2008), 158–72.

My aim in this chapter is to assist the modern reader in contextualizing Erasmus's reception of Origen and comparing it with that of his contemporaries.

As the final preliminary essay, I discuss (in chapter 4) Erasmus's critical assessment of Origen, based on a broad survey of Erasmus's other writings. What stance did Erasmus take toward Origen? Did he view him as a heretic and dangerous threat to the church, or as a substantially orthodox early Church Father who made the mistakes that are to be expected of a pioneer? Did Erasmus himself hold radical and suspect views respecting Origen, as some scholars claim? I endeavor to let Erasmus speak for himself. It seems necessary to discuss Erasmus's broader assessment of Origen in this manner, since he does not express all his opinions about Origen in the brief unfinished prefaces to his edition of Origen. For instance, Erasmus's reflections on Origen's orthodoxy are not incorporated in any way into his prefatory material to his Origen edition, where Erasmus focuses on displaying Origen's virtues. Yet they had been discussed openly elsewhere in Erasmus's corpus. For the sake of completeness and balance, I felt it necessary to compile some of these Erasmian reflections.

Chapter 4 also provides a specific introduction to and overview of the content of Erasmus's prefatory material that is translated and annotated in the subsequent chapter. There was not room in the footnotes for chapter 5 to contain all the discussion that is really necessary to understand the content and significance of Erasmus's text. Therefore I have anticipated the reader's first contact with Erasmus's prefaces by discussing their content in advance. The result of this arrangement is that the reader—at least the one who refuses to skip directly to chapter 5—begins to encounter commentary on Erasmus's prefaces to his edition of Origen before actually reading his text.

The heart of this volume is then provided in chapter 5, where I offer the first English translation of Erasmus's *Life of Origen* and of the remainder of the prefatory material to his 1536 edition of Origen's writings. Erasmus's first Catholic biographer, Beatus Rhenanus, said of Erasmus's editions of the writings of the Church Fathers that Erasmus saved the best for last in his Origen edition. Rhenanus highly esteemed Erasmus.[9] In a letter to the young Ulrich Zwingli, he said of Erasmus: "It seems to me that [Pope] Leo X does not properly understand how great Erasmus is; he thinks perhaps that he is

---

9. His *Life of Erasmus* is found in J. C. Olin, ed., *Desiderius Erasmus: Christian Humanism and the Reformation: Selected Writings of Erasmus with his Life by Beatus Rhenanus and a Biographical Sketch by the Editor*, 3rd ed. (New York: Fordham University Press, 1987). See also Enenkel, "Beatus Rhenanus' Second Vita Erasmi," 25–40.

just one of us. Erasmus is not to be measured by common standards; he has risen far above the summit of human greatness."[10] Rhenanus's exalted opinion of Erasmus was shared by Friedrich Nausea, bishop of Vienna, whose views will be recorded in the appendix. While I admit to sharing such admiration of Erasmus, at the least it seems safe to say that Erasmus's edition of Origen deserves more attention than it has hitherto received. I have supplemented the translation with clarifying annotations. Modern scholars who have become familiar with Erasmus's editions of the Church Fathers recognize them as watershed moments in the history of the discipline of patristic studies. Yet they have not been the subject of much research, and they are not referenced in standard Catholic patrologies such as those by Bardenhewer and Quasten.[11] My hope is that when his editions become better known in the English-speaking world, his learning and expertise as a patristic scholar will become more widely acknowledged and respected.

Recently, Siecienski summarized the attitude of Henri de Lubac toward Origen in these terms: "[Origen's] strong desire to constantly observe the rule of faith, to follow the tradition, and be an obedient child of the church, was not, according to de Lubac, the mark of an arch-heretic. For this reason he argued that Origen's name could not justly be put alongside those who had made a conscious break with the church—intention did count for something."[12] To the best of my knowledge, de Lubac's stance toward Origen was largely adopted by Crouzel, Daniélou, von Balthasar, and Ratzinger. It emphasizes Origen's churchman-like attitude.[13] This seems quite similar to Erasmus's overall assessment of Origen. Intention matters; emotional disposition cannot be wholly ignored when assessing someone's orthodoxy.[14] It appears to me, therefore, that Erasmus was a Catholic scholar, exegete, and theologian who perhaps was five centuries ahead of his time. His emphasis, for example, that an irenic attitude toward the question of Origen's orthodoxy is more helpful to the church is now favored in Catholic theology of the

---

10. Cited in P. S. Allen, *Erasmus: Lectures and Wayfaring Sketches* (Oxford: Clarendon Press, 1934), 13.

11. A nice overview of Erasmus's patristic editions is found in Backus, *The Reception of the Church Fathers in the West*.

12. A. E. Siecienski, "(Re)defining the Boundaries of Orthodoxy," in *Tradition and the Rule of Faith: Festschrift for Joseph T. Lienhard*, ed. R. Rombs and A. Y. Hwang (Washington, D.C.: The Catholic University of America Press, 2010), 298.

13. See also Voderholzer, *Meet Henri De Lubac*, 70.

14. Erasmus wrote to Latomus on Origen's behalf: "Origen has none of that feigned effusiveness that makes us look fearfully for the hidden trap: his language is entirely straightforward and churchmanlike" (CWE 71:67).

post-Vatican II period.[15] Moreover, Erasmus's view that in any case the question of Origen's orthodoxy should be assessed according to the standards of orthodoxy of *Origen's* day, not ours, is now universally accepted in the wake of John Henry Newman's writings on the development of dogma. Yet such an approach was not widely accepted in Erasmus's day, when the ancient theologians were not read historically but through the prism of the scholastic doctors and their judgments (which were subject to the limitations of their knowledge about antiquity). Because of his vastly superior knowledge of ancient sources, Erasmus's viewpoint in his *Life of Origen* and his other reflections upon Origen's contribution to Catholic theology seem to anticipate the ideas not only of Newman but also of twentieth-century Catholic *ressourcement* theologians, who were most appreciative of the Church Fathers and who were the architects, so to speak (or rather, divine instruments) of the Catholic renewal of the Second Vatican Council.

In the wake of the initial theological confusion that occurred immediately after the Second Vatican Council, C. J. De Vogel upheld Erasmus to contemporary Catholics as a theologian who bears the following message: "A total adherence to the Church of Rome, which implies an integral acceptance of dogma and tradition—the latter not to be taken in the non-theological sense of the term (which would exclude sound criticism), but in the sense it has in classical Catholic theology, which both presupposes and implies such a criticism."[16] I strongly concur with this assessment of Erasmus's overall significance for Catholic theology and catechesis today, however rare it is to find the total meaning of his life's work articulated in this way. The concern of this book and translation is to assist modern readers in obtaining a better appreciation of both Erasmus and Origen in the modern church.

In the appendix, I provide a historical essay on Erasmus's reputation as a Catholic theologian in the sixteenth century before, during, and after the Council of Trent, including assessments of him by the popes who held office during his lifetime. I include John Colet, Thomas More, and John Fisher among these Catholic contemporaries. I also discuss Erasmus's condemnation by Carafa (Pope Paul IV) and his partial rehabilitation in the final session of the Council of Trent. While this material is not directly related to the theme of Erasmus's edition of Origen, it may still be of interest to a number of readers, and much of this research is new.

---

15. See, for example, Pope Benedict XVI's weekly general audiences of April 25 and May 2, 2007.

16. "Erasmus and His Attitude towards Church Dogma," in *Scrinium Erasmianum*, ed. J. Coppens, 2 vols. (Leiden: Brill, 1969), 2:132.

ERASMUS'S
LIFE *of* ORIGEN

1

ERASMUS'S PROGRAM *for* THEOLOGICAL RENEWAL

Erasmus of Rotterdam (1466–1536) was an Augustinian priest ordained in 1492.[1] I mention Erasmus's priesthood as a point of fact not because his biographers are unfamiliar with it but because my experience leads me to think that many educated Christians I have encountered are unaware of Erasmus's ordination and express surprise when they hear of it. Secondly, like Martin Luther but unlike Luther's associate Philipp Melanchthon or the French humanist scholar Jacques Lefèvre d'Etaples, Erasmus held a doctorate in theology, his degree being granted by the University of Turin on September 4, 1506. It is true that the degree does not seem to have been very important to him; he rarely mentions having a doctorate and seems to have taken little pride in it.[2] But the possession of this degree meant that when

1. He had received permission from his superiors to live outside the monastery, and had obtained a dispensation from the Pope that freed him from adhering to the statutes of the Augustinian order. See CWE 4, ep. 517, for the details. In my judgment the best biography of Erasmus is L. Halkin, *Erasmus: A Critical Biography*, trans. John Tonkin (Oxford: Blackwell, 1993). Halkin does not give much attention to Erasmus's patristic scholarship, and says almost nothing about Erasmus's anti-Protestant apologetic writings. Moreover, he seems to interpret the Council of Trent far differently than I do. However, for the most part I agree with de Lubac that Halkin's Erasmus is the true Erasmus. The standard source for Erasmus's original text is LB. A modern critical edition (ASD) of Erasmus's works is in production.

2. In CWE 2, ep. 145, Erasmus explains to Anna van Borssele, from whom he was endeavoring to raise funding for his studies, that a reason he needed to obtain a doctorate in theology was not so much to make himself more learned as to give his name authority. "One has to follow the present-day fashion, since nowadays not only the vulgar but even the most highly

his right to write and speak on theological questions was challenged by conservative Catholic theologians, or by the newly arisen Protestant Reformers, all of whom belittled his authority by calling him a "Grammarian," having a degree meant that he had a legal right to discuss such questions. My modest intention in mentioning Erasmus's priesthood and doctorate is simply to indicate that officially speaking Erasmus was a Catholic theologian, a title he is often denied by his disparagers. According to de Lubac it is crucial to recognize Erasmus's status as a theologian in order to understand him.[3]

On the other hand it is fairly well known that Erasmus was a highly respected leader of a theological renewal movement within the Catholic church that had spread throughout Europe. Often designated as "Renaissance humanism" or "Christian humanism," it held as one of its central ideas that of *ressourcement*, the revitalization of Catholic Christianity by a transformative encounter with its sources of scripture and the writings of the early Church Fathers. In the appendix to this book, I will cite testimonials from several of Erasmus's contemporaries, including popes and future saints, confirming the esteem in which he was held in his own day. The present chapter will be devoted to clarifying the basic ideas of Erasmus's theological method, so that we may better understand the role that the Church Fathers generally, and Origen in particular, played in that method. It seems to me that the authenticity of Erasmus's Catholicism is integrally related to the question of his attitude toward the medieval inheritance, which he is often accused of completely repudiating. Therefore I wish to give significant attention to this matter in this initial chapter.

The Late Medieval Theological Curriculum

I believe that Erasmus's goal was to restore to theology the primacy of the study of scripture in its original languages under the principal tutelage of the Greek and Latin Church Fathers. In certain respects this aim implies a methodological break with the prevailing scholasticism and with medieval methods of doing theology in which the text of the Latin Vulgate was considered by many to be sacrosanct and the only valid version of scripture. Cur-

---

reputed scholars are unable to regard anyone as a learned man unless he is styled *magister noster*—though Christ, the prince of theologians, forbids this [cf. Mt 23:10]." Erasmus depicts Origen similarly, as an extremely learned scholar who was ordained in order to give his name greater authority.

3. Cf. Henri de Lubac, "Preface" to G. Chantraine, *Mystère et Philosophie du Christ selon Erasmus*, in *Theology in History*, 44.

ricular primacy was accorded to the writings of the scholastic doctors and to those of the pagan philosopher Aristotle. Under the old medieval system of theological education, all first-year students of theology were required to hear a course of cursory lectures on the Bible delivered by a more advanced (but not yet graduated) student of theology. The Bible was not totally unavailable in this system, but it was not given as much priority as was given to disputation. Congar reports that in the rules for the University of Paris for 1387, for example, scripture bachelors were authorized to exchange the study of two books of the Bible for two disputations.[4] In addition to the defect of the relative neglect of the study of the Bible, the reading of the original texts of the Fathers had diminished because of the expansion of the use of the works of Aristotle and the scholastics. Citing the great Dominican medievalist H. Denifle, Congar says that in the fifteenth century "the great works of the Fathers are hardly ever consulted, since theology had become a work of logic. Apparently only some extracts and purely moral works are in use."[5]

It is possible to know with great precision the nature of Erasmus's curricular disputes with the reigning scholastic theologians at Louvain, since the debate between them survives. Jacob Latomus of Louvain (1475–1544) published a book in 1519 entitled *De trium linguarum et studii theologici ratione* (*Concerning the Method of Three Languages and of Theology Study*), criticizing Erasmus's proposals (described in detail immediately below). Later in this chapter, I will discuss Latomus's dialogue in more detail. For now it is important to hear Latomus's opinion about what role the Bible should play in the theologian's education and what authors he believed should comprise the "core curriculum" of university-level theological studies. This information offers us a window into the late medieval theological curriculum and forms the background of Erasmus's *Methodus*.

Latomus argued that theology students should not be allowed to study either the Bible or the works of the early commentators such as Origen, Cyprian, Tertullian, Ambrose, Jerome, Hilary, Augustine, etc., until they had become thoroughly acquainted with scholastic writers, who were to be the foundation of theological education. Erasmus summarizes Latomus's views with a touch of sarcasm:

Latomus' speaker eventually allows his student to touch the works of the early commentators such as Origen, Ambrose, and Augustine, but only after he has become thoroughly acquainted with scholastic writers. So completely does he prefer

---

4. Congar, *A History of Theology*, 138.
5. Ibid.

these authors to their predecessors that our old scholar wants his theologian to study them before he touches the books of either the Old or the New Testament. He is concerned about the risk of a student's reading Cyprian, Hilary, Jerome, and Ambrose before Scotus, Durand, and Holcot, then being unable to stomach these modern writers without feeling sick.[6]

For Latomus the Bible takes second place to the scholastics in theological studies, and the Church Fathers come in a very distant third. In this same dialogue Latomus's spokesman criticizes Pico della Mirandola (1463–94), who had expressed regret over having spent six whole years studying nothing but Aquinas, Scotus, and Albert the Great, rather than scripture and the Fathers. Erasmus writes in response to Latomus's critique of Pico:

> But I have heard the best theologians making the same complaint as Pico, and lamenting not that they had spent time on scholastic theology but that they had spent so much time on this one field of study and this alone. But I cannot keep back my amazement at this wonderfully gentle old professor [Latomus's spokesman in the dialogue]: he excuses his theology student from the study of grammar, languages, and the orators; he does not want the poor boy to be "tormented" by the poets, by reading the Holy Scriptures, or even the early teachers, whom the church numbers amongst its holy doctors; then, as soon as he reaches the moderns, he overwhelms the unhappy youth with a pitiless flood of required reading, demanding that he read every page of authors such as Peter Lombard, Alexander of Hales, Thomas Aquinas, Scotus, Bonaventure, William of Paris, Maurice of Armagh, Isidore, Holcot, Pierre d'Ailly, Gerson, Ockham, Durand, Aymon, Gabriel, Nicholas of Lyra, Carrensis, Aegidius, Adrian, Tartaretus, Bricot ... in short, every one of those who ever have taught this form of theology, are teaching it now, or are likely to teach it in the future. He does not spare a single book, though a whole human life would not be long enough to read them all.[7]

According to the reigning paradigm, at least at Louvain, the stem and stern of theological studies are the modern scholastic authors. The important passages of the Bible can be learned via the medieval glosses; the most important thoughts of the Church Fathers can be encountered indirectly in the medieval excerpts from their writings; acquisition of the biblical languages is not necessary.

Erasmus resented this approach and regarded it as outmoded due to the rebirth of learning and languages that had come with the Renaissance, and wrong-headed insofar as scholastic theology dealt primarily with speculative

---

6. *Apology against Latomus* (CWE 71:70–71).
7. *Apology against Latomus* (CWE 71:77–78).

issues, drawing heavily on Aristotle for aid. Erasmus believed that theology should include dogma and some scholastic speculation, but should also address moral and pastoral problems that would assist in the goal of having a parish clergy that was competent to assist parishioners in dealing with issues of morality and personal spiritual life. In clear contrast with Latomus, Erasmus believed that scripture and the ancient Church Fathers were more reliable guides to the faith than any of the scholastic doctors and should be given priority over the scholastics. Yet, as the above quotations make clear, Erasmus's aim was not to banish the scholastic (medieval) theologians from theological studies, nor to reject authentic doctrinal developments that originated from the scholastic theologians that the church had assimilated as her dogma (such as Scotus's brilliant argument, opposed by the followers of Thomas Aquinas, in support of the doctrine of the Immaculate Conception of Mary). Certain aspects of the late scholastic *method* were imbalanced and needed correction; but the theological *substance* of medieval theology was to be preserved. It was not scholastic theology *per se* that was the problem, but the imbalanced isolation of these studies from other new and more crucial fields of study.

To reach this end of seeing Catholic theology renewed through a more direct encounter with scripture and the Fathers, Erasmus published epoch-making works of Christian scholarship. He edited the first published Greek New Testament in 1516, dedicated to Pope Leo X and approved by him.[8] The Greek text was accompanied by a new Latin translation on facing pages as well as by scholarly annotations to the entire text of the New Testament.[9] These annotations are thoroughly infused with references to the textual readings and exegesis of both the Greek and Latin Fathers, as well as to Aquinas and to a host of other medieval authors, whenever their interpretive assistance was available in the commentaries they left behind.[10] Erasmus's New Testament is a neglected monument in the field of Catholic biblical scholarship.[11] His goal was to link the church's sacred text to her most approved ancient interpreters, while inviting the scholastics to the table as well.

---

8. In the appendix, I quote extensively from Pope Leo X's epistles in which he approved of Erasmus's scholarly publications.

9. The original Greek and Latin text of his New Testament is available in LB 6.

10. A modern facsimile edition of his New Testament Annotations has been produced by Anne Reeve and M. A. Screech, *Erasmus' Annotations on the New Testament: Facsimile of the Final Latin Text with All Earlier Variants*, 3 vols. (Leiden: Brill, 1986–93). For a sample listing of his multiple sources see the index of Desiderius Erasmus, *New Testament Scholarship: Annotations on Romans*, ed. R. Sider, trans. J. Payne, A. Rabil, R. Sider, W. Smith (CWE 56).

11. The neglect can be illustrated by the fact that it is not even mentioned in two well-

6   PROGRAM *for* THEOLOGICAL RENEWAL

Erasmus's *Method of True Theology* (1518)

Erasmus's principles for theological renewal are articulated most clearly and concisely in his work *Ratio verae theologiae* (1518), "The Method of True Theology," a work that has not yet been published in English.[12] A shorter version of this work was originally prefixed to his Greek-Latin New Testament (1516) with the title *Paraclesis*. Erasmus published an expanded version of the *Paraclesis* separately beginning in 1518.[13] Boyle writes of it: "If the *Paraclesis* of 1516 was the 'trumpet blast' of his theological renaissance, then the *Ratio* of 1518 was its full orchestration."[14] Several important theologians of modern Catholicism defended Erasmus's theological method against misrepresentation. The first was Henri de Lubac, who devoted a lengthy essay in his *magnum opus* to defending Erasmus against an entire historiographical tradition in France that had presented him in a false light.[15] From what I can tell, de Lubac's views are hardly known today.[16] G. Chantraine's great book on Erasmus's theological method was prefaced by de Lubac.[17] Finally, Louis Bouyer boldly endeavored to defend Erasmus by focusing a major section of his book on Erasmus on the analysis of Erasmus's *Ratio verae theologiae* (1518). Bouyer suggests that the title of Erasmus's work might be paraphrased as "An

---

known essays in *Jerome Biblical Commentary*, ed. R. E. Brown et al. (Englewood Cliffs, N.J.: Prentice Hall, 1968). In his essay "Modern New Testament Criticism," John Kselman, who was a graduate student at the time of writing, fails to mention Erasmus's work in his survey of the history of New Testament scholarship (7–20). Likewise, Raymond Brown's essay on "Hermeneutics" (605–23) in the same volume fails to mention Erasmus's New Testament.

12. It is available in English translation, however, in a doctoral dissertation by D. M. Conroy, *The Ecumenical Theology of Erasmus of Rotterdam: A Study of the Ratio Verae Theologiae* (PhD diss., University of Pittsburgh, 1974). Louis Bouyer's monograph, *Erasmus and His Times*, analyzes Erasmus's *Ratio verae theologiae*.

13. It is found in LB 5:75–138. A modern edition of his original Latin text (1518) plus German translation by G. B. Winkler is available in the third volume of *Erasmus von Rotterdam, Ausgewählte Schriften*, 8 vols., ed. W. Welzig (Darmstadt: Wissenschaftliche Buchgesellschaft, 1967).

14. M. O'Rourke Boyle, *Erasmus on Language and Method in Theology* (Toronto: University of Toronto Press, 1977). She reports (62) that the *Ratio* was issued by nine different presses during Erasmus's lifetime.

15. Henri de Lubac, *Exégèse Médiévale: Les Quatre Sense de L'Ecriture*, Second Part (Paris: Aubier, 1964), 427–87. De Lubac concludes that Bouyer and Halkin's depictions of Erasmus are the truth in contrast with Renaudet and Huizinga.

16. They are only very briefly summarized in B. Mansfield's *Erasmus in the Twentieth Century: Interpretations 1920–2000* (Toronto: University of Toronto Press, 2003), 142–43.

17. *Mystère et Philosophie du Christ selon Erasmus* (Gembloux: Duculot, 1971). De Lubac's preface is translated in *Theology in History*, 44–48.

Introduction to Theological Studies."[18] In this work Erasmus proposes a new approach to the study of theology, one that in some respects breaks with the recent past but recovers the ancient past. In any case it differs significantly from the scholastic curriculum that was current in the day and that is clarified in the citations given above at the head of this section where Latomus's curricular preferences are stated.

Bouyer summarizes Erasmus's aims as follows: "What Erasmus obviously had in mind in his *Method* was to further the renovation of theology by the restoration of positive theology, that is, of the scrutiny of the very sources of the Catholic faith."[19] Boyle agrees with this synopsis: "What distinguishes the *Ratio* immediately is the emphatic restoration of biblical exegesis as normative theology. The prolix catalogue of biblical pericopes which composes the bulk of the treatise announces a renaissance of true method, countering human speculation which filled decadent scholastic commentaries on scholastic commentaries in an involution of spirit."[20] Christocentrism is perhaps the most apt way of describing Erasmus's theological approach, in the sense that his theological manual is utterly focused on expounding the teachings and works of Jesus exhibited to us in the four gospels.[21] To Erasmus, the Scotistic theological method in particular, in which he himself was trained at the University of Paris in the 1490s, had lost its focus on Jesus. It was too abstract, philosophical, casuistic, and intellectualist. It seemed intended to produce invincible debate champions, not scholars of humble Christ-like character. McNally describes the old scholasticism in these words:

Under the weight of a tired tradition the theology of the late medieval schools, apart from the work of a few exceptional doctors such as the illustrious Nicholas of Cusa (d. 1464) and Gabriel Biel (d. 1495), was basically committed to a conventional style, method, and form; involved in logical constructs whose significance was mostly academic, it was too often concerned with recondite speculation. Systematic, propositional, and dialectical in spirit, it resented the style and method which characterized the approach of the new humanism, and the full weight of its scorn was directed against all that this modern theology promised to accomplish through philology and history.[22]

---

18. Bouyer, *Erasmus and His Times*, 157.   19. Ibid., 172.
20. Boyle, *Erasmus on Language*, 63.
21. Halkin, *Erasmus: A Critical Biography*, 285: "Christocentrism was the golden rule of Erasmus's spirituality as well as of his theology."
22. McNally, "The Council of Trent and Vernacular Bibles," 205.

8 PROGRAM *for* THEOLOGICAL RENEWAL

The scorn McNally speaks of will be described in greater detail later in this chapter in the section on Jacob Latomus. The innovation of scholasticism was to change the goal of theology from pastoral and practical piety to theoretical and dialectical intellectualism. Erasmus objects to the prevalent neglect of emotional and moral issues that a theologian as priest must be competent to address.

For Erasmus, theology is a discipline that needs to be carried out on one's knees. He writes: "Your reading ought frequently be interrupted by prayer that implores the help of the Holy Spirit and by thanksgiving that appreciates his blessing, as you realize that you have made progress."[23] Jesus Christ is the goal and the theologian's ambition should be piety, that is, purity of heart and conformity into the image of Christ. Erasmus's *Ratio* is above all a beautiful meditation on Christ's teaching in the gospels and the New Testament epistles. I am aware of no treatise from the scholastic period that can be compared with Erasmus's discussion in terms of its Christocentrism, though many of the thoughts expressed in Thomas à Kempis's *Imitation of Christ* bear a number of striking resemblances.[24]

Erasmus writes: "So let this be your one and only objective, let this be your prayer, let this be your one purpose—that you be changed, caught up, inspired and transformed into that which you are learning."[25] Erasmus says that just as the people of Israel were required to purify themselves before they heard the Word of God (Ex 19:10), and Moses and Aaron needed purification from all earthly desires (Ex 20:21), so much the more does the theologian need to prepare his heart for the divine gift so that he may be worthy of being taught by God.

Simple and dovelike let the eye of faith be that perceives nothing but the things of heaven [Mt 6:22]. May there be added to this a very intense desire to learn. This unique pearl [Mt 13:46] must not be loved in a vulgar manner or cherished in common with others. It requires a thirsting soul, one thirsting for nothing else [Ps 42:1–2]. Let those about to step on this sacred threshold be far from all arrogance; let them be removed from all pride. The spirit which enjoys humble and not unruly dispositions instantly recoils from such things. Sublime is the palace of this Queen if you gain access to the inner precincts. However, you will have to enter only through a very lowly doorway [Mt 7:13–14]. You must stoop to be admitted.[26]

---

23. *Methodus* (*Ratio*), trans. Conroy, 79–80 (LB 5:77).

24. R. L. DeMolen, *The Spirituality of Erasmus of Rotterdam* (Nieuwkoop: De Graaf Publishers, 1987), 66–67, has brought out the similarity between Erasmus's spirituality and that of Thomas à Kempis.

25. *Methodus* (*Ratio*), trans. Conroy, 79 (LB 5:77).

26. Ibid., 76–77 (LB 5:76).

Erasmus compares the study of theology with pilgrimages to holy places which demand religious veneration, where we kiss everything devoutly, venerate everything humbly, and act just as if God were present all around us. In the same way, in theological studies we should be reverent with everything and must remember that we need to act in a much more spiritual manner when we are going to enter the inner shrine of the divine Spirit.

What you are permitted to see, admire it with humility; whatever still remains veiled, adore with simple faith and from a distance hold it in reverence and let evil curiosity be far away. You will even be allowed to see certain mysteries precisely because you have reverently withdrawn yourself from gazing at them. Perhaps this is what Moses taught us when he veiled his face in order not to behold the Lord speaking to him from the bush [Ex 3:6].[27]

Erasmus's vision of theology has the mystery of God as its central object. Only by means of the Holy Spirit can this mystery be penetrated. The theologian must be submissive to the Holy Spirit who alone prepares one to understand scripture. To be submissive to him means to have one's heart purified. One's soul must be at peace, and one's mind must thirst after understanding alone. To venerate the mysteries without succumbing to "evil curiosity" is the aim of theology. Chantraine writes in summary of Erasmus's intent: "The interior teacher [*doctor*], who is the Holy Spirit, thus elevates, for the person who is submissive to his action, the capacity for comprehending. The understanding of Scripture, which St. Paul calls prophecy, is knowledge that is capable of transforming."[28]

The theologian's moral and intellectual transformation takes place through prayer and contemplative study of scripture. Therefore, Erasmus challenges the aspiring theologian to learn scripture by heart, and to do so from direct study of the Bible and not indirectly from medieval summaries of biblical passages or from commentaries. "Make your heart itself into a library of Christ. From it, like from the provident householder, you can bring forth "new things and old" (Mt 13:52) as they should be needed. For these things which come forth from your own heart, as it were, practically alive, penetrate far more vividly into the souls of your listeners than those things which are gathered up from a hodgepodge of other authors."[29] The priest and teacher of theology should have the scriptures always in his hands, always by his side,

---

27. Ibid., 77–78 (LB 5:76–77).
28. G. Chantraine, "The Ratio Verae Theologiae (1518)," in *Essays on the Works of Erasmus*, ed. R. L. DeMolen (New Haven, Conn.: Yale University Press, 1978), 180.
29. *Methodus* (*Ratio*), trans. Conroy, 341 (LB 5:132).

and he should commit them to memory. It is not that Erasmus disapproves of the study of commentaries, but he thinks that our knowledge of the Bible should not be obtained indirectly but directly from meditation on the sacred text. This will inflame the hearts of one's students and parishioners more powerfully than second-hand citations.

Erasmus commends the study of commentaries as well, and says that Origen's are the most outstanding, "who has raised this morning star so high that no one after him dares to put his hand to this task!"[30] Moreover, there is Tertullian, Erasmus says: "a man so prodigious and learned in Sacred Literature that not without cause was Cyprian accustomed to call him master!"[31] If Cyprian revered Tertullian's writings in this way, and Jerome, as everyone knows, praised Origen to the skies, then Erasmus feels that his contemporaries should be emboldened to study even these non-canonized teachers of the ancient church whose writings have been preserved. Indeed, Erasmus says, nothing prevents the aspiring theologian from arriving at the point these ancient saints and scholars have arrived at if he travels by the same route, namely through the intensive and contemplative study of scripture. Erasmus adds:

> I do not say these things because I want to be an authority for anyone at all, in order that, after going beyond the commentaries of the ancients, one might claim authority for himself or even attain to a knowledge of the Holy Scriptures. In fact, the work of the ancients should relieve us of part of the labor; we are aided by their commentaries so long as we only select the best among them, such as Origen, who is the foremost, so that no one else can be compared to him. Then after him there is Basil, Nazianzus, Athanasius, Cyril, Chrysostom, Jerome, Ambrose, Hilary and Augustine. We should, hereafter, read even these authors with critical judgment and discretion, although I wish them to be read with reverence. They were human beings: some things they did not know; they were deceived in some matters; at times they got tired; they gave their utmost to overcoming heretics by whose arguments everything at that time was stirred up; they presented certain topics for the ears of those to whom they were then speaking.[32]

So for Erasmus it is incumbent upon the aspiring theologian to study the sacred text directly and obtain his knowledge from that source. Secondly one should become conversant with ancient exegesis, even though Erasmus ad-

---

30. Ibid., 342 (LB 5:132). Origen's *Commentary on Romans* is surely uppermost in Erasmus's mind here, since the *Commentary on John* was not known during Erasmus's day, and to my knowledge he had not yet discovered Origen's *Commentary on Matthew*.
31. Ibid.; cf. Jerome, *De Viris Illustribus*, 53.
32. *Methodus* (*Ratio*), trans. Conroy, 342–43 (LB 5:133).

mits that sometimes the Fathers go astray in their excessive zeal to refute heretics. Not everything they wrote is of lasting value. It is noteworthy that Erasmus's idea that one must learn the content of scripture directly from the sacred text itself and not indirectly through the theologians is a point about which Cardinal Marcello Cervini will remind the theologians of the Council of Trent.[33] This obviously was no accident but shows the direct influence of Erasmus's ideas upon Cervini.

Knowledge of the Original Languages

In terms of the practical linguistic training of theologians, Erasmus was inspired by the Renaissance movement, by the historical examples of Origen (d. 254) and Jerome (d. 420), as well as the explicit recommendation of Augustine (d. 430) in De doctrina Christiana 2.11 to commend the knowledge of the original languages of scripture. "Now with regard to those literary studies, with whose aid we more skillfully attain to these virtues, our primary concern must without question be to learn thoroughly the three languages of Latin, Greek and Hebrew, because it is evident that all the Sacred Scriptures have been recorded in these languages."[34] Erasmus expresses his firm belief that theology needs to be built on the foundation of a philological and historical study of scripture. Since scripture is divinely inspired and was originally written in Hebrew and Greek, the theologian should make it his goal to acquire the knowledge of these languages. Erasmus's proposition assumes that the knowledge of the Latin Vulgate alone has become inadequate for the training of a theologian. He does not say outright that knowledge of the biblical languages is so vital to a theologian that no one could be a theologian without them, but he does insist that in interpreting the scriptures and explaining their mysteries a theologian risks running into serious trouble without the assistance of the original languages. Chantraine clarifies the theological rationale for this:

---

33. Cf. McNally, "Trent and Vernacular Bibles," 206. Cervini became Pope Marcellus II (1555). McNally cites an oration by Cardinal Madruzzo at the Council of Trent in defense of the use of scripture in the vernacular, in which the cardinal says that no age, no sex, no condition, no station should be prevented from reading scripture. Everyone who loves Christ can make his heart a library where the book of Christ rests. McNally calls this speech "a high-water mark in the history of the Bible in the Catholic Church," "words the like of which had rarely, if ever, been heard in the ecclesiastical synods of the Middle Ages" (221). McNally appears to be unaware that Madruzzo's words are derived from the exhortations found in Erasmus's prefaces to the New Testament and from the passage from the *Ratio* cited above.

34. Cf. *Methodus* (*Ratio*), trans. Conroy, 81 (LB 5:77).

Rendered submissive to the prophetic Holy Spirit, human reason receives at the outset inspired Scripture. In an effort to understand Scripture in its spiritual sense, human reason strives in the first place to understand it literally in Hebrew, Greek, and Latin. If one wants to apply himself seriously to theology and if one has some talent in that area, he must learn these three languages. Such knowledge is humble in itself. It has the humility of the incarnate Word.[35]

The worship and adoration of the Word implies respect for the literal sense of scripture, since the Word of God is made known in the historical meaning. The biblical languages are indispensable to the theologian, as is the knowledge of grammar and rhetoric, because the theologian must become familiar with the "style" of the Holy Spirit. The chief reason for studying the profane disciplines is to learn the figures of speech and the nature of rhetoric in order to make theological application of this classical education in the study of scripture.

Weaknesses of Scholastic Theology

Language Deficiencies

Erasmus observes that the scholastic theologians of the medieval and late medieval period were at a disadvantage in that they lived in an epoch before the rebirth of linguistic knowledge that occurred during the Renaissance. They lacked fluency in Greek and Hebrew, which led to mistakes in their interpretation of scripture, and they showed no interest in acquiring the knowledge of these languages. In his annotation on Romans 4:17, Erasmus calls attention to the assistance that he received from Thomas Aquinas's *Super epistolam ad Romanos Lectura* and says that Aquinas would have also made other observations of even more importance if his knowledge of languages had allowed, but he knew only one language, "and not even that one fully."[36] But, Erasmus says, Aquinas deserved to live in an epoch when knowledge of the biblical languages was flourishing.[37] Elsewhere in the *Ratio* Erasmus faults some of the scholastics for misusing scripture at times. This is due sometimes to their need to rely on catena collections, not merely for their knowledge of the Fathers, but even for their knowledge of scripture.

---

35. Chantraine, "The *Ratio Verae Theologiae* (1518)," 180–81.
36. Cf. *Annotations on Romans* (CWE 56:118).
37. Cf. *Annotations on Romans* (CWE 56:10).

Excessive Use of Aristotle

Erasmus also censures some scholastic theologians for the excessive use of Aristotelian philosophy. He names some authors of "empty sophistic discourses" and "extremely confusing summaries and anthologies," but he does not exempt the classical scholastics Thomas Aquinas and Duns Scotus from criticism.[38] Erasmus writes:

> Chrysippus is blamed for having allowed entire tragedies to appear in his commentaries, which he wrote on logic.[39] How much more justifiably will someone blame us, when he sees more than the complete works of Aristotle are contained in the commentaries of theologians! If someone should cry out that one is not a theologian without an exact knowledge of these authors, then I will console myself with the example of so many outstanding men such as Chrysostom, Cyprian, Jerome, Ambrose, Augustine and Clement, among whom I would rather be an unimportant rhetorician than be a theologian among certain others who appear to themselves as more than human beings.[40]

By "commentaries of theologians," Erasmus means the commentaries on Peter Lombard's *Sentences*, the writing of which had become standard as an approach to theological studies. Erasmus clarifies his position in his *Apology against Latomus* in a passage that shows that it is not the use of Aristotelian philosophy in theological studies *per se* that concerns him, but the excessive use:

> We certainly find nothing to criticize in turning the philosophy of Aristotle to the needs of our study of theology. What we resent is rather the setting the whole corpus of Aristotle's works at the very core of theology, and giving almost as much, if not more weight to his authority than to that of the Gospels. If only we were content with Aristotle's *Dialectic*: but what a supplement we have added to it and how we add to that every day![41]

Not all medievals were guilty of this excess singled out by Erasmus, namely of incorporating the writings of the pagan Greek philosopher Aristotle on such a massive scale and placing them at the very core of theological studies. Erasmus's critique would apply far less to Peter Lombard, William of St. Thi-

---

38. Cf. *Methodus* (*Ratio*), trans. Conroy, 105 (LB 5:83). Specifically, in the 1518 edition, Erasmus names Bartholus, Baldus, Averroës, Duranti, Holcot, Birkhead, and Tartaretus. It appears that Erasmus deleted all these names in later editions.

39. Chrysippus of Soli (ca. 280–207 BC) succeeded Cleanthes as head of the Stoa in 232. His extensive writings argued for all aspects of Stoicism and Stoic logic.

40. Cf. *Methodus* (*Ratio*), trans. Conroy, 107 (LB 5:83).

41. *Apology against Latomus* (CWE 71:77).

erry, Bernard, and even Bonaventure than to Albert the Great, Thomas Aquinas, Duns Scotus, and the later scholastics of the fourteenth and fifteenth centuries.[42] In his *Controversy with Albert Pio*, written in 1529, Erasmus defends the validity of this critique, which he had also expressed in his edition of Jerome's writings:

> What is my complaint in the scholia of volume II [of his edition of Jerome] except that too much human philosophy is applied to scholastic theology? This is a criticism of Thomas, but most particularly of Scotus. The correctness of this view is clearly shown by the fact that now a good many schools commit themselves neither to Thomas nor to Scotus, but are shifting to a more sober study of Scripture.[43]

Erasmus concedes here that he has not exempted Thomas and Scotus from his criticism. Yet he defends himself by saying that his criticism has been well-received in a number of places. Later in this chapter I will discuss the Catholic institutions of this pre-Protestant period that had introduced the curricular changes Erasmus mentions here. It is noteworthy that when Erasmus was censured by the theologians of the University of Paris for allegedly condemning scholastic theology in its entirety, in his own defense Erasmus first cited from the works of Jean Gerson (1363–1429), who had made similar complaints about the quarrelsome nature of theology in his day.[44] Erasmus clarified: "Through the fault of some practitioners, we have a theology which is thorny with superfluous difficulties. Let anyone deny this after he has considered how much human philosophy Thomas and those like him have imported into theology, how much thorny matter Scotus also added on his part, to say nothing of the others."[45] It seems safe to conclude that the excessive utilization of Aristotle's writings by some scholastic theologians is one of the scholastic innovations criticized by Erasmus.

To clarify Erasmus's criticism, it is perhaps worth pointing out that Thomas Aquinas's *Summa theologiae* comprises 512 questions and contains 4,300 citations from Aristotle, 8,000 from Christian authors (mostly from Augustine and Pseudo-Dionysius), and 25,000 from the Bible.[46] There are

---

42. I am aware that most of Aristotle's writings were not available in Latin translation for Peter Lombard to use in his *Sentences*. Whether he would have used them had they been available to him, I do not know. My point here, however, is simply to observe that Erasmus's criticism of the excessive use of Aristotle does not apply to all scholastic theologians, but only to those guilty of this excess. Consequently, modern Thomist historians of theology should cease misrepresenting Erasmus by repeating the idea that he globally repudiated the schoolmen.

43. CWE 84:256.   44. See note 80 below.
45. CWE 82:248.
46. J. Verger, "L'exégèse de l'Université," in *Le Moyen Age et la Bible*, ed. P. Riché and G. Lo-

1,700 citations of Pseudo-Dionysius in Aquinas.[47] If my arithmetic is correct, this means that Aquinas averages 8.4 citations of Aristotle per question, and 3.3 citations of Pseudo-Dionysius per question. In contrast, Bonaventure's *Breviloquium* comprises 72 chapters and contains 45 citations of Aristotelian texts versus only 10 of Pseudo-Dionysian texts. Thus Bonaventure cites Aristotle 0.6 times per chapter. (I have not found statistics available for Duns Scotus's writings.) Anyone familiar with the ancient Church Fathers realizes that they scarcely cite Aristotle at all, and when they do it is normally to criticize him.[48] I do not see how one can avoid the conclusion that the scholastic mode of theologizing differs significantly from the patristic mode. Yet in spite of this excess, Erasmus still refers to the scholastics as "us." They are members of the same Catholic and Christian family as Erasmus and his contemporaries; they are indeed the rightful heirs of the Church Fathers, though they invented an innovative theological method that differed radically from the Fathers. The scholastics are the lawful predecessors of the current generation of Catholic theologians, yet the discipline they have influenced and shaped is outmoded in certain respects and needs to be steered now in a new and better direction.

Methodological Doubt

In addition to the problems of linguistic deficiencies and the excessive use of Aristotle, Erasmus offers another specific critique of the scholastic method of theology which deserves special attention. In this particular case it seems that once again Erasmus's main target is Duns Scotus. On the basis of personal experience, Erasmus was convinced that the practice of methodological doubt in scholastic theology led to real uncertainty in matters of faith. Generally the scholastic method of doing theology was to raise doubts even to the articles of faith and then provide answers to the objections raised.[49] Trained as they were in dialectics, some of the scholastics discussed

---

brichon (Paris: Beauchesne, 1984), 217–18. This passage is cited in D. Farkasfalvy, *Inspiration and Interpretation: A Theological Introduction to Sacred Scripture* (Washington, D.C.: The Catholic University of America Press, 2010), 141n2.

47. Cf. P. Casarella, "On the 'Reading Method' in Rorem's Pseudo-Dionysius," *The Thomist* 59, no. 4 (1995): 633–44, cited in W. Riordan, *Divine Light: The Theology of Denys the Areopagite* (San Francisco, Calif.: Ignatius, 2008), 63n94. A number of modern scholars have observed that for Thomas Aquinas the authority of [Pseudo-]Dionysius ranks higher even than that of Augustine himself. Cf. Riordan, *Divine Light*, 62–63, citing De Gandillac, *Oeuvres completes*, 18.

48. See the essay on "Aristotelianism" in Angelo Di Bernardino, ed., *Encyclopedia of the Early Church*, 2 vols. (New York: Oxford University Press, 1992), 1:73–76 [hereafter "EEC"].

49. This assessment would evidently not apply to Bonaventure's *Breviloquium*, which "breaks

every theological issue in the form of questions. They formulated arguments for and against before setting forth their own views. Erasmus writes:

> It appears to be not only superfluous but also dangerous that, concerning these matters which pertain to the vital activity of the faith, one should explore them so anxiously with human arguments. For whoever so carefully and so curiously assembles reasons by which he either attacks or safeguards what has been handed down to us for believing and not for discussion seems to doubt somewhat. And it quite frequently happens that such men, by investigating everything with more curiosity than devotion, come across certain reasons which wrench loose and weaken the vigor of faith. I personally know several people who, on account of Scotus' reasonings in which he deals with the evidence for the Eucharist, have admitted to having been seduced to the extent that they truly wavered in spirit and were scarcely able to shake off this doubting.[50]

When Erasmus mentions "evidence for the Eucharist" here, he means the Catholic belief in the real presence of Christ in the eucharist. Erasmus expresses real pastoral concerns that have arisen in response to seeing men's faith shaken as a result of reading Scotus's discussions.[51]

Erasmus finds it objectionable that there is nothing in scholastic disputations which is not called into doubt. Duns Scotus in particular discusses even the most approved articles, like the sacramental status of the eucharist, on both sides with equal probability. Erasmus faults Scotus for supplying arguments opposing the truth that sometimes have more strength than those

---

the bonds of Scholastic theology." D. Monti, quoting Gerken, in *Works of St. Bonaventure IX, Breviloquium* (Saint Bonaventure University, N.Y.: Franciscan Institute Publications, 2005), xxii.

50. *Methodus* (*Ratio*), trans. Conroy, 351–52 (LB 5:134–35). For a helpful discussion that includes a description of "Scotus' reasonings" about transubstantiation, see J. F. McCue, "The Doctrine of Transubstantiation from Berengar through Trent: The Point at Issue," *Harvard Theological Review* 61, no. 3 (1968): 385–430.

51. To me it seems noteworthy that in contrast with this quite serious criticism of Duns Scotus on the subject of the eucharist, in *CWE* 9, ep. 1334, Erasmus praises Thomas Aquinas's discussion of the eucharist as his theological masterpiece. The passage is found in Erasmus's dedicatory epistle to his edition of the writings of Hilary of Poitiers. Erasmus says of Hilary's treatise *De Trinitate*: "He seems to have exerted all his energy, however, to manifest and put forth in this work whatever he could by his natural ability, by his eloquence, and by his knowledge of Holy Scripture. For we see that it was usually the ambition of distinguished writers as well as of outstanding painters and sculptors to leave in some one work a finished and complete example of their art by which posterity might be able to evaluate what they would have been able to do if they had wished to exert their fullest powers. Virgil seems to have attempted this in the *Georgics*, Ovid in his *Medea*, Cicero in *De oratore*, Augustine in *De civitate Dei*, Jerome in his commentaries on the prophets, *Thomas Aquinas on the subject of the Eucharist*, Bernard on the Canticle" (emphasis added).

in favor of it. With his overly subtle arguments, Scotus even endangers the church, undermines her dogmas, and gives a handle to heretics. With the advantage of hindsight, one might paraphrase Erasmus's concern with this epigram: "Scotus laid the egg that Luther, Zwingli, Capito, Oecolampadius, and Calvin hatched." In other words, the scholastic writers supplied the reformers of Wittenberg, Zürich, Strasbourg, Basel, and Geneva with the arguments they would eventually use against the church. It is not that this was the original intention of the scholastic writers, but this was the use to which their writings were put by the reformers.

Bejczy very insightfully observes that Erasmus's criticism of scholasticism on this point contradicts the idea that Erasmus "consistently favored a rhetorical approach to theology aimed at discussing the truth without providing definite answers, as did the scholastics."[52] In fact, the situation is precisely the reverse. Erasmus wants to see Catholic dogma embraced, not called into question and endlessly debated and discussed using the scholastic method. This is not a plea for fideism, nor is it the case that Erasmus thinks that the scholastic theologians themselves actually doubted the truth of the questions they discussed. It is rather that in Erasmus's judgment they sometimes provided more forceful arguments against the truth than in favor of it. Erasmus had witnessed the detrimental effects of this in persons he knew.

Corroboration of Erasmus's Criticisms by John Fisher and Thomas More

If Erasmus has expressed what appears to me to be a legitimate pastoral concern about the detrimental effects on personal faith of excessive scholastic questioning, John Fisher makes reference to a concrete example of an individual who actually took the next step dreaded by Erasmus and abandoned the Catholic faith after being trained in the scholastic method. At the beginning of his treatise in defense of the Catholic doctrine of the eucharist against the Protestant reformer John Oecolampadius, Fisher reflects on scholastic theological methods in ways that are reminiscent of Erasmus.

Every time I read the treatise that Oecolampadius wrote on the words of the Lord's Supper, I feel that I am involved in those scholastic exercises where it is the custom to argue on both sides of any case at all. There is nothing at all that is so true and

---

52. Istvan Bejczy, *Erasmus and the Middle Ages: The Historical Consciousness of a Christian Humanist* (Leiden: Brill, 2001), 76.

readily admitted by everyone that those who are accustomed to disputations will not attempt to oppose it, producing from any sources arguments that are probable on their face, so to ensnare the defender of the real truth that for the most part he cannot easily extricate and free himself, though he would like to. What is truer or more certain than the existence of God? And yet if you bring this truth into disputation, those who are skilled in the art of deception will assail it in so many ways, will attack it with so many clever arguments, will spring upon it with so many sophisms; and by gathering together deceits from so many sources, and scraping together so many passages, as many as have any appearance of probability, they will bring upon their listeners such a cloud of darkness that there will be danger of their persuading the inexperienced that what before seemed most true to them is most false.[53]

Fisher seems to imply that at least some of the contemporary Catholic practitioners of scholastic methods of disputation are actually men who are skilled in deception, sophisms, and clever deceits. (Erasmus clearly would have agreed with this opinion.) To Fisher it seemed that the Protestant reformer Oecolampadius has imitated decadent scholastic methodology in his discussion of the mystery of the Lord's Supper, using similar sophisms, prattling, deceit, and falsehoods, to contend that the true body and blood are not present in the eucharist.

It is also noteworthy that Thomas More, in his *Letter to Dorp*, criticizes some of the monstrous absurdities and quibbles that have crept into theological studies using logic and dialectics. Thomas More writes:

Yet these quibbles, which do not even merit the label "sophistic," are not seen as sophistical trifles; instead, they are numbered among the most recondite treasures of dialectic. They are not learned by boys as things to be unlearned later on; instead, they are introduced even by old men into the innermost shrine of theology. Some of them use these quibbles to pad out perplexed theological inquiries; from these quibbles they contrive such ridiculous propositions that nowhere on earth could you find such a rich crop of laughing matter, although I would much rather see those who talk this sort of drivel converted to sanity than take pleasure myself in the drivel they talk while insane.[54]

It appears to me that More's criticisms of contemporary theological methods are less moderate and more subversive than Erasmus's.[55] The main target is neither Lombard, nor Thomas Aquinas nor Duns Scotus (though they

---

53. T. Marie Dougherty, *St. John Fisher's De Veritate Corporis et Sanguinis Christi in Eucharistia, The Prefaces: Text and Translation with Introduction and Notes* (PhD diss., The Catholic University of America, 1969), 46–48.

54. CW 15.37.

55. Thomas More's *Letter to Dorp* was proscribed by a Catholic inquisitor in a Madrid *Index*

PROGRAM *for* THEOLOGICAL RENEWAL   19

are not completely excluded), but scholastics of the era contemporary with Fisher, More, and Erasmus. Yet it was Lombard's *Sentences* combined with the translation of Aristotle's writings into Latin that began the whole scholastic enterprise. If a line can be drawn between the concerns of Erasmus, John Fisher, and Thomas More in respect to their criticism of contemporary scholastic theological method, I am not able to discern it.[56]

Erasmus backs up his criticism with citations from John Chrysostom, who in his homilies deters us from the excessive use of philosophy and from lingering with excessive curiosity over questions about the faith. Erasmus continues:

> Who then would attempt to explain the nature of God with so many subtleties? Who would fabricate so many riddles about charity such as these: What is its essence? In how many ways is it received? Where and to what extent is it proper to practice it? Now, is this questioning not harmful since it lingers while in the face of reality itself? And in fact, you will more quickly discover this charity among the uneducated than among those who endlessly dispute about it![57]

Debating the definition of charity is a poor excuse for learned men to fail to practice it. Erasmus illustrates his point with an anecdote from his own life. He says that he once had a disputation with a certain theologian, who was an educated and faultless human being, who had, however, lingered too long over Scotistic arguments. They talked about the sacraments and could not agree with each other. The man turned to Erasmus's assistant and said: "Even if Erasmus should desire to teach Greek, he cannot do it in only a few days! And how can it happen that he immediately understands what a sacra-

---

librorum expurgatorum of 1584 because of the harsh criticisms it contains of contemporary Catholic theologians (see CW 15:cxviii). A published version (1563) of More's *Letter to Dorp* omits the following passage: "My dear Dorp, I am so far from praising such men that I even think these theologians in name, not in fact, should be forced, as the Romans compelled bad officials to give up their public employments, to resign from the office they occupy so undeservingly" (CW 15:cxxiii; 76, lines 15–19). To me More's indignation seems justifiable, but it would be unjust to interpret his words literally, as the censor apparently did who struck the passage out of the work.

56. In two important books by E. Surtz, *The Praise of Wisdom: A Commentary on the Religious and Moral Problems and Backgrounds of St. Thomas More's Utopia* (Chicago: Loyola University Press, 1957) and *Works and Days of John Fisher*, substantial coincidence of thought and attitude is demonstrated between Thomas More, John Fisher, and Erasmus, in the realms of religion, society, theology, education, needed church reforms, and morality. For the handful of instances where Surtz attempts to depict Erasmus as more radical and less reliably orthodox than More or Fisher, he does not provide convincing textual evidence for this and ignores other evidence that points in the opposite direction.

57. *Methodus* (*Ratio*), trans. Conroy, 352 (LB 5:135).

ment is?" Erasmus concludes from this exchange: "It is an unusual situation, indeed, if we must dispute for ten years so that we might understand what a sacrament is, since it is quite necessary for everyone to use the sacraments for salvation."[58] Once again, in light of statements like this, it seems ironic that Erasmus has been accused of having too low a view of the sacraments. It is he who is insisting upon an end to the debates about their necessity for salvation.

Thomas More has written a passage in his *Letter to Dorp* that is strikingly similar to Erasmus's words and that shows the close bond between the two men. More finds Dorp's statement unendurable that modern scholastic problems are more useful to Christ's flock than knowledge of scripture.

> For if you claimed that those problems were worth knowing, I would certainly not disagree; if you set them alongside the works of the ancients, I would say you were going too far; since in fact you rank those kitchenmaids of yours not just as high as but indeed even higher than the Bible itself, holy queen of all genres of literature, you must pardon me, Dorp, but by Jove I cannot keep from sending them packing with that line from Terence, "Get lost, you tramps, and take those grand airs with you!"[59]

According to the testimony of Thomas More, contemporary scholastics at the University of Louvain, including Martin Dorp in the period prior to his conversion to Erasmian humanism, ranked their questions ahead of the Bible in importance. This is certainly confirmed by the text from Jacob Latomus cited above. Dorp had said: "How else are we to know how we ought to administer the sacraments, what their forms are, when we ought to absolve and when we ought to refuse absolution to a sinner, how much restitution we must make and how much we can keep?" To this More replies:

> Dorp, do you really think that all the old holy fathers, who were as learned as they were devout, were completely ignorant of all those points which you suppose to be found only in modern compilers of problems. Were Jerome, Ambrose, and Augustine stark blind when it came to the form and matter of the sacraments? And so for more than a thousand years—note that more than a thousand years separate the passion of Christ and the time of Peter Lombard, whose *Sentences*, like the Trojan horse, poured forth this entire army of problems—for so many years, no, for so many centuries, was the Church without sacraments? Did it not have the same ones? Was it so long unknown when we ought to absolve the sinner and when we ought to refuse absolution?[60]

---

58. *Methodus* (*Ratio*), trans. Conroy, 353–54 (LB 5:135).
59. Thomas More, *Letter to Dorp* (CW 15:63–65). The quote is from Terence, *Phormio*, 930–32.
60. Thomas More, *Letter to Dorp* (CW 15:63–65).

More goes on to say that he thinks that whatever is necessary for salvation has been transmitted to us, first of all through scripture itself, then through its first interpreters, then too by the customs transmitted from hand to hand, as it were, by the ancient Fathers, and finally through the sacred decrees of the church. However, the casuistry that was developed in the scholastic period went far beyond what is really essential to the church.

Erasmus and More see a clear contrast here between the approach to truth of the Church Fathers and the method of systematic doubt introduced and espoused by some of the scholastics and their successors. Erasmus again quotes Chrysostom, who said: "Consequently, we are commanded to search the Scriptures so that we may not always be searching but that we may cease searching once we have been confirmed by their authority." Erasmus appends to this:

It was not said to them that they should add this: "Search the philosophy of Aristotle. Perhaps the resurrection of the dead can be taught with its assistance." But rather: "Search the Scriptures" (Jn 5:39). Therein Paul shows to what extent the investigation of the Holy Writings is to be employed and toward what goal the learning of theology is to be directed, when he says: "The goal of instruction is love from a pure heart and a good conscience and unfeigned faith" (1 Tm 1:5). Therefore, we must deeply ponder Sacred Literature as far as our diligence leads us to those matters which Paul has mentioned.[61]

In summary, Erasmus prefers the Bible to Aristotle. He proposes that the practice of raising doubts about established dogma should be mitigated; he hopes to see the neglected treatises and exegesis of the orthodox Greek and Latin Fathers engaged directly and formatively in theological studies (as opposed to the proof-texting approach that utilizes catena collections or excerpts from a very limited number of Church Fathers, as found in Lombard's *Sentences*). Erasmus clearly feels that his contemporaries have much to learn about theological method from the ancients, such as Chrysostom.

Contrasting the Fathers with the Scholastics

The learning and holiness of the Church Fathers and the superiority of their writings over those of the medieval period was so obvious to Erasmus that he was deeply tormented by the loss of so many of their works. He wrote, "I can scarcely refrain from tears as I read the lists of ancient authors

---

61. *Methodus* (*Ratio*), trans. Conroy, 355 (LB 5:135).

and see what wealth we have lost. My grief increases when I compare the quality of our losses with what we now commonly read."[62] Many scholastics ignored the great theologians and exegetes of antiquity with the exception of Augustine and Pseudo-Dionysius. Much of the Greek tradition of exegesis was a sealed book to the scholastics, with John Damascene being the major exception. To Erasmus this neglect had gone on long enough. Another outburst of feeling is found in the dedication of several works of Athanasius in Latin translation as an annex to Erasmus's *Chrysostomi lucubrationes*.[63] Erasmus writes to bishop John Longland:

Every hunter, reverend bishop, has his favorite quarry. I count myself the luckiest of men, because recently I tracked down a manuscript containing many of the writings of St Athanasius. I think it is of the greatest importance for the well-being of Christendom that we lose none of the writings left us by that eloquent champion of the church. This great man deserved not just to have an immortal name, but to live on, immortal in a mortal world, and to survive entire.[64]

The passage undoubtedly reveals the driving inspiration of Erasmus's life: to help the church by making available the writings of the ancient Fathers. One can only be grateful for Erasmus's many hunting expeditions in monastic and university libraries that yielded quarry such as he describes here. In the *Ratio* Erasmus encourages the theology student to directly engage the writings of the Greek and Latin Church Fathers. Let him contrast and compare those old theologians such as Origen, Basil, Athanasius, Chrysostom, and Jerome with these more recent ones.

He will see how with the former a golden river, so to speak, is flowing, whereas here among the latter some tiny rivulets flow and these are neither altogether pure nor commensurate with their source.[65] Among the former thunder the oracles of eternal truth; with the latter you hear the little chatter of humans, whose narratives vanish like empty dreams the more closely you inspect them. With the former you will be directed on the right course toward the harbor of evangelical truth; with the latter you tire yourself struggling among the windings of human questions or you dash yourself against the Scylla of pontifical power or into the Syrtes of Scholastic teachings or into the Symplegades (unless you would prefer to make it the Charyb-

---

62. CWE 5, ep. 676:32–35. 63. Basel: Froben, 1527.
64. CWE 12, ep. 1790.
65. It is worth noting that Plutarch, in his *Life of Cicero*, says that Cicero had described the works of Aristotle (now mostly lost to us) as "a river of gold." Erasmus's contemporary scholastic theologians viewed Aristotle (in Latin translation) similarly, but they disdained the direct study of the Church Fathers, whom Erasmus regarded as the real river of gold.

dis) of divine and human law.[66] With the former supported by the firm foundations of the Scriptures the building rises upward; with the latter through the futile sophistry of man or, even at times, his cringing flattery is as fickle as a huge make-shift scaffolding which is built up to a monstrous size. With the former you will be, as it were, very delighted and satisfied in the gardens of supreme happiness; while with the latter you will lacerate and torture yourself among the barren thorn bushes. With the former everything is filled with majesty, while with the latter there is just nothing magnificent so that you will find much shabbiness and so little worthy of theological dignity.[67]

Here the direct use of patristic sources is contrasted with the scholastic method of extracting proof-texts from the writings of the Fathers in order to prove human propositions. Rummel is surely correct when she says that Erasmus "disdains medieval glosses and commentaries and recommends instead source reading and patristic writings."[68] With regard to Erasmus's critique of the "more recent" theologians in this passage, Bouyer comments: "It is easy to see the underlying criticism, which comes out fully later on, of what scholastic theology had become in the course of the fourteenth and fifteenth centuries."[69]

While he does promote the direct use of the writings of the Church Fathers, Erasmus adds a caveat, namely that we should not be so attached to any single church-approved exegete as to consider it wrong to dissent from him on some particular point. In other words one must never confuse the exegetical opinions of the Fathers with dogma and the common opinion of the church. By no means does Erasmus regard the Fathers as infallible interpreters of scripture. Lengthy sections of the *Ratio* are devoted to showing weaknesses and blind spots in the exegesis of the ancient Fathers. At times Erasmus says that their reactionary polemics against heretics, or the excessive influence of Origen's allegorism, has resulted in untenable and erroneous interpretations of scripture. So, just as he had identified what he regarded as weaknesses in the scholastic theologians, he equally expresses cautions about the Fathers.

66. Scylla was a six-headed sea-monster with a ring of barking dogs around her belly in the Straits of Messina opposite Charybdis, a whirlpool, past which Odysseus had to sail. The Syrtes were notoriously dangerous shoals and shallows off the Libyan continental shelf of North Africa. The Symplegades were the Clashing Rocks which guarded the entrance at the Bosporus to the Black Sea, past which Jason sailed.
67. *Methodus (Ratio)*, trans. Conroy, 99–100 (LB 5:82).
68. Rummel, *Erasmus and His Catholic Critics*, 1:83.
69. Bouyer, *Erasmus and His Times*, 158.

Erasmus endeavored to promote the study of the Church Fathers particularly during the last twenty years of his life (1516–36). With the assistance of a team of collaborators, Erasmus published critical editions of the writings of Jerome (1516), Cyprian (1520), Arnobius (1522), Hilary (1523), John Chrysostom (1525), Irenaeus (1526), Athanasius (1527), Ambrose (1527), Faustus of Riez (1528), Augustine (1529), Gregory Nazianzen (1531), Basil (1532), and Origen (1536).[70] With the exception of Augustine, most of these authors were scarcely known or utilized by scholastic writers. The editions of the Greek Fathers included Erasmus's own original Latin translations of selected works or translations done by his colleagues. The eighth volume (of ten) of Erasmus's *Opera Omnia* is comprised entirely of his own translations (into Latin) of the writings of the Greek Fathers Origen, Athanasius, Chrysostom, and Basil of Caesarea. L. Bouyer writes: "Although for most of these labors he had a whole team of scholars working under his guidance, there is still something quite stupendous in the sheer extent of this work of bringing ancient exegesis and the ancient biblical theology up to date."[71] In the field of patristic studies Erasmus's achievement has scarcely been appreciated. The standard Catholic patrologists do not take Erasmus into consideration in their respective surveys of ancient Christian literature.[72] On the other hand the Jesuit historian J. O'Malley noticed with respect to Erasmus's expertise in the Fathers: "His knowledge of them staggers us even today, and his editions of their works represent a watershed in the history of patristic studies."[73]

Retention of the Scholastics in the Erasmian Program

In light of the rebirth of knowledge brought by the Renaissance, Erasmus challenged the *status quo* and proposed a new theological method, or rather proposed changing and supplementing the old theological method by giving far greater precedence to the study of scripture, knowledge of its original languages, and the direct engagement with the exegesis of the Church Fathers. He was firmly supported in this endeavor by Thomas More and John Fisher, the only two canonized saints of the period acquainted with Eras-

---

70. For a the brief discussion of each of Erasmus's patristic editions, see Jan den Boeft, "Erasmus and the Church Fathers," in *Reception of the Church Fathers*, ed. Backus, 2:537–72.

71. L. Bouyer, "Erasmus in Relation to the Medieval Biblical Tradition," in *The Cambridge History of the Bible*, ed. G. Lampe (Cambridge: Cambridge University Press, 1969), 2:500.

72. O. Bardenhewer, *Geschichte der altkirchlichen Literatur*, 5 vols. (Freiburg im Breisgau: Herder, 1913–32); J. Quasten, *Patrology*, 4 vols. (Utrecht-Antwerp: Spectrum, 1975).

73. Introduction to Erasmus's *Enchiridion* (CWE 66:xxvii).

mus who expressed an opinion about the matter. One of these men (Fisher) died as a cardinal-elect of Pope Paul III. The other (More) had been commissioned by the bishop of London to protect England from Protestant heresies.[74] In other words, Fisher and More's agreement with Erasmus should be received not as feigned flattery from his friends but as mature theological assessments.

Yet Erasmus also was careful to explain that he was not advocating disdain for the classical scholastic authors, or a *sola scriptura* principle for theology, or some sort of nostalgic return to the epoch of the New Testament or of the Fathers, to the complete detriment of medieval Catholicism. In his *Methodus* he criticized scholastic theology on particular methodological points, just as he had criticized patristic exegesis on particular hermeneutical points, but in neither field does this entail a global rejection. He makes this very explicit:

Indeed, let no one interpret what we have said as intending by this to condemn entirely those who have left us nothing except questions or to disapprove of Scholastic disputations from which the truth is quite often elicited not differently than when fire is produced from the collision of flint stones. Rather we only request moderation and discretion in these debates. Moderation will cause one not to inquire into everything; discretion will cause one not to investigate anything he may choose.[75]

Erasmus goes on to say that much worthwhile reading is also contained in the books of the "modern" (scholastic) authors, but these should be dipped into moderately, according to one's age, and dealt with soberly and chastely. For the scholastic method was completely unknown among theologians at one time. Erasmus explains his aims in his *Apology against Latomus*: to link linguistic skills, elegant expression, and knowledge of ancient authors with the traditional methods of study.[76] Erasmus was aware that his proposed method could not totally supplant the scholastic one, nor did he wish to challenge the established logic and replace it with a superior one. On this latter point Christine Christ-Von Wedel notes the contrast between Erasmus and the Italian humanist Lorenzo Valla.[77]

---

74. See Christopher J. Malloy, "Thomas More on Luther's Sola Fide: Just or Unjust?," *Angelicum* 90 (2013): 761–98.

75. *Methodus* (*Ratio*), trans. Conroy, 361–62 (LB 5:136–37).

76. Cf. *Apology against Latomus* (CWE 71:38).

77. Lorenzo Valla (1406–57) was the most acute critical philologist of the first half of the fifteenth century. He proved that the *Donation of Constantine* was a forgery in his work *De false credita et ementita Constantini donatione declamatio* (1440). He wrote a work entitled *Elegantia linguae latinae*

As far as Erasmus was aware of them, he was not convinced by Valla's attempts to refute [sic] Aristotelian philosophy through linguistic analysis. An awareness of his own modest ability in this field held him back from making any similar attempts. Instead, Erasmus contented himself with pointing out the defects of the Scholastics and on emphasizing the merits of the Church Fathers. To that end, in his own editions and *Annotationes* of the New Testament he attempted to make the work of the Church Fathers more accessible. His philological-historical exegesis was groundbreaking, but he did not create a new dialectical method or come up with new ways to do without Scholastic logic; indeed, he did not even attempt a frontal attack on the Scholastic method. He only attempted to assign it to its proper place.[78]

This accurate assessment shows that Erasmus's approach to theology worked in continuity with theology's inherited language and definitions and was far more traditional than either Valla's or Luther's approach. Indeed, Christian Dolfen formulated the question of his doctoral dissertation from the above-cited passage of Erasmus.[79] He endeavored to put Erasmus's words to the test and to ask whether Erasmus sincerely had no intention of repudiating scholastic writers. Dolfen's inductive study of Erasmus's writings led him to the conclusion that Erasmus indeed meant what he said. He did not repudiate scholastic method entirely but, like Jean Gerson before him, recommended that it should be practiced with greater moderation and that it should be complemented by the new philological and patristic knowledge that was becoming available.[80] Dolfen's study proved that Erasmus had largely integrated the theology of high scholasticism into his own writings.

Erasmus's Admiration of Thomas Aquinas

In spite of his strictures about excessive Aristotelianism in some scholastics, including Aquinas and Scotus, Erasmus seems to have held Thomas

---

(*Elegance of the Latin Language*) which has been called a landmark in the history of Renaissance philology. He wrote an oration in praise of Thomas Aquinas, as well as *Annotations on the Greek New Testament* in which he made comments that were critical of the Vulgate translation at times. Erasmus discovered the latter work in a library and published it in 1505. Valla published a first-ever Latin translation of the Greek historian Thucydides (Venice, 1485).

78. Christine Christ-Von Wedel, *Erasmus of Rotterdam: Advocate of a New Christianity* (Toronto: University of Toronto Press, 2013), 29.

79. C. Dolfen, *Die Stellung des Erasmus von Rotterdam zur scholastischen Methode* (Osnabrück, 1936), 9 and 108.

80. Jean Gerson (1363–1429) was a nominalist (Ockhamist) theologian and chancellor of the University of Paris (successor of Peter of Ailly). He attacked vain curiosity in theology and especially the Scotists. He authored *The Mountain of Contemplation* (1397); *On the Spiritual Life of the*

Aquinas in especially high esteem.[81] For instance, the *Annotations on Romans* in the final edition of Erasmus's New Testament (1535) contains 139 explicit citations from Origen, 124 from Chrysostom, 113 from Theophylact, 106 from Ambrosiaster, 67 from Augustine, 48 from Jerome, 21 from Thomas Aquinas, and 14 from Lorenzo Valla.[82] In light of the common opinion that Erasmus "had nothing but disdain for the scholastics," it seems noteworthy that the number of engagements with medieval scholastic Thomas Aquinas exceeds those from the Renaissance humanist Lorenzo Valla.[83] Does one cite an author with such frequency for whom one has "nothing but disdain"? In his *Ratio* Erasmus highly commends Thomas Aquinas, whom he describes as "the most enlightened among all the more recent theologians."[84] Erasmus says that in his opinion, no other modern authors can be compared with Aquinas.[85] Erasmus cited Thomas Aquinas more often in his New Testament *Annotations* than did John Fisher in any of his published works.[86] In his *Annotation* on Romans 1:4, Erasmus praised Thomas Aquinas in these words:

[He was] on any count a great man, and not only in his own time. For there is no recent theologian, at least in my opinion, who is his equal in diligence, more distinguished in ability, more solid in learning; and he certainly deserved to obtain a knowledge of languages as well, and everything else belonging to the study of good literature, inasmuch as he so skillfully used the resources available to him in his day.[87]

Soul (1394); and *On the Unity of the Church* (1409). Nine complete editions of Gerson's works were published at Cologne, Strasbourg, Basel, and Paris between 1483 and 1521. See James L. Connolly, *John Gerson: Reformer and Mystic* (Louvain: Herder, 1928).

81. See Jean-Pierre Massaut, "Erasme et saint Thomas," in *Colloquia Erasmiana Turonensia*, ed. J.-C. Margolin (Paris: Vrin, 1972), 2:581–611.

82. A. Godin, "Fonction d'Origène dans la pratique exégètique d'Erasme: Les Annotations sur l'Épitre aux Romains," in *Histoire de l'exégèse au XVIe siècle*, ed. O. Fatio and P. Fraenkel (Geneva: Libraire Droz, 1978), 17. Godin did not include Aquinas in his tally. See also Scheck, *Origen and the History of Justification*, chap. 5. The index of CWE 56 (Erasmus's *Annotations on Romans*) references Thomas Aquinas's *Super epistolam ad Romanos lectura* with "*passim*"; see 10–11, 17, 86–87, 134, 202, 224–27, 262, 302, 312, 318, 322, 374, 433–34.

83. A very helpful study is Bejczy, *Erasmus and the Middle Ages*. His thesis is that Erasmus's attachment to tradition is consistent with the outlook on history which he had developed in his early years. The Protestant Reformation did not change Erasmus into a conservative, but accentuated an existing attitude.

84. *Methodus* (*Ratio*), trans. Conroy, 85 (LB 5:78).

85. Ibid. Cf. H. C. Porter, "Fisher and Erasmus," in *Humanism, Reform and the Reformation: The Career of Bishop John Fisher*, ed. B. Bradshaw and E. Duffy (New York: Cambridge University Press, 1989), 91.

86. Cf. R. Rex, *The Theology of John Fisher* (New York: Cambridge University Press, 1991), 63.

87. CWE 56:10.

It is clear that Erasmus found limitations in Aquinas's linguistic knowledge, namely his entire lack of Greek and imperfect knowledge of Latin. Yet he regards Thomas's intellectual abilities as truly superior. A character in Erasmus's *Antibarbari* who seems to represent Erasmus's own opinion expresses admiration of Aquinas's secular learning: "That most noble writer Thomas Aquinas brought out commentaries on the pagan philosopher Aristotle, and even in his theological *Questions*, where he is reflecting about the first principle and about the Trinity, he offers evidence from Cicero and the poets."[88]

This is not to say, of course, that Aquinas held for Erasmus the same authoritative position that he acquired in the nineteenth and twentieth centuries, which to my understanding was largely the result of the promotion of Aquinas by Pope Leo XIII in the encyclical *Aeterni Patris* (1879) and the papal imposition of Thomistic thought on Catholic seminaries, a trend that ended after the Second Vatican Council.[89] I do not believe that Franciscan or Augustinian theologians attributed such supreme importance to Aquinas, though he was respected as a leading theologian. Non-Dominicans, including Erasmus, respected Aquinas for his holiness and his greatness as a theologian but did not attribute to him the theological principate that he later acquired. The Franciscans had their own intellectual heroes, such as Bonaventure, Scotus, and Ockham.

Implementation of Erasmus's Program

In the *Ratio*, Erasmus gives some examples of the successful implementation of the Renaissance Christian humanist program for the renewal of Catholic theology. These examples pertain to the pre-Reformation period in Europe. He observes that in some academies, the scholastic method had begun to be considered more sparingly and moderately, as for instance, among the Britons at Cambridge and among the Brabanters at Louvain.[90] Notice how for Erasmus it is a question of moderating, not eliminating, the use of scholastic methods of theology. Elimination would be the achievement of the Reformation in Wittenberg, Germany, under the leadership of Martin Luther, and of Cromwell's injunctions in England in 1535, when the

---

88. CWE 23:112, 114–18.

89. See Gerald A. McCool, *From Unity to Pluralism: The Internal Evolution of Thomism* (New York: Fordham University Press, 1989), and *Catholic Theology in the Nineteenth Century: The Quest for a Unitary Method* (New York: Seabury Press, 1977).

90. Methodus (Ratio), trans. Conroy, 362 (LB 5:136–37).

universities "swept away large tracts of the medieval curriculum."[91] The reform of theology at Cambridge University alluded to here by Erasmus was the work of Bishop John Fisher himself, its chancellor.[92] Fisher supported Erasmus's educational reforms, and vice versa. Neither Fisher nor Erasmus promoted the total abandonment of the old scholasticism in their embrace of the new humanism. Rather, they wanted to preserve the best of both in a new synthesis. It is interesting and noteworthy to observe, however, that for John Fisher, in dramatic contrast with Erasmus, the best of scholasticism was represented by John Duns Scotus, not Thomas Aquinas.[93] Fisher's statutes for St. John's College provided for regular lectures in Greek and Hebrew, but they also laid down that the questions for academic disputation were to be taken from the Subtle Doctor, Duns Scotus.[94] Clearly Fisher preferred his countryman Duns Scotus to the Italian Aquinas. Fisher said that it was Scotus "whose acumen recommends itself most strongly to me."[95] Surtz correctly describes the new situation at Cambridge as "not a drastic measure like the elimination of the Schoolmen but rather the expansion of the curriculum to allow for the new humanism."[96]

The "humanistic" educational reforms supported the introduction of the Hebrew and Greek languages into theological studies and displayed openness to the science of textual criticism of the Latin Vulgate. Erasmus says that by embracing the new humanism, scholastic studies do not, for that reason, flourish in a lesser degree: "rather, they flourish more authentically."[97] This statement resembles an explanation of his life work he gave to Ludwig Baer in 1529:

> I exhorted the theologians that, leaving aside their little questions which have more of ostentation than of piety, they should betake themselves to the very sources [fontes] of the Scriptures and to the ancient Fathers of the Church. Moreover, I did not wish that scholastic theology should be abolished, but that it should be purer and more serious. That, unless I am mistaken, is to support, not to hurt it.[98]

---

91. Rex, *Theology of John Fisher*, 14.

92. See ibid., 13–29, and E. Surtz, "John Fisher and the Scholastics," *Studies in Philology* 55, no. 2 (1958): 153.

93. See the recent article by Daniel J. Heisey, "Papal Teaching on John Duns Scotus," *American Theological Inquiry: A Biannual Journal of Theology, Culture & History* 7, no. 2 (2014): 3–11.

94. Cf. Surtz, *Works and Days of John Fisher*, 177.

95. Quoted by Rex, *Theology of John Fisher*, 63.

96. Surtz, *Works and Days of John Fisher*, 190.

97. *Methodus (Ratio)*, trans. Conroy, 362 (LB 5:137).

98. CWE 15, ep. 2136, to L. Baer (March 30, 1529); *Opus epistolarum Desiderii Erasmi Rotero-*

Richard Fox, bishop of Winchester, to whom John Fisher dedicated his work *De Veritate Corporis et Sanguinis Christi in Eucharistia*, also supported Erasmian educational reforms. Fox was the founder of Corpus Christi College at Oxford, whose first statutes were published in 1517. He had founded the college out of his own private resources and those of his friends. The foundation of the college was an important step forward for the Renaissance in England, since Fox established the first lectureship in Greek at either Oxford or Cambridge and employed the famous Spanish humanist scholar Juan Luis Vives as reader in Latin. These English examples, both of which were pre-Reformation, may be assessed as positive fruits of the Erasmian program of theological renewal in Catholic universities.

Erasmus's allusion to the "Brabanters" at Louvain refers to the establishment of the Trilingual College at Louvain. The brothers Jerome (d. 1517) and Giles (d. 1536) Busleiden dedicated their large inheritance to providing decent salaries to those who taught Hebrew, Greek, and Latin languages in a new college they founded that was independent of the faculty of theology.[99] Their endeavor was strongly supported by Stephen Poncher, bishop of Paris and archbishop of Sens. Yet strong tensions persisted with the theological Faculty at Louvain. It is interesting to observe that Thomas More responded to the Louvain theologian Martin Dorp's allegation of Erasmus's alleged alienation from universities by saying that Erasmus's feeling for universities is shown by the fact that he studied in Paris, Bologna, and Rome. Both Oxford and Cambridge cherish Erasmus, More says, and urge him to join their faculty, to adopt him as one of their theologians. More adds that he himself prefers Oxford and Cambridge as universities to Louvain and Paris, since the former embraced the new humanism.[100]

Jacob Latomus Masson's Critique of Erasmus

In spite of the neglect of the Bible and the Fathers under the old system, and in spite of what appears to me to be the moderate nature of Erasmus's recommendations that were aimed to correct this problem and steer Catholic

---

dami, eds. P. S. Allen, H. M. Allen, and H. W. Garrod (Oxford: Oxford University Press, 1906–47), 8:120–21.

99. *Methodus* (*Ratio*), trans. Conroy, 82 (LB 5:77–78). See H. de Vocht, *History of the Foundation and Rise of the Collegium Trilingue Lovaniense* (Louvain: Bibliothèque l'Université, Bureaux du Recueil, 1951–53); and de Vocht, ed., *Jerome de Busleyden, founder of the Louvain Collegium Trilingue, his life and writings, edited for the first time in their entirety from the original manuscript* (Turnhout: Brepols, 1950).

100. Letter to Dorp (CW 15:21–23).

theology in a better direction without making a breach with the past, Erasmus's *Methodus* provoked a strong negative reaction from the Louvain theologian Jacob Latomus Masson (1475–1544). As we have already noted above, Latomus published a book in 1519 entitled *De trium linguarum et studii theologici ratione* (*Concerning the Method of Three Languages and of Theology Study*), criticizing Erasmus's proposals about the centrality of scripture in theological studies, the need for language acquisition beyond Latin, and direct use of the writings of the Church Fathers in theological studies.[101] Latomus declared that since the ecumenical councils and the popes had defined the content of the Catholic faith, the church really had no further need of the biblical text. He opposed letting anyone, even students of theology, study and interpret the Bible without expert guidance, and to his mind that guidance must be provided by the scholastic doctors, certainly not by the Church Fathers. Latomus simply rejected Renaissance humanism's call *ad fontes* (to the sources). He insisted that the genuine sense of the New Testament writings was to be found in its purest form in the expositions, glosses, or commentaries of the scholastic writers.[102] Rummel summarizes Latomus's ideas as follows:

> Masson [= Latomus] thinks that the writings of the Fathers are dangerous material, to be handled only by experienced theologians.... patristic authors could not provide guidelines for interpreting Holy Writ. On the contrary, they themselves must be interpreted in light of church doctrine and by means of dialectic, the tool of scholastic theologians. Patristic studies come late in the training of the theologian: scholastic texts, however, are a mainstay throughout his studies. Indeed the professional theologian cannot do without the scholastics.[103]

Erasmus viewed the study of the Fathers as indispensable to the health of the church and her renewal, something that was to be pursued as an end in itself by virtue of the church's approval of their writings. Latomus in contrast viewed the direct study of the Fathers' writings as potentially dangerous and productive of heresy. The Fathers' thought needed to be filtered and refracted through the prism of the scholastic doctors whom he regarded unqualifiedly as more reliable.[104]

---

101. Cf. E. Rummel, *Erasmus and His Catholic Critics*, 2 vols. (Nieuwkoop: De Graaf, 1989), chap. 4 of vol. 1. Erasmus's response is found in *CWE* 71.

102. Cf. Rummel, *Erasmus and His Catholic Critics*, 1:92.

103. Cf. ibid., 1:83.

104. In his answer to the censures of the Paris theologians (*CWE* 82:248–49), Erasmus replied to the assertion that the scholastic method of theology is better equipped than the humanist method to protect the church against heresy as follows: "And if scholastic theology is so powerful that it does not allow anyone to fall into error, I wonder from where John Huss and

Additionally, Latomus ridiculed the idea that theologians needed to learn Greek and Hebrew in addition to Latin. His response to Erasmus's use of Augustine's opinion in *De doctrina Christiana* 2.11 was to say that Augustine's intention in that passage was restricted to the need to consult the original text only on those occasions when the diversity of Latin translators required it. In Augustine's day there was indeed a diversity of translations, but Augustine's point is no longer relevant, since now the Latin Vulgate provides a standard text.[105] Therefore, for Latomus the Vulgate is good enough, and new translations of the Greek New Testament (that is, Erasmus's and Lefèvre's) are not warranted.[106] Significantly (some might say tragically), Latomus's critique on this point was supported by the theological faculty of Louvain and Paris. De Lubac quotes the "official conclusion" of the doctors of the Sorbonne by Dean Boussart: "The new translations of the Bible [by Lefèvre d'Étaples and Erasmus] that are being made from Greek or Hebrew into Latin are not useful to the Church, but pernicious ... and so in no way to be permitted or tolerated, but rather in every way to be eliminated from the Church through the prelates of the Church."[107]

In support of Latomus and in opposition to Erasmus, the Carthusian theologian Pierre Couturier (Petrus Sutor, 1475–1537) claimed that "the knowledge of Greek or Hebrew is not more useful for studying the Bible than that of Italian or Spanish."[108] Sutor said that wanting to translate the holy books anew was to undertake a "vain, impious, temerarious and scandalous" work; to pretend to amend the Vulgate was an "abomination," it was "to blaspheme against Saint Jerome and against the Holy Spirit who had inspired him." Even simply to call attention to the faults of a copyist was "to insult God."[109] Rummel identifies this point as a core issue that divided Erasmus

---

Wyclif, and also Luther, Oecolampadius, and Balthasar, drank up such a quantity of erroneous bilgewater, since they were all imbued with scholastic theology."

105. Cf. Rummel, *Erasmus and His Catholic Critics*, 1:79. T. A. Collins, "Cardinal Cajetan's Fundamental Biblical Principles," *CBQ* 17 (1955): 374, notes in his defense of Cardinal Cajetan, who was attacked by Parisian theologians in a manner similar to the way Erasmus was criticized by Latomus, that Pope Pius XII, in *Divino afflante spiritu* (1943), cites this precise teaching of Augustine to sharply criticize biblical scholars who neglect the study of original texts. Such scholars can "in no wise escape the stigma of levity and sloth." The same encyclical gives great praise to Catholic exegetes of the sixteenth and seventeenth centuries who studied the Bible in its original texts. It seems that Erasmus (and Cajetan), at long last, have been officially vindicated.

106. Cf. Rummel, *Erasmus and His Catholic Critics*, 1:92.
107. De Lubac, *Medieval Exegesis*, 3:201.
108. Ibid., 3:202. Cf. Rummel, *Erasmus and His Catholic Critics*, 2:61–73.
109. De Lubac, *Medieval Exegesis*, 3:202.

from his Catholic critics. To his critics, "the Vulgate was an inspired text; to criticize it was tantamount to criticizing the Holy Spirit who had been at the translator's side."[110]

Sutor's belief in the verbal dictation by the Holy Spirit of the Latin Vulgate stands miles apart from the claims of Jerome himself, who did not treat his own revised translation with any particular respect, but felt free to cite scripture according to other versions and expound it according to other versions.[111] De Lubac even shows that Sutor's narrow superstitious mentality regarding the verbal inspiration of the Latin Vulgate differs from the more open attitude found in the earlier medieval period, when readings that diverged from the Vulgate were not automatically condemned.[112] John Fisher, who recruited the first two lecturers in Greek and the first lecturer in Hebrew at Cambridge, plainly rejected Sutor's mentality and even preferred to use Erasmus's new Latin translation in his theological works.[113] Interestingly, Fisher's praxis differed markedly from Erasmus's own, who continued to use the Vulgate in his theological disputations with Protestants.[114] Erasmus's praxis confirms that he viewed his new translation as intended for private rather than public usage in the church. In any case the fact remains that Sutor and his colleagues prevailed at least over the theology faculty at the University of Paris.

Some bishops at the Council of Trent represented views that approximate those of Latomus and Sutor regarding the divine inspiration of the Latin Vulgate, but their opinions were never officially promulgated as church dogma.[115] Yet after Trent such views remained dominant in Catholic theology between 1550 and 1950, a period in which it was deemed unacceptable to challenge

---

110. Rummel, *Erasmus and His Catholic Critics*, 1:xi.

111. See A. Souter, "Notes on Incidental Gospel Quotations," *JTS* 42 (1941): 12–18.

112. De Lubac, *Medieval Exegesis*, 3:200–203.

113. Surtz, *Works and Days of John Fisher*, is clearly nervous in reporting that John Fisher considered Erasmus's Greek text infallible (150). Fisher used it in public lectures, disputations, sermons, and exegesis (133). The Council of Trent, which convened a decade after Fisher's death, determined that only the Latin Vulgate was to be used for such purposes. Surtz excuses Fisher by the fact that Fisher died before the Council had made this determination.

114. In CWE 76:3, P. Macardle, the translator of Erasmus's *Discussion of Free Will*, has noted: "Erasmus almost invariably quotes from the Vulgate, even where his own translation, the *Novum instrumentum* of 1516 (revised as the *Novum Testamentum* in 1519) comments on the shortcomings of the Vulgate and substitutes radically different readings. Only in one or two instances, recorded in the notes, are *Novum Instrumentum* or *Novum Testamentum* readings found in *De libero arbitrio*; it seems that Erasmus wished to conduct this debate [with Luther] on the basis of the received biblical text, presumably so as not to add philological to theological controversy."

115. Cf. McNally, "Trent and Vernacular Bibles," 218–19.

the authority of the Latin Vulgate text directly. The ice only began to thaw in 1943, when Pope Pius XII published *Divino afflante spiritu* in which he officially sanctioned the study of scripture in its original languages and interpreted the Tridentine decree on the "authenticity" of the Vulgate as meaning "juridical" not "critical" authenticity. After that, scholars like de Lubac contributed to the discussion by questioning why so many modern historians, both Catholic and not, found the standard of Catholic orthodoxy to be embodied in Erasmus's critics, such as Latomus, Beda, Sutor, Egmondanus, Dirks, rather than in Erasmus and his supporters, such as Fisher, More, and the popes of his day.[116]

From what I can determine, both Erasmus's and Latomus's views pertaining to the proper mode of theological education had representation at the Council of Trent, though to my knowledge that council made no dogmatic determinations about such matters. To my mind it is noteworthy, however, that Thomas More firmly supported Erasmus's position. He writes in his *Letter to Dorp*:

For I think that the principal reason that all of the most ancient interpreters of scripture have been neglected for so long by so many is simply that the corrupt judgments of less gifted intellects persuaded first themselves and then others as well that no honey remains to be found beyond what is amassed in the beehives of those compilations [commentaries on Peter Lombard's *Sentences*], and therefore, content with the hives alone, they neglect and scorn everything else.[117]

More's words amount to being a very strong commendation of Erasmus's life work, which was devoted to making the writings of the ancient interpreters of scripture, so neglected by the scholastics, accessible to the sixteenth-century church. In my opinion one of the great defects of the later form of scholasticism represented by Latomus is its reductionism and obscurantism. When scholastic theology is isolated from other fields of study, such as biblical studies and patristics, when it pre-packages and oversimplifies complex data by the method of proof-texting, it thereby delimits the teaching role of the Church Fathers to the citations preselected in Lombard's *Sentences* and expanded upon by his subsequent commentators. The result is not merely the misinterpretation of many passages that have been removed from their original contexts, but the substantial neglect and silencing of the church's most ancient interpreters of scripture.

---

116. *Exégèse Médiévale*, 4:464–66. Lubac further notes that Huizinga is among those who want to justify Erasmus's great Catholic critic, Noël Béda.

117. Thomas More, *Letter to Dorp* (CW 15:67).

The Critique of Luther and Melanchthon

Clearly Erasmus's challenges and theological recommendations met pointed opposition from certain extremely conservative, or rather, obscurantist Catholic theologians, especially in Louvain and Paris. Yet his program was embraced and implemented in the great pre-Reformation English Catholic universities of Cambridge and Oxford, until the Protestant revolution under Henry VIII killed it there. On the other hand, his theological vision can also be clearly distinguished from the first phase of the Protestant movement, for example, from Martin Luther's ideas that are set forth his *Disputation against Scholastic Theology* (1517), in which Luther utterly repudiates Thomas Aquinas, Duns Scotus, William of Ockham, Pierre d'Ailly, and Gabriel Biel as teachers of the church.[118] Luther's ideas were defended and reformulated by his twenty-four-year-old convert, Phillip Melanchthon, in his *Loci Communes* of 1521, a work that Martin Luther said deserved to be added to the canon of scripture.[119] Even though Luther's words there are obviously hyperbolic, such a statement shows that Luther fundamentally agreed with Melanchthon's ideas. What has seldom been noticed in modern scholarship is the way Melanchthon's views, so hyperbolically praised by Luther, stand in direct contradiction to the proposals of Erasmus's *Ratio*. Melanchthon tells his first-generation Lutheran students that they will not be able to grasp Paul's doctrine if they study the ancient Catholic exegetes of Paul's writings. Instead, he recommends the Lutheran *sola scriptura* principle.

For on the whole I do not look very favorably on commentaries, not even those of the ancients.... Anyone is mistaken who seeks to ascertain the nature of Christianity from any source except canonical Scripture. For how much of its purity the commentaries lack! ... The writers of commentaries did not suppress their mental faculties [*psychikon*] as to breathe forth nothing but the spiritual. If you delete from Origen his awkward allegories and his forest of philosophical jargon, how little will remain? Yet with few exceptions the Greeks follow this author as do some apparently distinguished Latin writers, such as Ambrose and Jerome.[120] After their time, one could almost say that the more recent an author is, the less Scriptural he is. In a

---

118. J. Pelikan and H. T. Lehmann, eds., *Luther's Works*, 55 vols. (Philadelphia: Muhlenberg, 1955–86), 31:5–16 [hereafter "LW"].

119. *De Servo Arbitrio*, in *Luthers Werke: Kritische Gesamtausgabe* [*Schriften*], 65 vols. (Weimar: H. Böhlau, 1930–85), 18:601.4–11 [hereafter "WA"] / LW 33:16.

120. His Latin reads "Qui videntur esse columnae," "those who seem to be pillars"; cf. Gal 2.9.

word, Christian doctrine has degenerated into Scholastic trifling, and one does not know whether it is more godless than it is stupid.[121]

Melanchthon continues: "So it has come about that apart from the canonical Scriptures, there is no reliable literature in the Church. In general, whatever has been handed down in the commentaries reeks of philosophy."[122]

Notice how Melanchthon simply denies that the nature of Christianity can be grasped from the exegetical writings of the Church Fathers. He includes the Church Fathers among the "scholastic triflers" and has asserted a separation between the Word of God given in the New Testament and its most ancient reception in the church. Melanchthon claims that not even the ancient "pillars," Ambrose and Jerome, are to be trusted as interpreters of scripture. He was apparently aware (from studying Erasmus's *Annotations* on the New Testament) that these Latins were heavily dependent on the Greek writer Origen in their exegetical works, a matter I will explore in chapter 3. Yet the Catholic church's approval of their writings does not intimidate this young layman. The church, Melanchthon claims, has no reliable literature except the Bible. These Lutheran ideas are radically contrary to Erasmus's views. In early Lutheran thought scripture is radically separated from its first interpreters on the grounds of the *sola scriptura* principle. Implicit in this slogan is the idea that Melanchthon and Luther have replaced the ancient Fathers as authoritative guides into the meaning of scripture. A modern Melanchthon expert concurs: "That Melanchthon saw Luther and himself as fulfilling the same theological function as the Fathers is incontestable."[123]

It is interesting to note that both Luther's adherent Melanchthon and the conservative Catholic theologian Latomus are in apparent agreement in the idea that the exegesis of the Fathers is potentially dangerous material for beginning students of theology, but they argue this point for completely different reasons, and obviously they do not agree in their assessment of scholasticism. For Melanchthon, who is a faithful student of Luther on this point, scholastic theology perpetuates the fundamental dogmatic errors that are present in the scriptural exegesis of the Fathers. Both epochs allegedly fundamentally misunderstood Pauline doctrine, which Luther and Melanchthon claim to have now brought back into the light. Paul's true doctrine equates to

---

121. *Loci Communes* (1521), in Wilhelm Pauck, *Library of Christian Classics* vol. 19: *Melanchthon and Bucer* (Philadelphia: Westminster, 1969), 19–20 [hereafter "LCC"]

122. Ibid., 23.

123. R. Keen, "Political Authority and Ecclesiology in Melanchthon's *De Ecclesia Autoritate*," *Church History* 65 (1996): 3.

the Lutheran "law-gospel" dialectic. Moreover, the Bible is alleged to be the only source needed for ascertaining the nature of "the gospel," provided that the Bible is interpreted by he and Luther. Melanchthon's distrust of ancient Catholic exegesis of scripture is consonant with the view of Martin Luther, who wrote to Melanchthon: "No one has expounded St. Paul better than you, Philipp [Melanchthon]. The commentaries of St. Jerome and Origen are the merest trash in comparison with your annotations [on Romans and Corinthians]. Be humble if you like, but at least let me be proud of you. Be content that you come so near to St. Paul himself."[124]

In both Luther and Melanchthon this dismissive attitude toward ancient Catholic exegesis is coupled with a complete repudiation of scholasticism. Melanchthon continues in his *Loci Communes* (1521): "What, I ask you, did the Scholastics accomplish during the many ages they were examining only these points? Have they not, as Paul says, become vain in their disputations (Rom 1:21), always trifling about universals, formalities, connotations, and various other foolish words? Their stupidity could be left unnoticed if those stupid discussions had not in the meantime covered up for us the gospel and the benefits of Christ."[125] In contrast with Melanchthon and Luther, Erasmus held that fundamental religious truth had always been preserved through the age of scholasticism. He treats the scholastic authors as earlier members of his own spiritual community, men who had allowed theological studies to deviate from the better standards and principles of the Fathers and who had gone to excessive lengths to utilize Aristotle in theological studies. Yet Erasmus viewed the scholastics as a part of the same Catholic family with himself and his contemporaries, who as the heirs of the scholastic theologians needed to be steered in a better direction.

In contrast, Melanchthon equates the scholastics with the pagan philosophers rejected by Paul. They are not really members of the Christian family because they have blocked access to the knowledge of salvation. Later on, Melanchthon asks: "But where, I ask, has Scholastic theology remembered the promises even in one work? This omission accounts for the fact that their theology obscures the grace of Christ, and makes of him not a pledge of mercy, but a legislator, and a much more exacting one than even Moses is considered to be."[126] These are damning indictments not merely of excesses in the method, but of the dogmatic substance of scholastic theology. It is

---

124. WA 10.2:309–10.
125. *Loci Communes* (1521), in *Melanchthon and Bucer*, ed. Pauck, 21.
126. Cf. ibid., 104.

no wonder that the Wittenberg reformers will completely ban the schoolmen from their revised theological curriculum. Melanchthon reproduces Luther's published statements and presupposes that Luther's teaching is identical with the Christian doctrine of grace. This dogmatic critique of scholasticism differs fundamentally from Erasmus's criticisms of the excesses of scholastic theology.[127]

Thus Erasmus's principles of theological renewal met with opposition on at least two fronts. Some Catholic "conservatives" especially in France and Belgium opposed it for the way it seemed to threaten the status quo by recommending a broader knowledge of languages—something these theologians had no interest in obtaining—and allegedly opened the floodgates to heresy by allowing direct study of the writings of the Church Fathers rather than the safer and more controlled proof-texting approach to the Fathers used by the scholastics. These contemporary Catholic opponents of Erasmus, who did not speak for the church but for themselves and in some cases for their theological faculties, also held superstitious views about the divine dictation of the Latin Vulgate translation. Yet we have also seen that during the same period, John Fisher and Thomas More were firm proponents of Erasmus's theological method and took steps to see it implemented in English Catholic universities.

On the other hand, first-generation Lutherans opposed certain aspects of Erasmus's theological vision, especially the way it gave primacy to the church's ancient exegetes as guides into the mind of scripture and the apostle Paul. Such a commendation posed a threat to Luther's alleged prophetic stature and authority. It is fairly well known, of course, that later in his career Melanchthon would cease regarding Luther as such an infallible guide to scripture and would distance himself not only from Luther but from some of his own scathing indictments of ancient Christian exegesis.[128] Moreover, later generations of Lutherans and almost all other Protestant communities would develop their own forms of scholasticism and would repudiate these early Melanchthonian/Lutheran views about the decadence of early Christian interpretation of Paul.[129] But those developments are not relevant to the present discussion, which is focused on the first Christian reactions to Erasmus's *Methodus*.

---

127. For a more detailed discussion, see Scheck, *Origen and the History of Justification*, 177–204.

128. Cf. G. Graybill, *Evangelical Free Will: Phillipp Melanchthon's Doctrinal Journey on the Origins of Faith* (Oxford: Oxford University Press, 2010).

129. See Scheck, *Origen and the History of Justification*, 183–89, 205–16.

Modern Catholic Critiques of Erasmus's Program

A number of Erasmus's modern Catholic critics do not display an accurate knowledge of his writings but misrepresent him, often by relying upon hostile secondary sources. What makes this particularly unlucky for Erasmus is that the names of at least some of these modern scholars are associated with impeccable Catholic scholarship. Yet no scholar should be regarded as omniscient or infallible, and no lifetime is adequate to the task of mastering every facet of the Catholic theological tradition. It is far easier simply to damn Erasmus to the limbo of "crypto-Protestantism" or "proto-modernism" than to read what he actually says.

Regrettably, the church historian Hubert Jedin, in his study of the Council of Trent, admitted that he was unable to consult Dolfen's dissertation cited above before writing his own damning assessment of Erasmus's allegedly un-Catholic theology.[130] Reading Dolfen would have saved Jedin from making the fundamental mistake of claiming that Erasmus's criticisms of scholastic method implied a complete rejection of scholastic theologians. I believe that Jedin's erroneous interpretation of Erasmus has helped perpetuate the myth of Erasmus's alleged total rejection of scholasticism.[131] In the appendix I will provide more evidence that points to Jedin's deep prejudices against Erasmus.

Another example of a modern Catholic theologian of outstanding credentials and reputation who has unjustly condemned Erasmus out of ignorance is Yves Congar, who in his famous essay claims that "the Erasmian program was not content to reform or complement Scholasticism. It was to replace it and, in short, to suppress it."[132] J. W. O'Malley makes essentially the same claim as Congar but he goes a step further and claims that the Nouvelle Théologie theologians of the pre-conciliar period had similar aims: "Just as Erasmus had wanted to displace medieval scholasticism with a biblical/patristic theology, the twentieth-century *ressourcement* wanted to do essentially

---

130. H. Jedin, *A History of the Council of Trent*, 2 vols. (St. Louis, Mo.: Herder, 1961), 1:159. In several passages Jedin casts aspersions on Tridentine bishops who recommended that Erasmus's writings be placed in the hands of future priests (1:161, 363; 2:100n1).

131. Dominic Baker Smith observes that Jedin, in his *magnum opus*, A History of the Council of Trent, "has little time for Erasmus" (CWE 65:xiv). Such words imply that Jedin has assessed Erasmus unfairly and prematurely.

132. *A History of Theology*, 149. Congar's opinion is shared by J. K. Farge, "Noel Beda and the Defense of the Tradition," in *Biblical Humanism and Scholasticism in the Age of Erasmus*, ed. E. Rummel (Leiden: Brill, 2008), 156n61.

the same."[133] Thus is Erasmus erroneously converted into an Anglican-style Protestant by his Catholic antagonist Congar, and by his admirer O'Malley, whereas Erasmus himself explicitly denies what these scholars say of him. In my view O'Malley is wrong both about Erasmus and about the twentieth-century *ressourcement* theologians.[134] Congar's view is essentially the same as Alberto Pio's, to whom Erasmus responded in his own lifetime in these words: "On the basis of these mutilated and misunderstood passages he [Pio] takes it for granted that I condemn all of scholastic theology absolutely, that the name of Aristotle is amazingly hateful to me, that I am of the opinion that philosophy should be separated altogether from the study of theology. In fact, in my writings I combat those who are of this opinion."[135] Erasmus had criticized the excessive use of Aristotle in theology. He had critiqued weaknesses and excesses in scholastic theology, not the thing itself. Whose word shall we take about Erasmus's intentions?[136]

Yet Congar goes even further than O'Malley in his defamation of Erasmus and claims he and the humanist movement were "anti-Scholastic," "anti-theological," and prepared the way for Spinoza's view of religion without dogmas.[137] If Erasmus was "anti-Scholastic" because he criticized excesses in the scholastics, then he was also "anti-Patristic" since he criticized excesses in the Fathers. I find it somewhat embarrassing that a theologian of Congar's stature would describe as "anti-theological" a New Testament scholar like Erasmus who had edited so many editions of the Greek and Latin Church Fathers. What does this imply about the Fathers themselves? Were they also "anti-theological," because they did not incorporate Aristotelian and Pseudo-Dionysian metaphysics into their works to the extent that Aquinas did?

---

133. O'Malley, *What Happened at Vatican II?*, 41.

134. See the helpful article by Aidan Nichols, "Thomism and the Nouvelle Théologie," *The Thomist* 64 (2000): 1–19.

135. *Controversy with Alberto Pio* (CWE 84:260).

136. In my judgment, J. W. O'Malley's generalizations about Erasmus's alleged relentless opposition to and hatred of the scholastics, in his article, "Erasmus and Luther, Continuity and Discontinuity," 51–53, are flawed, exaggerated, and misleading. O'Malley's later article, "Erasmus and Vatican II: Interpreting the Council," is an improvement, but he still exaggerates Erasmus's criticism of scholasticism and overlooks Erasmus's positive assessments and actual use of scholastic theologians. I find it astonishing that O'Malley, in the latter article, claims that the Second Vatican Council itself "repudiated Scholasticism" in a manner that was just as drastic as Erasmus's alleged repudiation of it (209). O'Malley is simply wrong in both respects. On the other hand, O'Malley is very solid in his recognition that Erasmus was deeply committed to Catholic dogma, to the sacraments, and to the church.

137. *A History of Theology*, 150.

Yet the influence of prejudices like these remains very much in force today in Catholic theology, though they are becoming more and more discredited in Erasmus studies. Congar remained ignorant of Erasmus's writings throughout his career and continued to depend on hostile secondary sources until the very end.[138] In my view Congar and his Dominican colleagues wish to blame the Protestant Reformation on Erasmus in order to turn our attention away from the reality that all the leading Protestant "reformers" had been thoroughly trained in scholastic theology. Erasmus actually pointed out this fallacy to his own critics on the Paris theological faculty, who had censured him and blamed the existence of Protestant schisms on Erasmus's plea for making available vernacular translations of scripture. Erasmus writes in response:

> It is not laypeople who have caused the uproars of our times but learned men, whose authority is followed by the people, since John Huss and Wyclif were expert scholastic theologians, and Balthasar, the Doctor of Anabaptism, was a scholastic Doctor. So also are Luther and Oecolampadius. All the heresies in the world arose almost entirely either from philosophy or from Holy Scripture wrongly understood; and no one is restrained from reading philosophical books, but Scripture is forbidden to us.[139]

The real tragedy in Congar's (and Jedin's) animosity toward Erasmus is that a careful reading of Congar's own writings shows that he and Erasmus are in fundamental agreement in their criticism of the weaknesses of scholasticism (though Congar is not aware of this, because he does not know Erasmus's writings). Congar himself says that the scholastics, including Aquinas, lacked a historical sense.[140] That is, they lacked the ability to read a text from the perspective of its original historical context. Yet in spite of this defect, according to Congar, Aquinas's commentaries on Romans and John are still good samples of biblical exegesis.[141]

Erasmus clearly concurs with both these assessments of Aquinas. Indeed Erasmus engages Aquinas in his *Annotations* on Romans and John. Congar further claims that the extreme use of Aristotle even by the classical scholastics has "all the elements of a false method, the danger of developing theology in a purely dialectical and deductive manner, using the bibli-

---

138. This is proven in his later work—*True and False Reform in the Church*, trans. Paul Philibert (Collegeville, Minn.: Liturgical Press, 2011)—where Congar, in reliance upon Renaudet, defended Luther and Zwingli's disparaging views of Erasmus (328).

139. CWE 82:136–37.   140. *A History of Theology*, 139.

141. Ibid.

cal texts in an accidental manner simply for decorative purposes."[142] This opinion too is shared by Erasmus. Moreover, according to Congar, even the best of the scholastic writers make use of the writings of the Church Fathers in a manner that is not exempt from the practice of "citing to support a thesis systematically developed for itself and by purely logical processes, one or two fragmentary texts, extracts of extracts, borrowed from authors of widely different historical context. These texts, treated thus, present merely a caricature of the positive datum."[143] Once more, Erasmus had anticipated this criticism in passages cited above. Congar actually stands very near to Erasmus in his theological assessments, but he does not know it.

142. *A History of Theology*, 140.
143. Ibid.

INTRODUCTION
to ORIGEN

In this chapter I will briefly survey the life, writings, and exegetical method of Origen of Alexandria (185–254), who was probably the most important and influential Christian theologian of the pre-Nicene church.[1] Born the eldest of seven children to Christian parents in Alexandria, Egypt, Origen received a thorough education in scripture and Greek literature from his father Leonides, a saint and martyr who was imprisoned and later beheaded in 202 during a persecution of the Christians that took place under the emperor Septimus Severus (193–211). Longing for martyrdom himself, Origen survived this purge, though his life was often in great danger. Evidently, the anti-Christian legislation only affected converts, not those who were already baptized.[2] Eusebius reports that Origen even wrote a letter to his imprisoned father, exhorting him not to shrink back from offering the supreme witness of the faith, for the sake of his family. His duty to God, in other words, must take precedence over his familial duty.

Forty years later, while preaching in Caesarea, Origen looked back upon

---

1. "Pre-Nicene" means prior to the Council of Nicaea (325), the ecumenical council at which the heresy of Arianism was condemned and Christ was declared to be consubstantial = *homoousios* ("one in being") with the Father. The most important primary source for Origen's life and work is Eusebius, *Historia Ecclesiastica*, book 6 [hereafter "HE"]. See the fine edition: *Eusebius: The History of the Church from Christ to Constantine*, trans. G. A. Williamson, ed. Andrew Louth (Harmondsworth: Penguin Books, 1989). There are many outstanding secondary sources on Origen's life and thought. As a starting point, I recommend H. Crouzel, *Origen: The Life and Thought of the First Great Theologian*, trans. A. S. Worrall (Edinburgh: T&T Clark, 1989), and J. McGuckin, ed., *The Westminster Handbook to Origen* (Louisville, Ky.: Westminster John Knox Press, 2004).

2. See *Historia Augusta, Severus* 17.1.

his spiritual heritage and made the following confession in a rare autobiographical reflection: "Having a father who was a martyr does me no good, if I do not live well myself and adorn the nobility of my descent. That is, I must adorn his testimony and confession by which he was illustrious in Christ."[3] By this Origen evidently means that being physically related to a saint or a martyr will not avail with God in the final judgment, since each of us will be held accountable for his or her own life. Origen's humility, exemplified in these words, his hunger for holiness, and his zeal for martyrdom, which is reminiscent of the outpourings of Ignatius of Antioch, are defining characteristics of his personality. He once preached: "If God would consent to let me be washed in my blood, receiving a second baptism by accepting death for Christ, I would surely go from this world.... But blessed are they who merit these things."[4] He even wrote a treatise on the subject, the *Exhortation to Martyrdom*. The latter work, however, was unknown to Erasmus in the sixteenth century.

After Leonides's martyrdom the family's goods were confiscated. In order to support his mother and siblings, Origen became a teacher of Greek grammar and literature. He studied philosophy in depth and gained a reputation for his learning, even in the pagan world. Demetrius, the bishop of Alexandria, then put him in charge of instructing catechumens, and for some time Origen maintained dual teaching responsibilities, both secular and ecclesial. He later gave up teaching secular literature, sold his library for a meager sum of money, and dedicated himself completely to Christian catechesis. In Alexandria this activity went on during the persecutions, and many of Origen's pupils and converts were persecuted and even killed, while he accompanied them to the execution site. Later in Caesarea, Origen's giftedness as an exemplary Christian teacher was remembered with nostalgia and great emotion by one of his most famous pupils, Gregory Thaumaturgus (the Wonderworker), in the *Panegyric to Origen*.[5] Gregory highlighted the fact that Origen's actions corresponded to his words, and that his sincere and Spirit-filled Christian discipleship is what led many others to imitate him. At the beginning of the fourth century, the future martyr Pamphilus of Caesarea also noted that Origen was very humble and had a deeply Christian character.[6]

---

3. *Homilies on Ezekiel* 4.8.
4. *Homilies on Judges* 7.12; cf. *Homilies on Numbers* 10.2.1.
5. Cf. *St. Gregory Thaumaturgus: Life and Works*, trans. M. Slusser, Fathers of the Church [hereafter "FOTC"] 98 (Washington, D.C.: The Catholic University of America Press, 1998).
6. Cf. *Apology for Origen* 3.

Origen lived a life of strict asceticism and self-denial in conscious imitation of Christ and the apostles. According to some reports, Origen took Matthew 19:12 literally and castrated himself in order to protect his chastity, since many of his students were female. This story is increasingly doubted by modern scholars as second-hand hearsay. Most recently, J. McGuckin rejected the tradition as "a smokescreen of Pamphilus's own invention, canonized by Eusebius."[7] The reason for doubt is that the story seems to contradict several passages in Origen's writings, where he ridicules such a crassly literal interpretation of Jesus's words.[8] It seems justifiable for McGuckin, in his historical reconstruction of Origen's life, to prefer primary sources (Origen's own statements) to secondary sources (Eusebius's account) in this manner. Yet the tradition about Origen's castration still seems probable to me, since it is recorded by Eusebius, who was a fervent admirer of Origen. Eusebius knew men and women who had known Origen personally. Moreover, it does not seem consistent with Pamphilus's upright Christian character to suggest that he would have invented this story as a "smokescreen."

At some point Origen traveled to Rome to visit the very famous and ancient church there. Jerome preserves the tradition that Origen heard Hippolytus preach a sermon in Rome, and the future martyr (Hippolytus) acknowledged the presence of his distinguished guest.[9] Origen later moved to Palestine, where, Eusebius reports, Bishop Theoctistus of Caesarea allowed him to preach, even though Origen was still a layman. Then, Origen was ordained a priest in Palestine by the local bishops, a canonically irregular procedure in that it took place without permission from Demetrius (Origen's bishop in Alexandria) and it was carried out in spite of the mutilation he had deliberately undergone. According to Eusebius it was for these reasons, the canonical irregularities, that Origen was expelled from the church of Alexandria. However, doctrinal issues seem to have been involved as well in Origen's excommunication which Eusebius may have wanted to minimize out of his partiality for Origen. Yet they are attested by Origen himself in his own *Letter to Friends in Alexandria*, which is cited by both Rufinus and Jerome.[10] The doctrinal issue referred to in that letter was Origen's alleged belief that the

---

7. *Westminster Handbook to Origen*, 7.
8. Cf. *Commentary on Matthew*, ad loc; *Hom in Nm* 25.3.5.
9. Cf. Jerome, *De viris illustribus* 61.
10. Cf. Jerome, *Apology against Rufinus*, 2.18, in *Nicene and Post-Nicene Fathers: First Series*, from *A Select Library of Nicene and Post-Nicene Fathers of the Christian Church* (Grand Rapids, Mich.: Eerdmans, 1994), 3:511 [hereafter "NPNF1" for First Series and "NPNF2" for Second Series].

devil would ultimately be saved, something Origen vehemently repudiates as a misrepresentation of his teaching in the same letter.[11]

Origen was consulted in theological discussions, one of which now survives, *The Dialogue with Heraclides* (although this work, as a recent discovery, was unknown to Erasmus and his contemporaries and does not appear in Migne). Unfortunately, only two letters from Origen's once vast correspondence are extant. He journeyed to Arabia and to Antioch, where he had been summoned by Julia Mammaea, the mother of the emperor Alexander Severus, who wanted to learn more about Christianity from him. Such involvements show Origen's substantial reputation among his contemporaries, both Christian and pagan. In 250, shortly after completing his two longest works, his *Commentary on the Epistle to the Romans* and the *Contra Celsum*, Origen was arrested during Decius's persecution. He was imprisoned and severely tortured on the rack. Eusebius writes the following description which is based on first-hand eyewitness evidence:

As for Origen, the terrible sufferings that befell him in the persecution, and how they ended, when the evil demon, bent on his destruction, brought all the weapons in his armory to bear and fought him with every device and expedient, attacking him with more determination than anyone he was fighting at the time—the dreadful cruelties he endured for the word of Christ, chains and bodily torments, agony in iron and the darkness of his prison; how for days on end his legs were pulled four paces apart in the torturer's stocks—the courage with which he bore threats of fire and every torture devised by his enemies—the way his maltreatment ended, when the judge had striven with might and main at all costs to avoid sentencing him to execution—the messages he left us after all this, messages full of help for those in need of comfort—of all these things a truthful and detailed account will be found in his own lengthy correspondence.[12]

The bulk of that "lengthy correspondence" does not survive, but it is clear that Origen, like his father, refused to deny his Lord Jesus Christ in order to be released from prison. Had he died during that term of imprisonment or been sentenced to capital punishment, he of course would have been canonized as a martyr. Instead, it was the emperor who died, the anti-Christian measures expired, and Origen was released from prison, but in broken

11. See the very helpful discussion by Mark S. M. Scott, "Guarding the Mysteries of Salvation: The Pastoral Pedagogy of Origen's Universalism," *Journal of Early Christian Studies* 18, no. 3 (2010): 350–51; H. Crouzel, "A Letter from Origen to 'Friends in Alexandria,'" in *The Heritage of the Early Church: Essays in Honor of George Vasilievich Florovsky*, ed. D. Neiman and M. Schatkin, trans. J. D. Gauthier (Rome: Pontificio Istituo Orientale, 1973), 135–50.

12. Eusebius, HE 6.39; trans. Williamson.

health. He died a few years later at the age of 69, probably in 254. Origen was thus initially ranked among the church's "confessors" (a person who confesses and adheres to the Christian religion in spite of persecution), whereas his father had been a martyr.

Anyone familiar with at least this perspective on Origen's story (granting that other viewpoints are possible) can readily understand why he would have been so admired by many Christians of subsequent generations. His life had been a living sermon, characterized in every respect by heroic Christian virtue and discipleship. His death was the nearest approach to martyrdom that one can make, and he died in the bosom of the church, as a priest who had been ordained by the holiest and most illustrious bishops in Palestine (Theoctistus of Caesarea and Alexander of Jerusalem). He was a respected scriptural scholar, churchman, and apologist, granting that some of his theological speculations had been deemed controversial even during his lifetime. He was revered by other bishops, such as Gregory Thaumaturgus and Firmilian of Caesarea in Cappadocia. His substantial orthodoxy was defended by the martyr Pamphilus, as well as by bishops and theologians of later generations, such as Athanasius, Didymus, Basil, Gregory Nazianzen, John of Jerusalem, John Chrysostom, Hilary, and Ambrose. Origen's tomb was still being shown to crusaders in the thirteenth century at Tyre, in the Cathedral of the Holy Sepulchre.

Origen's Surviving Works

One of the great tragedies of church history is that the vast majority of Origen's writings do not survive. This owes to the condemnation of "Origenism" at the Fifth Ecumenical Council in 553, which will be discussed in greater detail later in this chapter and in the next. Von Balthasar strikingly compared the destruction of Origen's writings to the shattering of a perfume vessel into a thousand pieces that filled the whole house (of the church) with its fragrance.[13] Some of the missing titles are known from Jerome's *Epistles* 33 to Paula. Of Origen's major extant works, table 2-1 shows their approximate length.[14] Origen's massive text-critical project, the *Hexapla*, where he dis-

---

13. Origen, *Spirit and Fire: A Thematic Anthology of His Writings*, trans. R. Daly (Washington, D.C.: The Catholic University of America Press, 1984), 2.

14. Most of these calculations are found in C. P. Hammond, "The Last Ten Years of Rufinus's Life and the Date of his Move South from Aquileia," *JTS* 28, no. 2 (1977): 428–29, who points out that these are very rough estimates owing to the inconsistent length of the additional

Table 2-1. Extent of Surviving Text of Origen's Works

TITLE (ANCIENT LATIN TRANSLATOR)	LENGTH IN COLUMNS[1]
Against Celsus*	493
Commentary on Romans (Rufinus)	455
Commentary on John*	405
Commentary on Matthew*[2] (on Mt 16:13–22:33)	382
On First Principles I–IV (Rufinus)	296
Homilies on Numbers (Rufinus)	220
Commentary Series on Matthew[2] (on Mt 22:24–27:66)	199
Homilies on Leviticus (Rufinus)	169
Commentary on the Song of Songs (Rufinus)	136
Homilies on Joshua (Rufinus)	123
Homilies on Genesis (Rufinus)	117
Homilies on Jeremiah* (Jerome)	107
Homilies on Exodus (Rufinus)	100
Homilies on Luke (Jerome)	99
Homilies on Ezekiel (Jerome)	96
Homilies on Psalms 36–38 (Rufinus)	90
On Prayer*	73
Pamphilus's Apology for Origen (Rufinus)	72
Homilies on Judges (Rufinus)	40
On Martyrdom*	36
Homilies on Isaiah (Jerome)	35
Homilies on the Song of Songs (Jerome)	21
Homily on 1 Samuel (Rufinus?)	17
TOTAL	3,781
Spurious Works Attributed to Origen	
Anonymous Commentary on Job	149
Dialogue of Adamantius on the Orthodox Faith* (Rufinus)	85

1. Number of columns in Migne, PG 11–17.
2. Traditionally called homilies.
* Indicates that the work survives in Greek as well.

played in parallel columns up to eight texts and translations of the OT, does not survive except in fragments. Many of its readings, however, were preserved in Jerome's commentaries on the Old Testament.

Origen's Homilies

According to the estimates in the table 2-1, Rufinus of Aquileia was responsible for translating approximately 50 percent of the authentic surviving works of Origen (1,835 columns). Jerome translated nearly 10 percent of the corpus that survives (358 columns). The reader will also notice that 33 percent (1,234 columns) of Origen's surviving writings are homilies on scripture. This illustrates how deeply Origen was connected to the church of his day as a priest, catechist, and pastor of souls. Origen's homilies represent the oldest surviving corpus of Christian sermons. As such they were in their Latin translations a source of inspiration to Christians of later generations in the western church.[15] It is chiefly in these homilies that he practices his "allegorical" method of interpretation, about which I will say more below. Origen's reflections on the institutional church in his homilies are extremely valuable as a sort of window into the rites and customs of the church of the third century.[16] Erasmus was well aware of this value. For instance, in his discussion of the historical evolution of the sacrament of confession in his *Response to the Annotations of Edward Lee*, Erasmus points out: "Origen was criticized for having deviated from the teaching of the Catholic faith in some of his opinions, but he was never reprehended by anyone for not holding the correct view on penitence."[17] Erasmus cited this as evidence in support of his own historical observation that the contemporary (sixteenth-century) practice of private confession to a priest had evolved and developed from the way the sacrament had been practiced in the early church. Erasmus's point was not to challenge the validity of the development of sixteenth-century sacramental customs, or to deny that the fundamental structure of the sacrament is discernable throughout the ages, but simply to point out the fact of historical development as a means of correcting abuses that were occurring

---

material found in the footnotes of Migne. For example, the figures for *On First Principles* are too generous. Sometimes my independent estimates have differed significantly from Hammond's.

15. Pope Benedict XVI commended the writings of Origen to his Catholic audience. See his weekly general audiences of April 25 and May 2, 2007.

16. This aspect is one of the main focuses of J. Daniélou's book, *Origen*, trans. W. Mitchell (New York: Sheed and Ward, 1955).

17. CWE 72:372.

in connection with the sacrament. Although many of his contemporaries criticized him for his observations and claimed that he was denying the sacrament, today the magisterium of the Catholic church recognizes the historical development of this sacrament.[18]

Some of Origen's homilies were translated by Jerome (347–420), who had initially planned to translate the bulk of Origen's writings into Latin, but later gave up the idea.[19] The greater part was translated by Rufinus of Aquileia (345–411).[20] Unlike Jerome, Rufinus maintained a clear and stable attitude toward Origen, whom he always esteemed as his revered teacher. He believed that Origen was the outstanding exegete and theologian of the early church and that a translation of Origen's works would be of considerable profit to the church in the west. After his death in 411, Rufinus's translations and ecclesiastical services were highly praised by Gennadius, Palladius, John Cassian, and Cassiodorus. Unfortunately, a conflict with the eloquent but intemperate Jerome damaged Rufinus's reputation in the west until quite recently. This may show, as the ancient Greek historian Plutarch points out with respect to Minos of Crete, how dangerous it is to incur the hostility of someone who is mistress of eloquence and song.[21] Jerome's defamation of Rufinus's character and orthodoxy was written during the tragic and unproductive Origenist con-

---

18. See *Catechism of the Catholic Church*, nos. 1447–49 (Città del Vaticano: Libreria Editrice Vatican, 1994). Pope Benedict XVI, *Jesus of Nazareth Part Two: Holy Week: From the Entrance into Jerusalem to the Resurrection* (San Francisco, Calif.: Ignatius, 2011), speaking of the confession of sins commended in Jas 5:16, writes: "Admittedly, one cannot equate this confession of sin, found in the life of early Christian communities in areas influenced by Jewish Christianity, with the sacrament of Confession as it was to develop in the course of later Church history: it is merely a 'step on the way' toward it" (74).

19. Jerome reports this aspiration in the preface to his translation of Origen's *Homilies on Ezekiel*. See my new translation in Origen, *Homilies 1–14 on Ezekiel*, Ancient Christian Writers, no. 62 (Mahwah, N.J.: Paulist Press, 2010), 24. The best secondary works on Jerome are J. N. D. Kelly, *Jerome: His Life, Writings, and Controversies* (New York: Harper and Row, 1975), and M. Hale Williams, *The Monk and the Book: Jerome and the Making of Christian Scholarship* (Chicago: University of Chicago Press, 2006).

20. See the still unsurpassed study by F. X. Murphy, *Rufinus of Aquileia (345–411): His Life and Works* (Washington, D.C.: The Catholic University of America Press, 1945).

21. In his *Life of Theseus*, Plutarch reports that neither Homer nor Hesiod availed Minos, in spite of their high praise of his character. Homer calls him "Jupiter's familiar friend"; Hesiod, "the most royal Minos." Yet because the Greek tragedians in Athens showered down abuse upon him, from the vantage point of the stage, depicting him as a very wicked man characterized by cruelty and violence, this is the reputation of him that endured in the west. My point is that Rufinus's reputation likewise suffered terribly from Jerome's abuse of him in spite of the fact that most other ancient writers highly praised Rufinus's character.

troversies of the late fourth and early fifth centuries. Thankfully Rufinus did not allow himself to become discouraged by this quarrel, and by his patient and selfless translation effort, carried out at the request of his religious superiors, he saved from certain destruction some of the most precious writings of Christian antiquity. As de Lubac has noted, Rufinus's translations were "destined to form Latin minds for many years to come."[22]

Excursus: The Fidelity of Rufinus's Translations of Origen

Erasmus was very advanced in his critical skills, but he was also an extreme partisan of Jerome, and he treats Rufinus dismissively and unfairly in the prefaces to his edition of Origen, above all for his alleged ineptitude as a translator of Origen. Jerome had condemned Rufinus's translation technique, particularly for the work *On First Principles*, in epistle 124 and in his *Apology against Rufinus*, works written at the height of the Origenist controversy. By his own free admission, Rufinus suspected that the Greek manuscripts of Origen's writings had been tampered with by heretics, an idea that Jerome reasonably doubted.[23] Because of this suspicion, in his Latin translations Rufinus sometimes omitted or altered the wording of the original in order to make the text conform more adequately to Origen's plainly orthodox statements found elsewhere in his writings. For obvious reasons Rufinus was concerned to defend Origen against the charge of "proto-Arianism."[24] Yet Rufinus denies on repeated occasions that he had added anything of his own. He says that he simply restored Origen to himself.

In past research I have conjectured that Rufinus's translation procedure may have been blemished by an honest text-critical misjudgment on his part. He mistakenly believed that the spurious *Dialogue of Adamantius on the Ortho-*

---

22. De Lubac, *History and Spirit*, 45–46.

23. Rufinus documents his suspicions in the prefaces to *On First Principles*, in his *Apology against Jerome*, and in his work *On the Adulteration of the Works of Origen* (NPNF2 3:421–27). See my new translation of the latter in Pamphilus, *Apology for Origen* and Rufinus, *On the Falsification of the Books of Origen*, trans. Thomas P. Scheck, FOTC 120 (Washington, D.C.: The Catholic University of America Press, 2010).

24. See: R. Williams, "Damnosa hereditas: Pamphilus's Apology and the Reputation of Origen," in *Logos: Festschrift für Luise Abramowski zum 8. Juli 1993*, ed. H. C. Brennecke, E. L. Grasmück, and C. Markschies (Berlin: W. De Gruyter, 1993), 151–69. For a good discussion of Rufinus's method of translation, see R. Heine's introduction to Origen, *Homilies on Genesis and Exodus*, FOTC 71 (Washington, D.C.: The Catholic University of America Press, 1982), 27–39.

dox Faith was an authentic work of Origen.[25] Buchheit thought that Rufinus falsified the authorship of this work deliberately.[26] However, Hammond has shown that this is wrong and that Rufinus had good reasons for his mistaken attribution of this work.[27] As late as the nineteenth century, the *Dialogue of Adamantius* was judged to be an authentic work of Origen. Rufinus himself had translated this work into Latin with the intention of exhibiting Origen as a champion in the fight against heresy. This *Dialogue*, which makes use of the writings of Methodius (d. 312 AD), was unknown to Erasmus and was first printed in Latin in 1556.[28] The work contains statements such as "I believe that ... God the Word is consubstantial and eternal" and "the blessed Trinity is consubstantial and inseparable."[29] Such formulations seem to point to the recent determination of the Council of Nicaea (325).[30] Yet Rufinus thought these were Origen's own expressions. He therefore evidently felt free to borrow such formulations and put them into Origen's mouth in certain thematically related texts, whenever he was convinced that heretics had inserted their own corruptions into Origen's original text. When judged by modern rubrics of translation, Rufinus had no right to do this, even if we assume that the *Dialogue of Adamantius* is an authentic work of Origen. But when he is assessed according to ancient standards of literary criticism, Rufinus's practice is perhaps more excusable; but in any case its result is that passages in which Rufinus's Latin Origen speaks with the language of Nicaea are probably not to be trusted. Erasmus rightly surmised this on the basis of Rufinus's other surviving translations, and his criticisms of Rufinus on this point are justified. In modern times L. Ayres has plausibly suggested that the historical Origen may have avoided *homoousios*-language because it was remi-

25. The work is found in *Patrologiae Cursus Completus: Series Graeca*, ed. J.-P. Migne, 161 vols. (Paris, 1857–66), 11:1713–1884 [hereafter "PG"].

26. V. Buchheit, "Rufinus von Aquileja als Fälscher des Adamantiosdialogs," *Byzantinische Zeitschrift* 51 (1958): 319.

27. Hammond, "The Last Ten Years of Rufinus's Life," 391.

28. Cf. F. Hort, "Adamantius," in *A Dictionary of Christian Biography*, eds. W. Smith and H. Wace, 4 vols. (London: John Murray, 1887), 1:39–41. [hereafter "DCB"].

29. Cf. PG 11:1718: "Deum unum, eumque conditorem et effectorem omnium esse credo: Deumque Verbum qui ex eo natus est, qui ejusdem est ac ille essentiae, qui semper est, qui extremis temporibus hominem ex Maria assumpsit [I believe that there is one God and that he is the founder and creator of all things; and [I believe] that God the Word, who was born from him, who is himself of the same substance, who is eternal, assumed a human nature from Mary in the last days]." Cf. PG 11:1883: "Ejusdem enim essentiae est, inseparabilisque beata Trinitas [For the blessed and inseparable Trinity is of the same substance]."

30. Cf. Hort, "Adamantius," DCB 1:40.

niscent of the perceived materialism of some Gnostic writers. "Thus, *ousia* language in most forms seemed to Origen unsuitable for application to the divine existence."[31] In my previous works of scholarship I have assumed that the real Origen did not use the language of consubstantiality to describe the Godhead.

On the other hand it should probably be noted that I. Ramelli has recently complicated the whole discussion by claiming that Origen was indeed "the forerunner and inspirer of the Nicene formula μία οὐσια, τρεῖν ὑποστάσειν [one essence, three persons], which is also consistent with his designation of the Son as ὁμοοῦσιον [consubstantial] with the Father."[32] She claims that Origen's Trinitarian heritage is to be found not in "Arianism" but in Athanasius, Marcellus of Ancyra, Eusebius, Didymus, and above all Gregory of Nyssa and the Cappadocians. I welcome Ramelli's challenge to the modern discussion, even if it may end up undermining some of my own theories. My only concern here is briefly to introduce the reader to the very complex problem of the survival of Origen's writings in Greek and Latin versions.

Apart from such Christological and Trinitarian passages, I believe that Rufinus's Latin translation can be received as generally reliable.[33] A modern expert in the field, C. P. Hammond Bammel, offers the following cautions to modern readers of Rufinus's translations.[34] She says that in his translations of Origen, Rufinus is speaking with his own voice to the readers of his time. He has reflected upon the thoughts of Origen and expressed them in his own words to his readers. In Rufinus's translations we are listening to a Latin speaker, schooled in rhetoric, of the time around 400, and no longer to a Greek, educated in philosophy, of the first half of the third century. Rufinus's language was less polished and less technical than Origen's. "His readers stood on a lower intellectual level than Origen. The difficult concepts had to be explained and simplified for them.... Rufinus' aim was to edify his readers, not to show off his erudition; thus he often simplifies problems or covers over difficulties. Inevitably his standpoint was different from that of

---

31. L. Ayres, *Nicaea and Its Legacy: An Approach to Fourth-Century Trinitarian Theology* (Oxford: Oxford University Press, 2004), 24.

32. I. Ramelli, "Origen's Anti-Subordinationism and its Heritage in the Nicene and Cappadocian Line," *Vigiliae Christianae* 65 (2011): 29.

33. This has been confirmed recently for a different work of Origen by M. Beyer Moser, *Teacher of Holiness: The Holy Spirit in Origen's Commentary on the Epistle to the Romans* (Piscataway, N.J.: Gorgias Press, 2005).

34. C. Hammond Bammel, *Der Römerbrieftext des Rufin und seine Origenes-Übersetzung* (Freiburg im Breisgau: Herder, 1985), 44–45.

Origen."[35] For all its caution, this modern assessment is quite favorable to Rufinus, in terms of judging his general reliability, especially in comparison with the thoroughgoing hostility of Erasmus toward him that the readers of this book will encounter in chapter 5.

Survey of Origen's Other Surviving Writings

Contra Celsum (*Against Celsus*), which survives intact in Greek, is Origen's *magnum opus*.[36] As his longest extant writing and final work, it comprises the most important written defense of Christianity from antiquity. It is a work of Christian apologetics that retains its relevance, vitality, and interest even to modern readers. It was included in Erasmus's edition of Origen in the Latin translation by Christopher Persona. *Contra Celsum* has caused misunderstanding because it contains remarks by Origen where he argues that the allegorization of the biblical narratives is no more unreasonable than the allegorization, or rationalization, of the Greek myths which was fashionable in the erudite Greek world of his day. Some scholars have extrapolated from this that Origen's exegetical principles were derived from Neo-Platonic allegorization of Homer and that he viewed the Bible stories as myths. However, de Lubac and others have demonstrated what did not escape the notice of Erasmus either, that, in spite of the widespread scholarly preoccupation with Origen's *ad hominem* remarks here, these statements simply do not become principles which are found in Origen's exegesis.[37] A similar precaution can be applied to Origen's theoretical hermeneutical principles found in the fourth book of *On First Principles* (also called *Peri Archon* or *De Principiis*). De Lubac argued that scholars should observe Origen "at work," in his actual exegesis, to determine the principles of his hermeneutics rather than focus exclusively on Origen's articulated theory or his *ad hominem* arguments. What makes the modern misapprehension of Origen all the more tragic is that in the very book *Against Celsus*, and in all his other works, Origen refuses to treat the Bible, or any part of it, as a Platonic myth. He defends historical Christianity against the attacks of Gnosticism, down to the very details concerning the dimensions of Noah's Ark.[38]

The martyr Pamphilus of Caesarea, for example, in his *Apology for Origen*, demonstrates from indisputably authentic texts that Origen defends

---

35. Ibid.
36. See Origen, *Contra Celsum*, trans. H. Chadwick (Cambridge: Cambridge University Press, 1980).
37. De Lubac, *History and Spirit*, 33–42.
38. Cf. *Homilies on Genesis* 2.1.

God's direct creation of the first man, Adam, and of Eve from one of Adam's ribs; he accepts the literal truth of Enoch's translation to heaven, Noah's flood and the Ark, the Tower of Babel, Abraham's hospitality to angels, Abraham's wife changed into a pillar of salt, the ten plagues of Egypt, the passage through the Jordan, the rock struck by Moses, Joshua's making the sun stand still in the sky, the stories of Balaam, Gideon, and Deborah, Elijah's assumption into heaven, the resuscitation of the son of the Shunamite woman, the backward movement of the shadow under Hezekiah, and the historicity of Daniel, Judith, and Esther.[39] A multitude of Origenian texts confirm that in the overwhelming majority of instances, Origen believed in the historicity of the literal accounts of scripture.[40] I will say a bit more about this below.

Origen's treatises *On Prayer* and *On Martyrdom* are important thematic treatments that exemplify the way Origen grounded theology in the explanation of scripture. They too remain stimulating reading to this day, though they were unknown to Erasmus and his predecessors. Pamphilus's *Apology for Origen* (309) is listed in this chart because it is a work comprised mainly of excerpts from a diverse selection of Origen's writings, many of which are no longer extant. Composed by the martyr Pamphilus (d. 310), with the collaboration of Eusebius of Caesarea, the author defends Origen's orthodoxy against the attacks of some contemporaries (probably Methodius of Olympus). It survives in Rufinus's Latin translation and was included in Erasmus's edition and in that of his predecessors. Other more recently discovered works of Origen are not listed in this chart and include the previously mentioned *Dialogue with Heraclides* and his treatise *On the Passover*. I will continue the discussion of Origen's commentaries on scripture after speaking briefly about his method of exegesis.

Origen's Allegorical Method of Exegesis

The Catholic theologian L. Bouyer spoke very highly of Erasmus's grasp both of Origen's hermeneutical principles and of patristic exegesis in general. Referring to Erasmus's summary in his *Ratio Theologiae Verae*, Bouyer writes:

The most developed of these counsels in itself constitutes a whole dissertation on the literal meaning and the spiritual allegorical meaning. In it Erasmus reveals so

---

39. Cf. Pamphilus, *Apology for Origen*, 123–63. De Lubac, *History and Spirit*, 40, comments: "From the beginning, Origenian allegory had been violently attacked, but Pamphilus had no trouble in warding off these objections."

40. Cf. de Lubac, *History and Spirit*, 103–18.

profoundly penetrating a knowledge of the Fathers that it anticipates the best of the most modern works, such as those of Père de Lubac on Origen [*History and Spirit, Medieval Exegesis*]. His views are far removed from the abstract views systematized by Thomas Aquinas, on the literal meaning and the various figurative meanings.[41]

I strongly concur with Bouyer that Erasmus had obtained a profound grasp of patristic exegesis that surpasses the medievals by far and that he has anticipated de Lubac's analyses of Origen's contribution to Catholic theology and exegesis, to which we now turn.

Interpretation of the Old Testament

Origen's spiritual exegesis of the Old Testament is grounded upon and inspired by the historical revelation of the Christian mystery. The presupposition of all ancient Christian exegesis is that the coming of Jesus Christ, the incarnate Word of God and Messiah of Israel, has brought the fulfillment of the long-awaited time of salvation (cf. Mk 1:15), of the Mosaic law (cf. Mt 5:17; Rom 13:10), and of the Old Testament scriptures (cf. Mt 26:31, 54; Lk 22:37; Jn 13:18; Acts 3:18; Rom 1:2; 1 Cor 15:3–4). In light of the historical fulfillment, the Old Testament must now be received as a period of preparation for the messianic or ecclesiastical age. It was a period of divine pedagogy (cf. Gal 3:23–25). The fulfillment of the Old Testament promises in the New Testament implies that what was imperfect and incomplete in the Old Testament has now been surpassed; indeed the fulfillment introduces a certain obsolescence of the ceremonial and ritual aspects of the law. The Christian principle admits that Old Testament moral precepts remain in force, and that the Old Testament played a positive role in that it procured religious education for the Jews and led them to Christ. But the law was a temporary and provisional regime from which Christians have now been set free.

Origen's basic hermeneutical principles for interpreting the Old Testament derive from Christ himself. Jesus taught his followers that he had not come to destroy the law but to fulfill it (cf. Mt 5:16–17). He said that the Old Testament predicts and prefigures him and the spiritual realities that constitute the New Testament (cf. Lk 24:27). For instance, Jesus announced the beginning of his public ministry as a fulfillment of Isaiah 61 (cf. Lk 4:16–21). He explained the meaning of his life and death using the rites of the Sinai cov-

---

41. Cf. L. Bouyer, "Erasmus in Relation to the Medieval Biblical Tradition," in *The Cambridge History of the Bible*, vol. 2: *The West from the Fathers to the Reformation*, ed. G. Lampe (Cambridge: Cambridge University Press, 1969), 503–4.

enant (cf. Lk 22:20). Jesus viewed the bronze serpent fashioned and lifted up by Moses in the wilderness as a symbol and foreshadowing of his own death on the cross and ascension into heaven (cf. Jn 3:13–15). Jesus related his miracles directly to the literal fulfillment of prophecies made by the prophet Isaiah (Mt 11:5; Lk 7:22; cf. Is 35:4–6). Jesus understood his own betrayal, suffering, death, and resurrection as the will of God that fulfills the prophecies (cf. Mk 14:27–28; Lk 22:37). Origen endeavors quite simply to sit at Jesus's feet, as a devoted pupil, and to learn from him how to read and interpret the Old Testament. The four evangelists witness to Christ's authority in this respect and develop this way of reading the Old Testament, as predicting and prefiguring Jesus Christ, as do the book of Revelation and the Catholic epistles.[42]

Following the antecedent Christian tradition (Irenaeus, Justin Martyr), Origen believed that through his coming, Jesus created a new meaning of the law. In order for us to assimilate it into our lives, it is necessary that Jesus enter into us, that we ourselves be recreated in him. Exegesis is thus for Origen a specifically Christian exercise. Origen regards Paul and the author of Hebrews as the supreme exemplars of the Christian exegete. Indeed, Paul is the creator of the term "allegorical exegesis."[43] In Galatians 4:21–31, for example, Paul uses an allegorical interpretation from the life of Abraham to bolster his argument. Abraham's son Isaac was born to Sarah, Abraham's wife, by miraculous divine intervention, because Sarah was infertile and very old (cf. Gn 21:1–3). Abraham's son Ishmael was born to Hagar, Sarah's slave girl, with whom Abraham had relations when Sarah was unable to conceive (cf. Gn 16). Although Ishmael was born first, he and his mother were driven from Abraham's home. They went out to the desert, where they made their home and where Ishmael is said to have become ancestor of various tribes who lived in the Sinai desert near Egypt (cf. Gn 16:21). In Galatians, Paul takes this famous story and allegorizes it: the Jews saw themselves as God's chosen people, the children of Abraham and Isaac. Paul argues that actually those Jews who are now insisting on the law, given on Mount Sinai, correspond to Ishmael, son of the slave woman. Christians, on the other hand, who trust in the miracle-producing promises of God, correspond to Isaac. Paul sees the Christians, whether they descend from Jewish or Gentile backgrounds, as the true spiritual family of Abraham, as the true Israel (6:16).

Origen reveres the evangelists, Paul, and the author of Hebrews. In his homilies he wants to perpetuate and develop their interpretive meth-

---

42. Cf. Mt 2:15; 1 Cor 5:7, 9:9, 10:4; Eph 5:31–32; Heb 9:5, 12:17; 1 Pt 1:19, 2:6–9; Rv 14:8.
43. Cf. de Lubac, *History and Spirit*, 77–86.

ods when treating the Old Testament texts. Origen brings this Christological and ecclesiological interpretive program to bear on the smallest details of the Old Testament text. De Lubac argues that in light of his rootedness in Paul and the evangelists, nothing authorizes the reader of Origen to see in his method a concern to "Hellenize." Rather, Origen tells his hearers to go back to the gospels and to Paul to find examples of "spiritual interpretation."[44] Programmatic texts for Origen's hermeneutics are Matthew 5:17 ("I have not come to abolish [the law and the prophets] but to fulfill them),", Hebrews 10:1 ("For since the law has but a shadow of the good things to come instead of the true form of these realities"), 1 Corinthians 10:11 ("Now these things happened to them as a warning, but they were written down for our instruction, upon whom the end of the ages has come"), Romans 15:4 ("For whatever was written in former days was written for our instruction, that by steadfastness and by the encouragement of the scriptures we might have hope"); and 2 Timothy 3:16–17: "All scripture is inspired by God and profitable for teaching, for reproof, for correction, and for training in righteousness, that the man of God may be complete, equipped for every good work." Especially in light of Paul's claims about the Old Testament in these passages, Origen asks: what foreshadowing, what warning, what instruction, what encouragement, reproof, correction or exhortation, do we find in these narratives?[45] What this implies is that Origen, following Jesus, is far from scorning or eliminating history, as has often been charged. He maintains it intact and defends it, but he seeks the truth of it in terms of its deeper significance in the light of Christ.

In addition to adhering closely to the New Testament patterns of interpretation of the Old Testament, it is also evident that Origen had an almost excessive admiration of ancient Jewish methods of exegesis. He mentions a Jewish convert to Christianity, the son of a Palestinian rabbi, who taught him influential principles of scriptural interpretation.[46] Links to the renowned Philo of Alexandria are not difficult to find in Origen's works. Indeed, it is to Origen that the west owes the survival of Philo's writings.[47] Origen also subtly praises the type of symbolic interpretation found in the intertestamental Jewish books such as 1 Enoch, a work that is quoted in the New Testament book of Jude 14.[48] Thus it is clear that many tributaries fed into Origen's ex-

---

44. Cf. *Hom in Num* 7.5.3.   45. *Hom in Num* 7.1.1.
46. *Hom in Num* 13.5.1.
47. See D. Runia, "Philo of Alexandria," in *The Westminster Handbook to Origen*, ed. McGuckin, 169–71.
48. Cf. *Hom in Num* 28.2.1.

egetical method, rather than merely Jesus and Paul. Yet Origen did not derive his principles from pagan thought or from intertestamental Jewish exegesis or from the rabbis. Of fundamental importance to him was the pattern of interpretation inaugurated by Jesus and found in the New Testament itself. To Origen, the question for the homilist is not whether the stories in the Old Testament literally occurred in history. For the most part Origen assumed that they did. But in the light of the coming of Christ, he subsequently asks: why were these narratives preserved by the Holy Spirit in the church? What spiritual lessons and warnings do these stories offer the Christian? How can our souls be edified by these readings? As H. Crouzel reminds us, "In spite of the spontaneous reactions of many modern scholars it must not be concluded from the fact that Origen allegorizes a story that he does not believe in the historicity of the literal account, which is perfectly compatible with the quest for a spiritual meaning."[49] Similarly, Tillemont writes:

[Origen] has been blamed for having, throughout his writings, explained the whole of Scripture through allegory without following the letter. If he had claimed that the events reported by Scripture had not happened, he would assuredly have been worthy of blame. But if, assuming these events to be true, he tried to find in them more spiritual and elevated meanings by relating them to Jesus Christ and to the Church, he was only doing what Saint Paul taught through his words and through his example, and what Saint Augustine, Saint Gregory the Great, and nearly all the other Fathers tried to do after him.[50]

Doubtless, the fact that the followers of Marcion denied that the Old Testament narratives had any use whatsoever played a role in inspiring Origen to find a practical and spiritually edifying use even for seemingly insignificant details in the text of the Old Testament.[51] However, of much more fundamental importance was the influence of Paul, who had confronted the way the Jews and the Judaizing Christians sought to hold Christians to the observances of circumcision, Passover, unleavened bread, rules about food and drink, feasts, new moons, and the sabbath by means of a literal interpretation of the Old Testament. Such Jews and Judaizers saw no meaning more profound than the immediate one in the Old Testament ceremonial law. Allegorical interpretation, inaugurated by Jesus and Paul, equipped the Christian reader to handle Jewish objections like this. Indeed, P. Martens has recently shown that Origen's principal objections to Jewish literal exegesis of

49. Crouzel, *Origen*, 63.
50. Tillemont, *Mémoires*, 3:555; cited by de Lubac, *History and Spirit*, 81–82.
51. Cf. *Hom in Num* 27.2.1.

scripture focus on two issues in particular: the obligation to continue to adhere to Jewish ceremonial law (sabbaths, sacrifices, food laws, etc.) and the identity of Jesus as the Messiah.[52] Origen's critique of Jewish exegesis is not abstract and categorically dismissive of Jewish interpretation, but particular and focused on these specific dogmatic issues.

We can now fruitfully compare Origen's principles for interpreting the Old Testament with those of Erasmus. In the *Ratio* (1518), Erasmus writes:

> For whatever was either commanded or forbidden or permitted to the Jews cannot simply be applied to the life of Christians. It is not that there was something in the books of the Old Testament that does not pertain to us, but that most of these things were handed down for the time being as a symbol and a foreshadowing of things to come (cf. Heb 8.5) and it would be dangerous if they were not understood allegorically, for example, circumcision, the Sabbath, the choice of foods, sacrifices, hatred of one's enemy, war accepted and conducted in this spirit, polygamy, and other things similar to these, which have in part ceased to be permitted and in part like shadows, faded away, in the brilliant light of the Gospel.[53]

Here we see the fundamental concord between Erasmus and Origen in their approach to Old Testament interpretation. To Christian interpreters beginning with the authors of the New Testament, the practice of allegorical interpretation of the Old Testament is what distinguishes Christianity from Judaism, the New Covenant from the Old (Mosaic) Covenant. Erasmus simply aligns his exegetical principles with those of the ancient Christian exegetes.

One can nevertheless concede, as Erasmus himself also points out, that Origen goes too far at times and plays games with allegorical exegesis that lead to forced and far-fetched interpretations.[54] Origen sometimes expresses himself provocatively and his reasoning lends itself to misunderstandings. Attacks on Origen's doctrine of history and allegory by orthodox churchmen began during his own lifetime, which would seem to indicate that this concern was not merely a matter of misrepresentation of his views but of genuine concern to remain faithful to tradition.[55] Origen's interpretation of the first three chapters of Genesis leaves the reader with the impression that he utterly denies the historical factuality of the garden of Eden, which is not quite true.[56] His main concern in such texts, I believe, is directed against an

---

52. Cf. Martens, *Origen and Scripture*, 140–48.
53. Methodus (Ratio), trans. Conroy, 121 (LB 5:85).
54. Cf. LB 5:124–26.
55. Cf. Origen, *Hom in Ezek* 6.8.3.
56. Cf. de Lubac, *History and Spirit*, 19–22.

anthropomorphic interpretation of the narratives, as if God has a physical body, plants trees like a gardener, and walks around in the cool breeze like a man. However, even when we concede that Origen's language can be easily misunderstood to imply that he abandons history entirely, it is nevertheless clear from a careful reading of his writings that Origen by and large defends the veracity of the historical facts recorded in scripture.

When Origen does allegorize narratives, it is noteworthy that he does not claim finality for his spiritual interpretations, and in fact he often offers more than one. Frequently, he challenges his hearers to pursue their own investigations into the mystical meaning. It is also evident that Origen's linguistic terminology is significantly different from that of moderns. His understanding of "allegory" or "spiritual understanding" is far more extensive than it is for modern scholars. It is virtually the equivalent of "figurative." De Lubac writes: "Anytime he encounters an anthropomorphism, a metaphor, a parable, a figurative expression, he says that is must be taken in the spiritual sense."[57] This shows that Origen's notion of "literal" is diminutive in comparison with ours. Meanings that modern exegetes would consider to be included in the literal sense, Origen identifies as allegorical or spiritual meanings.

On the other hand, even scholars who are largely sympathetic to Origen's exegetical achievement have criticized his system of interpretation on two points.[58] First, while reacting against Gnosticism, he remained under its influence as seen by the way he invests meaning in biblical expressions that is foreign to the authentic sense. Second, he was unduly influenced by the allegorism of Philo, which led him to propose the idea that all passages of the Old Testament have a symbolic sense. To me these criticisms seem to be largely valid. Erasmus will repeat, or rather, anticipate, these criticisms without attributing them to Gnosticism or Philo, though not in the prefaces to his edition of Origen but rather in his early work, *Ratio* and other writings, as I will discuss in chapter 4. Erasmus will express strong disapproval of the way Origen often unnecessarily undermines the literal meaning in the gospels in his quest for allegory, and will lament the baneful influence Origen had upon subsequent exegetes like Hilary and Ambrose in this connection. On the other hand, the modern patristic scholar, J. Lienhard, argued that Origen's main exegetical achievement was to assure the Old Testament

---

57. Ibid., 129.
58. These are identified and discussed by de Margerie, *An Introduction to the History of Exegesis*, 107–12.

a permanent place in the Christian church. Origen did this not by an abstract theory but by working his way through the entire Old Testament, book by book, sentence by sentence, and word by word. Origen provided the church with the first Christian commentary on virtually the entire Old Testament. "Seldom, if ever again, would there be any doubt that this book had its proper and rightful place in the Christian church."[59] This is a fitting tribute to one of Origen's central contributions to Christian thought. It also shows the irony and silliness of Erasmus's being accused of having a disparaging view of the Old Testament—Erasmus, the great promoter of Origen's Old Testament exegesis.[60]

Origen the Moralist

There is also a strong moral thrust in Origen's exegesis that deserves mention, especially since it affected Erasmus very deeply. De Lubac writes that Origen follows in the footsteps of Paul, who in his first letter to the Corinthians strongly inculcated the necessity of Christian moral effort after baptism: "Let us not fear to affirm that Origen is in fact a moralist, whose exegesis is constantly oriented toward morality. For what is important in his eyes is, not to speculate on the profound meaning of the Bible, but to receive it with a living faith and to 'adapt one's conduct to the words of truth.'"[61] Origen endeavored to equip his hearers for spiritual warfare against Satan and his demons and the vices they incite. De Lubac writes: "What he thus describes, that to which he exhorts, particularly in his homilies, under the symbols of the Old Testament, is spiritual combat."[62] "He conceived the Christian life above all as a combat initiated at baptism, and it is to this combat that he did not cease to exhort his listeners."[63] Origen believed that from the

---

59. J. T. Lienhard, "Origen and the Crisis of the Old Testament in the Early Church," *Pro Ecclesia* 9, no. 3 (2000): 362.

60. The misleading claim that Erasmus would have preferred to see the Old Testament perish was made by R. Bainton, *Erasmus of Christendom* (New York: Charles Scribner's Sons, 1969), 143. Though repeated by many, for instance, by Ronald E. Heine, *Reading the Old Testament with the Ancient Church: Exploring the Formation of Early Christian Thought* (Grand Rapids, Mich.: Baker, 2007), 17, it is based on a crassly literal interpretation of some hypothetical statements of Erasmus in his private letters that have been lifted out of their original context. The same modern scholars ignore Erasmus's public, programmatic, and non-hypothetical statements, not to mention his actual use of the Old Testament in his theological works.

61. De Lubac, *History and Spirit*, 211; quoting C. Bigg.

62. Ibid., 171.

63. Ibid., 212.

day when the divine Word is introduced into a soul, the Christian must be engaged in a struggle of virtues against vices. Before the Word came to attack them, the vices remained in peace, but as soon as it undertook to judge them one by one, then a great movement arose and a merciless war was born.[64] De Lubac expands on the significance of this:

> If there is a traditional theme in Christian morality and asceticism, that is it. Now it is to Origen that we owe its name: "spiritual combat." It is also to him that we owe its symbolism. A wholly biblical symbolism. Through his spiritual interpretation, Origen transposes the history of Israel's wars, its captivities, its deliverances, its victories, in order to apply them to the Christian life. All of Scripture is for him the book of the Lord's combats.[65]

It is precisely this theme of the Christian life as spiritual combat, of course, that Erasmus incorporated so profoundly into his *Enchiridion*, or *Handbook of the Christian Soldier*. Godin has shown the depth of Erasmus's assimilation of Origen.[66] The same theme is deeply present in Erasmus's other spiritual writings, which shows that Origen, both directly and indirectly, was one of the great teachers of Catholic spirituality in the first half of the sixteenth century.

Origen's Exegesis of the Gospels

We now return to our survey of the remainder of Origen's writings. About 42 percent (1,577 columns) of Origen's surviving works are commentaries on scripture. Origen's commentaries on Song of Songs and Romans became classics in the west.[67] Those on Matthew and John, which survived only in fragmentary form, seem to have been less well known, although Origen's exegesis of Matthew was thoroughly assimilated into Jerome's *Commentary on Matthew*. Origen's *Commentary on John* was not included in Erasmus's edition of Origen or in the editions of Origen's writings prior to Erasmus. It was first edited by Daniel Huet in 1688.[68] Erasmus was the first to publish a

---

64. Cf. *Homilies on Exodus* 3.3.

65. De Lubac, *History and Spirit*, 214.

66. See A. Godin, "The Enchiridion Militis Christiani: The Modes of an Origenian Appropriation," trans. H. Gibaud, *Erasmus of Rotterdam Society Yearbook* 2 (1982): 47–79.

67. For a study of the legacy of Origen's Commentary on Romans, see Thomas P. Scheck, *Origen and the History of Justification* (Notre Dame, Ind.: University of Notre Dame Press, 2008).

68. Two Latin translations of it were made in the sixteenth century, one by Ambrosius Ferrarius of Milan in 1551 and the other by Joachim Perionius. Cf. Origen: *Commentary on the Gospel According to John, Books 1–10*, translated by R. Heine, FOTC 80:28; *Ante-Nicene Fathers* (Grand Rapids, Mich.: Eerdmans, 1969), 10:294 [hereafter "ANF"].

translation of a substantial fragment from Origen's *Commentary on Matthew*. All four of these commentaries (Song of Songs, Romans, John, Matthew) show Origen "at work" in the verse-by-verse exposition of individual books of the Bible. Of these great commentaries of Origen, all but the commentary on Romans place their main focus on bringing out the spiritual and allegorical meaning of the text. For even in his exegesis of the gospels, Origen's interpretation focuses on the symbolism that he thinks is inherent in the narratives, not on the literal historical meaning. This is not to say that Origen denies the history of the gospel narratives, but he seeks to transcend it.[69] Sometimes, however, the way Origen endeavors to reconcile discrepancies between the gospels tends to undermine the literal factuality of one of the parallel narratives in the other gospels. Origen believed that Jesus wanted to make the actions reported to us by the evangelists symbolic of his own spiritual operations within us. As in the case of his Old Testament interpretations, Origen interprets the gospel narratives as symbolic of deeper realities.[70] According to Origen, everything in the gospels, Christ's birth, his growth, his maturity, his passion, his descent to hell, his resurrection and ascension, not only took place at a given time, but also continues to act in us even today.[71]

Origen's Exegesis of Paul's Writings

Origen's *Commentary on Romans* is his second longest extant work, and therefore merits careful consideration. Surprisingly, this text approaches being a literal exposition of Paul's argument from beginning to end. This is not to say that Origen is doing purely scholarly work in the modern sense in his exegesis of Paul, or in any of his commentaries and sermons. He is always a man of the church, attentive to the present pastoral situation and concerned with the needs of souls. Yet he adopts a more literal and historical approach in interpreting Paul's writings, since his "allegorical" method of exegesis applies first and foremost to the interpretation of the Old Testament, secondarily to the gospels, but it does not fundamentally apply to the letters of Paul, except in exceptional passages. In a classic study of the Pauline exegesis of

---

69. Origen was severely criticized for this interpretive tendency by the eastern Orthodox scholar, G. Florovsky in his "Origen, Eusebius and the Iconoclastic Controversy," *Church History* 19 (1950): 87–90.

70. Cf. de Lubac, *History and Spirit*, 223–80.

71. Cf. *Homilies on Luke* 7.

the ancient church, M. F. Wiles observed: "The basic divergence between an allegorical and a more literal approach to Scripture is far less relevant to the interpretation of Paul's writings than it is to that of the Old Testament or of the Gospels."[72] With specific reference to Origen's *Commentary on Romans*, several modern theologians who have reviewed the English translation of Origen's *Commentary on Romans* have observed this with a sense of surprise. For instance D. Brattston writes: "Scholars interested in the Alexandrian school of allegorical exegesis will be disappointed because there are surprisingly few examples of this method in the commentary."[73] Similarly, an American patristic scholar was equally surprised: "It should be noted first that the allegorical exegesis which is usually associated with Origen is rarely present in this commentary. Instead we see Origen as an Alexandrian *grammaticus*."[74]

The reason for the lack of allegorical exegesis in Origen's exposition is that Paul's letter to the Romans is itself a Christian theological interpretation of the Old Testament in its literal argument. Paul himself explains the gospel in his text, that is, the Christological meaning of the Old Testament. Paul informs us, or at least alludes to the Christian meaning of Abraham's faith and circumcision (chap. 2, chap. 4), of the propitiatory (3:25), of Adam (chap. 5), of the law (chap. 7), of God's choice of Jacob over Esau and of God's dealings with Pharaoh (chap. 9), of God's dealings with Elijah (chap. 11), of the offering of sacrifices (chap. 12), of the Hebrew prophecies concerning the identity of the Messiah and the inclusion of the Gentiles among God's people (chap. 15), etc. Elsewhere (Gal 4) Paul explains the allegorical meaning of Abraham's wives Sarah and Hagar. Working upon such Pauline material, Origen does not need to dig beneath the letter on his own to find Christian meaning, since it is on the surface and of ready application. The epistles of Paul themselves are Christian theology, which is not the case for much

---

72. M. F. Wiles, *The Divine Apostle: The Interpretation of St Paul's Epistles in the Early Church* (Cambridge: Cambridge University Press, 1967), 10.

73. D. Brattston, *Churchman* 116, no. 2 (Summer 2002): 189.

74. R. Heine, *Adamantius* 9 (2003): 433. In the preface to his translation of *The Commentaries of Origen and Jerome on St Paul's Epistle to the Ephesians* (Oxford: Oxford University Press, 2002), Heine writes: "The loss of so much of Origen's exegetical work is one of the tragedies of ancient Church history. This is especially true of his exegesis of the Pauline epistles for, from what can be surmised from the pieces that remain of this exegesis, he seems to have applied allegorical interpretation, which most modern exegetes find distasteful in his work, sparingly to Paul's epistles and to have concentrated more on philological issues, moral questions, and, of course, theological speculation" (vii).

of the Old Testament according to the letter. Origen's goal in interpreting the Pauline epistles, then, is to clarify and explain Paul's terms and the train of his thought as carefully, literally, and historically as he can. Once again, Henri de Lubac can be called upon to clarify matters:

> Indeed, we see that Origen uses this word "allegory" with much more reserve in regard to New Testament writings. For that matter, all his exegesis takes on a different appearance. Except for a few isolated reflections, his commentary on the Letter to the Romans, for example, in no way resembles his explanation of the texts from the Hexateuch.[75] We cannot be surprised to observe that the form taken by his theological elaboration is the interpretation of the Holy Books and that precisely, through its characteristic reflection on Scripture as well as on the Christian Event that accomplishes it, *the Pauline doctrine is itself a theology*. Origen imitates and extends the movement of the Apostle, in whom he sees above all the foremost of exegetes.[76]

In interpreting the Old Testament, Origen "imitates and extends" the interpretive patterns of Paul. But in interpreting Paul's own letters, Origen explains them literally. These sorts of clarifications and distinctions are only beginning to be appreciated in modern accounts of patristic exegesis, which normally does not distinguish patristic exegesis of Paul's writings from that of the Old Testament. But they are principles that are of fundamental importance and that were well known and understood not only by Wiles and de Lubac, but in my estimation by Erasmus as well.

Erasmus's thorough acquaintance with Origen's principles and practice of biblical exegesis explains, for instance, why he suspected that Luther and Melanchthon were unfamiliar with Origen's writings. The Wittenberg reformers spoke disparagingly of Origen's "allegorical exegesis," but they did so with specific reference to his *Commentary on Romans*, in which allegory is scarcely used. Erasmus responded that they had no right to criticize or reject something or someone with whom they were not familiar. In a letter to Erasmus written on January 5, 1519, the twenty-two-year-old Melanchthon admitted that he had disparaged Erasmus's *Paraphrase on Romans*, where the influence of Origen's exegesis was very strong.[77] Erasmus replied to Melanchthon on April 22, 1519, stating that no one will easily pass judgment on that work (his *Paraphrase on Romans*), "who has not been through all the an-

---

75. By "Hexateuch," he means Origen's homilies on Genesis, Exodus, Leviticus, Numbers, Deuteronomy, and Joshua.

76. De Lubac, *History and Spirit*, 262–63 (emphasis added).

77. Cf. CWE 6, ep. 910.

cient commentators with his eyes well and truly open."[78] As Wengert correctly recognizes, Erasmus's subtle rebuke assumes that Melanchthon (at least at this early stage in his theological career) "does not have the requisite knowledge of the Fathers to judge Erasmus's paraphrase."[79]

Unfortunately, Melanchthon still had not really learned anything new a couple years later when he wrote his *Loci Communes* (1521). There he writes with respect to Origen's Pauline exegesis: "If you delete from Origen his awkward allegories and his forest of philosophical jargon, how little will remain?"[80] A modern reader might well reply that there is very little allegory or "philosophical jargon" in Origen's *Commentary on Romans*. Only in his later years did Melanchthon begin to become familiar with Origen's exegesis of Romans.[81] From what I can tell, Luther never found time to read Origen's exegesis of Paul and engage it constructively, though he did find time to condemn it. My main concern here is to stress that Erasmus's advocacy and defense of Origen's exegesis of Romans is riveted on the way he thinks Origen profoundly and accurately understands the train of Paul's literal argument. It is certainly not an unqualified endorsement of Origen's allegories or philosophical ideas, even though a number of self-proclaimed champions of orthodoxy in the sixteenth century, both Catholic and Lutheran, accused Erasmus on this point.

Origen's Speculations and Dogmatic Errors

To conclude this chapter I will briefly recount the reasons for Origen's reputation as a "heretic." Origen's first book, *On First Principles*, became his most controversial treatise.[82] It was the main source of posthumous accusations against Origen's orthodoxy. In this work Origen became the first Christian theologian to attempt a theological reflection on the essential doctrines of the Christian faith, beginning with the Trinity, using the tools of reason,

---

78. Cf. CWE 6, ep. 947.

79. T. Wengert, "'Qui vigilantissimis oculis veterum omnium commentarios excus serit': Philipp Melanchthon's Patristic Exegesis," in *Die Patristik in der Bibelexegese des 16. Jahrhunderts*, ed. D. C. Steinmetz (Wiesbaden: Harrassowitz, 1999), 117.

80. *Loci Communes*, in *Melanchthon and Bucer*, ed. Wilhelm Pauck (Philadelphia: Westminster Press, 1969), 19.

81. I have analyzed this in *Origen and the History of Justification*, 173–204.

82. For a good discussion of some of the textual issues involved in this work and its modern editions, see R. Rombs, "A Note on the Status of Origen's *De Principiis* in English," *Vigiliae Christianae* 61 (2007): 21–29.

scripture, and apostolic tradition.[83] His stated aim is to defend the church's faith against the heretics. Two centuries after Origen's death, in 543, some of Origen's opinions that are discussed in On First Principles were condemned by emperor Justinian. In 553, fifteen anathemas were laid down against Origenian doctrines by the Fathers of the Fifth Ecumenical Council, but outside the official sessions of the council. The condemned doctrines included Origen's theories about the pre-existence of human souls and of Christ's soul, the spherical shape of resurrected bodies, the animate nature of the stars and heavenly bodies, the suggestion that Christ may have to be crucified in the future age on behalf of demons, the view that the power of God is limited, and the conjecture that the punishment of demons and impious men is only temporary.[84] None of these views are clearly exhibited in Origen's surviving texts. H. Crouzel, a very competent expert on Origen, states that the action of emperor Justinian in 543 was really directed against sixth century "Origenists," and not against the historical Origen.[85] This would mitigate the authority and relevance of the action with respect to Origen.

Origen's tainted reputation was well known even prior to this conciliar action. In his work De haeresibus, Augustine (d. 430) makes clear what he believes to be the errors in Origen that no Catholic can deny:

> But there are other teachings of this Origen which the Catholic Church does not accept at all. On these matters, she does not accuse him unwarrantably, and cannot herself be deceived by his defenders. Specifically, they are his teachings on purgation, liberation, and the return of all rational creation to the same trials after a long interval. Now what Catholic Christian, learned or otherwise, would not shrink in horror from what Origen calls the purgation of evils? According to him, even they who die in infamy, crime, sacrilege and the greatest possible impiety, and at last even the devil himself and his angels, though after very long periods of time, will be purged, liberated and restored to the kingdom of God and of light.[86]

---

83. See B. Daley, "Origen's De Principiis: A Guide to the Principles of Christian Scriptural Interpretation," in Nova et Vetera: Patristic Studies in Honor of Thomas Patrick Halton, ed. J. Petruccione (Washington, D.C.: The Catholic University of America Press, 1998), 3–21.

84. This summary is taken from the Anathemas against Origen (from the book against Origen written by Justinian), reproduced in DS 403–11.

85. Crouzel, Origen, xii. I believe that Crouzel's account is based on de Lubac, Medieval Exegesis, 1:161–84.

86. Augustine, De haeresibus, chap. 43, in The 'De haeresibus' of St. Augustine, ed. R. Deferrari, trans. L. G. Müller, Patristic Studies 90, (Washington, D.C.: The Catholic University of America Press, 1956).

C. Bammel describes Augustine's general attitude displayed here as "marked by cautious restraint and avoidance of personal polemics; his interest is directed to the teachings in question rather than to the individual."[87] Augustine continues by referring to his recently-written *City of God*, where he says he has discussed these matters thoroughly, as well as Origen's error about the pre-existence of souls.[88] This shows that from the very beginning of Latin theology, clear passages from famous works of Augustine had publicized Origen's errors in the west. In the medieval period, Thomas Aquinas identified as Origen's principal eschatological error not his purgatorial conception of the afterlife *per se*, but his misapprehension of the "volitional powers of the damned."[89] Modern scholars have argued that Origen's position on universalism resists neat schematization.[90]

In Origen's defense—but not in defense of the condemned views—one might say in reply to Augustine's assertions that it appears that with the exception of his doctrine of pre-existence of souls, Origen did not dogmatically *assert* any of these heterodox views, but instead he tentatively put them forward for the sake of discussion as interpretive possibilities in his attempt to refute the arguments of his Gnostic opponents. Origen surely does not seem to have had any intention of consciously violating the church's rule of faith, and there was no obstinacy in his erroneous views. Erasmus had observed this, following in the footsteps of Pico. There are even modern scholars who deny that Origen held these views in the form in which Augustine lists them. For example, C. Bammel writes:

The teachings of Origen which Augustine denounces in his later works are in fact a travesty of Origen constructed by anti-Origenists. Augustine would not have found them in this form in the exegetical works available to him in Latin translation, nor even unambiguously expressed as "teachings" in Rufinus' translation of *De principiis*. Such denunciations no doubt partly have the function of a safeguard enabling the denouncer to retain the useful insights of Origen and continue reading him without risking being accused as an Origenist.[91]

In light of Bammel's critique, it would seem more accurate to say, therefore, that Origen affirmed the logical possibility of restoration of all rational crea-

---

87. "Augustine, Origen and the Exegesis of St. Paul," *Augustinianum* 32 (1992): 346.
88. Cf. *City of God* 21.17.
89. Cf. *De Malo* 16.5, *De Veritate* 24.10, and *Summa Theologiae* I, q. 64, a. 2.
90. See Mark S. M. Scott, "Guarding the Mysteries of Salvation: The Pastoral Pedagogy of Origen's Universalism," *JECS* 18.3 (2010): 347–68.
91. "Augustine, Origen and the Exegesis of St. Paul," *Augustinianum* 32 (1992): 346n26.

tures, and also of the possibility of failure of such a hope, but he did not assert its inevitability.[92]

My aim in this brief survey of Origen's life, writings, exegetical method, and posthumous condemnation has been to aid the reader in understanding Erasmus's assessments of the ancient Alexandrian theologian and (obviously) not to resolve the complicated issues that have been discussed. From here we turn now to the matter of Origen's legacy in the western Catholic church.

92. Cf. Daniélou, *Origen*, 289.

ORIGEN'S LEGACY *in the* CATHOLIC EXEGETICAL TRADITION

Origen's legacy in the west continues to be underestimated and misleadingly portrayed. Very recently, a prominent Erasmus scholar, J. K. Farge, made the following claim: "Origen was seldom cited and little known in the medieval western tradition until Giovanni Pico della Mirandola [1463–93] championed his work in the fifteenth century."[1] To this assertion Farge adds that Erasmus "readily overlooked Origen's errors in order to profit from his insights into Christian exegesis and theology." The latter claim is most certainly correct, as I shall demonstrate in the next chapter. Erasmus clearly supported the irenic approach to receiving Origen's exegesis that the Cappadocian Fathers had recommended, and that had been practiced by Ambrose, Hilary, and the early Jerome. But to me it seems astonishing that the former opinion is still being propagated well into the twenty-first century in the light of de Lubac's findings to the contrary. Contrast Farge's claim with de Lubac's: "The entire western tradition is witness to an 'extraordinary interest' in the works of Origen. They enjoyed an immense popularity."[2] Elsewhere de Lubac describes Rufinus's project of translating Origen into Latin as a feat that "saved from definitive ruin some of the most precious monuments of Christian antiquity, *destined to form Latin minds for many years to come.*"[3] Or again, thanks to Rufinus's translations:

1. J. K. Farge (CWE 13:231).
2. De Lubac, *Medieval Exegesis*, 1:173.
3. De Lubac, *History and Spirit*, 45–46 (emphasis added).

Origen would be read, particularly on the Hexateuch and on the Song of Songs, with the same tractable diligence as Ambrose on the life of the Patriarchs and David, as Augustine on the Psalms, and as Gregory on Ezekiel and the Book of Job. From now on nobody could say, without ignoring the evidence, that "his [Origen's] colossal effort had not been fruitful." He was destined to be, almost directly, one of the foremost educators of the Latin Middle Ages. His "vision" of the Bible and of the Christian life was destined to govern the underpinnings of its customs and methods. Together with Saint Augustine, he was destined to be "the doctor of the spiritual sense of history." More than any other figure in the fields of hermeneutics, exegesis, and spirituality, he would be the grand master.[4]

Is it reasonable to think that de Lubac is speaking here of Origen's influence only upon minds born after Pico della Mirandola? On the contrary, de Lubac's very next chapter, entitled "The Latin Origen: The Reading of Origen in the Middle Ages," documents the Latin Origen's pervasive influence through the centuries. Such evidence is ignored by those who claim that Origen was unknown until Pico. This is not to deny Pico's impressive contribution to Origen's legacy or to contest the great role that the printing press played in disseminating knowledge in the fifteenth and sixteenth centuries.

Inspired by de Lubac's observations, I studied William of St. Thierry's (1085–1148) *Commentary on Romans* and found that the first half of it was largely copied from Origen's, whom he explicitly identifies as his "teacher" in the preface.[5] A similar pattern of assimilating Origen is seen in Peter Abelard's (1079–1142) *Commentary on Romans*.[6] It is true that Thomas Aquinas does not seem to have known or made direct use of Origen's *Commentary on Romans* in his own *Lectures on Romans*. The handful of passages in the *Summa Theologiae* in which he refers to Origen appears to be derived from some sort of catena source and not directly from Origen. But neither does Aquinas make use of Jerome's *Commentary on Ephesians* in his own commentary on that Pauline epistle. Does that prove that Jerome's exegesis was unknown during the medieval period? In any case Aquinas appears to be more of an exception than the rule. It seems that when detailed examinations of medieval authors are conducted by scholars who are equally familiar with Origen's works, the result often shows that the Latin Origen was well known in medieval times. Knowledge of Origen in the west clearly did not begin with Pico in 1486, but

---

4. De Lubac, *Medieval Exegesis*, 1:159.

5. In my book *Origen and the History of Justification*, I researched the legacy of Origen's *Commentary on Romans* in the west, including William's reception of Origen (104–28).

6. See Peter Abelard, *Commentary on the Epistle to the Romans*, trans. Steven R. Cartwright FOTC Medieval Continuation (Washington, D.C.: The Catholic University of America Press, 2011).

more than a thousand years earlier when his writings were turned into Latin. It is not easy to dismiss de Lubac's evidence on this matter, since he appears to have read everything pertaining to this topic.

Another common misunderstanding among modern scholars is that Erasmus himself stood apart from his contemporaries as some sort of Catholic *sui generis* who held radical views respecting Origen. It seems correct to say that Erasmus was advanced beyond many of his contemporaries in his knowledge not only of Origen but of the Greek and Latin exegetical tradition as a whole. Clearly he was unique in his detailed knowledge of Greek and Latin authors, and he unashamedly exploited these minds in his own exegesis, believing that benefit would come to the church by greater knowledge of ancient exegesis and theology.[7] In contrast many of Erasmus's contemporaries had read only scholastic compendia and chains of extracts from the Fathers based on Lombard's *Sentences*. Their exposure to the Fathers was thus limited to the proof-texts supplied there.[8] This is probably why Erasmus's exegesis of Paul (Romans), for example, initially provoked a negative reaction from some of his contemporaries who did not share his esteem for the ancient exegetes, since they were not familiar with them.

Two of the more famous responses to Erasmus's interpretation of Romans came from the future Protestant reformer Martin Luther and from the Catholic theologian John Eck of Ingolstadt, both of whom advised Erasmus to reread Augustine's writings if he really wanted to understand Romans.[9] Erasmus ignored Luther but replied to Eck, saying that he had been unable to read Eck's critique of him with a straight face, since he was already quite familiar with Augustine. The reality was not that Erasmus needed to obtain greater familiarity with Augustine, but that Eck needed to read more widely than Augustine. It is in this letter to Eck where Erasmus's famous words are recorded: "Other men's experience I know not; but in myself at least I find good reason to say that I learn more of Christian philosophy from a single page of Origen than from ten of Augustine."[10] "Christian philosophy" is a

---

7. A nice expression of Erasmus's enthusiasm for publishing the ancients is found in CWE 12, ep. 1790, the dedication of several works of Athanasius in Latin translation: "I think it is of the greatest importance for the well-being of Christendom that we lose none of the writings left us by that eloquent champion of the church. This great man deserved not just to have an immortal name, but to live on, immortal in a mortal world, and to survive entire."

8. Thomas More complained about this vehemently in his *Letter to Martin Dorp* (CW 15:69).

9. Eck's reaction to Erasmus's exegesis of Romans is found in CWE 5, ep. 769 (February 2, 1518). Erasmus's response is given in CWE 6, ep. 844. Luther's first criticism of Erasmus's exegesis is found in CWE 4, ep. 501.

10. CWE 6, ep. 844.

deliberate archaism drawn from the Church Fathers that Erasmus uses frequently to refer to the wisdom of Christ of which Paul speaks (cf. 1 Cor 2:6). In this context it is equivalent to "Christian theology." The term includes not only doctrinal and exegetical views but embraces the Christian person's intellectual, moral, and religious character shaped by Christ.[11]

As a Catholic theologian and exegete, Erasmus was certainly endeavoring to broaden out the theology curriculum to include the writings of the Greek Fathers, including Origen, and the Latin Fathers who were seldom cited by the scholastics, such as Jerome, Hilary, and Ambrose. He wanted to challenge the monopolization of theological studies by partisans of Augustine's writings alone. To traditionalist theologians who ascribed theological and exegetical supremacy to Augustine alone, Erasmus's program looked like an attack on the doctor of Hippo. It was in reality a more genuinely Catholic approach to theology than that method practiced by the scholastics and their successors, which essentially equated theological speculation with Augustinian theological speculation. Erasmus believed that other voices besides Augustine's should be summoned to aid us in the interpretation of scripture. In *Hyperaspistes* II Erasmus writes the following to Luther: "Only Augustine excludes foreknown merits as the reason why Jacob was chosen and Esau rejected, and his interpretation makes original sin the cause of the hatred. For my part, Augustine is a man to whom anyone may grant as high a status as he likes; but I would never attribute so much to him as to think he sees further in Paul's epistles than the Greek interpreters."[12] So I do not wish to deny Erasmus's uniqueness as a Catholic interpreter of Paul or underestimate that reality. He stands above the partisan quarrels of those who wish to see Augustine standing alone on the pillar of theological studies.

However, it seems unfair to insinuate that Erasmus's aims in promoting and defending Origen and the Greek interpreters of Paul were to subvert the Catholic theological tradition. On the contrary he was aiming to see it revitalized. One possible source of this idea is that the co-founder of the Lutheran

---

11. The term has been much misunderstood and maligned (in a pagan, moralistic, or intellectualist sense) by his critics spanning from Luther to Sauer, Renaudet, and Lortz, who are evidently unfamiliar or unsympathetic with the use of this term in the patristic tradition. Cf. de Vogel, "Erasmus and Church Dogma," 114n31; Bouyer, *Erasmus and His Times*, 142. It is noteworthy that the term "Christian philosophy" is used approvingly to describe Christian wisdom and revelation under the first article of the Creed, "I believe in God," in the *Catechism of the Council of Trent* (Roman Catechism). Cf. *Catechism of the Council of Trent for Parish Priests*, trans. J. McHugh, C. Callan (Rockford, Ill.: Tan Books, 1982), 16.

12. CWE 77:535.

church, Philipp Melanchthon, on the basis of Erasmus's profound respect for Origen's insights into the mind of Paul, polemically described Erasmus as a "sworn adherent of Origen's philosophy."[13] Melanchthon had plagiarized the epithet "sworn adherent" from Erasmus himself, who had previously described Melanchthon as a "sworn adherent" of Martin Luther's theology.[14] By describing Erasmus this way with respect to Origen, Melanchthon was avenging himself. At least one modern scholar agrees with Melanchthon, however, and claims that Erasmus was indeed Origen's "most avid" sixteenth-century supporter.[15] The truth, however, as I will discuss below, is that Erasmus was quite moderate in his support of Origen when he is compared with some of his Catholic contemporaries. And contrary to Melanchthon's claim, Erasmus's support for Origen did not focus on Origen's philosophy but on his exegesis, especially of Paul's epistles and of the Gospel of Matthew, and on his morally edifying homilies; moreover, Erasmus was by no means an isolated figure in his display of admiration and respect for Origen. I will demonstrate these points carefully in this and in the next chapter.

Origen's Influence upon Jerome

Even if one were to concede that Origen's name was "seldom cited and little known in the medieval western tradition" until Pico came along in 1486, Origen's importance would not thereby be diminished, since his scriptural interpretations were profoundly assimilated by the most important Latin exegetes: Hilary, Ambrose, and Jerome. No scholar familiar with the writings of Hilary, Ambrose, and Jerome would dare deny this. It was the highly independent-minded Greek-less Augustine who was uninfluenced by Origen's (and Jerome's) exegesis in his own scriptural commentaries. It is noteworthy that Augustine, in his own commentary on Paul's epistle to the Galatians, chose not to learn anything even from Jerome's erudite exegesis of Galatians, though he clearly had access to Jerome's work and had already severely criticized some of Jerome's interpretations in his written correspondence. E. Plumer finds Augustine's neglect of Jerome "astonishing" and writes:

---

13. For a discussion of this issue, see chap. 6 of Scheck, *Origen and the History of Justification*.

14. Cf. Desiderius Erasmus, *Hyperaspistes I* (CWE 76:180–81; LB 10:1283) and *Hyperaspistes II* (CWE 77:546; LB 10:1441).

15. Cf. T. Wengert, *Human Freedom, Christian Righteousness: Philip Melanchthon's Exegetical Dispute with Erasmus of Rotterdam* (Oxford: Oxford University Press, 1998), 59, 140.

At the very least, one would have expected him [Augustine] to borrow some linguistic point or other from Jerome, particularly as we find Augustine very soon afterwards emphasizing the importance of linguistic expertise for the interpreter of the Bible, painfully conscious of his own lack in this regard, and (no doubt thinking primarily of Jerome) commending the work of the Hebraists to biblical interpreters [De Doctrina Christiana 2.11.16; 2.16.23]. Yet where is the evidence of Augustine's having taken his own advice?[16]

Plumer's observation and question shows the originality of Augustine's exegesis and its innovative nature, which did not endear him to Jerome or John Cassian.[17] It also illustrates the point that works can be well known to authors who choose not to use them and learn from them. In this instance, Jerome's *Commentary on Galatians* was well known to Augustine, who, however, has left behind no evidence for this in his own commentary.

Origen's influence on Jerome, in contrast, is comparable to Homer's influence on Virgil, or Menander's influence on Terence. It is impossible to conceive of these Latin authors apart from the influence of the Greek models. Since Erasmus was the greatest promoter of Jerome's writings in the sixteenth century, having published an edition of them in 1516, it makes sense to include in this chapter a study of the influence of Origen upon Jerome, which was well known to Erasmus. Therefore I shall first briefly survey Jerome's life and scholarship, focusing on the theme of Origen's influence upon his theology and exegesis. I begin by offering a chart that shows the approximate length (in Migne columns) of Jerome's translations of Origen's homilies and of his own commentaries on scripture (see table 3-1). Only Jerome's exegetical works are included here.

After his baptism in Rome during Lent in 367, Jerome traveled to Gaul, where, in Trier, he made a decision to pursue the monastic life and made copies of some works by Hilary of Poitiers (d. 368). This appears to be the beginning, at least retrospectively, of Jerome's theological and exegetical formation

---

16. Augustine, *Commentary on Galatians*, trans. E. Plumer (Oxford: Oxford University Press, 2003), 53.

17. Jerome's exegetical dispute with Augustine is well known. I discuss it briefly in the introduction to my translation of *St. Jerome's Commentaries on Galatians, Titus and Philemon* (Notre Dame, Ind.: University of Notre Dame Press, 2010), 31–37. Augustine seems not to have been John Cassian's pet theologian. Notice the comparatively less effusive praise of him in Cassian's work, *De incarnatione Domini contra Nestorium*. Cassian mentions Hilary as "a man in possession of all virtues and marks of distinction, and remarkable both for his life and eloquence"; Ambrose: "an outstanding priest of God who always sparkled like a jewel on God's finger and did not draw back from the hand of the Lord"; Jerome: "a teacher of Catholics whose writings sparkle like divine lamps throughout the whole world"; Augustine: "a priest of the town of Hippo."

Table 3-1. Length of Jerome's Translations of Origen's Homilies and of Jerome's Own Commentaries on Scripture

DATE	TITLE	DEDICATEE(S)	LENGTH IN COLUMNS[1]
379–82	Origen's 9 Hom in Isaiah	[none]	35
	Origen's 14 Hom in Jer	[none]	96
	Origen's 14 Hom in Ezek	Vincentius	96
383–84	Origen's 2 Hom in Cant	Damasus	21
386–87	In Philemonem	Paula and Eustochium	17
	In Galatas	"	130
	In Ephesos	"	115
	In Titum	"	45
388–89	In Ecclesiasten	"	107
392	Origen's 39 Hom in Lk	"	99
392–93	In Nahum	"	41
	In Michaeam	"	79
	In Sophoniam	"	50
	In Aggaeum	"	29
	In Habacuc	Chromatius, bishop of Aquileia	63
396	In Ionam	"	35
	In Abdiam	Pammachius	21
397	In Visiones Isaiae	Amabilis, bishop	53
398	In Mattaeum	Eusebius of Cremona, monk	201
406	In Zachariam	Exsuperius, bishop of Toulouse	124
	In Malachiam	Minervius and Alexander, bishops	37
	In Osee	Pammachius	131
	In Ioelem	"	41
	In Amos	"	107
407	In Danielem	Pammachius and Marcella	93
408–10	In Isaiam	Eustochium	661
410–14	In Ezechielem	"	475
414–16	In Hieremiam	Eusebius of Cremona	223

1. Number of columns in Migne's PG 11–17 or PL 22–30.

from the writings of Origen.[18] The influence of Origen on Jerome deepened over time and is evident in several of Jerome's works. In *On Famous Men* 54, Jerome briefly describes Origen's life and literary output in very admiring fashion, as a complement to his summary in *Epistle* 33. In *On Famous Men* 100, Jerome reports that the Latin Hilary had imitated the Greek Origen in his commentaries on the Psalms, but also added some original material. Moreover, in his *Commentary on Job* Hilary had translated freely from the Greek of Origen's commentary. Repeatedly, Jerome will encounter theologians and exegetes of untainted orthodoxy who adopted an irenic attitude toward Origen and recognized that he was the church's exegete *par excellence*. In addition to his antiquity and to his Spirit-filled fidelity to New Testament modes of Old Testament interpretation, Origen's word-perfect knowledge of the Greek Bible was famous. Jerome later remarked that he would gladly trade his knowledge of scripture with Origen, who "knew the Scriptures by heart."[19] Also, the many years of labor Origen had invested in creating the *Hexapla*, a six-column edition of the Old Testament, left an indelible impression on subsequent Christian scholars who became aware of Origen's indefatigable research. In his early writings, Jerome adopted the same irenic stance toward Origen that had been represented by men such as Pamphilus the Martyr, Eusebius of Caesarea, Hilary, Didymus, Ambrose, Rufinus, Gregory Nazianzen, and John Chrysostom. For example, the early Jerome described Origen as the "greatest teacher of the Church after the apostles," a man endowed with "immortal genius," who was of "incomparable eloquence and knowledge"; Origen "surpassed all previous writers, Latin or Greek."[20] Moreover, in his translations of Origen at this early stage of his career, Jerome endeavored to protect Origen's reputation from malicious misrepresentation, especially against the anachronistic charge of proto-Arianism. Jerome did this by glossing his translations of Origen, removing passages that might be subject to misunderstanding in the post-Nicene church, and by adding clarifications directly into his translation of Origen's text.[21]

When Jerome moved to Aquileia in northeastern Italy, he continued to

18. Hale Williams, *The Monk and the Book*, 45, states that Jerome "discovered" Origen at a later date while under the influence of Gregory Nazianzus in Constantinople. For full documentation, see P. Courcelle, *Late Latin Writers and Their Greek Sources*, trans. H. E. Wedeck (Cambridge: Cambridge University Press, 1969), 100–127.

19. *Ep* 84.8.

20. Jerome, *Hebrew Names*, preface; *Vir Ill* 54.8; *Ep* 33.4 to Paula; Jerome's preface to his translation of Origen's *Homilies on Song of Songs*.

21. See Alfons Fürst, "Jerome Keeping Silent: Origen and His Exegesis of Isaiah," in *Jerome of Stridon: His Life, Writings and Legacy*, ed. A. Cain and J. Lössl (Aldershot: Ashgate, 2009), 141–52. I have integrated Fürst's observations into my new English translation of Jerome's translation of

study scripture and theology and lived as an ascetic for seven years. In 374 he began living as a hermit in the desert of Chalcis, a region located slightly east of Syrian Antioch.[22] During this period Jerome made the acquaintance of a converted Jew named Baranina, who introduced him to the Hebrew language. Jerome went to Antioch in 379 and was ordained to the priesthood by bishop Paulinus. He heard lectures there from Apollinaris of Laodicea, an Alexandrian grammarian, who had mastered Greek literature and philosophy and had written an important apologetic work in thirty books, *Against Porphyry*. Apollinaris's work does not survive but had a formative influence on Jerome. In *Epistles* 84.3, Jerome said that he had learned biblical interpretation from Apollinaris, though he distanced himself from Apollinaris's heterodox understanding of the incarnation.[23]

From Antioch Jerome went to Constantinople, where he became a pupil of Gregory Nazianzen (d. 390), whose eloquence he respectfully mentions in his *Commentary on Isaiah* at 3.3. This saintly Cappadocian Father likewise encouraged Jerome to combine Bible study with the assimilation of Origen's scriptural exegesis. Jerome adopted Origen's comprehensive pattern of life, scholarship, and asceticism as a model for his own life. At this time he completed his translations of Origen's *Homilies on Jeremiah, on Ezekiel, and on Isaiah*.[24] He also translated Eusebius of Caesarea's *Chronicle of World History*. These projects were finished around 381. Eusebius was another Greek Christian author deeply indebted to Origen's works. Thus both directly and indirectly, Jerome was formed theologically and exegetically under Origen's massive influence on ecclesiastical literature. Jerome also translated Origen's *Homilies on the Song of Songs*, which he dedicated to Pope Damasus. At about this time he also wrote his *Commentary on Ecclesiastes*, a work that essentially reproduces Origen's interpretation of this book.[25]

Origen's Homilies on Isaiah found in Appendix 1 of Jerome's *Commentary on Isaiah*, Ancient Christian Writers 68 [hereafter "ACW"] (New York: Newman Press, 2015).

22. For a study of the letters Jerome wrote during this period, see A. Cain, *The Letters of Jerome: Asceticism, Biblical Exegesis, and the Construction of Christian Authority in Late Antiquity* (Oxford: Oxford University Press, 2009).

23. Apollinaris said that the Son of God did not fully assume human flesh but that the divinity itself took the place of the human mind and spirit.

24. See Origen, *Homilies 1–14 on Ezekiel*, trans. Thomas P. Scheck, ACW 62 (Mahwah, N.J.: Paulist Press, 2010). The *Homilies on Jeremiah* are available in FOTC 97, trans. John Clark Smith (Washington, D.C.: The Catholic University of America Press, 1998). See also my translation in Jerome, *Commentary on Isaiah; Origen: Homilies 1–9 on Isaiah*, ACW 68.

25. See the new translation of St. Jerome's *Commentary on Ecclesiastes* by R. J. Goodrich and D. J. D. Miller in ACW 66 (Mahwah, N.J.: Newman Press, 2012).

Returning to Rome in the early 380s, Jerome undertook important scholarly activity under the patronage of Pope Damasus. After the death of his patron, Jerome traveled to Palestine and visited the holy sites. He also made a brief visit to Egypt, where he stayed for thirty days with Didymus the Blind (d. 398). Soon he would publish his own translation of Didymus's *Treatise on the Holy Spirit*. Jerome was well aware that Didymus as well had been immersed in the writings of Origen and he wanted to make this material available to Latin readers.[26] Unfortunately Jerome was inspired to translate Didymus partly by a base motive: he aimed to show Latin readers that Ambrose, bishop of Milan, whom he intensely disliked, had plagiarized much of his own book on the Holy Spirit from Didymus. Rufinus of Aquileia would later expose Jerome's ill will and come to Ambrose's defense in his *Apology against Jerome* 2.22–25.[27] It seems ironic that Jerome would accuse Ambrose on this point, since he himself practiced the same method of exegesis throughout his life.

In 385 Jerome settled in Bethlehem, where he set up a monastery. Being within range of Caesarea, he traveled there frequently to consult its magnificent library, which included a copy of Origen's *Hexapla* in which the entire text of the Old Testament was displayed in six columns in the Hebrew and various Greek versions.[28] This work assisted Jerome enormously in his biblical translations and commentaries, since he could consult its Greek versions for assistance in translating and comprehending the Hebrew text. Jerome copied and otherwise obtained important manuscripts of the scriptures and the writings of Origen and other Greek writers. It was at this time, in the early Bethlehem period, that Jerome completed commentaries on Ephesians, Philemon, Galatians, and Titus.[29] In 398 he published his influential Com-

26. See A. Cain, "Origen, Jerome, and the *Senatus Pharisaeorum*," *Latomus* 65, no. 3 (2006): 727–34; R. A. Layton, *Didymus the Blind and His Circle in Late-Antique Alexandria* (Urbana: University of Illinois Press, 2004).

27. Cf. NPNF2 3:470–71. For an assembly of passages in Jerome that attack Ambrose, see D. Hunter, *Marriage, Celibacy, and Heresy in Ancient Christianity: The Jovinianist Controversy* (Oxford: Oxford University Press, 2007), 234–36. There is now a fine translation of Ambrose's *Exposition of the Holy Gospel according to Saint Luke with Fragments on the Prophecy of Isaias*, trans. Theodosia Tomkinson, 2nd ed. (Etna, Calif.: Center for Traditionalist Orthodox Studies, 2003).

28. For a description of the library see the article on "Disciples of Origen" in *Westminster Handbook to Origen*, ed. McGuckin. For a description of Jerome's own library, see Williams, *Monk and the Book*. For a reconstruction of Origen's *Hexapla* on Isaiah, see PG 16.2:1611–86 and *Origenis Hexaplorum Quae Supersunt*, Tomus II, ed. Fridericus Field (Hildesheim: Olms, 1964).

29. See Heine, *Commentaries of Origen and Jerome on Ephesians*; Scheck, *St. Jerome's Commentaries on Galatians, Titus and Philemon*.

mentary on Matthew.[30] All of these New Testament commentaries are heavily indebted to Origen's Greek exegesis.[31]

The Origenist Controversy

During the decade of the 390s and beyond, Jerome became embroiled in "Origenist" controversies which began in Palestine and spread to Rome and Constantinople. The Palestinian controversy was instigated by Epiphanius, bishop of Salamis. He and his cobelligerent Theophilus of Alexandria were responsible for deposing John Chrysostom from his bishopric of Constantinople. Jerome was complicit in this action, having translated Theophilus's violent invective against Chrysostom into Latin.[32] Epiphanius entered Palestine in 393 and accused Jerome's bishop, John of Jerusalem, as well as the monk Rufinus of Aquileia, of being "Origenist" heretics, because they refused to sign a petition circulated by a monk named Atarbius declaring Origen to be a heretic. Jerome reversed his earlier irenicism toward Origen and signed the petition. A quarrel ensued which led Epiphanius to violate canonical norms by ordaining Jerome's brother Paulinian to the priesthood in Palestine. John of Jerusalem responded by excommunicating Jerome and his monks. Reconciliation was temporarily achieved in 397, through the mediation of Melania, and Jerome was reinstated, but an even worse controversy over Origenism was soon to break out in Rome and Constantinople. The best primary sources of information are the respective apologies written by Rufinus and Jerome.[33]

Many modern writers have analyzed this episode in Jerome's career, in which he changed sides from being one of Origen's most vocal advocates and defenders into being Origen's most immoderate and violent accuser. In a very learned treatment, F. X. Murphy concluded that in spite of Jerome's

---

30. See Jerome, *Commentary on Matthew*, trans. Thomas P. Scheck, FOTC 117 (Washington, D.C.: The Catholic University of America Press, 2008).

31. A. Harnack, *Der kirchengeschichtliche Ertrag der exegetischen Arbeiten des Origenes* (Leipzig: Hinrichs, 1919), 65, complained of the lack of studies of Jerome's commentaries to determine Origen's influence upon them. In an appendix to the same work, Harnack himself undertook an examination of Jerome's commentaries on Galatians, Titus, and Philemon for this purpose. I have endeavored to integrate Harnack's conjectures and conclusions in the notes to my translation, *St. Jerome's Commentaries on Galatians, Titus and Philemon*.

32. Cf. Kelly, *Jerome*, 260–63.

33. Good discussions are found in de Lubac, *Medieval Exegesis*, vol. 1; Kelly, *Jerome*; and Murphy, *Rufinus of Aquileia*. See also my introductions to *St. Jerome's Commentary on Matthew* (FOTC 117) and *St. Pamphilus's Apology for Origen* (FOTC 120).

inflamed rhetoric about his alleged repudiation of the "heretic" Origen, Jerome did not really differ from his orthodox contemporaries in his deep reverence for Origen as the church's exegete *par excellence*. Murphy writes: "It was a needless controversy. In reality, the two men [Jerome and Rufinus] were agreed on their attitude toward Origen. Their misunderstandings were due to the machinations of their friends."[34] I would perhaps place more direct responsibility on Jerome's contentious and volatile personality than Murphy does, since, independently of his friends, Jerome continued to rage against both Origen and Rufinus until the day of his death. The worst and most slanderous of Jerome's anti-Rufinus polemic is found in his *Commentary on Jeremiah* which is his final work and was written well after Rufinus had died. In any case Jerome's accusations of Origen applied only to a handful of doctrinal conjectures.

Henri de Lubac says that Jerome's rhetoric against Origen and Rufinus during the Origenistic controversy is "somewhat untruthful" since he makes a distinction between Origen the dogmatist and theologian, whom he allegedly repudiated, and Origen the exegete and philosopher, whom he allegedly admired. Yet Jerome had once called Origen "Master of the Churches." De Lubac suggests that Jerome's distinction was as artificial as it was facile, and that Jerome was well aware of this, when he advanced other defensive schemes.

A "faithful interpreter" could easily have made some false steps. But how, at the same time, could he be so culpable? Besides, was there not quite often a dependence on his doctrine? Was theology not, in fact, identically the science of Scriptures? Praising the interpreter did not mean that reference was made only to his critical erudition. It meant that one talked of his homilies and his commentaries, not of the *Hexapla* or the scholia.... How, therefore, are we to understand that so faithful an interpreter of all the Scriptures had at the same time corrupted them, to the point of becoming a purveyor of heterodox doctrine? And, as Rufinus had long before objected to Jerome: "Who that was once Master of the Churches could be said to have been a heretic?" [*Apol* 1.21].[35]

The fact is that Jerome was caught in disingenuous behavior during the Origenist controversies, and that Rufinus really occupied the high ground. Jerome was inconsistent and even untruthful with respect to his attitude toward Origen. Moreover, it seems ironic that Jerome would eventually find

---

34. Murphy, *Rufinus of Aquileia*, 110.
35. De Lubac, *Medieval Exegesis*, 1:177–78.

fault with Rufinus's method of translating Origen, when it was directly from Jerome that Rufinus learned the method.[36] Until the day of his death Jerome resented Rufinus as the one who had exposed to the world Jerome's own inconsistency with respect to Origen and for other matters, such as his Judaizing view of the Old Testament canon.[37] To conceal all this, Jerome endeavored to darken both Origen's and Rufinus's reputation to posterity, and he was largely successful during the centuries in which genuine historical criticism of the issues was asleep. Origen would eventually be listed among the heretics by the emperor Justinian at the Fifth Council of Constantinople in 543. As a result his Greek writings would be mostly destroyed. Jerome and Epiphanius were culpable in this affair, since it is they who planted the seeds for Origen's ruin.

Origen as the Master Exegete

Gregory Thaumaturgus (213–75) was a pupil of Origen who describes his teacher's method and influence on him with great emotion, calling attention to Origen's divinely inspired ability to explain the Old Testament prophets according to their divine meaning:

And he [Origen] became the interpreter of the prophets to us, and explained whatsoever was dark or enigmatical in them ... and set them in the light, as being himself a skilled and most discerning hearer of God, who alone of all men of the present time with whom I have myself been acquainted, or of whom I have heard by the report of others, has so deeply studied the clear and luminous oracles of God, as to be able at once to receive their meaning into his own mind, and to convey it to others.... To speak in brief, he was truly a paradise to us after the similitude of the paradise of God.[38]

Notice how Gregory observes that Origen was so attentive to the voice of the Holy Spirit, he had so carefully studied the divine scriptures, that he was able to comprehend their meaning and convey it to others. A remarkably similar report concerning the first attempts in Christian learning of the great Cappadocians, Gregory Nazianzen and Basil of Caesarea, is preserved by Rufinus of Aquileia (345–411) in his translation of Eusebius of Caesarea's *Church His-*

---

36. See the Fürst article cited above and the first appendix of my translation of Jerome's *Commentary on Isaiah*.

37. See my brief discussion in the introduction to *St. Jerome: Commentary on Isaiah; Origen: Homilies 1–9 on Isaiah* (ACW 68).

38. Gregory Thaumaturgus, *Panegyric to Origen* 15 (ANF 6:36).

tory. Rufinus appended his own additions to the work, in order to bring the work up to date and cover the eighty-year period between Eusebius's final redaction and Rufinus's day. In 11.7, Rufinus writes:

[Gregory] removed Basil from the professor's chair which he was occupying and forced him to accompany him to a monastery, where for thirteen years, they say, having put aside all the writings of the worldly pagans, they gave their attention solely to the books of holy scripture, the understanding of which they did not presume to derive from themselves but *from the writings and the authority of those of old, who were themselves known to have received the rule of understanding from apostolic tradition.* They sought the treasures of wisdom and knowledge hidden in these vessels of clay by *examining their commentaries on the prophets in particular.*[39]

The italicized sentences refer chiefly to Origen's exegetical writings on the prophets, which were the most celebrated of the ancient Christian commentaries. Rufinus is testifying to the fact that the Cappadocians—and we should recall that Jerome studied for a time directly under Gregory Nazianzen and that it was Gregory who encouraged Jerome to translate Origen's homilies on the prophets—believed that the church's scriptures should not be separated from her most ancient interpreters, who were transmitters of apostolic tradition and modes of exegesis. Rufinus's summary is strikingly in alignment with the words of Gregory Thaumaturgus cited above.

M. Hale Williams has insightfully noticed how in the latter passage Rufinus's description of Gregory Nazianzen and Basil resonates on several levels with aspects of Jerome's career. "First there is a renunciation of pagan literature in favor of the Bible and Christian exegesis.... Then, there is the Cappadocians' deference toward their illustrious predecessors. Rufinus's understanding of the proper mode of Christian scholarship, based on the authority of tradition rather than on individual creativity, seems remarkably like that articulated by Jerome in his programmatic statements on the commentary."[40] This latter insight is verified in Jerome's commentaries on the prophets where he repeatedly says that it is his wish to transmit to his readers what men of the church before him have taught.

It appears to me, then, that in his own scriptural commentaries, Jerome, in spite of his intermittent outbursts against Origen's alleged heresies, was endeavoring to carry on the legacy of the Cappadocians by his reliance upon Origen's exegesis. Jerome admits as much in *On Famous Men* 75, where

39. *The Church History of Rufinus of Aquileia, Books 10 and 11*, trans. P. Amidon (New York: Oxford University Press, 1997), 70–71 (11:7).
40. Williams, *Monk and the Book*, 130.

he reports that he possessed Origen's twenty-five-book *Commentary on the Twelve [Minor] Prophets*, transcribed by the hand of the martyr Pamphilus himself, "which I hug and guard with such joy, that I deem myself to have the wealth of Croesus." Since Jesus said, "For where your treasure is, there will your heart be also" (Mt 6:21), we can assume that Jerome's heart was found in the possession of Origen's commentaries. Throughout all periods of his life, he recommends Origen's works for study. In 392 Jerome responded to critics who accused him of dependence on Origen in his own exegetical writings with these words:

They say that I made excerpts from Origen's works, and that it is illegitimate to touch the writings of the old masters in such a way. People think that they gravely insult me by this. For myself, however, I see in this the highest praise. It is my express desire to follow an example of which I am convinced that it will please all men of discernment and you too.[41]

Aided by the Holy Spirit, Origen had reflected deeply on the Christian meaning of the Old Testament, that is, its meaning in the light of the Paschal mystery. He had transmitted this meaning to posterity in his Greek writings. His Greek successors, the Cappadocian Fathers, assimilated this perspective into their own works. Jerome carried this legacy forward into the Latin tradition, first of all by translating of significant number of Origen's homilies, then by composing his own Latin commentaries in dependence on Origen's Greek exegesis. Courcelle summarizes the influence of Origen's writings upon Jerome's corpus this way:

The range of his reading in Origen is therefore extensive and his knowledge of this writer far exceeds our own, since the majority of Origen's works are lost. To Jerome, Origen appears as the indispensable source. If he writes a commentary on a book or merely on a verse of Scripture, Jerome searches out a corresponding homily by Origen on such a book or verse. If by chance he cannot find such a homily, for instance in commenting on a passage of Psalm 126, he apologizes, saying that Pamphilus no longer possessed the homily. But he regrets the thought that Origen did write it and that time destroyed it. Similarly, he notes that the twenty-sixth of Origen's thirty books on Isaiah cannot be found.... If Jerome knows that Origen did not make any particular commentary on a book of Scripture, for instance the Book of Daniel, he looks for explanations in another of Origen's works, namely the *Stromateis*. But he feels particularly satisfied when he has at his disposal for a single subject (as in the

---

41. *Commentariorum in Michaeum, libri 2,* in *Patrologiae Cursus Completus: Series Latina*, ed. J.-P. Migne, 221 vols. (Paris, 1878–90), 25:1189 [hereafter "PL"].

case of the Psalms, Isaiah, and Hosea) a large amount of Origen's works to compile. It is therefore not surprising that Jerome's contemporaries were even then charging him with compiling Origen.[42]

Without Origen, there would have been no Jerome. Origen's exegetical writings underlay Jerome's and are the principal source of Jerome's commentaries. This is a reality of which Erasmus was very much aware.

Medieval Era

Many other Christian exegetes and theologians during the medieval era made use of Origen's Latin exegesis. The following evidence only scratches the surface and focuses on a single work of Origen, namely his *Commentary on Romans*. In his *Institutiones* Cassiodorus (490–583) named Origen's *Commentary on Romans* as the first work to be recommended to those inquiring about the ecclesiastical authors who can provide the safest guidance for understanding the individual books of the Bible. "Of [the epistles of] Saint Paul the first of all and the one destined to be more admired is known as the one 'to the Romans,' which Origen clarified in twenty books in the Greek language; which however the above-mentioned Rufinus translated very eloquently into Latin, reducing it to ten books."[43] P. Courcelle notes how Cassiodorus rates Origen very highly, without minimizing the dangers of the doctrine. He considers his contemporaries' severity too excessive, for they prohibit even the reading of his commentaries. "Without mentioning any of his dogmatic works, he carefully collected all the texts and translations by Origen that he could find, protecting himself by following St. Jerome's example.... Although he possessed a number of Latin commentators, he did not lose sight of the quality of Origen's works. To him, Greek Christian literature seemed like an inexhaustible reservoir for Latin exegesis."[44] Other scholars who drew from this reservoir include Notker the Stammerer (840–912), who compiled a catalog of the most important theologians to which he gave the following title: "Observations on the illustrious men who made a careful exposition of Sacred Scripture and gave opportune explanations of certain decisions on the part of divine authority."[45] In this work he wrote: "On the Epistle to the Romans, Ori-

---

42. Courcelle, *Late Latin Writers and Their Greek Sources*, 111–12.
43. PL 70:1120–21. "Sancti Pauli prima omnium et admirabilior destinata cognoscitur ad Romanos, quam Origenes viginti libris Graeco sermone declaravit; quos tamen supradictus Rufinus in decem libros redigens, adhuc copiose transtulit in Latinum."
44. Courcelle, *Late Latin Writers and Their Greek Sources*, 356, 359.
45. Cited in de Lubac, *Medieval Exegesis*, 1:28.

gen wrote many wonderful things."[46] The *Glossa Ordinaria*, a twelfth-century compilation of scriptural glosses traditionally attributed to Walafrid Strabo, cites Origen's *Commentary on Romans* on Romans 3:3, 4:15, and 8:3, though the influence is more extensive than these explicit citations.[47]

From what I have been able to ascertain, Origen's Latin writings were consulted only minimally by Peter Lombard (d. 1160), Bonaventure (d. 1274), and Thomas Aquinas (d. 1274).[48] However, his *Commentary on Romans* is woven deeply into the fabric of Peter Abelard's (d. 1142) *Commentary on Romans*. In his study of the history of interpretation of Romans 1:17, H. Denifle found that two western scripture scholars who used Origen's *Commentary on Romans* very extensively were Sedulius Scottus (fl. 840–60) and Augustinus Favaroni of Rome (d. 1443).[49] Such evidence suggests that even deeply committed Augustinian theologians were capable of admiring Origen's exegesis of Paul. Indeed, the high Augustinian William of St. Thierry's (d. 1148) openly admitted in the preface to his own *Exposition on Romans* that he had copied his "teacher" Origen extensively.[50] Evidence such as this suggests that Origen's Pauline exegesis was viewed as Catholic exegesis, even by deeply committed Augustinians. The clouds of suspicion that hung elsewhere over Origen's orthodoxy did not render suspect his *Commentary on Romans* or his understanding of the mind of Paul. As an exegete of Paul, Origen was normally cited as a Catholic authority of good reliability.[51] None of this evidence supports the

46. *In Epistolam ad Romanos multa et mira scripsit Origenes. De int. div. Script.* (PL 131:997c), cited in de Lubac, *Medieval Exegesis*, 1:388.

47. PL 114:477, 483, 495. Cf. E. Matter, "The Church Fathers and the Glossa Ordinaria," in *Reception of the Church Fathers*, ed. Backus, 1:83–111.

48. For specific references, see the respective essays in Backus, ed., *Reception of the Church Fathers*.

49. PL 103. Cf. de Lubac, *Medieval Exegesis*, 1:167: "Sedulius Scottus appropriates large blocks of the commentary on the Letter to the Romans. He goes so far as to reproduce, word for word, a phrase in which Origen, speaking in the first person, gives the opinion that the Hermas mentioned by Saint Paul is the author of the Pastor and that this work is divinely inspired." On Augustinus Favaroni, see H. Denifle, *Die abendländischen Schriftausleger bis Luther über Justitia Dei (Rom. 1, 17) und Justificatio* (Mainz: Franz Kirchleim, 1905), xv, 11–12, 220–35. On Favaroni, see N. Toner, "The Doctrine of Original Sin according to Augustine of Rome (Favaroni) (d. 1443)," *Augustiniana* 7 (1957): 100–117, and *Augustiniana* 8 (1958): 349–66.

50. See S. Cartwright, "William of St. Thierry's Use of Patristic Sources in His Exposition on Romans," *Citeaux* 54, nos. 1–2 (2003): 27–53; A. Rydstrom-Poulsen, "William of Saint-Thierry's Use of Origen in His Commentary on Romans," *Cistercian Studies Quarterly* 42, no. 1 (2007): 1–10; T. Scheck, "William of St. Thierry's Reception of Origen's Exegesis of Romans," *Adamantius* 10 (2004): 238–58; Scheck, *Origen and the History of Justification*, chap. 4.

51. Cf. C. Verfaillie, "La doctrine de la justification dans Origène d'après son commentaire de l'Épître aux Romains" (PhD diss., University of Strasbourg, 1926), 8.

idea that "Origen was seldom cited and little known in the medieval western tradition until Giovanni Pico della Mirandola championed his work in the fifteenth century."[52]

The Pre-Erasmus Published Editions of Origen's Writings

Erasmus was the heir rather than the author of an impressive Origen renaissance in the Catholic church which the printing press had enabled.[53] Moreover, his support for Origen was critical, theologically mature, and measured in comparison with the views of some of his contemporaries, and unlike others he never denied the presence of serious doctrinal errors in Origen's writings. A brief survey of the pre-Erasmus published editions of Origen's writings will clarify this and provide the reader with an opportunity to see the foundation upon which Erasmus's *Edition of Origen* was built. Much of the material that follows is not well known in English language scholarship, which justifies its inclusion here.

Cristoforo Persona, Marsilio Ficino

The first printed edition of a work of Origen appeared in 1481, a Latin translation of Origen's *Contra Celsum* by Cristoforo Persona (1416–85).[54] This was the first new Latin translation of Origen since antiquity and was dedicated to Pope Sixtus IV (d. 1484). Persona's translation made available to the Latin west that writing of Origen that constitutes alongside Augustine's *City of God* the most important Christian apologetic work of antiquity. The edition was well received and had a decisive influence.[55] It was reprinted in Venice (1514) and became established through the Merlin (1512) and Erasmus (1536) editions of Origen's writings.

The great Italian philosopher Marsilio Ficino (1433–99) had enumerated Origen's virtues and praised his doctrine in chapter 35 of *De Christiana Re-*

---

52. J. K. Farge (CWE 13:231).

53. The excursus in this section represents a reworking with permission of 158–72 of my book, *Origen and the History of Justification*. It is largely based on M. Schär, *Das Nachleben des Origenes im Zeitalter des Humanismus* (Basel: Helbing and Lichtenhahn, 1979), where the original texts are cited.

54. *Origenis proaemium Contra Celsum et in fidei Christianae defensionem*, liber 1 (Rome: Georgius Herolt de Bamburga, 1481), in Ludwig Hain, *Repertorium bibliographicum ... usque ad annum MD.*, 4 vols. (Stuttgart: 1826–38), cat. #12078, cited in Schär, *Das Nachleben des Origenes im Zeitalter des Humanismus*, 112–26.

55. Pico della Mirandola possessed it. Cf. Schär, *Das Nachleben des Origenes im Zeitalter des Humanismus*, 126.

ligione in 1477.[56] Ficino was drawn to Origen's Platonism rather than Aristotelianism. "He cherished the idea of man's ontological position in the center of the great chain of being, thus sharing in material and spiritual creation. Ficino knew that Origen was deeply committed to all these."[57] Ficino clearly paved the way for the staunch and learned support of Origen by Pico della Mirandola, the philosopher who was so admired by Erasmus's close friend Thomas More.

Pico della Mirandola (1463–93)

Pico was one of the central figures of the Italian Renaissance.[58] In 1486 he published nine hundred theses and attached an introduction to them entitled by the publisher *A Speech about the Dignity of Man*, in which he postulated among other things that the creation of humanity in the image of God is the source of human dignity. Because the human being possesses free will, he has the capacity for divinization through contemplation. One of Pico's theses stated: "It is more reasonable to believe that Origen is saved than damned." When thirteen of Pico's theses were declared heretical, including the one just cited, Pico wrote an *Apology* for his condemned theses entitled *A Disputation about Origen's Salvation*. The official reaction was so hostile that Pico fled to France in order to avoid being arrested and sent to Rome for trial as a heretic. He was briefly arrested in France but was soon released. He returned to Italy only because he was secure in his family principality of Mirandola, and then in Florence was secure as the protégé of Lorenzo de Medici. I regret that in my earlier study of Origen's legacy, I failed to report the details of the persecution Pico faced for his views.

Pico's opponents argued that it was not permissible to hope for the salvation of Origen because the church had already condemned him, and the church is incapable of error; nor is it permissible to question the rightness of the act of condemnation, since just as when the church canonizes someone it declares that he or she has been received in heaven, so when it condemns someone as a heretic it declares that he is in hell. On March 31, 1487, Pico countered this argument with a full defense of his thirteen the-

---

56. Cf. ibid., 109–11.

57. Cf. D. Nodes, "Origen of Alexandria Among the Renaissance Humanists and Their Twentieth Century Historians," in *Nova Doctrina Vetusque: Essays on Early Christianity in Honor of Fredric W. Schlatter, S.J.*, ed. D. Kries and C. Brown Tkacz (New York: Peter Lang, 1999), 54.

58. Cf. de Lubac, *Une controverse sur Origène à la Renaissance: Jean Pic de la Mirandole et Pedro Garcia* (Paris: Vrin, 1977); Schär, *Das Nachleben des Origenes im Zeitalter des Humanismus*, 126–43.

ses. Pico's *Apology* was dedicated to his patron, Lorenzo de Medici. Some of Pico's arguments may be summarized here.[59] The theologians of the pontifical commission who condemned Pico's theses have said that Pico's conclusion, that it is more reasonable to believe Origen saved than to believe him damned, is "rash and blameworthy, that it smells of heresy, and that it goes against the decision of the universal Church." Pico will endeavor to show that their judgment is mistaken and that his thesis is not contrary to the decision of the church. Pico is aware that doctrines deriving from Origen had been condemned by two early church councils. Of the Synod of Alexandria (400), which included Origen's name in a list of anathemas, Pico said that it had the authority of a regional council but not that of the universal church. In any case it was theologically suspect because of its entanglement in regional politics. Of the Second Council of Constantinople (553), Pico sensed that it seems to have had in view teachings loosely attributed to Origen which were the real target of condemnation.

Turning to specific issues, Pico said that except on the doctrine of the pre-existence of souls, highly esteemed Church Fathers and the writings of Origen himself unanimously testify that Origen neither believed nor wrote heretical views. Disputed passages should be viewed as heretical interpolations. (Here Pico was following Rufinus's theory described in the preface to his Latin translation of *De Principiis* and in the epilogue to his translation of Pamphilus's *Apology for Origen*, to the effect that heretics had inserted interpolations into Origen's writings.)[60] Moreover, Pico continued, no guilt accrues to Origen for the error on the doctrine of the soul's pre-existence, since up to the time of Augustine there was no clarity on the church's position regarding the origin of souls. Pico is quite correct on this point, which is one that Rufinus had made in his *Apology to Pope Anastasius*.[61]

Pico went on to say that even if Origen had represented heretical views that contradicted subsequent church teaching, he did not do this by way of dogmatic assertion, but always hesitantly, as one conducting scholarly research (*neque dogmatice neque assertive sed dubitative semper et inquisitive*). Pico added that even if Origen had taught errors, this was no mortal sin, for there was no malicious or perverse intent and will, but mere intellectual error. And

---

59. They are found with Latin text in Schär, *Das Nachleben des Origenes im Zeitalter des Humanismus*, 132–34, and summarized by D. Nodes, "Origen of Alexandria among the Renaissance Humanists and Their Twentieth Century Historians," in *Nova Doctrina Vetusque*, ed. Kries and Tkacz, 56–57; de Lubac, *Theology in History*, 61–66.

60. See my new translation in FOTC 120.

61. Cf. NPNF2 3:431.

many saints taught errors, that is, doctrines that were later condemned by the church as heretical, and yet they were still canonized. Not even Jerome accused Origen of malicious or heretical intentions. Pico continued, if Origen had committed mortal sin, there were indications that he repented before his death, and therefore he cannot be conclusively damned.[62] Moreover, even if nothing were known of his repentance, it would still be pious and reasonable to hope for his redemption. For, while it is true that the church condemned the doctrines attributed to Origen and also Origen as a teacher, it has never issued a decree concerning the damnation or redemption of his soul, nor is the church qualified to do so. For it is God alone who judges the living and the dead. Further, even if the church did teach the damnation of Origen's soul, we are not obligated to believe the same. For such matters are not essential for salvation and do not touch the substance of the faith.

Pico's defense of Origen is impressive from a modern point of view, even if he himself faced persecution for it. It is not completely original, but various elements of it were advocated by Eusebius, Pamphilus, Jerome, Didymus, Rufinus, and even Athanasius, all of whom Pico cited as his authorities. Referring to Pico's *Apology*, Schär makes the interesting observation that Pico seldom cites Origen's works directly. Instead it is the voices of other ancient Fathers that are heaped up in Pico's work.[63] Apart from the second-hand citations from Origen's *Letter to Certain Friends in Alexandria* (a letter that is cited by Rufinus and Jerome in their respective *Apologies*), the sole source of Origen's words of which Pico makes immediate and strikingly frequent use is Rufinus's translation of Origen's *Commentary on the Epistle to the Romans*. Schär counted eight citations from this work.[64] Schär credits Pico with establishing the "Origen renaissance" in Italy and with making a significant contribution to the requirement of tolerance for later ages.[65] Yet Schär seems to exaggerate the originality of Pico and, more generally, the newness of this revival of Origen under Pico, and does not seem sufficiently cognizant of the extent of Origen's popularity throughout the medieval era and early Renaissance. Nodes has observed, "It seems that Schär overstates the limitations of Origen's revival when he writes that with the condemnation of Pico's thesis, and in the heat of the Savonarolan austerity campaign, the newly opened Origen

---

62. For a detailed discussion of the dispute over Origen's supposed fall and repentance, see de Lubac, "The Dispute in Modern Times about the Salvation of Origen," in de Lubac, *Theology in History*, 57–116.
63. Schär, *Das Nachleben des Origenes im Zeitalter des Humanismus*, 136.
64. Ibid.
65. Ibid., 142.

revival suddenly stops."[66] On the contrary Pico was an influential authority and many of his arguments used in defense of Origen would be picked up by Aldus Manutius and Jacques Merlin and to a more limited extent by Erasmus.[67] This is why O'Malley reports that Pico's apology was received favorably in some religious circles.[68]

Aldus Manutius's Edition of Origen's Homilies (1503)

Some of Pico's views were assimilated into the edition of Origen's *Homilies on the Heptateuch* (Genesis, Exodus, Leviticus, Numbers, Joshua, Judges) published by Aldus Manutius (Venice, 1503).[69] Aldus Manutius (1452–1515) was perhaps the most famous Venetian printer and was known intimately by Erasmus, who had stayed at his house in 1507. His edition was dedicated to Fra Egidio (Giles) da Viterbo (1469–1532), the famous humanist, outstanding Augustinian-Eremite preacher, and later cardinal. Egidio delivered the famous opening address to the Fifth Lateran Council on May 3, 1512.[70] Aldus's edition confined itself to Origen's homilies on the Old Testament. Aldus gave his edition two prefaces, one of which is signed by him and quotes several times from Pico's *Apology for Origen*. Here he adopted the commonplace assessment of Origen derived from Jerome, "*Ubi bene dixit, nemo melius; ubi male, nemo peius* [When Origen spoke well, no one has ever said it better, when he spoke badly, no one has ever spoken worse]." The second preface of Aldus's edition was anonymous but has been reasonably attributed to Jerome Aleander (1480–1542), the brilliant young humanist scholar who later became the papal legate to the Diet of Worms (1521), which condemned Martin Luther. Aleander would eventually become a cardinal. He was also a one-time friend and colleague of Erasmus, but later a bitter enemy.[71] It is noteworthy they they shared a common admiration for Origen.

E. Wind provides the following evidence for the identification of Je-

---

66. Nodes, "Origen of Alexandria," 60.

67. See I. Pusino, "Der Einfluss Picos auf Erasmus," *Zeitschrift für Kirchengeschichte* 46 (1927): 75–96.

68. Cf. J. O'Malley, "Preaching for the Popes," in *The Pursuit of Holiness in Late Medieval and Renaissance Religion, Papers from the University of Michigan Conference*, ed. C. Trinkhaus and H. A. Oberman (Leiden: Brill, 1974), 408–43.

69. On this edition, see Schär, *Das Nachleben des Origenes im Zeitalter des Humanismus*, 143–52.

70. For an English translation, see John C. Olin, *Catholic Reform: From Cardinal Ximenes to the Council of Trent, 1495–1563* (New York: Fordham University Press, 1990), 47–60.

71. Cf. Rummel, *Erasmus and His Catholic Critics*, 2:111–13.

rome Aleander as the author of the second preface.[72] The preface author envies Origen because Jerome (Aleander's namesake) had been his bard, just as Alexander (= Aleander) the Great, standing at the tomb of Achilles, had envied him because his fame had been sung by Homer. As early as 1499, Aleander had engaged in a public debate with the title "De natura angelica."[73] Wind further observes that Aleander's youthful proficiency in Hebrew, Greek, and Latin was extolled by Aldus in his dedication of the edition of Homer (1504); and in 1521, in his oration at the Diet of Worms, Aleander protested against a comparison of Luther to Origen. To me Wind's evidence for authorship by Jerome Aleander seems persuasive.

In this second preface the twenty-three-year-old Aleander invites the reader to drink deeply from Origen's homilies, "the supreme fountain of saving wisdom." Aleander adds a passionate eulogy of Origen addressed to the Christian reader:

Whoever thou art, faithful soul, who desirest to be built together for the heavenly Jerusalem that rises with living stones [cf. 1 Pt 2:5]: enter these sacred grounds ... where there is the well of living waters flowing flowing from the heights of Lebanon, irrigating all the surface of the earth and issuing into life eternal.... Let me speak with daring: for many things have I read, yet nothing, in my opinion, was I ever granted to see which was so noble, so mysterious, so profound, so perfect, so suited to every age, condition and degree. But I better be silent about this than say little; for if I had a hundred tongues for praise, I would not yet be able to touch the lowest hem of his [Origen's] garment. For if you will come close and unfold and see for yourself—you, too, will say with the Queen of Sheba [cf. 1 Kgs 10.6-7]: True is what I heard in my own country about these sayings and about this wisdom great in the extreme; and I did not believe those who told me of it until I came myself and saw with my own eyes, and found that the better part of it had not been reported to me: for greater is this wisdom than the renown of it, which I heard. Truly, to have come here is sufficient. And for us too it is time to sound the retreat. Let Origen himself, setting out from the shore, offer the sails to the winds and lead us seaward.[74]

Whereas the first preface by Aldus was characterized by caution and restraint, here we encounter a burning enthusiasm for Origen that is virtually boundless. With intense and passionate emotion, the young humanist scholar promotes Origen as a deeply Christian writer and an exceptionally gifted homilist.

72. Wind, "The Revival of Origen," 423.
73. Ibid., citing E. Jovy, *François Tissard et Jérôme Aléandre* (1899), 1:139.
74. Cited by Wind, "The Revival of Origen," 423. The last sentence alludes to Jerome's preface to his translation of Origen's *Homilies on Ezekiel* and Rufinus's preface to Origen's *Commentary on Romans*.

Egidio (Giles) of Viterbo

Aldus hoped to place Origen under the protection of Egidio (Giles) of Viterbo, who had himself expressed an opinion about Origen in his *Historia Viginti Saeculorum*. On the one hand, Giles could repeat Jerome's view that Origen was a "heretic." Yet Giles could also speak very highly of Origen's person, and he confessed that he was impressed by the virtues and insights of those whom the church had condemned.

> When we study the writings of the ancient heretics, would it not seem that nothing could be more saintly, more chaste, more sacred than they, except for the one or two points on which they differed from other right believers? For to speak alone of Origen, whom Jerome and the Church condemn, what could be more chaste, what purer, what more exalted in the rejection of human frailty, what more inspiring, more forceful and more felicitous in desiring, observing and revealing things divine? So that Jerome said he was unique after the Apostles and deserved, and should receive, a place before all mortals.[75]

Clearly the author of these words is no stranger to the writings of Origen. Egidio admits that Jerome and the church condemn Origen, but this applies to only a few points of his teaching. The greater part of Origen is received by the church.

Theophilus Salodianus (Venice, 1506)

The *Editio Princeps* of Origen's *Commentary on Romans* was printed in Venice in 1506 by the printer Simon de Lueres (Simone da Lovere).[76] The editor was a friar named Theophilus Salodianus (of Salò, Italy), who was a member of a mendicant order devoted to Jerome. His dedicatee is a patron, "the very brilliant knight Alexander," for whom Theophilus provides what Hammond has described as a "charming description" of his joy at the discovery of the manuscript in a monastic library in the city of Fiesole (Italy) and of his painstaking effort to restore and correct the manuscript.[77] Theophilus says he was searching for manuscripts of Jerome. This fits well with his being a monk dedicated to Jerome. He mistakenly attributes the Latin translation of Ori-

---

75. Cited by Wind, "The Revival of Origen," 416. Jerome said this in the preface to his translation of Origen's *Homilies on Ezekiel*.

76. See Schär, *Das Nachleben des Origenes im Zeitalter des Humanismus*, 153–60.

77. C. P. Hammond, "Notes on the Manuscripts and Editions of Origen's Commentary on the Epistle to the Romans in the Latin Translation by Rufinus," JTS 16 (1965): 356. For a translation of this preface, see Scheck, *Origen and the History of Justification*, 164. The Latin text is given in Schär, *Das Nachleben des Origenes im Zeitalter des Humanismus*, 154n446.

gen's *Commentary on Romans* to Jerome rather to Rufinus. This was partly due to the corruption of the end of the manuscript, which is the only place where Rufinus's name originally appeared. In fact many manuscripts substituted Jerome's name for Rufinus's. (Erasmus will be the first Renaissance scholar correctly to identify Rufinus as the translator of this work.) Elsewhere in the preface Theophilus complains about the lack of attention of past generations, who had allowed the text to decay to its present condition. This captures well the spirit of Christian humanism during the Renaissance, which sought to restore and purify the monuments of Christian and classical antiquity. Theophilus's text of Origen's *Commentary on Romans* was adopted in both the Merlin (1512) and Erasmus (1536) editions. Westcott reports that Origen's *Homilies on Canticles, Isaiah, Jeremiah, Ezekiel, Matthew* (16), *Luke* (6), *John* (2), with the books *on Job* and *Canticles* were printed at Venice (1513).[78]

Jacques Merlin (Paris, 1512)

In 1512, a four-volume complete Latin edition of Origen's works appeared under the editorship of Jacques Merlin (1470?–1541), who was assisted by Josse Bade and John Parvus.[79] This was not only the first French printing of Origen's works but also the first complete edition of the writings of Origen that were available in Latin translation.[80] The principal editor, Jacques Merlin, had acquired the degree of doctor in theology at the Sorbonne in 1510. Afterward he became a member of the theological faculty and was active in the diocese of Paris. He was known as an outstanding preacher and later became a staunch opponent of French "Lutherans." Next to his Origen edition, his most important publication was a collection of council acts and

78. Cf. Westcott, "Origenes," 140.

79. In my book *Origen and the History of Justification*, 168, I mistakenly attributed Merlin's birth year to 1490 and vastly understated his age at the time of his editorial work on Origen.

80. J. Merlin, *Operum Origenis Adamantii tomi duo priores, cum tabula et indice generali. Venumdatur cum duobus reliquiis eorumdem tomis in edibus Joannis Parvi et Jodocii Badii Ascensii* (Paris, 1512); cf. Schär, *Das Nachleben des Origenes im Zeitalter des Humanismus*, 193. The contents of this edition are as follows (cf. Westcott, "Origenes," 140): Part I: Dedicatory Letter; general index; *Homilies on Genesis* (17), *Exodus* (13), *Leviticus* (16), *Numbers* (28), *Joshua* (26), *Judges* (9), *1 Kings* (1). Part II: *Commentaries on Job* (three books; this is the *Anonymus in Iob* that Erasmus will expose as an Arian work, as explained in chapter 4), on *Psalms 36* (5 homilies), *Ps 38* (2 homilies), *on Canticles* (2 homilies, with a second, spurious commentary), *on Isaiah* (9 homilies), *on Jeremiah* (14 homilies), *on Ezekiel* (14 homilies). Part III: Merlin's *Apology for Origen*; *Homilies on St. Matthew* (35), *on St. Luke* (39); Miscellaneous Homilies (10); *Commentary on the Epistle to the Romans* (10 books); Jerome's notice of Origen (*De Vir. Ill*). Part IV: Trithemius's notice of Origen; *Against Celsus* (8 books); *On First Principles* (4 books); *Laments*; Pamphilus's *Apology for Origen*; Rufinus's *On the Falsification of Origen's Books*; *A Commendation of Origen* by Jodocus Badius, the original publisher of the work.

papal decrees.[81] From 1522 to 1528 Merlin was engaged in a bitter dispute with Noël Béda, a theologian of the Sorbonne, over the *Apologia* for Origen, which appeared in Merlin's edition of Origen's works. The dispute was intensified when Merlin publicly ridiculed Béda for attempting to stifle the works of Erasmus. Eventually the case was allowed to drop.[82] A first-hand account of its outcome in which Beda was suppressed is preserved.[83]

Merlin's edition of Origen is dedicated to Michael Boudet (d. 1529), the bishop of Langres. The third part of the edition begins with an impassioned panegyric of Origen, in which Merlin praises the Alexandrian highly as a teacher of the church. Origen is said to hold the same place among philosophical theologians (*inter theosophos*) as the sun among the stars, the eagle among birds, and Atlas among the giants. Origen is preeminent, just as Pythagoras, Socrates, Plato, and Aristotle stand out among the philosophers; Homer, Vergil, Menander, and Terence among the poets; Sallust, Herodotus, and Livy among the historians; and Lysias, Gracchus, Demosthenes, and Cicero among the orators. Merlin exclaims that no one was holier, more scholarly, more eloquent, and more universally learned than Origen.

> You, O my Adamantius, have planted the best seed of Christianity in moistened ground. By the splendor of your doctrine the entire world receives an unfailing illumination. You tear down the intricate curtain of the tabernacle and separate the linen from the purple. You reveal the feet and countenance of the Cherubim and you unfold their wings. You lead out wheel from wheel. You are eyes for the blind, feet for the lame. In short, the service Abraham offered to the angels, Joseph to the Egyptians, Moses to the Israelites, Job to those who are suffering, Daniel to the captives, you perform for the worshipers of Christ.[84]

Merlin's preface resembles Aleander's (cited above) and is remarkable for its Ciceronian eloquence, its biblicism, and its passionate enthusiasm for Origen. Merlin praises the apologetic achievement of Origen as displayed in his work *Contra Celsum*: "No one who approached him went away uninstructed; no one who came to him with the intention of fighting against the truth departed the victor."[85] He extols the good fortune of Greece in possessing such a great star. But the Greeks were blind, he says, referring to the harassment Ori-

---

81. Cf. Schär, *Das Nachleben des Origenes im Zeitalter des Humanismus*, 194.
82. See Farge's article on Merlin in CE 2:435–36.
83. Cf. Erasmus, CWE 12, ep. 1763. For a recent assessment of Beda, see Mark Crane, "Competing Visions of Christian Reform: Noel Beda and Erasmus," *Erasmus of Rotterdam Society Yearbook* 25 (2005): 39–57.
84. Schär, *Das Nachleben des Origenes im Zeitalter des Humanismus*, 198n169.
85. Ibid., 198n170.

gen faced in his lifetime and his subsequent condemnation; for they charged with innumerable errors the one God had sent. Mistreated and abused by the Greeks, Origen fell into the hands of robbers. Instead of embracing him they sent him into exile. In Origen Merlin sees the traveler in the parable of the Good Samaritan whom the Levite and the priest pass by. Merlin wants to be like the Good Samaritan to Origen, to bind his wounds and restore him. He requests that his patron bishop, Michael Boudet, do the same.[86]

A unique feature of Merlin's edition is the defense of Origen's orthodoxy that Merlin mounts in these prefaces. This aspect of his edition certainly distinguishes it from Erasmus's later edition. Like Pico before him, Merlin named this part of his edition the "Apology," and it caused him immediate difficulties with a very persistent conservative Catholic opponent, Noël Béda.[87] In the "Apology" Merlin reveals a detailed knowledge of the history of the Origenist controversy in the ancient church. He asserts that Pope Gelasius (492–96) had prematurely and unfairly condemned both Rufinus and Origen based on Jerome's testimony alone.[88] Merlin argues that it is illicit to condemn a man (whether Origen or Rufinus) based on the testimony of one witness. Therefore the pope was obligated to listen to a series of sworn witnesses. "For a judgment which affects everyone requires the approval of everyone."[89] By this statement, Merlin means that a sentence of condemnation by a pope demands the agreement of the entire church. This reflects a thesis of conciliarism, which was still a burning issue at the beginning of the sixteenth century. Schär has observed that in making these statements, Merlin is clearly placing the council over the pope. Nor is this really surprising when we recall that Merlin himself was the first editor of the texts of the councils.[90]

Merlin defends Origen's orthodoxy on the question of Origen's alleged assertion of a universal restoration of all rational creatures. Invoking numerous citations from Origen's homilies and from the *Commentary on Romans*, Merlin tries to prove that Origen's eschatological views were incontestably orthodox.[91] According to Merlin, Origen did not teach that the devil would be restored nor did he assert that the fire of hell would be of limited duration. Merlin followed

---

86. Ibid., 198.   87. Ibid., 200.
88. Pope Gelasius, at a council at Rome in 494, drew up a list of books to be received in the church, in which he said of Origen's translator Rufinus: "He was a religious man, and wrote many books of use to the Church, and many commentaries on the Scriptures; but since the most blessed Jerome defamed him on certain points, we take part with him [Jerome] in this and in all cases in which he has pronounced a condemnation." Cited by Fremantle, NPNF2 3:410. The pope's judgment was taken by many to be an official endorsement of the late Jerome's condemnation of Origen.
89. Schär, *Das Nachleben des Origenes im Zeitalter des Humanismus*, 202.
90. Ibid., 203.   91. Ibid.

Rufinus's claim in asserting that the errors found in *De Principiis* were heretical interpolations. He also repeated Pico della Mirandola's line of defense, that Origen had spoken hesitantly and inquisitively. Like Pico, Merlin encouraged his readers to think well on the subject of Origen's eternal salvation.[92]

Startlingly, Merlin's "Apologia" for Origen totally absolves Origen of error, even on the question of the pre-existence of souls. In contrast with Pico, Origen's great fifteenth-century defender, who conceded that Origen taught error in his doctrine of the soul's pre-existence, Merlin defends Origen even on this point. Moreover, it is surprising that Merlin is completely silent about the condemnation of Origen in 553 at the Fifth Ecumenical Council, a matter that Pico had discussed. Schär conjectures that Merlin's faith in the authority of the councils over that of the pope resounds in this silence. For whereas Merlin consistently expresses doubt about the binding authority of papal decisions, conciliar decisions are sacrosanct for him, since they are an expression of the general will of the church. Thus for Merlin to report the condemnation of Origenism at the Fifth Ecumenical Council in 553 would be to undermine the legitimacy of his own edition of Origen's writings.[93] This was not entirely candid of him, and he was judged as an imprudent scholar by later generations. De Lubac says of Merlin: "Intending to exalt Origen, he expressed himself, as Huet would say, 'without sufficient prudence' concerning Pope Gelasius as well as Saint Jerome and his language was not the product of a considered theologian."[94] In my book on Origen, I tried to excuse and defend Merlin by pointing out that he was, I thought, only twenty-two years old when he published his edition of Origen's writings.[95] This was a miscalculation on my part. Merlin was at least twenty years older than this. Though he may have lacked prudence in his enthusiasm for Origen, I still believe that he was also provoked by the excessive and obscurantist aggression of his opponents.

Merlin concludes his preface with the wish that Origen "may rise like a morning star for the entire Church" and that this edition "may soon be turned by the hands of many."[96] Insofar as his edition became standard for scholars north of the Alps, this wish was fulfilled. No fewer than six reprints appeared before 1536. This is the edition that Catholic theologians and the Protestant reformers would have used until it was replaced and superseded by Erasmus's edition of 1536.

92. Ibid., 204n211.
93. Ibid., 205.
94. De Lubac, *Theology in History*, 68.
95. Scheck, *Origen and the History of Justification*, 168.
96. Schär, *Das Nachleben des Origenes im Zeitalter des Humanismus*, 204n211.

ERASMUS'S RECEPTION *of* ORIGEN

As a scholar and theologian devoted to Jerome, Erasmus was familiar with the influence of Origen's writings on the formation of the saint.[1] Erasmus's special interest in Origen was inspired and deepened by a personal friendship with a priest of the Franciscan tradition named Jean Vitrier, a man whom Erasmus regarded as the saintliest individual he had ever met and whose brief biography he composed in his epistle 1211.[2] It was Vitrier—a contemporary Francis of Assisi, in Erasmus's estimation—who had spoken to Erasmus of Origen in these terms: "There can be no doubt that the Holy Spirit dwelt in a heart that produced so many books with such learning and such fire."[3] During a retreat at Courtebourne in 1501, Erasmus read in manuscript Origen's homilies on the Hexateuch and his *Commentary on Romans*. One immediate result was the composition of the *Enchiridion*, Erasmus's first great devotional work. This book is infused with citations from these particular works of Origen.[4] Prior to publication Erasmus asked Vitrier to read

---

1. Erasmus published the first complete edition of Jerome's writings in 1516. For a translation of some of the prefatory material, including Erasmus's *Life of Jerome*, see CWE 61.

2. For a translation of this letter, see CWE 8 as well as John C. Olin, ed., *Christian Humanism and the Reformation: Selected Writings of Erasmus with his Life by Beatus Rhenanus and a Biographical Sketch by the Editor*, 3rd ed. (New York: Fordham University Press, 1987), 157–79. Cf. A. Godin, *Erasme lecteur d'Origène*, 21–32; A. Godin, *Erasmus, vie de Jean Vitrier et de John Colet, traduction et présentation* (Angers: Editions Moreana, 1982).

3. CWE 8, ep. 1211.

4. Cf. A. Godin, "The *Enchiridion Militis Christiani*: The Modes of an Origenian Appropriation," trans. H. Gibaud, *Erasmus of Rotterdam Society Yearbook* 2 (1982): 47–79.

his *Enchiridion* in manuscript. Vitrier did so and approved the work, which gave Erasmus the courage to publish it.[5]

Erasmus was moved by the way Origen's allegorical interpretations of the Old Testament gripped the emotions of the Christian reader. For instance he praised the emotion with which Origen's homily on Genesis 22 was written: the story of Abraham's offering of Isaac in obedience to God's command.[6] There is nothing sterile, dry, or spiritless in Origen's homiletical style, says Erasmus; he touches our spirit. Erasmus was inspired by the reading of Origen's *Commentary on Romans* to attempt to write his own commentary on Paul's epistle. At the end of the *Enchiridion* (1503), Erasmus speaks of a commentary on Romans he has in preparation which is based upon a thorough study of Origen, Ambrose [= Ambrosiaster], Augustine, and others, his goal being "to adorn the Lord's temple with rare treasures ... so that by means of these treasures fine intellects could be kindled into a love for Holy Scripture."[7] This work was left unfinished until 1514. In that year, after sustaining a back injury, Erasmus made a vow to the apostle Paul to complete a commentary on Romans if he should be healed.[8] When in answer to this prayer, Erasmus received relief from his back pain, he fulfilled his vow and eventually published his *Paraphrase* and *Annotations on Romans*. These examples show that the writings of Origen played a direct role in inspiring Erasmus to become an author himself.

In my study of Erasmus's use of Origen's *Commentary on Romans* in his *Paraphrase* and *Annotations on Romans*, I found that in his interpretation of Paul's letter, Erasmus was indebted to Origen throughout the text of the entire epistle. He tends to follow Origen especially where Origen interpreted Paul in a way that was favorably received by subsequent orthodox exegetes, even if this meant dissent from Augustine (famously on Rom 5:12), who, Erasmus observed, sometimes stood in isolation from the Greek and Latin tradition of exegesis.[9] Erasmus prefers the consensual patristic interpretation

---

5. Cf. *CWE* 9, ep. 1341A. Again I recommend Halkin and McConica for helpful expositions of Erasmus's aims in the *Enchiridion*.

6. See *Ratio theologiae verae* (1519), LB 5:81–82.

7. Cf. *CWE* 66:127. John Dolan's lacunar paraphrase of this passage in *The Essential Erasmus* suppresses the specific reference to Erasmus's commentary in preparation.

8. *CWE* 3, ep. 301.

9. I gave an example in the previous chapter, Erasmus's words to Martin Luther in *Hyperaspistes* II (*CWE* 77:535): "Only Augustine excludes foreknown merits as the reason why Jacob was chosen and Esau rejected, and his interpretation makes original sin the cause of the hatred. For my part, Augustine is a man to whom anyone may grant as high a status as he likes; but I would

of Paul's letter to the Romans, a consensus founded by Origen but represented by many others including Jerome, Ambrosiaster, and Chrysostom. Above all in his lengthy works written against Luther, *Hyperaspistes* I and II, Erasmus defends this ancient consensus against Luther's imbalanced interpretations of the same epistle, who endeavored to radicalize the Augustinian interpretation of Paul's text into a double-predestination doctrine that completely eliminated free will and human cooperation from the process of salvation. Luther's doctrine may have some fragile basis in late Augustinian texts, but it has nothing in common with the Greek tradition of exegesis, as Luther himself recognized, and it does not really represent Augustine's views.

For Erasmus one of Origen's greatest achievements was in his supplying an abundance of material that was received with approval in later Catholic exegesis.[10] Not all of Origen's original writings survive, but it is clear to Erasmus that Origen was an important source from which Greek writers, such as Chrysostom, Theophylact, Basil, and Gregory Nazianzen, and Latins such as pseudo-Jerome [= Pelagius], Ambrose, Hilary, and Jerome, drew their chief exegetical ideas.[11] In his prefatory letter to his edition of Ambrose's writings, Erasmus writes: "It must be confessed, but not in reproach, that the greater part of Ambrose's writings were drawn from Greek commentaries, especially Origen, but in such a way that he excerpted what was sound while disguising what was incompatible with orthodox Catholic teaching, or controversial, without adducing errors or betraying authors."[12] In contrast with the irenic Ambrose, who assimilated much from Origen without publicly reproaching his errors, Jerome, in his later period, according to Erasmus, "made it his business to see that the world knew about Origen's errors, but not about the sound points he made."[13] Erasmus thinks that Ambrose's irenic approach to Origen, which also happens to have been the method of the

---

never attribute so much to him as to think he sees further in Paul's epistles than the Greek interpreters."

10. CWE 13, ep. 1844. See P. S. Allen, *Opus Epistolarum Desiderii Erasmi Roteradami* (Oxford: Oxford University Press, 1928), 7:102: "Origenes omnibus fere Graecis scriptoribus materiam suppeditavit." Cf. *In Psalmum* 38 (LB 5:432B–435B): "Origen was a great doctor of the Church from whose sources the minds of nearly all the Greeks were irrigated."

11. Theophylact was not an ancient Greek Church Father but a Bulgarian bishop of the eleventh century. Erasmus did not know this in 1516, but by the time of the second edition in 1518, he had discovered Theophylact's identity and no longer made him out to be an ancient patristic authority. His writings were essentially a distillation of John Chrysostom's exegesis of the New Testament.

12. CWE 13, ep. 1855 (August 1527).

13. Erasmus, *Apology against Latomus* (CWE 71:67).

Cappadocian Fathers and of the early Jerome, has been more helpful to the church. Erasmus perceptively observes that Origen stands in a relation to the Greek and Latin exegetical tradition in a way that is analogous to the relation of Greek and Latin poets to Homer: as a principal source and fountainhead from which they drew many of their thoughts. Origen's relation to the Greek tradition is analogous to Tertullian's relation to the Latin tradition.[14]

Erasmus says that a more direct acquaintance with Origen's works will give us a better understanding and appreciation of the writings of the orthodox. In his prefatory letter to his Latin translation of Origen's *Commentary on Matthew*, Erasmus writes an illuminating reflection upon what he regards as the focal point of his own life's work.[15] He says that he prefers to spend his time restoring the ancient writers, from the reading of whom we benefit by obtaining a more accurate understanding of Chrysostom, Jerome, and others like them of more recent times, because we can recognize the various sources from which they drew.

In the same way no one adequately understands the poets and those who seasoned their writings, as it were, with the sayings of poets without being steeped in the poetry of Homer. One can have a more certain and more lively understanding of the commentaries of Thomas [Aquinas] by reading the authors from whom he borrowed. Among the early interpreters of Scripture pride of place is given to the Greek writer Origen and the Latin writer Tertullian; it is not certain which was the more learned, but certainly Origen was by far the more celebrated.[16]

Not only does an acquaintance with Origen's writings give us a better understanding of ancient and more recent writers who drew on him, but this widespread use of Origen's exegesis demonstrates Origen's substantial orthodoxy as a scriptural exegete. Erasmus makes this point explicit to Luther in response to a passage in *De Servo Arbitrio* where Luther attacked Origen's explanation of the causes of the hardening of Pharaoh's heart (Rom 9) as residing in the Pharaoh's bad use of his own free will. Origen had observed that the text of Romans 9:17 does not exclude Pharaoh's free will as the antecedent cause of God's judgment, since the scripture says, "for this very purpose I have *raised you up*," not "for this very purpose I have *made you*." Otherwise, Origen says, Pharaoh would not have been wicked, if God had *made* him like that.[17] In his *Discourse on the Free Will* (1524), Erasmus had cited Origen's inter-

14. CWE 13, ep. 1844.
15. *Fragmentum commentariorum Origenis in evangelium secundum Matthaeum* (Basel: Froben, 1527).
16. CWE 13, ep. 1844.
17. Origen, *Commentary on Romans* 7.16.7 (1146).

pretation with approval in order to refute Luther's claim found in his *Assertion of Article Thirty Six*, that man's free will does not even have the power to make its own paths evil, since "God does even bad deeds in the wicked."[18] Luther replied to Erasmus's tactic by using an *ad hominem* argument: he fulminates that no ecclesiastical writers have handled scripture more ineptly and absurdly than Origen and Jerome.[19] And so, in the *Hyperaspistes* II, which was Erasmus's detailed response to Luther's *De Servo Arbitrio*, Erasmus replies to Luther's accusation: "The Church has approved of this gloss of Origen; Jerome, together with orthodox teachers, follows it."[20] He specifically cites Jerome's commentary on Isaiah 63:17, which had offered the same interpretation as Origen.

It appears to me that the principle that is involved here is a programmatic one: Erasmus tends to follow Origen's exegesis particularly where Origen was himself followed by other writers whom church authority recognizes as orthodox. Conversely, Erasmus's distrust of Luther's theological judgments includes the fact that Luther sometimes attacks aspects of the Catholic exegetical tradition that have always received broad approval. A similar reaction is found in response to a passage in which Luther mocked Jerome's interpretation of Galatians 3:19. Erasmus writes: "How hatefully he [Luther] fumes against a man whose memory has been held sacred by God's church for so many centuries! Why is Jerome said to be dreaming about this passage when he is following, or rather translating, so many Greek Fathers? Why do not Chrysostom, Theophylact, and Ambrose also share in the beating, since they give the same interpretation?"[21] To Erasmus the consensual voice of writers approved by the church is the church's voice. It is well known that Jerome had adopted Origen's exegesis throughout his Pauline commentaries as he himself tells us in his prefaces.[22] Erasmus's point seems to be that for Luther to express such contempt for an interpretation that is represented by such a broad consensus of ancient Christian exegesis, both Latin and Greek, is not only arrogant, but reflective of a mind that does not wish to think well of the Catholic church.

---

18. Martin Luther's Assertion of Article 36 (WA 7:144; CWE 76:305).

19. Luther, *On the Bondage of the Will*, in Luther and Erasmus, *Free Will and Salvation*, ed. G. Rupp, LCC (Philadelphia: Westminster, 1969), 224.

20. LB 10:1392: "Hoc Origenis commentum approbavit Ecclesia, sequitur cum Orthodoxis Hieronymus."

21. *Hyperaspistes* II (CWE 77:668).

22. See Scheck, *St. Jerome's Commentaries on Galatians, Titus and Philemon*; Heine, *Commentaries of Origen and Jerome on Ephesians*.

Erasmus's Reflections on Origen's Orthodoxy

In various places scattered throughout his writings, Erasmus offers some reflections on the question of Origen's orthodoxy and heresy. His tone is not defensive of Origen but scholarly and measured. Erasmus never attempted to present Origen as totally orthodox, as Jacques Merlin did, but freely admitted that Origen taught some errors. In his *Exposition of Psalm 38* (*Enarratio Psalmi 38*), Erasmus writes: "Some people destroy the divine harmony by using the wrong instruments, which are not appropriate to it, as when they corrupt the heavenly wisdom with human philosophy or when they mix heretical errors with true doctrine. Origen was a lyre player of this type, and so were Tertullian and Arius who ruined their whole song because a single string was badly out of tune."[23] Here Origen is listed alongside the schismatic Tertullian and the heretic Arius for his corruption of the heavenly wisdom with human philosophy. Erasmus adds to this slightly later by saying: "At times Origen's playing is devoid of harmony when he produces the sounds of allegory but scorns the literal meaning; but the playing of the Jews is the most dispiriting because they just harp on at the historical sense."[24] Thus in addition to his errors stemming from erroneous human philosophy, in Erasmus's judgment Origen at times undermines the literal meaning of scripture through excessive allegorizing.

This particular criticism of Origen is also found in Erasmus's *Ratio* (1518) where he writes with respect to allegorical exegesis: "In fact, I must in general warn the reader, here, that in this matter Origen, Ambrose, Hilary and others who freely imitate Origen are frequently mistaken. Indeed, they sometimes remove the grammatical meaning in their zeal to teach an allegory, when it is not necessary. Therefore, whoever wishes to deal with Sacred Literature in a serious manner should observe moderation in all things."[25] The same thought is repeated in Erasmus's dedicatory letter to his edition of Hilary, where Erasmus faults Hilary for excessive and far-fetched allegorizing and says that "this failing is peculiar to Origen in nearly all his writings."[26] These quotes should serve to remind the reader that Erasmus was by no means completely uncritical of Origen's hermeneutics. Though in his *Enchiridion* of 1503 Erasmus had praised Origen's emotionally gripping Old

---

23. CWE 65:31.
24. CWE 65:32.
25. Methodus (Ratio), trans. Conroy, 309 (LB 5:126).
26. CWE 9, ep. 1334, to Jean Carondelet.

Testament homilies which utilized allegorical principles of exegesis, even here in his earliest published theological essay, Erasmus critiques Origen's baneful influence on the point of excessive use of allegorical exegesis.

In his *Exposition of Psalm 38*, Erasmus continues the critique of Origen by mentioning philosophical errors as well: "Origen was one of the great teachers of the church and his writings were a source of inspiration to almost all the Greek Fathers; in addition, he was the son of a martyr and he himself sought to attain martyrdom. And yet are not many things to be found in this man's writings which are more than heretical? The cause of his downfall was Platonic philosophy."[27] Whereas Jacques Merlin had endeavored to exonerate the extant writings of Origen against these sorts of reproaches, Erasmus concedes Origen's errors. Such passages seem to indicate that Erasmus supported the church's traditional view that Origen's writings contain heretical errors stemming from his Platonic philosophy. This is confirmed by a passage in his *Explanation of the Creed* (1533) in which Erasmus clarifies the added words "of whose kingdom there will be no end" with this remark:

It has been added because of some who have foolishly uttered certain outlandish blasphemies about the Platonic cycles. It was from this source that Origen drew his erroneous teaching (if indeed he really believed what he reported rather than asserted in his writings) that after many thousands of years the demons would become angels and the angels would become demons; that those condemned to hell would sometime or other be freed from suffering and return purified to a state of happiness; that, finally, Christ would be crucified again, and in this way the kingdom that Christ prepared for himself by his death would sometime come to an end. This blasphemy is too senseless to be refuted.[28]

The views described here are reported to be Origen's by Jerome in *Ep* 124 and by Augustine in *De haeresibus*. There are hints of them in Origen's surviving texts and in Jerome's rendering of Origen's exegesis in his own commentaries. Erasmus stands with both Jerome and Augustine in rejecting such views as blasphemous, as "too senseless to be refuted"; yet, unlike his ancient predecessors, Erasmus expressly wonders whether Origen really intended to assert these opinions dogmatically. Slightly later in the same catechism, Erasmus mitigates his critique of Origen with the following reflection: "Not all Greeks who asserted the belief that the Holy Spirit proceeds from the Father alone were heretics. Perhaps Origen was not a heretic either simply because, in his zeal for investigating truth, he questioned whether the Son and

27. CWE 65:43.
28. CWE 70:316.

the Holy Spirit have the same divine essence as the Father, or are created beings superior to all others."[29] Prior to the church's definition of the double-procession of the Holy Spirit from the Father and the Son, there were Greek Fathers who did not affirm this. They should not be treated as heretics. Similarly, in *De Principiis*, Origen raised questions about the scriptural basis for certain doctrines or verbal formulas, but he did so in the time period before the church had dogmatically defined those particular doctrines. Is this the same thing as to obstinately reject a dogma or formula that has already been defined? Erasmus clearly sees that these are two very different things. Since Origen lived well before the Council of Nicaea, perhaps he should not be judged anachronistically by the dogmatic standards of that council.

Erasmus expresses a more mitigating interpretation of Origen's errors in his *Apology against Latomus* (1518), where he reports that Latomus had criticized his preference for Origen's exegesis in his *Annotations on Romans*. Latomus has reservations about Origen, warning readers that "they might be easily deceived and, while innocently emulating the splendor of his style and his learning, drink in poisonous doctrines."[30] In other words, Latomus's pretext for attacking Erasmus's use of Origen is to protect Catholic orthodoxy. Latomus was scarcely prepared to allow even a seasoned theologian to read Origen's works. To this Erasmus replies: "Yet everyone, without exception, recognizes that Origen had the profoundest knowledge of the Scriptures and there are very few passages in his surviving books which are suspect.... If anyone was prepared to do the arithmetic exactly, he would perhaps find more mistakes in the works of Peter Lombard than in those of Origen which have come down to us."[31] Erasmus's opinion agrees with that expressed by Giles of Viterbo cited in the previous chapter, that Origen's theological errors are confined to "one or two points." Erasmus goes on to say that Origen has none of that feigned effusiveness that makes us look fearfully for the hidden trap. His language is entirely straightforward and churchman-like. Moreover, none of Origen's heretical doctrines are extant except in Jerome, "who made it his business to see that the world knew about Origen's errors, but not about the sound points he made."[32]

In a passage that is directed to Martin Luther, who had reviled Origen, Erasmus confirms his attitude toward Origen's errors, namely that when he

---

29. CWE 70:332.
30. Cited in Rummel, *Erasmus and His Catholic Critics*, 1:83.
31. CWE 71:72.
32. CWE 71:73.

did go astray he ought to be and in fact is pardoned for two reasons: "First, because he wrote to investigate such things, not to define them; and then because he wrote at an early period when it was legitimate to have doubts about many points which cannot now legitimately be considered ambiguous."[33] Erasmus's defense here repeats an idea found in his dedicatory epistle to his edition of Origen's *Commentary on Matthew* (1527), where he stresses that we must understand the Fathers in light of the opinions and customs prevailing in their own century, rather than measuring them by modern standards.[34] In a passage that appears to be a subtle criticism of Noël Béda's attack upon Jacques Merlin, Erasmus writes:

> We judge Origen according to the morals, usages, and beliefs of our times. If you wish to see the absurdity of this, reverse the scene and pretend that Origen lived in the present age, and that people like Scotus, Ockham, Thomas, Capreolus, Egidius, Gregory and the rest of that crowd lived in Origen's age; then recall from that age to this any one of them—let us say Thomas (who of this number falls less below the standard of the ancients, except that Augustine, whom he follows in most respects, was bold enough to disagree with all the ancient writers, both Greek and Latin). Who would allow him to make the dogmas of the church conform to the precepts of Aristotle and Averroes?[35]

Erasmus makes several important points here. One is that a weakness of Thomas Aquinas's theology is his mostly uncritical acceptance of all of Augustine's dogmatic statements, even when Augustine boldly dissents from all other ancient writers, both Greek and Latin. Such a monochromatic approach to Catholic truth presumes Augustine's exclusive and final authority. It does not permit continual dialogue with Augustine, and ignores the Greek theological tradition, thus abandoning the principle of the symphonic nature of orthodoxy. Augustine's late doctrines of irresistible grace and infant damnation would be cases in point.[36]

Erasmus is also aware that the ancients scarcely used Aristotle in comparison with Aquinas, nor would Aquinas have been allowed to practice such a theological method in ancient times. Erasmus goes on to say that the church has grown like an organism through the centuries. It has now passed through its infancy, its adolescence, its maturity, and perhaps its old age

---

33. *Hyperaspistes* II (CWE 77:449).
34. This is discussed by Bejczy, *Erasmus and the Middle Ages*, 29–30.
35. CWE 13, ep. 1844.
36. I have briefly discussed this in my article, "Pelagius's Interpretation of Romans," in *A Companion to St. Paul in the Middle Ages*, ed. Steven R. Cartwright (Leiden: Brill, 2013), 79–113.

as well. There is a very great variety of epochs and countries, yet in spite of this, some erroneously examine all ancient writings by the standards of the present age. For Erasmus this demonstrates ingratitude towards the ancient theologians, who lived and wrote when the church was young and undeveloped. These men of antiquity deserve our thanks, not criticism. According to Erasmus such a hypercritical attitude toward the ancients also displays a spirit that is harmful to those who wield it. Erasmus continues:

> There are many things that it would be height of impiety to call into question today, while in an earlier age inquiry into those same matters constituted religious fidelity. Origen supplied material for almost all the Greek writers, investigating every single point, affirming nothing that was not expressly stated in Scripture and often repeating his favorite word, "never" [sic].[37] Yet he has had no other reward for such services than the greatest hatred, which would not be the case if we were willing to judge each person according to his own age.[38]

Erasmus is here disputing with some of his contemporaries, both Catholic and Protestant. The conservative Catholic theologians Noël Béda of Paris and Jacob Latomus of Louvain were quite hostile to Origen, as were the Protestants Luther and Melanchthon. The pretext for their hatred of Origen was the concern to shield the faithful from poisonous doctrine. Unlike these contemporaries Erasmus seems to have had a clearer sense of the idea that Catholic doctrine has developed over the centuries. He noticed that many Fathers, in particular during the early period, had expressed ideas that would later be judged to be heterodox. There is no reason to make a fuss about this, he says, for we can admire authors without sharing all their ideas. Moreover, no author, ancient or modern, can escape the charge of heresy from an overzealous critic.

With regard to Origen, Erasmus goes on to say that in addition to his admirable zeal in knowing thoroughly and commenting on scripture, in which he has no rival, he possesses the peculiar quality of leaving in the mind of the gifted and well-trained reader various incentives and diverse material for meditation.[39] This makes Origen of unequaled importance for the formation

---

37. Erasmus uses the Greek term μήποτε here, which I believe in this context should be rendered "perhaps," not "never," as the *CWE* translation has rendered it. To use "never" misses Erasmus's (and Origen's) point, which is that Origen interpreted scripture tentatively and humbly, not combatively and assertively. "Consider whether *perhaps*" is a favorite phrase of Origen. In *CWE* 8, ep. 1232, Erasmus compared Origen and Tertullian as follows: "For he [Origen] as a rule is all argument and inquiry, while Tertullian is absolute and combative."

38. CWE 13, ep. 1844.

39. Ibid.

of the church preacher. Some writers dwell on commonplaces to the point of nausea, but Origen touches on one passage and then immediately turns off in another direction. This he does particularly in the tomes (commentaries) that he destined for the private reading of learned men, where he included some rather abstruse matters that would not be appropriate for general consumption. Origen intimates in more than one place that this was his intention.[40]

In another important discussion of heresy that is based on a figurative interpretation of Psalm 33 (34), Erasmus makes the point that in the determination of who is a heretic, emotional attachment to a heresy is of far greater importance than intellectual error. Although he does not name Origen in this passage, the text still seems relevant to the present discussion. Erasmus reports that later doctrinal standards would condemn as erroneous various views represented by the early theologians Irenaeus, Cyprian, Jerome, and even Augustine. Erasmus asks, if these men were saints, why did the Lord not "guard all their bones"? And if they were not saints, why does the church honor them as such? He replies:

A wounded or dislocated bone is one thing, but a broken bone quite another. A wounded bone can be healed, a bone out of joint can be put back in place, but a broken bone is scarcely curable. There are very few examples of a confirmed heretic's return to the church. But those whose error is a merely intellectual one and whose emotions have not been seduced are easily brought back to the path. This was the case with Paul, and so when he received a warning he at once returned to the path. Consequently, if the church had admonished those devout men, they would immediately have rejected their erroneous beliefs.[41]

It seems that Erasmus assessed Origen's errors, along with those of other ancient Fathers, as being primarily intellectual mistakes that were made in a period that was preliminary to subsequent doctrinal developments. He did not detect in him any emotional attachment to heresy or malicious intent. On the contrary, Erasmus rated Origen very highly in terms of the emotional disposition that is displayed in his writings. Interestingly, Erasmus used this same argument in defense of his own orthodoxy when some of his practical reform proposals and ecclesiastical advice were accused of heresy by critics at the Sorbonne. Rummel points out that on several occasions during his

---

40. Ibid. See the article by Mark S. M. Scott, "Guarding the Mysteries of Salvation: The Pastoral Pedagogy of Origen's Universalism," JECS 18, no. 3 (2010): 347–68, for confirmation of Erasmus's insight here.

41. CWE 64:367–68. The editor indicates that a fuller treatment is given by Erasmus in In Psalmum 38 (LB 5:432B–435B); cf. In Psalmum 22, 185n399 (CWE 63:xxxii).

controversy with Noël Béda, Erasmus stressed that intent was the mark that distinguished error from heresy. Accordingly he asked: "How can this be called impious when I propose it in a pious spirit?" "I have never knowingly diverged from the church, not even a finger's breadth."[42]

Recently a scholar has summarized the attitude of Henri de Lubac toward Origen in these terms: "[Origen's] strong desire to constantly observe the rule of faith, to follow the tradition, and be an obedient child of the church, was not, according to de Lubac, the mark of an arch-heretic. For this reason he argued that Origen's name could not justly be put alongside those who had made a conscious break with the church—intention did count for something."[43] According to de Lubac and Erasmus, intention counts for something; emotional disposition cannot be ignored when assessing someone's orthodoxy. There is a distinction between a Church Father who made mistakes but died in the bosom of the church, and a heretic or schismatic who divided the church asunder by his errors and contention. Origen more closely resembles the former than the latter, according to both Erasmus and de Lubac.

Erasmus's Edition of Origen (1536)

Having summarized the assessments of Origen's orthodoxy made in Erasmus's other published writings, which were not able to be incorporated into his edition of Origen, we now turn to a specific introduction to his edition of Origen. Erasmus's edition of Origen's writings was the last publication to come from his hand. It was published posthumously in September 1536 by the Froben Press two months after Erasmus's death in Basel on the night of July 11/12, 1536. The Froben Press produced it with the assistance of an old colleague of Erasmus, Beatus Rhenanus, who wrote the prefatory letter dedicating it, as Erasmus intended, to Hermann von Wied, archbishop of Cologne.[44] Beatus tells us how Erasmus worked on Origen after having edited Jerome, Cyprian, Augustine, and others, and comments that "sometimes the best are reserved till the end." He also gives us in his preface a moving account of Erasmus's failing health and death and a brief sketch of his life. The actual edition of Origen's writings comprised two volumes and was entitled:

All the extant works of Origen Adamantius, the outstanding interpreter of the Scriptures, works which have been partly translated and partly diligently examined

---

42. Rummel, *Erasmus and His Catholic Critics*, 2:54.
43. Siecienski, "(Re)defining the Boundaries of Orthodoxy," 298.
44. Cf. Allen, *Opus Epistolarum Desiderii Erasmi Roteradami*, 1:52–56.

for authenticity by Desiderius Erasmus of Rotterdam, with a preface covering his life, style of speaking, manner of teaching, and his works, with the addition of a dedicatory epistle by Beatus Rhenanus, the greater part of which contains information concerning what is known about the life and death of Erasmus himself, and a very detailed index.[45]

For the text of Origen's writings, Erasmus's 1536 edition incorporates the Latin texts of his predecessors, above all the Aldine (Aldus Manutius) edition of Origen's *Homilies on the Heptateuch* (Venice, 1503) and Jacques Merlin's four-volume edition of Origen's complete Latin works (Paris, 1512), the precise contents of which have been catalogued in chapter 3.

The edition of Erasmus is more complete than that of Merlin in that Erasmus incorporates his previously published translation of the substantial fragments that survive from Origen's *Commentary on Matthew*, which in their entirety comprise Origen's fourth longest extant work (PG 13:835–1600). Erasmus's translation, however, only covers the material found in PG 13:835–1015 (books 13–16).[46] That earlier translation was made from a Greek fragment supplied to Erasmus by Jerome Froben.[47] The fragment included some of the same text that had circulated widely in a Latin version rendered by an anonymous translator who Erasmus believed to be Rufinus. The fragment extended the commentary available in the Latin backward from Matthew 16:13 to 13:36.[48] Although Erasmus criticized what he regarded as falsifications and corruptions of the translator, Erasmus never doubted the authenticity of the fragment.[49] Godin observed that Erasmus's esteem for the authority of the *textus receptus* (the Byzantine textual type that he utilized in his Greek-Latin edition of the New Testament) was so great that he deduced the authenticity of the Greek fragment not by examining the codex itself, but from its substantial identity with the old translation.[50] Erasmus's first published edition

---

45. "Origenis Adamantii eximii scriptuarum interpretis opera, quae quidem extant omnia, per Des. Erasmum Roterodamum, partim versa, partim vigilanter recognita, cum praefatione de Vita, Phrasi, Docendi ratione, et Operibus illius, adiectis epistola Beati Rhenani nuncupatoria, quae pleraque de vita obituque ipsius Erasmi cognitu dicta continet, et indice copiosissimo."

46. LB 8:439–84 (corresponds to ANF 10:414–59). Origen's commentary on Mt 13:36–22:33 survives in Greek. From 12:9 (Mt 16:13) onwards, a Latin translation presumably made in the sixth century, has also been transmitted which continues to almost the end of book 25 of the commentary (Mt 27:63). See McGuckin, *Westminster Handbook*, 30.

47. Cf. Allen, *Opus Epistolarum Desiderii Erasmi Roterodami*, eps. 1767, 1774, and 1844. See also Godin, *Érasme lecteur d'Origène*, 569.

48. Cf. Sider, "Erasmus and the Search for Authenticity," 241.

49. Cf. CWE 13, ep. 1844.

50. Godin, *Érasme lecteur d'Origène*, 571. Godin's use of the term *textus receptus* is, of course, an

of his new translation of the Greek fragment of Origen's *Commentary on Matthew* had been accompanied by a dedicatory letter addressed to Nicholas of Diesbach and dated July 6, 1527.[51] Erasmus withdrew this dedication from the 1536 edition, possibly because he disapproved of Diesbach's sympathetic attitude toward the Reformation.[52]

The prefatory material in Erasmus's edition of Origen resonates with the irenic reception and advocacy of Origen by his editorial predecessors, yet it also differs from the earlier published editions of Origen's works in important respects. Most notably, Erasmus mercilessly (and unjustly) reproaches Origen's translator Rufinus, whereas Jacques Merlin had spoken respectfully of him. Second, Erasmus does not attempt to present Origen as totally orthodox, as Merlin did, who even appended what became a controversial *Apology for Origen* to his edition. Erasmus leaves these issues on the side and does not even discuss the question of Origen's orthodoxy in his prefaces, although he had reflected upon this abundantly in his other writings, as we have seen. Instead of an apology for Origen or a discussion of Origen's errors, Erasmus includes a *Life of Origen* and essays on Origen's education, written works, style of preaching and teaching, and a section in which he assesses the authenticity of certain works. Erasmus limits his prefatory discussions of Origen's works to those which survive in Latin translation. He is particularly concerned to discuss the matter of their authenticity and of the correct identity of the Latin translator, whenever these issues are in dispute.[53]

To be sure, Erasmus's essays about Origen, like Aleander's and Merlin's prefaces, display a deep sympathy for the man, as a pious churchman and an "outstanding doctor of the Church," whose life, scholarship, and service to the church are worthy of emulation. In Origen Erasmus observes the same combination of literary erudition and sanctity of life that he also found in the other Church Fathers.[54] He found these same qualities in a few of the

---

anachronism. Erasmus's Greek text in his New Testament of 1516 became the basis of subsequent editions of the Greek New Testament. The term *Textus Receptus* was first used in the preface of an edition of the Greek New Testament by the Elzevir brothers in 1633. Cf. B. Metzger, *The Text of the New Testament: Its Transmission, Corruption, and Restoration*, 2nd ed. (New York: Oxford University Press, 1968), 106.

51. CWE 13, ep. 1844.

52. Cf. ibid.

53. For example, Erasmus does not treat Origen's *De Principiis*, *Homilies on Ezekiel*, and *Homilies on Numbers* in this section. There was no controversy about the identity of the Latin translators of these works: *De Principiis* and the *Homilies on Numbers* are by Rufinus, and the *Homilies on Ezekiel* are by Jerome.

54. Cf. Boeft, "Erasmus," 537.

great men of his generation, such as John Reuchlin, Thomas More, John Colet, John Fisher, and above all Jean Vitrier, and he uses similar language to describe them all.[55]

Erasmus's *Life of Origen*: Historical Sources

Erasmus's account of Origen's life is based chiefly on Rufinus's Latin translation of Eusebius's *Historia Ecclesiastica* 6.[56] Boeft suggests that in all probability Erasmus used the edition that had been incorporated in Beatus Rhenanus's edition of the *Auctores historiae ecclesiasticae* (Basel: Froben, 1523).[57] Godin confirms that Erasmus's *Life* and Rufinus's translation of Eusebius's *Historia* have so many lexical and stylistic points of contact that the possibility of Erasmus's direct utilization of Eusebius's original Greek is formally excluded.[58] To base his life of Origen on this source was a wise move, for Eusebius's work is in fact the best primary source for Origen. This is owed in part to Eusebius's basic skills as an historian, though in modern times, the French scholar P. Nautin has challenged the historical reliability of Eusebius, attempting first to deconstruct Eusebius by identifying and evaluating his sources, and then to reconstruct Origen's life based upon the new conjectures, rather than on Eusebius's account.[59] Nautin's work has been favorably received by some scholars including J. Trigg, who describes it as epoch-making, a breakthrough parallel with the "advance" made over previous New Testament scholars by Bultmann and Dibelius when they applied form criticism to the gospels.[60] On the other hand, H. Crouzel is far more cautious and argues that Nautin's criticisms of Eusebius and his alternative reconstructions would be better if their hypothetical and debatable character were acknowledged.[61]

Eusebius (260–339), bishop of Caesarea, was born only a few years after Origen's death in 254 and was the warden of Origen's then extant library in Caesarea. He had access to over a hundred letters of Origen, comprising nine

---

55. Cf. Godin, *Erasme lecteur d'Origène*, 667–74.

56. Rufinus's Latin text is available in a modern critical edition: *Eusebius Werke: Die Kirchengeschichte* (*Die griechischen christlichen Schriftsteller der ersten drei Jahrhunderte* [hereafter "GCS"]), ed. E. Schwartz and T. Mommsen (Berlin: Akademie, 1999).

57. Boeft, "Erasmus and the Church Fathers," 569. See also John F. Amico, "Beatus Rhenanus, Tertullian and the Reformation: A Humanist's Critique of Scholasticism," *Archiv für Reformationsgeschichte* 71 (1980): 37–60.

58. *Erasme lecteur d'Origène*, 632.

59. Nautin, *Origène, sa vie et son oeuvre*, 20.

60. Trigg, *Origen: The Bible and Philosophy in the Third-Century Church*, 23.

61. Crouzel, *Origen*, 1–2.

volumes. All but two of Origen's letters have subsequently perished.[62] Additionally, Eusebius knew men who had known Origen, and he interviewed them personally. He states: "The facts here set forth are drawn from some of his letters and from the recollections of those of his friends who have lived on till my own time."[63] Nautin attempted to debunk this statement.[64] Yet, Eusebius's testimony speaks for itself. It is true that Eusebius was by his own admission an ardent admirer and defender of Origen. He had collaborated with the martyr Pamphilus in writing an *Apology for Origen* against Origen's detractors.[65] His defensiveness undoubtedly taints his objectivity in some respects, and the account in HE does at times read like hagiography. Indeed everything Eusebius has preserved deserves to be weighed carefully and read with critical eyes. Yet the fact that Eusebius openly acknowledges his admiration of Origen and does not refrain from recording discreditable facts about Origen, such as his self-castration, is to his credit. At the least we can say that Erasmus's decision to depend as closely as possible on Eusebius's account and Jerome's writings for his *Life of Origen* was a fortunate one and adds to the value of this biography as an historical narrative.

Rufinus's Latin Translation of Eusebius

Rufinus informs us in the preface that he had been asked by Chromatius, bishop of Aquileia, to translate Eusebius's *Church History* as a means of providing comfort and encouragement to Italian Christians.[66] In 401 the armies of Alaric, commander of the Goths, had broken into Italy and were wreaking havoc up and down the Italian countryside. Chromatius hoped that human minds would find relief and comfort in the stories of the sufferings of the early Christians. The stated aim of Rufinus's translation was the edification and comfort of believers. Rufinus does not inform his readers, however, that in order to reach that goal, he would deem it necessary to supply additional material to his translation that would clarify and supplement Eusebius's narrative and make it more comprehensible. Whereas modern translators would

---

62. Cf. Eusebius, HE 6.36.3. The surviving letters are those to Julius Africanus and to Gregory Thaumaturgus (PG 11:47–92).

63. HE 6.2.1, trans. Williamson.

64. Nautin, *Origène, sa vie et son oeuvre*, 20–21.

65. Cf. Eusebius, HE 6.36.4. See my new translation, St. Pamphilus, *Apology for Origen. Rufinus: On the Falsification of the Books of Origen*, FOTC 120 (Washington, D.C.: The Catholic University of America Press, 2010).

66. NPNF2 3:565.

tend to use footnotes to introduce such clarifications and additions, in antiquity it was not uncommon to introduce such material directly into Latin translations of Greek works. (Erasmus was completely unaware that Rufinus had done this in his translation of Eusebius.)

In a very helpful article, Oulton, the Loeb translator of Eusebius, has shown that in some cases, Rufinus had knowledge of facts that enabled him to distinguish and clarify what Eusebius had confused, while in others he had recourse to original documents. Rufinus also draws upon first-hand sources of knowledge for the subject in question.[67] Oulton asserts that Rufinus's additions deserve more weight and consideration than they have hitherto received, even in cases when he is the sole witness to something.[68] Rufinus supplied this additional material primarily in HE 6, which is the chapter that concerns Origen. Significantly, Oulton has shown that in almost every instance Rufinus has added accurate and illuminating historical information that can be confirmed from outside sources. Rufinus knew Origen's writings well, including his now-lost epistles, to which Eusebius had also had full access. He was also acquainted with the complete text of the *Apology of Origen*, written by Eusebius and Pamphilus, of which his Latin translation preserves for us only the first book. A priori we should expect that Rufinus had independent knowledge of some of the facts that Eusebius recounts concerning Origen, especially since he (Rufinus) had lived for many years in Egypt and Palestine.

Some modern scholars have sharply criticized Rufinus's methods as a translator on the basis of his tendency to make clarifying insertions and interpolations. While his general reliability is granted, Rufinus is often judged according to the criteria of modern literary criticism. This is not completely fair to Rufinus, who was not a modern translator, and who was not attempting to supplant the original Greek text of Eusebius's HE.[69] The following are some examples of Rufinus's translation procedure in this particular work. Eusebius's HE contains Greek translations from Tertullian's (Latin) *Apology*. When rendering these into Latin, Rufinus supplies Tertullian's original Latin text directly. He does not back-translate Eusebius's Greek rendering of Tertullian. Similarly, Rufinus renders Eusebius's biblical citations according to the old Latin version (the Latin translation of the Septuagint), which was the

67. Cf. Oulton, "Rufinus's Translation," 150–74.
68. Ibid., 153.
69. For a recent reassessment of Rufinus's aims, see M. Humphries, "Rufinus's Eusebius: Translation, Continuation, and Edition in the Latin Ecclesiastical History," JECS 16, no. 2 (2008): 143–64.

version of the Bible in use in Rufinus's churches. He follows this same procedure in his translation of Origen's *Commentary on Romans* as well. He refrains from creating a new Latin translation of Eusebius's biblical quotations. Such decisions were made, obviously, to save work for the translator. These particular instances are difficult to reprehend when judged by either ancient or modern standards.

Of greater moment, however, was Rufinus's decision to interpolate material into his author for the sake of clarification and to make additions that are not found in the original Greek text. Even in this connection, however, Rufinus's method did not necessarily violate the literary canons of antiquity, especially since he clearly announced his procedure in his prefaces.[70] His translation procedure was scarcely different from that which Jerome employed in his translation of Eusebius's *Chronicle* or of Origen's *Homilies on Isaiah*.[71] Yet Rufinus's methods frustrate modern textual critics who are attempting to reconstruct the original Greek text of Eusebius. For that task, Rufinus's translation is not very helpful. Hence, Mommsen states that the value of Rufinus's translation is low.[72] Both he and Oulton accused Rufinus of arbitrariness.[73] The charge seems valid from the perspective of modern textual criticism.

Erasmus's close dependence on Rufinus's translation explains why his *Life of Origen* is not always explicable on the basis of Eusebius's Greek text alone (modern English translations of Eusebius are based solely on the Greek text). Erasmus appears not to have known or consulted Eusebius's Greek original, and therefore he was not aware of the times when he was relying upon Rufinus's modifications and additions. In the notes appended to my translation in the next chapter, I clarify several examples of Rufinus's modifications of Eusebius.

---

70. Cf. Murphy, *Rufinus of Aquileia*, 163; M. M. Wagner, *Rufinus the Translator* (Washington, D.C.: The Catholic University of America Press, 1945), 29.

71. Cf. Humphries, "Rufinus's Eusebius," 163–64; A. Fürst, "Jerome Keeping Silent: Origen and his Exegesis of Isaiah," in *Jerome of Stridon: His Life, Writings and Legacy*, ed. A. Cain and J. Lössl (Aldershot: Ashgate, 2009), 141–52; A. Fürst, "Origen Losing His Text: The Fate of Origen as a Writer in Jerome's Latin Translation of the Homilies on Isaiah," in *Origeniana Decima: Origen as Writer: Papers of the 10th International Origen Congress*, ed. S. Kaczmarek, H. Pietras, A. Dziadowiec (Louvain: Peeters, 2011), 689–701.

72. *GCS* 2.3, part 3, ccli.

73. See Humphries, "Rufinus's Eusebius," 146–47.

Erasmus's *Life of Origen*

K. Enenkel has recently observed that early modern biographies functioned as para-texts meant to accompany, explain, and transmit other texts. In general they are persuasive texts. "They try to persuade the readers of certain (historical) facts, attitudes, and visions. If they accompany the works of early modern authors, they try to guide and influence the reception of those writings."[74] It appears to me that Erasmus did indeed have intentions like this in his *Life of Origen*. He aimed to guide the reader of his edition of Origen's writings in how to read Origen most profitably. I also note that the historian Plutarch (one of Erasmus's favorite writers) said in his *Life of Pericles* that virtue, by the bare statement of its actions, can so affect men's minds as to create at once both admiration of the things done and desire to imitate the doers of them. Moral good is a practical stimulus; as soon as it is seen, it inspires an impulse to practice, and influences the mind and character of the reader. Erasmus's *Life of Origen* seems also to be in many respects a statement of Origen's virtues. He calls attention to those aspects of Origen's life and career that he thinks are most worthy of emulation by his contemporaries.

Erasmus presents Origen as a heroic, humble, and learned saint and the embodiment of many of Erasmus's own Catholic reform ideals. He singles out qualities of Origen that he had praised in other Fathers as well. Thus his brief biography of Origen reflects his own experiences and idiosyncrasies. What Brady and Olin have said of Erasmus's *Life of Jerome* can also be applied to his *Life of Origen*.

> It is above all a plea on behalf of the ideas and reforms Erasmus held most dear. Jerome is an exemplar, a model to be followed: he is the ideal Christian scholar, the right kind of monk, the true theologian. To tell his authentic story and defend him against his critics is to argue the case for the reforms in theology and religious life that Erasmus sought. Indeed Erasmus identified with Jerome, and the life in many respects is his own justification and defense, an *apologia pro vita sua*. We love those in whom we see our own resemblance, Erasmus realized. But even as a personal projection—an aspect that should not be overemphasized—Jerome is a historic model, and Erasmus's portrait of him embodies a program and a plea for humanist reform.[75]

Of course the comparison of these two lives is made more complex by the fact that Jerome, though quite controversial and even marginalized during

---

74. Enenkel, "Beatus Rhenanus' Second Vita Erasmi," 27.
75. CWE 61:16–17.

his own lifetime, eventually became a canonized saint, and in the medieval period was even declared one of the four doctors of the Latin church (alongside Ambrose, Augustine, and Gregory the Great). His orthodoxy was beyond question in Erasmus's day. Origen, on the other hand, while recognized by some saints during his lifetime and in subsequent centuries as a great teacher of the church, was simultaneously accused by other saints of espousing various heretical views. Moreover, his followers, the Origenists, were eventually condemned by an ecumenical council. Thus the very name of Origen was controversial. In spite of this, it appears to me that there are still vast similarities between the portraits that reveal the extent to which Erasmus includes Origen among the church's outstanding teachers. In some cases it seems clear that Erasmus has projected contemporary events and conflicts into the writing of Origen's biography. He has actualized Origen's story and made it relevant to the contemporary church.

Origen's Double Name, Virtues, Homeland, Parents

Godin divides his discussion of Erasmus's *Life of Origen* into eight parts, which are set forth in accordance with the chronological succession of the ideas reflected as essential by Eusebius in HE 6.[76] I will follow Godin's helpful outline and briefly reflect upon the particular significance of these themes for Erasmus himself. Erasmus thinks that both names, Origen and Adamantius, were assigned to him from the very beginning of his life, in the same manner that some men of the Bible bear more than one name. In Origen's case, the names are wonderfully suited to this "outstanding doctor of the Church," for they contain auspicious prophecies of his future service. Erasmus discusses and makes conjectures about the meaning of both names. It is noteworthy that Erasmus had similarly described the name of Augustine (Aurelius Augustinus) as a name that predicts his future as a golden (*aurelius*) and venerable (*augustus*) theologian and bishop.[77] Erasmus admits that he does not know for certain Origen's native country but that it is likely he was an Alexandrian. He then adds a significant gloss to the effect that it does not so much matter where you are born or from whom you descend, but rather by whom you receive your education from infancy. This reflects an important thesis of Erasmus's most important educational writing, *De pueris statim ac liberaliter instituendis declamatio* (A Declamation on the Subject of Early Liberal Education

---

76. *Erasme lecteur d'Origène*, 633.
77. CWE 15, ep. 2157.

For Children) (1529).[78] In this work Erasmus offers a Christian reformulation of the classical ideal of liberal education.

Erasmus also points out that Origen's saintly father, Leonidas of Alexandria, was a martyr of the Catholic church. Erasmus describes Leonidas as a man "who was as pious as he was learned." Erasmus is rightly distrustful of later accounts that report that Leonidas was a bishop, since there is no evidence for this from antiquity. Erasmus praises Leonidas's prudence and far-sightedness in instilling the seeds of virtue into the heart of his son and in cultivating Origen's zeal for divine things, a natural capacity that was present even when Origen was a small child. Thus Leonidas is portrayed as a prototypical Christian educator according to the Erasmian ideals.

The reader of this section is reminded of the educational vision of Erasmus's close friend John Colet, who after his father's death, founded a school in London to educate boys. Moreover, in his *Methodus*, Erasmus praised the brothers Jerome (d. 1517) and Giles Busleiden (d. 1536), who dedicated their large inheritance to providing decent salaries to those who taught languages at the Trilingual College of Louvain.[79] In the same passage in the *Methodus*, Erasmus commended to posterity the memory of Stephen Poncher (d. 1524), bishop of Paris and later archbishop of Sens, who also strongly supported the education of the next generation. In Erasmus's judgment, men like this would surely qualify as modern counterparts both to Leonidas of Alexandria and to his son Origen.

Origen's Burning Desire for Martyrdom

Erasmus admires Origen's burning aspiration to be a martyr for Christ and notices that in his extant works Origen speaks with enthusiasm whenever he has the occasion to discourse on martyrdom. There is no doubt that Erasmus has identified an important emphasis in Origen's theology and spirituality: the prime importance of martyrdom. For Origen martyrdom is the highest form of being faithful to Christ in all circumstances, of uniting oneself with the passion of Christ in the present and the presence of Christ after death, and of participating in Christ's work of redemption through the routing of the devil's power. And since the martyr shows himself impervious to suffering in particular, he experiences by the grace of God a sort of foretaste of the resurrection in this life and thus continues the work of redemp-

78. CWE 26.
79. *Methodus*, trans. Conroy, 82.

tion in this world. Crouzel observes: "Origen always desired martyrdom and constantly made clear, in his *Exhortation to Martyrdom* as well as in his homilies, the esteem in which he held this crowning testimony to our belonging to Christ."[80]

Erasmus had long since assimilated the theme of the supreme importance of martyrdom into his own spirituality and theology. It is pervasive in the *Enchiridion*, which is a work that is simultaneously infused with citations from Origen.[81] His biography of Jean Vitrier emphasizes his subject's burning desire for martyrdom, in the footsteps of Francis of Assisi.[82] At the literal level, upholding martyrdom as the highest ideal means that Christians must be ready to face death for their beliefs. But for Erasmus the aspiration for martyrdom is achieved above all on the spiritual level by the interior martyrdom of mortification of the flesh and death to sin and vices.

Erasmus omits from his biography of Origen any mention of the final outcome of Origen's aspirations, when Origen was imprisoned and tortured during the Decian persecution and died shortly after his release as a result of the physical brutality inflicted upon him. Though technically Origen never became a martyr, he did endure prison and physical torture for the sake of Christ, and all of this is recounted in vivid detail by Erasmus's principal source, Eusebius, as we have seen in chapter 2. Erasmus's omission of this final episode of Origen's life seems surprising, even when we take account of the fact that we are dealing with an unfinished work.

Yet it also perhaps reveals Erasmus's deeper aims in writing this biography, which are not primarily hagiographical. For in Erasmus's judgment the greatest benefit that the church has derived from Origen is from his learned writings, not necessarily from his imprisonment and torture during the Decian persecution, however inspiring that episode may be to us. In his early work the *Antibarbari*, the characters in Erasmus's fictitious dialogue discussed this theme in greater depth. One character speaks of the incomparable benefit that has come to the church from the fact that the learned writings of the Church Fathers have been handed down to posterity. It is not merely their holiness of life or brutal deaths in some cases that have brought benefit, but their decision to write books; for worthiness of life or even a martyr's death will die with its possessor, unless it be commended to poster-

---

80. Crouzel, *Origen*, 52; cf. 136. Cf. Daniélou, *Origen*, 7.
81. Cf. Godin, "The Enchiridion Militis Christiani: The Modes of an Origenian Appropriation," trans. H. Gibaud, *Erasmus of Rotterdam Society Yearbook* 2 (1982): 47–79.
82. Cf. CWE 8, ep. 1211, to Justus Jonas.

ity in written works. But where there is learned scholarship, the speaker says, "nothing stops it from spreading out to all humanity, neither land nor sea nor the long succession of the centuries." The character of the dialogue then makes a comparison which he himself recognizes is "invidious":

> I am not disparaging the glory of the martyrs, which a man could not attain to even by unlimited eloquence; but to speak simply of usefulness to us, we owe more to some heretics than to some martyrs. There was indeed a plentiful supply of martyrs, but very few doctors. The martyrs died, and so diminished the number of Christians; the scholars persuaded others and so increased it. In short, the martyrs would have shed their blood in vain for the teaching of Christ unless the others had defended it against the heretics by their writings. The Christian religion found good letters a valuable safeguard in times of stress, and it will not be so ungrateful now, when it has peace and prosperity, as to thrust them off into exile—for it was through them that it attained peace and happiness.[83]

Obviously there is no disparagement of the glory of the martyrs in this passage. Rather Erasmus, under the persona of his dramatic character, is simply observing that the Fathers who, provoked by the heretics, wrote learned works for posterity have done a great service to the church, and we continue to reap the benefit. Origen's writings exemplify this, since they are largely written against ancient heresies.

Origen as Grammarian, Soldier of Christ, and Catechist

Erasmus expresses admiration for Origen's decision to become a "grammarian" or professional teacher of literature. The profession itself required a nearly perfect knowledge of all the liberal subjects. Erasmus himself had been disparaged and dismissed as a "grammarian" by some of his Catholic and Protestant critics. A passage from Thomas More's *Letter to Dorp* sheds some light on the technical terms and historical figures referred to in this section of Erasmus's *Life of Origen*. More tells Dorp that Erasmus is not to be banished from the theologians to the grammarians, as Dorp haughtily suggests. In any case, Erasmus

will by no means spurn the title "grammarian" which you ridicule more frequently than cleverly. Or rather, modest as he is, even though he deserves it more than anyone, he may hesitate to accept it, since he knows that "grammarian" means precise-

---

83. *Antibarbari* (CWE 23:83).

ly the same thing as "man of letters," whose area of study extends across every variety of literature, that is, every discipline.... Erasmus is certainly not one of those grammarians who have mastered no more than mere words, nor is he one of those theologians who know nothing at all outside a tangled labyrinth of petty problems. He is a grammarian of the same stamp as Varro and Aristarchus and a theologian of the same stamp as you, Dorp, that is, of the best. For he is not ignorant of those petty problems, and he has gone on to do what you too have done in such depth; he has gained something vastly more useful, a general command of sound literature, which means sacred letters especially but not at the expense of the rest.[84]

This passage from More is remarkable not only for the love and respect it shows Martin Dorp, but for the light it sheds on the ancient title of "grammarian."

According to Erasmus, the secular nature of the profession of grammarian indicates that Origen wanted to provide a living for himself and his family by his own labor rather than to turn to begging. This gloss amounts to an implicit criticism of the serious abuses that were occurring in the all-too-numerous mendicant orders. Origen is depicted as a foil to the abuses of the latter, and as a truer imitator of the apostle Paul, who earned his own keep by tent-making. And yet, Erasmus stresses, there was no question of covetousness on Origen's part, for his income was below the subsistence level. Erasmus also highlights that Origen combined in his teaching evangelical doctrine, perfect piety, and sanctity of life. Clear proof of this is the fact that some of his disciples became important church leaders; others, both men and women, became martyrs. Origen's outstanding virtue and learning even earned for him the respect of pagans, some of whom were so impressed that they undertook to imitate Origen's life by conversion.

Erasmus highlights Origen's function as a catechist in the church of Alexandria. He instructed pagans in the rudiments of the Christian religion. "He not only taught them the first principles of Gospel teaching, but also raised up many to the heights of perfect piety." Many of his pupils were crowned with martyrdom. Erasmus admires the way Origen hardened his flesh to the point of total endurance by means of vigils, fasts, sleeping on the hard ground, nakedness, and labors. His purity of life made his name beloved and admired, and very many undertook to imitate Origen. Erasmus notes the contrast between the admirable emphasis on catechesis in the early church and the comparative neglect of it in Erasmus's day. In Erasmus's judgment

---

84. Thomas More, *Letter to Dorp* (CW 15:14–15).

catechesis was in fact one of the most important responsibilities of Catholic priests. In his great work on preaching, *Ecclesiastes* (1535), he wrote:

> The most important function of the priest is teaching the Lord's flock, by which he may instruct them in sound doctrine, admonish, rebuke, console, and convict those he is offering up to the truth of the Gospel [cf. Rom 15:16]. A layman can baptize. The people can pray in their turn for the priest. The administration of the rest of the sacraments is not difficult, but the duty of teaching is both an extremely difficult and a very beautiful duty, since its advantage is clear for all to see. The priest does not always baptize, he does not always anoint, he does not always absolve, but the task of teaching is constant. Without it his other duties are unprofitable. For what good is it for adults to be baptized, if they have not been instructed by a catechist what force baptism has, what one must believe, how one should establish his life according to the Christian profession? What good comes from consuming the body and blood of the Lord if the people have not learned how this sacrament was instituted, what it effects in us, with what faith and purity it ought to be consumed?[85]

Erasmus himself accomplished a great deal in the field of Catholic catechetics in the sixteenth century, as I will mention also in the appendix.[86] His production began with the catechetical poem, *Christiani hominis institutum*, written to give instruction to the schoolboys at John Colet's St. Paul's School in London.[87] His colloquy *An Inquiry concerning Faith* is not without catechetical importance, based as it is on Rufinus's commentary on the Apostles' Creed. Erasmus's most important catechetical work was his *Explanation of the Apostles' Creed* (1533).[88] On the basis of his study of the latter work and its subsequent influence, Padberg concluded that Erasmus was one of the principal renewers of kerygmatic and catechetical preaching in the pre-Tridentine Catholic church. For Erasmus's catechism provided clear dogmatic answers in the fullest sense of the term for the precise moment of distress and danger to the church that Erasmus had faced.[89] Subsequent scholarship has

---

85. *Ecclesiastes* (LB 5:831C-D). For a study of this work, see R. Kleinhans, "Erasmus's Doctrine of Preaching: A Study of Ecclesiastes, sive de ratione concionandi" (PhD diss., Princeton Theological Seminary, 1968). A number of bishops at the Council of Trent made the suggestion that this work of Erasmus should be placed in every rectory library. Cf. S. Ehses, CT 5:147–48; noted in Dolan, *The Essential Erasmus*, 223. It is true that the Council did not officially adopt this suggestion or legislate its implementation, but the very fact that the suggestion was made indicates that an atmosphere sympathetic to Erasmian reform was present at the Tridentine Council.

86. Cf. R. Padberg, *Erasmus als Katechet* (Freiburg im Breisgau: Herder, 1956).

87. Cf. CWE 85:92–107.

88. CWE 70.

89. Padberg, *Erasmus als Katechet*, 127, 157. F. J. Kötter, *Die Eucharistielehre in den Katholischen*

independently confirmed Padberg's research. J. O'Malley writes: "Erasmus' heavy concentration on the creed was unusual for the age, and it should put to rest forever the old shibboleth that he was uninterested in dogma."[90] Thus, in highlighting catechesis as a matter of crucial importance to Origen and to Origen's bishop Demetrius, Erasmus is both recording historical fact and simultaneously challenging his contemporaries, whether priests, bishops or popes, to make catechesis a central concern of their apostolate, as it was of Erasmus's own.

Origen's Priesthood, Journeys, and Crisis with His Bishop

Erasmus describes how Origen was raised to the rank of priesthood, adding that at that time the dignity of priests was great, "although later they became worthless because of the multitude of them."[91] The criticism voiced here was shared by others. Among the *Gravamina* (*Grievances*) presented by German Catholic princes at the Diet of Worms in 1521 was listed the complaint that too many priests were being ordained, including base and uneducated persons. The first meeting of the nine bishops at Regensburg agreed that quality rather than simply numbers in candidates for the priesthood would be the greatest step in the reform of the church. J. Lortz saw this as the beginning of the Catholic reform in Germany.[92] Also, the document of the papal commission of Paul III, *Consilium de Emendanda Ecclesia* (1537) said that the worst abuse in the church was the indiscriminate ordination of men to the priesthood, from which practice came "innumerable scandals, contempt for the whole ecclesiastical order, and diminution of veneration of the divine mysteries."[93] Erasmus was in the mainstream in his criticism of this abuse.

Erasmus further describes Origen's conflict with his ecclesiastical superior Demetrius, the bishop of Alexandria. He follows Rufinus's version of

---

Katechismen des 16. Jahrhunderts bis zum Erscheinen des Catechisms Romanus (1566) (Münster: Aschendorff, 1969) recognizes the merits of Padberg's study (24) but thinks that Padberg has overstated the degree to which Erasmus's catechism provided clear dogmatic answers to all pressing questions (35).

90. This is found in the introduction to the new translation of Erasmus's *Catechism* (CWE 70:xxiii).

91. This passage is cited in chapter 5.

92. *The Reformation in Germany*, 1:117.

93. Cf. J. C. Olin, *The Catholic Reformation: Savonarola to Ignatius Loyola* (New York: Fordham, 1969), 188; *Consilium Tridentinum*, 12, 136.

Eusebius carefully, as well as Jerome's *On Illustrious Men*. Erasmus transmits the additional material supplied by Rufinus according to which Origen's purity of life had been universally acknowledged to the point that he was deemed worthy of the highest sacerdotal office (bishop). In his translation of Eusebius, Rufinus had added the following passage:

> When the chief bishops of note in Palestine, that is to say, Alexander of Jerusalem and Theoctistus of Caesarea, seeing his divine labors in the word of God, had ordained him presbyter and were deeming him even now worthy of the highest sacerdotal office [*ac summo eum sacerdotio iam iamque dignum probarent*], and their action was praised by all as most fittingly done, and men were saying that not even thus was fitting honor paid him for his wisdom and virtues, Demetrius was exceedingly vexed by this talk, and not finding in him any other cause of accusation, that thing which formerly Origen had done while still a boy and which Demetrius himself had praised when already a bishop, this he later brought forward as a ground of accusation, and now attempted to cast blame upon those who had ordained him.[94]

Oulton comments on the significance of Rufinus's additions to Eusebius by saying that whereas Eusebius attributes Demetrius's jealousy merely to Origen's growing reputation and his elevation to the priesthood, Rufinus seems clearly to indicate that both the church authorities and the people considered him worthy of the episcopate also (*summo sacerdotio dignum*). "This gives additional point to Demetrius's subsequent action, which was actuated not merely by annoyance at a *fait accompli*, but was also intended to bar Origen's elevation to the episcopate. The spreading of the scandal connected with his boyhood effectually prevented this."[95] Erasmus sees evidence of human weakness in Origen's bishop Demetrius in that this same man who was now accusing Origen had initially praised the devotion shown by Origen's youthful act of self-castration.

Origen's Physical Mutilation, Spiritual Castration

Erasmus transmits two ancient traditions regarding Origen's self-inflicted act. Epiphanius had reported that Origen deprived himself of incitements to lust by means of medicines applied to the genital area. In contrast Eusebius makes clear that a physical act of self-mutilation was involved. Erasmus follows Eusebius, but leaves the decision about this matter to the reader. Relying on his sources, Erasmus fails to acknowledge that anything but per-

---

94. Translated by Oulton, "Rufinus's Translation," 161–62.
95. Ibid., 162.

sonal, canonical, and disciplinary matters were involved in Origen's conflict with Demetrius. He does not mention any doctrinal issues. Erasmus appends a brief excursus on the lack of vigilance in the contemporary church, which in order to prevent dishonor to the church excludes the physically mutilated from the priesthood; and yet this same church tolerates priests who are spiritually mutilated and castrated by their being blind and lame in respect to the knowledge of scripture. The point is not to challenge the validity of ecclesiastical law respecting the physically mutilated, but to call attention to the importance of spiritual integrity.

Origen's Influence and Productivity as a Teacher in Caesarea of Palestine

Erasmus concludes his *Life of Origen* by calling attention to Origen's churchman-like spirit and behavior, which kept him in the bosom of the Catholic church all his life in spite of his being mistreated by his ecclesiastical superiors. Erasmus sees this as exemplary and a notable contrast with Tertullian, who left the Catholic church and joined a sect, and with Arius, who tore the church asunder by schism. There is plenty of evidence in Origen's extant writings that indicates that Origen viewed himself, from first to last, as a man of the church. According to Eusebius (HE 6.2.14), Origen had such a deep feeling for the unity of the church that he refused even to pray with heretics, for schism and heresy made him feel sick. In his *Homily on Joshua*, Origen said: "If I should do anything against the teaching of the Church and the rule of the Gospel, so that I create a stumbling block for you the Church, may the whole Church in one accord, acting in concert, cut me off and fling me, their right hand, away" (7.6). Another well-known text is *Homily on Luke* (16.6):

Although the heretics seek to expound it, they will be unable to succeed. But I hope to be a man of the Church. I hope to be addressed not by the name of some heresiarch, but by the name of Christ. I hope to have his name, which is blessed upon the earth. I desire, both in deed and in thought, both to be and to be called a Christian.[96]

In his *Homily on Ezekiel* (10.1) Origen repudiates the tactics of those who created schisms in the church, even in cases when their own original deposition had been unjust. He says that it is an infamy to be separated from the church and to leave the congress of the priesthood. Those who created schisms after

---

96. Origen, *Homilies on Luke, Fragments on Luke*, trans. J. Lienhard, FOTC 94 (Washington, D.C.: The Catholic University of America Press, 1996).

being deposed are storing up wrath for themselves, whereas those who humbly accept the judgment made against them will gain God's mercy.

Erasmus was deeply impressed by Origen's repudiation of heresy and schism in principle, and by his lifelong adherence to the Catholic church in spite of the conflicts Origen had experienced with bishops. Indeed, according to Godin, when Erasmus points out the contrast between Origen and Tertullian and Arius, he seems to be subtly alluding to the Protestants and even to his own departure from Basel.[97] When Basel became Protestant in 1529, Erasmus, the theologian Ludwig Baer, together with all the canons of the cathedral emigrated to the Catholic city of Freiburg im Breisgau, where the Edict of Worms had been rigorously enforced. Shortly before his migration, on March 25, 1529, Erasmus wrote to Alfonso Vergara, archbishop of Toledo, telling him that he had to move from Basel even if this caused grave danger to his life (due to his frail health): "We shall do what behooves an orthodox man, that is: we shall place piety before our personal well-being. For to stay here, where it is permitted neither to sacrifice nor to confect the Lord's Body, would inevitably mean professing what they profess."[98] As Reedijk rightly observes, "Erasmus's decision [to migrate] was dictated by inner conviction and spiritual necessity."[99] Thus, a perceptive and informed reader is able to see that Erasmus's later patristic editions of the 1520s and 1530s are subtle works of Catholic apologetics, by means of which Erasmus makes his own pleas with his contemporaries. Just as Erasmus's biography of the Franciscan priest Jean Vitrier was recorded in a letter addressed to one of Luther's associates, Justus Jonas, and served to offer Luther's adherents a contemporary model of true Catholic reform ideals, in contrast with Luther's schismatic methods, so here Erasmus seems to be alluding to the Protestant reformers—above all to Martin Luther, Melanchthon, Zwingli, Capito, and Oecolampadius—as the sixteenth-century counterpart to Tertullian and Arius. For by this time Luther and his disciples had separated themselves from the Catholic church into diverse sects (like Tertullian) and thrown the world into a horrendous schism (like Arius), all of which was accomplished by increasingly embittered writings.

In *Hyperaspistes* I (1526), Erasmus used the same word he uses here of Tertullian, "sect," to describe the divisions Luther had caused:

97. Godin, *Erasme lecteur d'Origène*, 653.
98. CWE 15, ep. 2134.
99. C. Reedijk, "Erasmus' Final Modesty," in *Actes du Congrès Erasme Rotterdam 27–29 Octobre 1969* (Amsterdam: North-Holland Publishing Company, 1971), 180.

> You [Luther] are indignant if we do not immediately abandon the teaching embraced and held by the Catholic church for so many centuries in the past and swear allegiance to you. I never had any inclination to join your conspiracy. But still, if I were growing weary of this church, as I wavered in perplexity, tell me, I beg you in the name of the gospel, where would you have me go? To that disintegrated congregation of yours, that totally dissected sect? Karlstadt has raged against you, and you in turn against him. And the dispute was not simply a tempest in a teapot but concerned a very serious matter. Zwingli and Oecolampadius have opposed your opinion in many volumes. And some of the leaders of your congregation agree with them, among whom is Capito. Then too what an all-out battle was fought by Balthazar and Zwingli! I am not even sure that there in that tiny little town you agree among yourselves very well.[100]

Thus for Erasmus the lesson to be learned from Origen's lifelong adherence to the Catholic church ran very deep indeed. Schism creates more problems than it solves. Erasmus himself had been mistreated by conservative theologians and repeatedly accused of heresy, but he refused to be provoked by this into schism. If the principle of schism from the Catholic church is accepted as valid, where does it end?

Erasmus's concluding statement about Origen is another remarkable autobiographical reflection: "He lived on amidst his most holy labors until the sixty-ninth year of his life." When he wrote these words Erasmus himself was almost certainly sixty-nine years old.[101] He was engaged in his most holy patristic studies of this "outstanding doctor of the Church." And in fulfillment of his own desire to die amidst such labors, he died thus engaged. A comment made in a letter of 1523 sheds light on this. Erasmus describes his own sufferings from kidney stones and his attitude toward death:

> Some men are born for themselves and for themselves they live. A nuisance to everyone else, they keep their felicity to themselves, and do nothing to please other people except by dying. Even then they have not lost their readiness to be a nuisance: they burden posterity with memorial rites and prayer and sacrifice and ceremonies and vestments and the ringing of bells, so that even after death they are a trouble to the living. Personally I would rather be a Hercules and die amid my labors.[102]

In his depiction of Origen's life and death, Erasmus has truly created a self-portrait.

---

100. *Hyperaspistes* I (CWE 76:142–43).
101. The standard study of Erasmus's birth year is H. Vredeveld, "The Ages of Erasmus and the Year of His Birth," *Renaissance Quarterly* 46 (1993): 754–809.
102. CWE 9, ep. 1347.

"Concerning the Education and Writings of Origen"

The second part of the prefatory material in Erasmus's edition of Origen is an essay on Origen's education and writings. Erasmus follows Eusebius and Jerome in finding in Origen a most versatile scholar who was extremely learned in many areas. He observes that Origen's entire life was devoted to studies. He compares Origen's erudition with that of Rome's greatest scholar, Marcus Varro, whose achievements in scholarship laid the foundation for the achievements of the Augustans (Livy, Horace, Virgil, Ovid, etc.). The comparison is deliberate, since Erasmus is fully aware of Origen's massive influence on the Catholic church's exegetical tradition. Erasmus contrasts Origen's lifelong immersion in a Christian education, which began in early childhood, with that of Augustine, who was estranged from the Catholic religion until his thirty-sixth year, and with that of Ambrose, who likewise came to baptism and priesthood from secular work as an adult. Erasmus mentions how Origen had learned everything so thoroughly that he was even admired and mentioned honorably in the works of pagan philosophers, estranged from Christ. He expresses regret that it is now impossible to know even the titles of all of Origen's works because of the zeal of those who destroyed them. On the other hand maybe this is fortunate, he reflects, for our ignorance of the titles of these lost works keeps us from bewailing the loss all the more. Erasmus said similar things about the loss of the works of other Church Fathers.

It is noteworthy that Erasmus mentions the loss and destruction of Origen's writings without anywhere having discussed the cause of this, which lay in the official condemnation of Origenism at the Fifth Ecumenical Council in 553. Of course Erasmus is quite familiar with this event, since information about Origen's condemnation was common knowledge, and both Pico della Mirandola's *Apology* and Jacques Merlin's edition of Origen's writings in particular had discussed it in detail. Moreover there was the verdict on Origen's errors by Augustine in *De haeresibus* and *City of God*.[103] Erasmus apparently did not feel the need to go over such familiar ground. He had already spoken clearly about these matters in his own catechetical writings and expositions of the Psalms.

Next Erasmus discusses the divisions of Origen's works, following Jerome's description of the same in the preface to Jerome's translation of

---

103. *De haeresibus*, chaps. 42–43, and *City of God* 11.23, 21.17.

Origen's Homilies on Ezekiel.[104] There Jerome described to his dedicatee, the priest Vincentius, the threefold division of Origen's works on scripture.

> The first are his Selections (Excerpta) which in Greek are called scolia (scholia). In these in a brief and summary fashion, he lightly touched on things that seemed obscure or that contained some difficulty. The second kind of work is homiletical in nature. The present translation is one of these. The third kind are those that he inscribed as τόμοι. We can call them commentaries.[105] Here he lowered all the sails of his genius to the blowing winds, withdrawing from the land and going out to middle of the ocean.[106]

Erasmus reflects the wording of this passage several times in his own survey of the life, education, and writings of Origen. In the present essay, Erasmus's survey of Origen's writings is not exhaustive but focuses on the works for which the authenticity of the work itself or the identity of its Latin translator is in dispute.

Erasmus mentions with approval Origen's endeavor to learn the Hebrew language. "For it is from these sources that the sacred books first came down to us, particularly those of the Old Testament." His description of Origen's efforts in this connection reflects that used by Jerome in Ep 25.12, where Jerome describes his own labors in learning Hebrew. Study of the original biblical languages was an important Erasmian ideal. Erasmus also calls attention to Origen's massive project of textual criticism, the Hexapla, in which Origen displayed the Hebrew text of the Old Testament alongside several of the ancient Greek translations of the same, in separate columns. Interestingly, Erasmus believes that the true title of this work should be ἐξαπλά, with smooth breathing on the initial vowel. He found this spelling consistently in the manuscripts. Erasmus believes that this word derives from ἐξαπλόω and means "to display, to unfold." Erasmus does not endorse the standard derivation from ἑξαπλά (with rough breathing), meaning "six-fold" and referring to the six columns of text, even though this was the understanding found in Rufinus's translation of Eusebius's HE. Immediately after making this suggestion, Erasmus pleads for tolerance of his opinion. He says that he should be allowed to convey his opinion to the public without becoming the subject

---

104. Cf. the prologue to Jerome's Commentary on Galatians, where he gives the same division of Origen's works in inverse order: volumina, tractatus et excerpta. See also Jerome's In Isaiam, prologue.

105. Literally "volumes" or "books."

106. Origen, Homilies 1–14 on Ezekiel (ACW 62), trans. Thomas P. Scheck (Mahwah, N.J.: Newman Press, 2010), 23.

of accusations. For this is in keeping with the Pauline injunction, "let each be content with his own judgment."

In Rufinus's version of Eusebius, HE 6.16.3–4, is found an important independent account of Origen's *Hexapla* that is much clearer and fuller than Eusebius's description.[107] Rufinus clarifies the arrangement of the columns in this order: Hebrew, Hebrew transliterated into Greek, Aquila, Symmachus, Septuagint, and Theodotion. This arrangement is far from clear in Eusebius's account. Also, Rufinus makes plain that Origen had discovered more than two additional Greek translations (in addition to Aquila, Symmachus, and Theodotion), whereas Eusebius had reported only two additional versions. Moreover, Rufinus says that Origen used these additional versions not merely in the Psalter, as Eusebius's claims, but elsewhere in the *Hexapla*. With respect to the *Hexapla*, Rufinus's account is more detailed than Eusebius's and was based on independent knowledge of the work.[108]

On the one hand Rufinus's additions and clarifications make it rather surprising that Erasmus does not support the traditional derivation of the word *Hexapla* from the "six-fold" arrangement of the work, since Rufinus explicitly assigns such a meaning to the word and clarifies the arrangement and contents of each of the six columns. On the other hand Rufinus's additions to Eusebius may partly explain why Erasmus was confused about this derivation of *Hexapla* from "six-fold," since Rufinus clarified that the work in fact had more than six columns throughout.

"Assessments" (*Censurae*)

The next section in the prefatory section of Erasmus's edition of Origen offers the reader his own scholarly assessment of the identity of the Latin translator of Origen's works and of the authenticity of certain works. Schär accurately remarked that these "assessments" show a "final sparkling testimony for the critical sense and enormous erudition" of Erasmus.[109] The Latin translation of Origen's *Homiles on the Heptateuch* and his *Commentary on Romans* had been wrongly attributed to Jerome. Erasmus correctly ascribes them to Rufinus, not Jerome, whose name had been gratuitously inserted into the earlier printed additions. Erasmus praises the style of the *Homilies on Genesis* as pure and fluent, but he nevertheless attacks Rufinus as an in-

---

107. GCS 2.2, part 2, 555.
108. Cf. Oulton, "Rufinus's Translation," 162–63.
109. Schär, *Das Nachleben des Origenes im Zeitalter des Humanismus*, 289.

competent translator. Erasmus correctly attributes the *Homilies on Leviticus* and *Joshua* to Rufinus. The latter had been previously published in Jerome's name. Also, in a lengthy "assessment," Erasmus was the first of his contemporaries to identify Rufinus, not Jerome, as the translator of Origen's *Commentary on the Epistle to the Romans*. Moreover, he correctly surmises that Rufinus was the translator of Origen's *Homilies on Psalms 36–38*.

The longest assessment is devoted to the *Commentary on Job* (*Anonymus in Job*) which previously had been attributed to Origen in Merlin's edition (Paris, 1512). Erasmus's assessment of this work is his longest, which indicates that the Origenian attribution was firmly anchored in the minds of Erasmus's contemporaries.[110] In what may be his most impressive critical breakthrough, Erasmus correctly identifies the author as an Arian.[111] He suspects that the author was Maximinus whose disputations with Augustine are extant.[112] In modern times Erasmus's conjecture that Maximinus was the author was defended by Meslin, but firmly rejected by Steinhauser.[113]

It is somewhat ironic that some of Erasmus's contemporary Catholic critics, such as Zuniga, Aleander, and Pio, as well as the Protestant Martin Luther, accused him of being an Arian. The accusation, ridiculous as it sounds of one who was the first publisher of Athanasius's writings, was based partly on the fact that Erasmus did not include the "Johannine Comma" (1 Jn 5:8,

---

110. Cf. Godin, *Erasme lecteur d'Origène*, 608.

111. *Anonymus in Iob* is now available in a critical edition: K. B. Steinhauser, ed., *Anonymi in Iob Commentarius, Corpus Scriptorum Ecclesiasticorum Latinorum* XCVI [hereafter "CSEL"] (Vienna: Verlag der Österreichischen Akademie der Wissenschaften, 2006). It was reprinted among the spurious works of Origen in PG 17:371–522. For a discussion of the work, see Quasten, *Patrology*, 4:101–5; Meslin, *Les Ariens d'Occident*, 201–26; and now Steinhauser's critical edition. *Anonymus* was written in Latin and interprets Job's text up to 3:19 in three books. In his edition, Steinhauser writes: "[Erasmus] certainly did not mince words in expressing his disdain for the unknown author of the prologue" (48). He agrees with Erasmus's judgment that the author of the prologue is someone other than the author of the commentary.

112. Maximinus the Arian is the one Latin Arian author whose personality can be partly reconstructed. He was born ca. 360 in Rome and became bishop of an Arian community, possibly in Illyricum. He debated publicly with Augustine at Hippo in 427 or 428. A stenographic account of the debate survives (*Collatio Augustini cum Maximino*, PL 42:743–814).

113. Cf. M. Meslin, *Les Ariens d'Occident* (Paris: Editions du Seuil, 1967), 226. Meslin's argument is based on a comparison of these works with Maximinus's disputation with Augustine. Meslin finds the following parallels: the same theology, identical scriptural versions, an analogous style, the same acquaintance with ancient Arian sources, a taste for a very developed biblical erudition, the same moralizing vision of economic problems, and an analogous prolixity. On the other hand, Steinhauser rejects the attribution of *Anonymous in Iob* to Maximinus as "clearly false" and attributes the work to Auxentius of Durostorum (42, 45 in his edition).

Vulgate) in the first edition of his published New Testament, since that reading was not found in his Greek manuscript. Although Erasmus's contemporary critics were silenced by living popes, who knew the truth of the matter, during the Counter-Reformation, Roberto Bellarmine resurrected these baseless slanders against Erasmus and claimed that Erasmus was an Arian.[114] The same slanders had been voiced by Martin Luther himself against Erasmus in an attempt to discredit his most formidable Catholic opponent.[115] In his *Controversy with Alberto Pio*, Erasmus said in response to such charges: "If I had in any way supported the insanity of the Arians, why would I express my hatred for their position in countless passages and declare forcefully and expressly that those who do not make profession among Christians are not to be regarded as such?"[116] Moreover, in his *Apology against the Spanish Monks*, Erasmus cites eighty texts in his writings where he defended the Trinity.[117] It is not that Erasmus was an Arian, but that his critics were either ignorant of what he had actually written or they were slanderous and malicious obscurantists.

Erasmus's opposition to Arianism is also manifested by the fact that he was the most productive Latin translator in the sixteenth century of the Greek writings of John Chrysostom, Athanasius, and Basil of Caesarea.[118] These Greek churchmen were among the ancient church's greatest opponents of Arianism. If Erasmus were an Arian, why would he devote such energy to translating works that strongly oppose Arianism? Irena Backus has recently demonstrated convincingly that the anti-Trinitarians of the late sixteenth century who appealed to Erasmus's *Annotations to the New Testament* for support of their own heresies were unjustified in doing so, since Erasmus, as opposed to the anti-Trinitarians, "accepted the Church's teaching and did not attempt to cancel it out by his textual or philological findings."[119] To me it seems rather odd that Erasmus has been accused of Arianism, when in fact, from a modern standpoint, probably no Catholic scholar in the sixteenth century did more to undermine Arianism than Erasmus of Rotter-

---

114. Cf. Mansfield, *Phoenix of His Age*, 53–54.

115. See Desiderius Erasmus, *Controversies: Spongia, Detectio Praestigiarum, Epistola Contra Pseudevangelicos, Epistola ad Fratres Inferioris Germaniae, Admonitio Adversus Mendacium, Purgatio Adversus Epistolam Lutheri*, ed. James D. Tracy and Manfred Hoffmann, CWE 78 (Toronto: University of Toronto Press, 2011).

116. CWE 84:277.

117. See Rummel, *Erasmus and His Catholic Critics*, 2:111–13.

118. LB 8 contains Erasmus's translations of Chrysostom (col. 1–326), Athanasius (col. 327–424), and Basil (col. 483–552).

119. Backus, "Erasmus and the Antitrinitarians," 66.

dam. He did so by setting the church's scriptural arguments against Arius on a much firmer historical foundation, and by exposing as Arian certain writings, such as *Anonymous on Job* and the *Incomplete Commentary on Matthew*, that had previously passed unnoticed as Catholic works. Erasmus's arguments are still effective today.

"Concerning Origen's Method of Teaching and Speaking"

The final section in the prefatory material of Erasmus's edition of Origen is entitled *De ratione docendi et phrasi Origenis*. Its theme is Origen's outstanding abilities as a preacher of the Word of God. In Erasmus's judgment, Origen was a model homilist and he gave Origen the first place in this regard in his *Ecclesiastes* (1535).[120] Erasmus introduces Origen with an adaptation of Horace's famous lines in praise of the eloquence of the Greeks, substituting "the Spirit" for Horace's "Muse," and "Christ" for "praise." Horace had written: "To the Greeks the Muse gave genius, to the Greeks the Muse gave the ability to speak with a well-turned phrase, desirous of nothing but praise."[121] Erasmus adapts this to Origen as: "To Origen the Spirit gave genius, to Origen He gave the ability to speak with a well-turned phrase, desirous of nothing but Christ."

Erasmus has imitated Jerome in this passage. In Jerome's *Commentary on Ezekiel*, book 14 (preface), Jerome compares Ezekiel's temple with the labyrinth of Crete, citing Virgil, *Aeneid* 6:29–30. Omitting at the beginning of the line the reference to Daedalus, the designer of the labyrinth, who gave a ball of thread to Ariadne to assist Theseus in finding his way out of the labyrinth, Jerome substitutes Christ. At the end of the line, in place of "ball of thread," Jerome substitutes the Holy Spirit.[122]

Erasmus commends in Origen the absence of contrived effects, of artificial rhetoric, and of formalism. He notices with admiration Origen's evident concern for the idea alone and his clarity of diction—a clarity that applies even in obscure matters! Erasmus considers meritorious the absence of numbers and subclauses in Origen's sermons. He contrasts Origen's simplic-

---

120. LB 5:1029.
121. Ars Poet 323–24.
122. The passage in Jerome reads: "[Christ] ... has himself unraveled the deceitful windings of the house, guiding the blind steps by the Holy Spirit." See my new translation of Jerome's *Commentary on Ezekiel* (forthcoming from Paulist Press).

ity with the grandiloquence and affectation of many of the Latin Fathers. He praises the natural way in which scriptural quotations are introduced, sometimes by simple allusion, and contrasts this with the style of some of the scholastics, who cite Aristotle every third sentence but never cite scripture, and when they do, they do not do it successfully. Erasmus also admires the liveliness and vigor of Origen's diction as well as the intimacy, moderation, and gentleness of his homilies. In his previous essay on Origen's education, Erasmus had observed that Origen's homilies were more like intimate conversations with the people than the thunderbolts of a censorious preacher.

Godin has analyzed Erasmus's essay and has shown remarkable resemblances between the picture Erasmus paints of Origen and his depiction of Jean Vitrier in his epistle 1211 to Jonas.[123] Both men, according to Erasmus, were in possession of an extraordinary memory. Neither of them misused the homily to demonstrate his own knowledge by means of innumerable citations, but rather allowed the scriptures to speak without interruption. Both Vitrier and Origen preached with a spirit of mercy and did not revile their audiences like censorious judges of morals. Both were characterized by Christian moderation and were estranged from insincere passion. Both preferred frequency to length in their preaching. Finally, of both men Erasmus makes the statement: "He loved what he was speaking about" (*Amabat, quod [quae] loquebatur*); that is, they both loved Christ, the divine Word. Godin has drawn the conclusion that Erasmus has melted Origen into the form of the Franciscan warden Vitrier. In Vitrier Erasmus saw *Origenes redivivus*, Origen come to life again. There are also noteworthy parallels between Erasmus's description of Origen here and his picture of John Chrysostom, as Erasmus depicts the latter in epistle 1800 (written in 1527), his dedicatory epistle to some of Chrysostom's writings. Moreover he describes Augustine similarly in epistle 2157.[124]

Erasmus seems to regard Origen's epoch as a sort of Golden Age in that the people heard the scriptures proclaimed in their original language (Greek). Back then, Erasmus says, even weavers "had the sacred codices at home and held them in their hands." This sentence is reminiscent of Erasmus's words in the *Paraclesis*, where he expressed the wish that the scriptures be translated into vernacular languages so that they could be read and understood by everyone. "Christ wishes his mysteries published as openly as possible. I would that even the lowliest women read the Gospels and the

---

123. Godin, *Erasme lecteur d'Origène*, 667–74.
124. CWE 15.

Pauline Epistles.... Would that, as a result, the farmer sing some portion of them at the plow, the weaver hum some parts of them to the movement of his shuttle, the traveler lighten the weariness of the journey with stories from this source."[125] The implication seems to be that in respect to knowledge of the original languages of scripture and to the individual possession of the scriptures in the vernacular tongue, Origen's epoch was idyllic. In the sixteenth century Erasmus was probably the greatest Catholic advocate for the use of vernacular translations of scripture. His views were represented and debated at the Council of Trent, but ultimately defeated.[126]

In his description of Origen's spiritual exegesis, Erasmus displays a profound and accurate understanding of Origen's hermeneutical principles. Erasmus says that Origen first explains the history "very clearly and briefly." Next, he incites the hearer to discover the more hidden allegory. Lastly he treats moral topics. Erasmus points out that Origen's movement toward the deeper allegorical meaning is inspired principally by the exegetical method of the apostle Paul (cf. Gal 4:21–31; 1 Cor 10:1–11) and not by Hellenistic or Jewish methods of interpretation or by arbitrary choice. Erasmus contrasts Origen's allegories specifically with those found in the philosophers, the Jewish Talmud and the Kabbalah of the Hebrews. The difference is that Origen's are rooted in the scriptures themselves, by comparing scripture with scripture. His homilies are lively and avoid tedium by their brevity.

A remarkable commentary on Erasmus's concluding words in this essay is found in a letter to Erasmus from his close friend, John Colet, in epistle 593 (June 1517).[127] Colet reports that he has recently been learning Greek himself, inspired by the publication of Erasmus's Greek-Latin edition of the New Testament. He expresses regret that Erasmus had sent a copy of Reuchlin's *De arte caballista* to John Fisher but not to himself. Colet admits that he is in any case ignorant of this recondite subject which aims to show the mysteries of the Hebrew language. The letter concludes with Colet's confession as to where he believes the heart of theological studies lies:

My dear Erasmus, of books and knowledge there is no end. Nothing can be better, in view of this brief life of ours, than that we should live a holy and pure life and use our best endeavors every day to become pure and enlightened and perfected. These things are promised us by Reuchlin's Pythagorical and Cabalistic philosophy; but in my opinion we shall achieve them in no way but this, by the fervent love and imita-

---

125. Translated in Olin, *Christian Humanism*, 101.
126. See McNally, "The Council of Trent and Vernacular Bibles."
127. CWE 4.

tion of Jesus.[128] Let us therefore leave all these complications behind us, and take the short road to the truth. I mean to do this as far as in me lies.[129]

I have wondered if Erasmus may have had Colet's thought in the back of his mind when he describes Origen's expositions of scripture, which are not drawn from the Talmud or Kabbalah of the Hebrews but from the Bible itself. In Erasmus's judgment, for all his great learning, Origen was above all a man who had taken the short road to the truth and had attained to the spiritual ideals articulated here by John Colet, namely to a holy and pure life. Origen's homilies are really familiar conversations with people whom he longs to see fervently loving and imitating Jesus, and through grace transformed into the image of Christ, along with himself.

---

128. John Reuchlin (1455–1522) of Pfortzheim was the champion of Hebrew learning of his day.

129. CWE 4, ep. 593.

ERASMUS'S PREFACES

Desiderius Erasmus of Rotterdam, *Concerning the life, style of speaking, teaching method and writings of Origen, with assessments of individual works.*

A Summary of the Life of Origen Adamantius

Origen had two names, also being called Adamantius,[1] an epithet apparently attributed to him by the literary sources not because his character suggested it—as Basil[2] was called "the Great" on account of the constancy of his genius, John of Constantinople[3] was called "Chrysostom" [golden mouth] on account of his charming eloquence, and Gregory Nazianzenus[4] earned the

---

This chapter consists of the prefaces to Erasmus's edition of Origen (1536) (LB 8:425–40).

1. Cf. Eusebius, HE 6.14.10; Jerome, Ep 33.3; Jerome, De viris illustribus 54.1. The Greek *adamantios* means "man of *adamas*, that is steel or diamond or some other material that cannot be 'tamed' (alpha privative plus *damazein*), to tame." Cf. Crouzel, *Origen*, 51. Originally this name probably referred to Origen's great capacity for work or to his spiritual strength.

2. Basil the Great (330–79) was one of the Cappadocian Fathers, and the older brother of Gregory of Nyssa. With Gregory Nazianzen, Basil published the *Philocalia*, an anthology of Origen's writings. He defended Nicene orthodoxy. Erasmus published an edition of Basil's writings in 1532. See den Boeft, "Erasmus and the Church Fathers," 566–67.

3. John Chrysostom (345?–407), following a brilliant preaching career as priest in the church of Antioch, where he stirred the crowds with his eloquence, became bishop of Constantinople in 398 and remained until his deposition in 404. His name means "golden-mouth." He was one of Erasmus's favorites among the Greek Fathers. Erasmus began publishing translations of Chrysostom's writings in 1525. See den Boeft, "Erasmus and the Church Fathers," 563–64; Lackner, "Erasmus von Rotterdam als Editor und Übersetzer des Johannes Chrysostomos."

4. Gregory Nazianzen (330–90) was a close friend of Basil the Great and Gregory of Nyssa, the other Cappadocian Fathers. He assisted Basil in the publication of the *Philocalia*, an anthology

nickname "the Theologian" on account of his lofty theological treatises—but because it had already been applied to him at the very beginning of his life.[5] And indeed, in holy scripture it is not infrequent that the same man is called by several names.[6] But if names are not bestowed on great men by chance but contain through divine providence prophetic forebodings of future things, both names[7] are marvelously suited to this outstanding doctor of the church. In fact to the Greeks *Origenes* signifies "mountain-born,"[8] if the first vowel is long, as it is in Ὠρείθυια, a girl who doubtless was named from the fact that she carried out her nefarious rites in the mountains.[9] Right from childhood, Origen thought nothing lowly but directed his attention to the perfection of the gospel, which the Lord taught while sitting on the mountain,[10] and to the sublime mysteries of the scriptures. When he explains holy scripture he does not crawl on the ground or settle for the earthly sense of the letter, but through allegories raises the hearer to the things above[11] and nearer to

---

of Origen's writings. Gregory wrote famous orations, some of which were translated by Rufinus of Aquileia. Jerome had met him in Constantinople and was inspired by his moderate devotion to Origen to translate a series of Origen's homilies. In 1531, Erasmus published a posthumous edition of Willibald Pirckheimer's translation of thirty of Gregory's orations. It was dedicated to Duke George of Saxony and contains a eulogy of Willibald Pirckheimer (d. 1530), Erasmus's long time humanist friend. See den Boeft, "Erasmus and the Church Fathers," 566.

5. Erasmus reproduces the view of Eusebius, HE 6.14.10. Jerome says that the name Adamantius signifies Origen's unwearied industry in producing innumerable books (Ep 43.1); cf. his Ep 33.3.

6. Cf. Gn 17:5, 17:15, 35:10; 2 Sm 12:25; 2 Kgs 25:7, 25:27; 2 Kgs 15:1–7; Mk 3:16–17. Origen himself discusses name changes in scripture in the preface of his *Commentary on the Epistle to the Romans*. Jerome mimics Origen's discussion in *Commentary on Philemon* 1–3.

7. That is, Origen and Adamantius.

8. In Greek "mountain-born" would be derived from ὄρος (mountain) and γένος (offspring, child, stock). Crouzel, *Origen*, 4n11, thinks that Origen's name derives from the Egyptian god Horus (son of Isis and Osiris) and means "offspring of Horus." It is a matter of debate whether this name provides evidence that Origen's parents were still pagans at the time of his birth, since there is no shortage of Christians in the first centuries who, though born Christians, had names derived from pagan deities.

9. According to legend, Oreithyuia, daughter of the Athenian king Erechtheus, was abducted by Boreas, the North Wind, while she was playing and dancing with Nymphs along the banks of the Ilisus River. Through the forced marriage she became the mother of the flying heroes Calais and Zetes. Cf. Apollonius Rhodius, *Argonautika* 1.211–18; Ovid, *Metamorphoses* 6.683. In Plato, *Phaedrus* 229cd, Socrates suggests a rationalization of the story, that a gust of the North Wind blew her over the rocks where she was playing with Pharmaceia. Erasmus seems to have made up the etymology of her name as if it came from ὄρειος (from the mountains) and θύω (to celebrate sacred rites).

10. Cf. Mt 5:1.

11. Cf. Col 3:1.

heaven.[12] Adamant, on the other hand, became proverbial for "invincible" because, though it is perfectly transparent, it yields not even to hard steel, nor to hammer-blows. But Origen's frame of mind was more than adamantine. Neither the harshness of life nor perpetual labors, nor hard poverty, nor the malice of his rivals, nor the fear of punishments, nor any form of death could distract him in the least from his holy purpose.

Nothing is known for certain about Origen's native country except that it is likely that he was an Alexandrian because his father was in prison there, and when his father's martyrdom had taken place, he left behind wife and children in the same place.[13] Now it is of some importance where you are born; but it is of greater importance of whom you are born; of greatest importance indeed is by whom you are educated from infancy. But this Origen had Christian ancestors all the way from his grandparents and great-great-great grandparents,[14] although the impious Porphyry[15] reports that he was descended from pagans.[16] His father was Leonidas,[17] a man as pious as he

---

12. Erasmus associates Origen's name with the mountain on which Jesus preached the Sermon on the Mount (cf. Mt 5–7).

13. Cf. Eusebius, HE 6.2.12. Epiphanius, Panarion 64.1.2 says that Origen was a native Egyptian. A. Rousselle, "The Persecution of the Christians at Alexandria in the 3rd Century," Revue historique de Droit français et étranger" 2 (1974): 222–51, gives reasons for thinking that Origen's mother was a native Egyptian and thus not of his Roman father's social class, which would help explain why Origen was able to carry on intensive catechizing activity during the persecution at Alexandria without much harassment. See also R. Heine, Origen: Scholarship in the Service of the Church (Oxford: Oxford University Press, 2010).

14. Erasmus's phrase "usque ab avis et atavis," which skips two generations of ancestors, seems to be an echo of Virgil, Aeneid 7.56, where Turnus is described as "avis atavisque potens." Both Virgil and Erasmus wish to emphasize a long line of ancestry.

15. Porphyry (232–305) was a Neoplatonist philosopher and pupil and biographer of Plotinus. He opposed Christianity in his work Against the Christians (now lost), which was refuted by Eusebius of Caesarea and Apollinaris of Laodicea. Jerome was familiar with the latter authors and refers to the "blasphemies of Porphyry" frequently. Eusebius quotes passages from Porphyry's work that concern Origen in HE 6.19.4–8.

16. Cf. Eusebius, HE 6.19.7.

17. Cf. ibid., 6.1.1. Technically, his name was Leonides, an Ionic form, not Leonidas, which was a Doric form and is more frequently used in literature because of its association with the famous Spartan general Leonidas. Eusebius reports that Leonides was "said to be Origen's father." Nautin took this as evidence that Eusebius did not know the name of Origen's father and arbitrarily assigned to Origen a well-known Alexandrian martyr for a father. More probable is the view that Leonides owed his fame to being the father of Origen. He was among the martyrs of Septimius Severus's persecution and was beheaded, which suggests that he was a Roman citizen. Father of seven sons, of whom Origen was the oldest, his martyrdom suggests that he was a prominent member of the church in Alexandria. Origen refers to his father's martyrdom in Homilies on Ezekiel 4.8.

was learned,[18] who, while the emperor Severus[19] was raging cruelly against those who professed the Christian name, was put to death after imprisonment and torture and obtained the crown of martyrdom. The young Origen was left behind with six brothers, no doubt in utter poverty. For the imperial treasury seized his father's otherwise sufficiently abundant resources. Some report that this Leonidas was a bishop, but do not add where he was a bishop. According to Suidas[20] there are two anonymous persons who wrote a summary of Origen's life; the first of them generally agrees with the things that Eusebius reports in the sixth book of his *Ecclesiastical History*, and Jerome in his *Catalogue of Illustrious Writers* [54]. The second mixes in some nonsense as if drawn from hearsay, scarcely fair, it seems, to Origen. He reports that Leonidas was a bishop, a fact whose truth or falsity we leave undecided. In any case, this Leonidas, a prudent and perceptive man, detected in the boy a natural capacity for divine things and the seeds of perfect virtue. And for that reason he sometimes used to tenderly kiss the naked chest of the sleeping child, as a treasure chest and workshop of the worshipful Spirit.[21]

But what we admire in men advanced in age and trained in the philosophy of piety[22] is what the mere youth displayed on his own and without being motivated by any kind of encouragement. For he burned with such great longing for martyrdom that he energetically strove to be his father's companion or precursor in that department of praise.[23] And he would actually have preceded him, if his mother had not taken away all his clothes secretly during the night, having a premonition that he wanted to run ahead at daybreak to the contests where many were being slaughtered.[24] Thus [LB 8:426] where

---

18. Erasmus describes Cyprian (read Rufinus) this way in his *Explanation of the Creed* (CWE 70:263).

19. Cf. Eusebius, HE 6.2.2. Lucius Septimius Severus (193–211) was the founder of the dynasty of the Severi that ruled in succession to the Antonines. In 202 Severus initiated the persecution against Christians in Alexandria during which Origen's father was killed and Clement of Alexandria took flight.

20. Suidas or Sudas (PG 117:1193–1424) refers to an anonymous late tenth-century Byzantine Greek work, an encyclopedic lexicographical compilation consisting of some thirty thousand headings. Under numerous headings it touches on problems of secular and sacred history and describes writers of classical and Christian antiquity. Erasmus is rightly distrustful of the work's reliability respecting Origen and Leonidas.

21. Cf. Eusebius, HE 6.2. Erasmus reports that his priest friend Jean Vitrier also believed that the Holy Spirit resided in Origen's heart. Cf. CWE 8, ep. 1211.

22. For the meaning of "philosophy of piety," see the discussion in chapter 3.

23. Cf. Eusebius, HE 6.2.3–5.

24. Cf. ibid., 6.2.5, and the more detailed account in Rufinus's Latin translation of Eusebius.

the fear of death had failed, modesty prevailed, in keeping the candidate for martyrdom[25] at home. I am not discussing for the time being whether such darting ahead is praiseworthy.[26] For now we are commending only his natural inclinations. Why, while his father was still in chains, he even urged him by letter to persevere in his most noble purpose, adding: "See to it, Father, that you act no differently for my sake."[27] And yet, children customarily call their parents back from a resolution like this, with tears, prayers, coaxing, and embraces. But in this boy piety conquered piety,[28] and religious ardor overcame natural affection; the strength of faith shook off the weakness of the flesh. Consequently, by no means an idle spectator, by his presence and his words he also regularly gave encouragement to others who were struggling in the contest or at risk before judges—to anyone he could.[29] He also rescued a number from the squalor of prison, fearing nothing for himself. To some he was a promoter of glory, to others a man of compassion.[30]

In a word, that youth so conducted himself as an elder that he seemed to be striving for and inviting his own death for the sake of Christ. Nor did he act any differently as he grew older, and he was frequently assailed by the treacheries of the ungodly, but the providence of God most high wanted that chosen instrument preserved to the fullest advantage of the Catholic church.[31] Indeed, even in his books you can sense a certain enthusiasm whenever an opportunity arises to speak about martyrdom.

And so the boy, now sixteen years old,[32] bereft of his father, as has been

---

25. In *CWE* 12, ep. 1738, the dedicatory epistle to his edition of Irenaeus, Erasmus also calls Irenaeus a "candidate for martyrdom."

26. Though the youthful Origen seemed to invite martyrdom in Alexandria, Origen expressed disapproval of such "darting ahead" in his *Commentary on John* 28.23, where he not only condemned any courting of martyrdom, but even makes it a Christian duty to avoid confrontation with authorities, if this can be done without committing apostasy. He recommends the policy of flight (cf. Mt 10:23) as a way of manifesting Christian charity to the enemies of the faith, for it saves them from committing a crime. Origen's mature position is moderate in comparison with that of the schismatic Tertullian, who in his *De Fuga* (written when he was a Montanist) condemned any kind of flight from persecution.

27. Cf. Eusebius, HE 6.2.6. Both the Greek Eusebius and Rufinus in his Latin translation use the plural: "for our sake." Origen's meaning is that his father must not commit apostasy in order to be released from prison for the sake of his family.

28. *Pietas vicit pietatem*, i.e., devotion to God conquered filial duty.

29. Cf. Eusebius, HE 6.3.3–4.

30. Rufinus's version of the events narrated in Eusebius, HE 6.3.4 is much fuller than Eusebius's and describes in greater detail the help Origen gave to the martyrs of Alexandria.

31. Cf. Acts 9:15; Eusebius, HE 6.4.3.

32. Literally "in his seventeenth year."

said, and left with a widowed mother and five[33] small brothers, did not turn to begging, in which some think a great part of holiness consists. Instead, by following the advice and also the example of St. Paul, he earned a living for himself by his own labor, so as not to be a burden to anyone, and he became a professional teacher of literature.[34] If anyone should say that this was undignified, more undignified still was the great Paul's sewing the skins of goats among the Corinthians for use in tent making.[35] Again, if anyone says that teaching literature has nothing remarkable about it, since today the colleges of the scholastics are overflowing with youths who teach literature, he should know that formerly it was a mature and difficult business. For not only was the teacher expected to explain declensions, conjugations, and constructions, but in addition to elegance of speech, in addition to the reading of very many authors, in addition to expertise in antiquity and in all the histories, knowledge of poetry, rhetoric, dialectic, arithmetic, geography, and music was required.[36] While still a mere boy Origen had thoroughly learned all these disciplines with astonishing intellectual adroitness. You would turn out three doctors of law with less trouble than one teacher of literature, of the sort that Aristarchus[37] was among the Greeks, and Servius[38] and Donatus[39] among the Latins. Nor did Origen teach privately in some obscure corner, but in the most renowned city of Alexandria, and that publicly, already at that time preparing himself for the office of bishop. In fact, once upon a time it was part of the responsibility of bishops to see to it that young children were educated in literature and the arts.

33. Both Eusebius, HE 6.2.12, and Jerome, De viris illustribus 54.1, report that Origen had six brothers.

34. Cf. Eusebius, HE 6.2.12–15.   35. Cf. Acts 18:3; 1 Cor 9:6, 9:15.

36. Erasmus may be thinking of Origen's own description of the diversity of educational tasks assumed by the teacher of literature in Homilies on Judges 6.2. Cf. Godin, Erasme lecteur d'Origène, 642n42.

37. Aristarchus of Samothrace (216–144 BC) belonged to the school of Aristophanes of Byzantium at Alexandria. He was tutor of Ptolemy VII and succeeded Apollonius as head of the Library of Alexandria. His work covered a wide range of grammatical, etymological, orthographical, literary, and textual criticism. He was the first scholar to write numerous commentaries and the first to write about prose authors. He published critical recensions of and commentaries on Homer, Hesiod, Archilocus, Alcaeus, Anacreon, and Pindar.

38. Servius (fourth century AD) was a grammarian and commentator, the author of a celebrated commentary on Virgil, based on an earlier work (now lost) of Aelius Donatus. He was one of the participants in Macrobius's dialogue, Saturnalia.

39. Aelius Donatus (fourth century AD) was the teacher of Jerome in Rome and the most celebrated Latin grammarian of his day. His two treatises on Latin grammar dominated European learning until the twelfth century. He also wrote commentaries on Terence and Virgil.

And meanwhile the noble-minded young man in the guise of a schoolmaster rehearsed his role as a catechist, in passing sowing seeds as it were of the Christian religion in the minds of his hearers. For when all of the other catechists had run away out of fear of persecutions, a certain number of pagans approached Origen, desiring to be instructed in the rudiments of Christian philosophy.[40] He not only taught them the first principles of gospel teaching, but also raised many up to the pinnacle of perfect piety.[41] From this number Plutarch attained the crown of martyrdom.[42] Heraclas,[43] the brother of Plutarch, was admitted to the government of the church of Alexandria after Demetrius,[44] on account of the admirable sanctity of his life.[45] Serenus,[46] while still a catechumen,[47] was slain for the name of Christ. Heraclides[48] likewise merited the glory of martyrdom, which also Hero obtained while still a neophyte.[49] A second Serenus was put to death after dreadful tortures [LB 8:427] bravely endured for Christ's sake.[50] For the sake of brevity I shall say nothing of the rest, among whom was Ambrose,[51] whom he

---

40. Cf. Jerome, De viris illustribus 54.2.

41. This sentence reflects an addition by Rufinus to the text of Eusebius HE 6.3.1 (cf. Eusebius, GCS 2.2, part 2, 525).

42. Cf. Eusebius, HE 6.3.2; 6.4.1. This Plutarch (not the Roman historian and author of Plutarch's Lives), the brother of Heraclas, was converted by Origen and martyred at the beginning of the third century.

43. Cf. ibid., 6.3.2. Heraclas, brother of Plutarch, attended the classes of Ammonius Saccas for five years before Origen began to do so. He was converted by Origen and was closely associated with him in the catechetical school of Alexandria and succeeded him as head when Origen left Alexandria. He later succeeded Demetrius as bishop of Alexandria. Julius Africanus attests to Heraclas's reputation as an intellectual. When he succeeded Demetrius as bishop of Alexandria, Heraclas maintained the adversarial standpoint taken against Origen.

44. Cf. ibid. Demetrius was bishop of Alexandria (189–231/32). He appointed Origen head of the catechetical school in Alexandria in 203.

45. Cf. Eusebius, HE 6.3.2; 6.26.1.

46. Cf. ibid., 6.4.2–3. Serenus is the name of two of Origen's pupils in Alexandria, both of whom were martyred at the beginning of the third century.

47. Rufinus alone in his translation of Eusebius tells us that this Serenus was martyred while still a catechumen.

48. Cf. Eusebius, HE 6.4.3. Heraclides was a pupil of Origen's at the catechetical school in Alexandria who was martyred while still a catechumen.

49. Cf. ibid. Hero was a pupil of Origen's who was martyred just after his baptism.

50. Literally "had his head wreathed" [with the crown of martyrdom]. Erasmus's phrasing reflects Rufinus's version of Eusebius. Cf. Eusebius, HE 6.4.3.

51. Ambrose of Alexandria (d. 250)—not to be confused with Ambrose of Milan (340–97) or with Ambrosiaster, the commentator on Paul of the late fourth century—was a rich and cultured man of noble birth who was converted by Origen from the Valentinian sect and became

brought back to the light of Catholic doctrine from the Valentinian heresy.[52] And further, for the moment I will leave unmentioned the women who exhibited an invincible spirit on behalf of the Christian religion, among whom Potamiena outshone the rest.[53] In this way the beloved[54] Adamantius fathered many adamant ones for the church, all the while chastening his body and subjecting it to slavery, lest perhaps while preaching to others, he himself should be rejected.[55] For he hardened his flesh to the point of total endurance by means of vigils, fasts, sleeping on the hard ground, nakedness, and labors.[56] By this wonderful purity of life and by continual services toward everyone and especially to those whose lives were at risk during the brutal persecutions, although he himself despised glory no less than money, he still created for himself a name, both famous and beloved, not only among Christians but also among pagans.[57] For outstanding virtue seizes even the impious with admiration and love of itself, and so it came about that very many undertook to imitate Origen.

Demetrius, the bishop of his city, weighed this carefully and assigned to the now eighteen-year-old young man a difficult and obviously mature duty, namely that of catechist.[58] In Alexandria, after the apostles, Pantaenus[59] first

---

Origen's patron in his writing and research. He followed Origen to Caesarea, and according to Jerome, *De viris illustribus* 56, became a deacon there. Origen dedicated many works to him, including his *Exhortation to Martyrdom*. He wrote *Contra Celsum* at Ambrose's initiative. Ambrose died around 250, leaving a wife and children.

52. Cf. Eusebius, HE 6.18. Valentinus was an Egyptian heretic of the second century who spread Alexandrian Gnosticism in Rome from 135 to 160. He exerted a considerable influence and was refuted in turn by Justin, Tertullian, Irenaeus, Hippolytus, and Origen. In addition to his basic Gnostic teaching that repudiated the God of the Old Testament as an inferior being, he taught a sort of natural predestination according to which salvation or damnation is based on the good or evil nature one allegedly receives at birth.

53. Cf. Eusebius, HE 6.5.1. Potamiaena was a Christian virgin martyred at the beginning of the third century. Another account of her martyrdom is recorded in Palladius's *Lausiac History*, chap. 3.

54. *Adamandus*. Erasmus is playing on Origen's name Adamantius.

55. Cf. 1 Cor 9:27.

56. Cf. Eusebius, HE 6.3.9–12; 2 Cor 11:27.

57. Cf. Eusebius, HE 6.3.13.

58. Cf. ibid., 6.2.3; Jerome, *De viris illustribus* 54.2.

59. Cf. Eusebius HE 5.10–11, 6.6, 6:13–14, 6:19; Jerome, *De viris illustribus* 36. Pantaenus (d. ca. 200) was born in Sicily and was converted from paganism to Christianity. He undertook a missionary journey to India and from 180 settled in Alexandria, where he taught as the first head of the catechetical school. His pupils included Clement of Alexandria and Alexander of Jerusalem. Clement probably inherited from him the tendency of combining Christian beliefs with the best doctrines of the various philosophical schools.

carried out this task, second Clement,[60] and third Origen.[61] Origen flourished in this post for several years. They were called catechists because they transmitted the doctrines of the Christian religion orally to those seeking baptism. Their pupils were called catechumens, whom you could call hearers.[62] The titles continue in the church to the present day, but the practice is not the same, because we are baptized as babies.[63] Some traces of the original custom remain, however, when male and female sponsors are brought in, whom some call godmothers and godfathers.

Therefore, what Origen had at first done secretly and out of personal zeal, he now began to do publicly by appointment. Up to that time he had not completely despised the humanities but even took care to learn mathematics. But now, since he was totally on fire for interpreting the divine word, he neglected the school of literature and sold his secular books to a friend, but on this condition, that the friend should pay him four obols a day.[64] In this way he provided for his subsistence but not in such a way that he could be suspected of being held captive by a desire to accumulate money. Actually from this one can reckon how far he was from indulging in luxuries, since four obols supplied him his food and clothing.[65] And yet Paul teaches

---

60. Eusebius, HE 6.6 asserts that Origen studied under Clement of Alexandria (150?–220?) as does Jerome, *De viris illustribus* 38. Modern scholarship is less certain about this, but H. Chadwick says that it is beyond all doubt that Origen read Clement's books and "absorbed his point of view." *Origen: Contra Celsum*, trans. H. Chadwick (Cambridge: Cambridge University Press, 1953), ix.

61. Cf. Eusebius, HE 6.6.1.

62. Catechumen refers to a candidate for baptism. In Origen's day candidates required a sponsor and for up to three years received catechetical instruction through scriptural exegesis and the refutation of heresies. See Origen's description of catechesis *Contra Celsum* 3.51.

63. Erasmus is correct in surmising that the normal practice in Origen's day was to defer the baptism of children of Christian parents until they were old enough to choose to be baptized. While there is some evidence (including from Origen's writings) for the practice of infant baptism in the early third century, by the middle of the fourth century it seems that the baptism of babies was generally abandoned for several decades. Between 329 and 354 there are many examples even of saints who had one or both parents Christians, but were nevertheless not baptized until they were grown up, such as Gregory Nazianzen, Jerome, Rufinus, Basil the Great, Ambrose, and Augustine. For a helpful study of the ancient catechumenate, see Josef A. Jungmann, *The Early Liturgy to the Time of Gregory the Great*, trans. F. Brunner (London: Darton, Longman & Todd, 1959), chap. 7; E. Yarnold, SJ, *Cyril of Jerusalem* (New York: Routledge, 2000), 34–40.

64. Cf. Eusebius, HE 6.3.8. Rufinus made an addition to Eusebius, HE 6.3.9, reporting that the books Origen disposed of were pagan writings and that the purchaser was a believing friend. Rufinus adds the reason Origen preferred that the payment should take the form of a small daily sum was because he did not wish to have a large sum of money in cash at home.

65. Cf. Eusebius, HE 6.3.9. Six obols were the equivalent of one denarius, which represented a very low daily wage in first-century Palestine (cf. Mt 20:1–16). Origen's salary was thus below the subsistence level.

that catechists have a right to be supported by the generosity of the catechumens.[66] Nor was Origen unaware of this, but in this he was imitating Pauline arrogance, so to speak, for he was unwilling to make use of his own rights.[67] And, what is more, when gifts were offered to him by his friends on their own initiative, he repeatedly refused them in order to set forth his gospel "free of charge."[68] And he did this to such an extent that, if it is permissible to say so, in a way he surpassed the apostle's generosity. For Paul, although he took nothing from the greedy Corinthians and from those who were swollen with opulence, so as not to diminish his authority among them, nevertheless sometimes took advantage of the spontaneous kindness of others.[69]

Furthermore, just as Origen daily surpassed himself in the ministry of the word and other religious duties, so the fragrance of his good name was diffused more widely from day to day, so much so that he was forcibly ordained by Alexander, bishop of Jerusalem[70] and Theoctistus, bishop of Caesarea,[71] whose authority in Palestine at that time was preeminent.[72] For at that time the dignity of priests was great, although later they became worthless because of the multitude of them. Origen was appointed as a substitute in place of Clement in the following circumstances. The churches of Achaea were being troubled by different heresies. Origen, now middle-aged, was sent to settle them, and this was done with an ecclesiastical letter as his authorization.[73] But while he was heading for Athens through Palestine he was

66. Cf. 1 Cor 9:6; Gal 6:6; 1 Tm 5:17–18. 67. Cf. 1 Cor 9:15.
68. Cf. 1 Cor 9:18. 69. Cf. Phil 3:8–13.

70. Alexander of Jerusalem (d. 250) was already a bishop in Cappadocia when he visited Jerusalem and stayed on to become the first recorded example of a coadjutor bishop, who was translated from one see to another. He was a friend of Clement and Pantaenus, and of Origen, whom he, together with Theoctistus, bishop of Caesarea, ordained to the priesthood in 230. This act created an outcry against Origen from bishop Demetrius of Alexandria. Alexander defended Origen against the accusations of Demetrius and set up a Christian library at Jerusalem (then called Aelia), a library Eusebius used in compiling his HE. Alexander was imprisoned under Severus at the beginning of the third century and finally died in prison at Caesarea during the Decian persecution.

71. Cf. Eusebius, HE 6.19.17. Theoctistus of Caesarea was bishop of Palestinian Caesarea and a friend and protector of Origen. Together with Alexander, bishop of Jerusalem, he allowed Origen to preach while still a layman and answered the protests of Demetrius of Alexandria. Later he ordained Origen a priest.

72. Cf. ibid., 6.8.4.

73. Cf. ibid., 6.23.4; Jerome, *De viris illustribus* 54.3. Erasmus's version of this incident reflects some additions made by Rufinus. Eusebius speaks of a journey of Origen to Greece through Palestine, taken "because of an urgent necessity in Church matters." Eusebius does not say what the "urgent necessity" was, but Rufinus tells us that Origen went to Achaea to win over the heretics who lived there. Jerome, *De viris illustribus* 54.3, corroborates Rufinus's statement. It is also

detained by the above-mentioned bishops and was ordained a priest so that he could conduct Christ's business with greater authority.[74] He received this rank, therefore, with the highest approval of everyone, who proclaimed that this honor was far beneath the merit of a man whose virtues entitled him even to the highest priestly office.[75] This expression of the people's opinion vexed the mind of Demetrius not a little, who succumbed to human weakness[76] (for this worm [of envy] often [LB 8:428] puts even the minds of the perfect to the test) and who began to spread charges against Origen and to blacken his brilliant reputation in letters circulated throughout the world.[77] And because he had nothing to criticize in the most pure life of the man, he charged him with an error from his youth, namely that when he was a very young man, out of some kind of fervent zeal but not according to knowl-

---

confirmed by a letter of Origen which Rufinus himself elsewhere quotes (PG 17:625). Cf. Oulton, "Rufinus's Translation," 164.

74. Cf. Eusebius, HE 6.23.4. It is noteworthy that Erasmus, in CWE 2, ep. 145, explained to Anna van Borssele that a reason he himself needed to obtain a doctorate in theology was not so much to make himself more learned as to give his name *authority*. "One has to follow the present-day fashion, since nowadays not only the vulgar but even the most highly reputed scholars are unable to regard anyone as learned man unless he is styled *magister noster*—though Christ, the prince of theologians, forbids this [cf. Mt 23:10]. In antiquity, on the other hand, no man was reputed to be learned merely because he had purchased a doctorate, but those who in their published books showed clear proof of sound doctrine were alone entitled to the appellation of doctors. But, as I have remarked, it is no use putting on a good performance if everyone hisses it. I must therefore put on the lion's skin, in order that those who judge a man by his title and not by his books, which they cannot understand, may believe that I too have learnt my letters."

75. That is, a bishopric. This section reflects several important additions of Rufinus to the text of Eusebius. Eusebius had described Origen's ordination to the priesthood by the bishops of Jerusalem and Caesarea, Demetrius's jealousy at Origen's growing fame, his disclosure of Origen's youthful indiscretion, and his criticism of those bishops who ordained Origen. But Rufinus adds that the bishops who ordained Origen to the priesthood (Alexander of Jerusalem and Theoctistus of Caesarea) also deemed Origen worthy of the episcopate. Thus, according to Rufinus's translation of Eusebius, Demetrius's action against Origen was intended to prevent Origen's elevation to the office of bishop.

76. Cf. Eusebius, HE 6.8.4. This conflict seems to have occurred in 230. Eusebius represents the quarrel between Demetrius and Origen as concerned with disciplinary matters (Origen's castration and ordination by a foreign bishop). Jerome (Ep 33) blames the quarrel on Demetrius's envy. There is no doubt that these were contributing causes to the rupture between Demetrius and Origen. Yet Origen himself seems to have admitted that doctrinal motives also played a role. Cf. *Letters to Friends in Alexandria* (NPNF2 3:426) and Jerome, *Apology against Rufinus* 2.18 (NPNF2 4:511). See the very helpful article by Crouzel, "A Letter from Origen to 'Friends in Alexandria.'"

77. Cf. Eusebius, HE 6.8.4–5; Jerome, De viris illustribus 54.3. In CWE 8, ep. 1211, Erasmus depicts John Colet in similar terms, as the victim of envy and detraction of his ecclesiastical superiors.

edge,[78] he had castrated himself, in order that he might teach the gospel philosophy freely and without endangering his chastity.[79]

It is said that he had also observed certain other precepts of the gospel in their literal sense, such as the one about not having two tunics,[80] and the one about casting away anxiety for tomorrow.[81] Some report that he deprived himself of the natural inclination to reproduce by means of medicinal herbs.[82] I think this is false; the deed was done with a knife. I suspect that this is what St. Augustine reports from Epiphanius in the catalogue of heretics: "The Origenists," he says, "are named after a certain Origen, not after the one who is known to nearly everyone, but after some other one. Concerning him or his followers Epiphanius says: 'The Origenists, hailing from a certain Origen, are characterized by shameful conduct. They are practitioners of unspeakable things, handing over their own bodies to corruption.'"[83] Thus far Augustine, who perhaps did not correctly understand the Greek of Epiphanius.[84] For φθείρειν and φθορά are terms used by the Greeks as much about profaners as about lewd persons. Epiphanius, moreover, was a man of virginal modesty and did not dare to name the genitalia. And Augustine had not yet heard about Origen's castration.[85] But let the reader make his own decision about this matter.

78. Cf. Rom 10:2.
79. Cf. Mt 19:12; Eusebius, HE 6.8.1–2. Crouzel notes that later in life Origen unequivocally disavows self-mutilation in the strongest terms, though without alluding to his own case (*Origen*, 51). For when Origen comments on Mt 19:12 in his *Commentary on Matthew*, he condemns the literal interpretation of Jesus's words as irrational.
80. Cf. Mt 10:10. Eusebius, HE 6.3.10.
81. Cf. Mt 6:34. Eusebius, HE 6.3.10.
82. This was the view of Epiphanius, *Panarion* 64.3.12.
83. Cf. Augustine, *De haeresibus*, chaps. 42–43 (PL 42:33). Augustine draws on Epiphanius, Philaster, and his own personal knowledge.
84. Epiphanius (315–403) described all heresies in his *Panarion*, a work that is of little historical value except where he transmits information supplied by Irenaeus and Hippolytus and from his own time. When composing his *De haeresibus*, Augustine used a summary recapitulation of the *Panarion* entitled *Anacephaleosis*, which he believed was written by Epiphanius himself. Scholars are not certain whether this faithful epitome was in fact written by Epiphanius.
85. Epiphanius, *Panarion* 64.3.11–12 reports several traditions about Origen's self-inflicted act. "Some say he severed a nerve, others that he invented a drug and applied it to his genitals to dry them up, others ascribe other inventions to him." But Augustine does not discuss any of these matters in his abbreviated translation *De haeresibus* 42–43, which is Erasmus's source. Godin confesses that he is unable to follow Erasmus's train of thought and asks: "By rejecting this thesis [of a medicinal act] that more or less implies premeditation in a sinful act, did Erasmus wish to stress by way of contrast the impulsive and therefore excusable character of Origen's act?" (*Erasme lecteur d'Origène*, 651). It is not clear to me how the medicinal act could be deemed more blameworthy than castration.

To return to the course of the story, Origen wanted to keep this deed a secret, yet it had somehow come to the notice of Demetrius, who then, at least, admired such remarkable virtue of mind and strength of spirit in the young man.[86] He also praised him highly and congratulated the church. For sometimes, as in more spirited horses, so from the faults of young men one catches a glimpse of a splendid natural capacity for virtue. It was a mistake but it proceeded from the young man's passionate zeal for piety. In any case, what Demetrius had previously praised highly he later objected to as a fault.[87] This physical mutilation became an obstacle to Origen's elevation to the summit of the priesthood [that is, the office of bishop], who would not have been admitted even to the rank of priest, if this fault had not been hidden. And even today vigilance is exercised to prevent anyone from being ordained a priest who is mutilated in any part of his body, lest the church suffer scandal. Would that precautions were taken with equal enthusiasm to prevent a man from being admitted to this rank unless his mind is pure! A man who lacks the knowledge of sacred literature has a mind that has been disgracefully mutilated, and one who is led by no love of piety has a mind mutilated more disgracefully still. He who is physically one-eyed dishonors the church, and does he not dishonor it who is blind to the knowledge of gospel philosophy? He who is physically lame disgraces the church, and does he not disgrace it who is inwardly "lame in both feet" according to the words of the prophets, indeed, who leans entirely on the world, and is a stranger to Christ except in name?[88]

But I return to our eunuch. As envy became a burden, he yielded, admittedly, to the insolence of his rivals and left Alexandria,[89] and yet Adamantius was everywhere the same, shining everywhere, and preaching the Gospel with inexhaustible zeal.[90] He did not attach himself to a condemned

---

86. Cf. Eusebius, HE 6.8.3.   87. Cf. ibid., 6.8.3, 5.
88. Cf. 1 Kgs 18:21; 2 Sm 9:3, 9:13.

89. Erasmus follows Jerome, Ep 33 in attributing Origen's ecclesiastical difficulties to the envy of his superiors. According to Daniélou, Demetrius banished Origen from Alexandria because he insisted that Origen was an incompetent catechist (*Origen*, 23). The synod convoked by Demetrius did not, however, declare Origen's ordination invalid, nor was it ratified by the bishops of Palestine and Arabia. Jerome alone (Ep 33.4) says that Rome consented to this censure of Origen.

90. In CWE 8, ep. 1211, Erasmus describes Jean Vitrier in very similar terms, as one who in spite of unjust treatment from ecclesiastical superiors remained what he had always been, teaching, comforting, and encouraging. Godin reasonably speculates that in this sentence and the following, Erasmus is alluding autobiographically to his own departure from Basel to the Catholic city Freiburg in 1529, when Basel became Protestant (*Erasme lecteur d'Origène*, 653).

sect, as Tertullian[91] did, who from orthodoxy became a follower of the blasphemer Montanus,[92] and against his own convictions, called Montanus the "guide of all truth."[93] For I cannot be persuaded that Tertullian, a man of such keen judgment, so trained in sacred literature, could have believed that Montanus was the Holy Spirit whom Christ promised to the apostles.[94] Nor did Origen throw the whole world into confusion with a horrible schism, as did Arius. He did not even contend with his detractors in embittered writing, but he shut the mouths of his slanderers by doing good, which is by far the most beautiful kind of victory, according to the advice of St. Peter.[95]

Now, he taught chiefly in Caesarea of Palestine where he instructed very many distinguished men in sacred literature, above all Firmillianus, bishop of Caesarea in Cappadocia.[96] Firmillianus, along with all Cappadocia, had invited Origen, and kept him there a long time.[97] Afterward, setting out for Palestine under the pretext of visiting sacred places, he again presented himself to Ori-

---

91. Tertullian (160–225?) was the first great Latin theologian, a native of Carthage (North Africa) and according to Jerome (*De viris illustribus* 35) the son of a proconsular centurion. He grew up in a pagan family, but was converted to Christianity around 197, perhaps attracted by the example of the martyrs. He wrote very important apologies and a masterpiece, *Against Marcion*. He sharply criticized the laxity of the penitential discipline of the church and eventually joined the Montanist sect, attracted by its moral rigorism. He became the most important representative of second-generation Montanism. Beatus Rhenanus published the first edition of Tertullian's writings in 1521, an achievement that Erasmus enthusiastically praised.

92. Montanus (fl. 155–80) was the founder of a heretical charismatic movement in Phrygia which called itself "The New Prophecy" and claimed that God spoke to his church through ecstatic prophets and prophetesses, whose authority was to be heeded rather than that of the bishops. It spread rapidly throughout the Roman Empire through the activity of the shepherd Montanus and his prophetesses Priscilla and Maximilla. Many bishops in Asia Minor opposed the movement. Tertullian went over to Montanism in 207 mainly because of its strong ethical rigorism.

93. Tertullian suggests this of Montanus in *De corona* 4. According to Godin, Erasmus probably intends this statement as a criticism of the Protestant reformers, Luther above all, who claimed to have all certitude of possessing the Spirit in his scriptural interpretations (*Erasme lecteur d'Origène*, 654).

94. This refers to Montanus's claim to be the mouthpiece of the Holy Spirit and the incarnation of the Paraclete promised in Jn 14:26 and 16:7.

95. Cf. 1 Pt 2:12, 2:15.

96. Cf. Eusebius, HE 6.27.1, 7.14.1; Jerome, *De viris illustribus* 54.5. Firmilian was bishop of Caesarea in Cappadocia for more than thirty years (ca. 230–68). He welcomed Origen in 232 or 233 and allowed him to preach in his churches. He later supported Cyprian of Carthage against Pope Stephen of Rome on the necessity of rebaptizing heretics, a view that was condemned at the Council of Arles in 314. Firmilian's only extant writing is a letter to Cyprian, preserved in Cyprian's Ep 75.

97. Cf. Eusebius, HE 6.27.1; Jerome, *De viris illustribus* 54.5.

gen as his student for a long time. Origen also taught Theodorus,[98] who later obtained the office of bishop, and Gregory, whom they call Thaumaturgus,[99] I think because he was famous for his miracles.[100] Likewise, he instructed Gregory's brother Athenodorus,[101] whom he led from worldly philosophy to the gospel [LB 8:429] philosophy, who also while still a young man was raised to the ecclesiastical governance. Origen was summoned to Antioch by Mammea,[102] the mother of Alexander Severus,[103] and she dismissed him honorably.[104] Jerome calls her a religious woman, he did not say "Christian."[105] Yet her son was Syrus, and he did very many things in his life not unworthy of a Christian man. Certainly Heliogabalus,[106] his father, was reproached for having Moses and a certain Christ in his household shrine.[107] Origen moreover

---

98. According to Eusebius, HE 6.30 and Jerome, De viris illustribus 65.1, this is the same person as Gregory Thaumaturgus. Nautin denies the identification of the two.

99. According to Eusebius, HE 6.30.1, Gregory Thaumaturgus (d. 270) was also called Theodore. He and his brother Athenodorus were born pagans in Neocaesarea in Pontus on the Black Sea, and studied rhetoric, before being converted to Christianity in Caesarea under Origen's influence. Both Gregory and Athenodorus went back to Pontus where Gregory became bishop of Neocaesarea and converted the pagan population. He composed a panegyric on Origen, which contains an account of Origen's gifts as a teacher. See Gregory's Address of Thanksgiving to Origen, trans. M. Slusser, FOTC 98 (Washington, D.C.: The Catholic University of America Press, 1998). Nautin rejected the traditional attribution of this writing to Gregory and assigns it to an unknown Theodore. The traditional identification is defended by Crouzel, Origen.

100. Eusebius attributes no miracles to Gregory (HE 6.30.1); however, Rufinus adds several stories of his miracles at HE 7.28.2. Cf. Humphries, "Rufinus's Eusebius," 160–61.

101. Cf. Eusebius, HE 6.30.1. Athenodorus, like his brother Gregory Thaumaturgus, studied rhetoric as a pagan, came to Caesarea in Palestine where he became a pupil of Origen, and returned to Pontus where he became a bishop. He participated in the second synod of Antioch (268) that condemned the teaching of Paul of Samosata.

102. Cf. Eusebius, HE 6.21.3–4. Julia Avita Mamaea was the mother of emperor Severus Alexander. Having heard of Origen's fame, she requested an interview with him in Antioch. The year of the interview is not certain. G. Williamson, Church History of Eusebius, 387–88, thinks it must have been in 231–33, not in 218 as is often supposed, when she was not yet the emperor's mother. Yet it is a commonplace to refer to historical personages by their subsequent titles, and so the earlier date cannot be excluded.

103. Cf. Eusebius, HE 6.21.3. Marcus Aurelius Severus Alexander was emperor from 222 to 235. Eusebius seems to have thought that he was a Christian; see HE 7.10.3.

104. Cf. Eusebius, HE 6.21.4.

105. Cf. Jerome, De viris illustribus 54.5.

106. Cf. Eusebius, HE 6.21.1. Heliogabalus was the name adopted by Aurelius Antoninus Marcus Elagabalus, born in 202 as Varius Avitus Bassianus. He ruled as emperor from 218 to 222 and regarded himself as the priest of the sun god, Elagabal, whose name he adopted. He was grandnephew of Julia Domna, the consort of emperor Septimus Severus.

107. Erasmus's source may be Severus Alexander, Historia Augusta, 4.29. It was actually He-

wrote a letter to Philip the emperor who was the first Christian among the rulers of Rome.[108] He wrote also to his mother.[109] He merely saw Rome,[110] which he calls "the great Church" in one of his letters.[111] That happened under the pontificate of Zephyrinus before he set out for Caesarea.[112]

And having just returned to Alexandria, he once again took Heraclas the presbyter as his partner in catechesis.[113] Jerome described this carefully, because some had spread it abroad that he had been expelled from his own church, that he fled first to Rome, then to Caesarea, when in fact he had never been expelled.[114] But after Demetrius manifested his hostility against him in his absence, he preferred to teach Christ in Palestine than to vie with a raging bishop in Alexandria.[115] Ambrose, whom, as I said, he recalled from the error of Marcion[116] to the purity of the Catholic faith, he regarded as a

---

liogabalus who prayed before the images of Orpheus, Apollonius of Tyana, and Jesus as his protective deities.

108. Cf. Eusebius, HE 6:34–36, 39. Julius Verus Philippus ("the Arabian") was emperor from 244 to 249. Eusebius seems to be correct in his belief that he was a Christian. He began his reign with the crime of collaborating in the death of his predecessor's (Gordian III) young son, but was subjected to penance by the bishop of Antioch, Babylas, which suggests that he was baptized. This public penance during an Easter vigil is attested by three independent witnesses: Eusebius, John Chrysostom, and the *Chronicon Paschale*. See H. Crouzel, "Le christianisme de l'empereur Philippe l'Arabe," *Gregorianum* 56 (1975): 545–50.

109. Eusebius states in HE 6.36.3 that Origen wrote to Philip and Philip's *wife*, Severa, not to Philip's *mother*.

110. According to Jerome, *De viris illustribus* 61, Hippolytus of Rome reports in his *Exhortation on the Praise of our Lord and Savior* that he is speaking in the church in the presence of Origen. Since Hippolytus was the first Christian writer to compose continuous commentaries on scripture, doubtless in that respect he provided a model for Origen. Erasmus's phrase "He merely saw Rome" seems to be an allusion to Ovid's comment in *Tristia* 4.10.50. After listing the famous Roman poets he venerated as gods and knew personally, including Macer, Propertius, Ponticus, Bassus, Tibulus, and Horace, he adds of Virgil, the most famous Latin poet of all: "Vergilium vidi tantum" ["I merely saw Virgil"]. Erasmus's imitation of Ovid may suggest that for him the Roman church occupies the highest rank.

111. Cf. Eusebius, HE 6.14.10.

112. Cf. ibid.; Jerome, *De viris illustribus* 54.4. Zephyrinus was bishop of Rome from 199 to 217.

113. Cf. Eusebius, HE 6.15.1; Jerome, *De viris illustribus* 54.4.

114. Jerome, *De viris illustribus* 54.   115. Cf. Jerome, *De viris illustribus* 54.3.

116. Earlier Erasmus reported the view of Eusebius, HE 6.18.1, that Ambrose was converted to orthodoxy from the heresy of *Valentinus*. Here he follows Jerome, *De viris illustribus* 56.1 who says that Ambrose had been a follower of *Marcion*. Marcion of Sinope in Pontus founded a quasi-Gnostic sect in Rome in the 140s. Scandalized by the problem of evil, he responded by thinking out a doctrinal system based on the irreconcilability of justice and grace, law and gospel, Judaism and Christianity, the God of the Old Testament and the Father of Jesus. He admitted two eternal and uncreated principles, a good God (the Father of Jesus) and a just but wicked god (the creator of the world and god

ἐργοδιώκτης, that is, a taskmaster.[117] Origen complains in a letter that he was pressured by him with such persistence that he was not given time to read or to revise what had been taken down by the stenographers.[118] The skill of stenographers consisted in taking down what was said in shorthand notes with such great rapidity that they could keep up not merely with the voice of a person dictating, but of a person speaking normally. This is why the Greeks call them "speed-writers." For there were also "fine-writers" who transcribed more fully things taken down in shorthand notes.[119] So Ambrose supplied the stenographers and the parchments, Origen the tongue.[120] Ambrose has been criticized by many because when dying he did not remember his friend Origen, who was old and poor.[121] From this it is clear that Origen had persevered in poverty to extreme old age, since it would not have been difficult for such a man to enrich himself if he had so desired. So great was Origen's modesty that only late in life did he allow what he was discussing to be written down.[122] So great was his zeal that he never took food without a reading,[123] for he considered it inappropriate that the inferior part of a man be refreshed, while the more excellent part is neglected. He lived on amidst his most holy labors until his sixty-ninth year.[124] He died in Tyre and was buried there.[125]

---

of the Jews). Marcion held docetic views of Christ's physical body. He repudiated the Old Testament in its entirety and taught his followers that the received form of the New Testament had been corrupted with interpolations by Judaizing Christians, whom he identifies as the Catholics of his day. He created his own New Testament canon, consisting of the Gospel of Luke and ten Pauline letters, which he edited to make these texts compatible with his own theology.

117. This is how Origen describes Ambrose in *Commentary on John* 5.1, borrowing the term from Ex 3:7. In *De viris illustribus* 61.3, Jerome attributes this term (which he evidently liked; cf. Ep 60 where he uses it of Nepotian) to a letter of Origen. Erasmus seems to be following Jerome.

118. Cf. Eusebius, HE 6.23.1–2.   119. Literally "calligraphers."

120. Rufinus's Latin account of the part played by Ambrose in supporting Origen's literary efforts is more elaborate than Eusebius's Greek original.

121. Jerome reports this criticism in *De viris illustribus* 56.6. In Ambrose's defense, one might suggest that all that this negligence proves is that Ambrose respected Origen's love for poverty.

122. Cf. Eusebius, HE 6.36.

123. This is reported by Jerome, Ep 43.1, who cites as the source of his information a letter of Ambrose to a friend in Athens. Godin, *Erasme lecteur d'Origène*, 659n112, is thus apparently mistaken when he claims that Erasmus has here projected onto Origen a customary table practice of John Colet reported in CWE 8, ep. 1211.

124. Cf. Eusebius, HE 7.1.1. Erasmus may have been sixty-nine years old himself when he wrote these words. For evidence that Erasmus was born in October 1466, see Vredeveld, "The Ages of Erasmus." On the other hand, A. C. F. Koch, *The Year of Erasmus' Birth and Other Contributions to the Chronology of His Life*, trans. E. Franco (Utrecht: Haentjins Dekker and Gumbert, 1969), argues for 1467 as the birth year.

125. Cf. Jerome, *De viris illustribus* 54.11; Ep 84.7. In the wall of the cathedral of Tyre, called

Concerning His Education and Written Works

There are those who report that Origen was self-taught.[126] I think that this is true insofar as he provided himself the greatest part of his learning. For the rest we read that he had studied philosophy for seven years with a certain Ammonius,[127] and while still a boy he used to pester his father with certain brief questions.[128] But since he was so eager to learn, there is no doubt that he strove to learn something whenever he could, and there were eminently learned men in Alexandria. But if Augustine attained such great erudition without the service of a teacher, what ought we to think concerning Origen's intellect, the like of which learned Greece, the mother of the most fortunate minds, has scarcely ever possessed?[129] Indeed, things are learned more easily and more profitably when they are understood right from an early age. No part of Origen's life was wasted with respect to his studies. St. Augustine was estranged from religion up to his thirty-sixth year,[130] and both as a catechumen and also after his baptism, he wasted some of his time in secular studies.[131] Ambrose, when he was an adult, was taken out of civil service and summoned at one and the same time to baptism and a bishopric. Both were compelled to learn by teaching.

Origen's natural talent was sufficient for learning everything thoroughly to the point that those who occupied themselves with nothing else in life oth-

---

the Cathedral of the Holy Sepulchre, Origen's name and epitaph, carved on a marble column and adorned with precious stones, could still be read as late as 1283, according to Crouzel, *Origen*, 35.

126. I have not found the source of Erasmus's statement. Diogenes Laertius attributes this adjective "self-taught" to Epicurus in *Vitae philosophorum*.

127. Cf. Eusebius, HE 6.19.6; Jerome, *De viris illustribus* 55. Ammonius Saccas (d. 242) was an Alexandrian philosopher, the teacher of Longinus and Plotinus, as well as Origen. He was brought up a Christian, according to Porphyry, but became a pagan. Eusebius and Jerome say that he remained a Christian until the end of his life. See M. Edwards, "Ammonius, Teacher of Origen," *Journal of Ecclesiastical History* 44 (1993): 169–81. I have not found the source of Erasmus's information that Origen studied *seven years* with Ammonius.

128. Cf. Eusebius, HE 6.2.9.

129. In his 1512 edition of Origen's writings, Jacques Merlin had extolled the good fortune of Greece in possessing such a great star as Origen.

130. Obviously Erasmus means that Augustine was estranged from the Christian religion and Christian writings, not religion in general. Augustine's mother Monica was a Christian and always hoped to attract him to her faith, which he dismissed as childish and intellectually unsatisfying. The *Confessions* reveal that Augustine was keenly interested in religion and spent some years on the fringes of Manicheism.

131. From his secular studies Augustine obtained a masterful knowledge of Latin rhetoric and a somewhat inadequate understanding of contemporary Platonism.

er than dialectic and other disciplines of this kind brought to him any complicated question they might have. And even famous philosophers, though they were estranged from Christ, frequently mentioned Origen honorably in their books, respectfully acknowledging him as teacher and master.[132] In any case, we would know for sure how many books he either dictated or wrote on sacred scripture, if the letter survived that Jerome, as he himself testifies, wrote to Paula, the mother of Eustochium, in which he reviewed all the monuments of Origenian genius[133] and compared him with Marcus Varro:[134] he too was in every respect a most learned man [LB 8:430] as well as a prolific writer.[135]

So great was the eagerness for blotting out Origen entirely that they did not even allow the titles of his works to survive. Now we may know only what was translated into Latin or quoted by the ancients. Perhaps it is better for us not to know the titles of his lost books. It keeps us from grieving too much. But whatever he left is divided up in a threefold classification,[136] since some works are called *Scholia*,[137] others *Homilies*,[138] and others *Tomes*.[139] In Latin you could call *Scholia* short leisure compositions. Whenever he lacked the

---

132. Cf. Eusebius, HE 6.19.1.

133. The original, like the English, contains a jingle: *Origenici ingenii*.

134. Jerome records a list of Origen's works in Ep 33 to Paula. However, those who copied the letters of Jerome did not transcribe more than the opening lines of this list. Thus in Erasmus's day, the list of Origen's books was not extant. In the mid-nineteenth century, the complete text of Jerome's letter was rediscovered by Sir Thomas Phillipps in a manuscript at Arras. Since then, it has appeared in the editions of Jerome's letters. Even so, the list of Origen's writings given by Jerome is not exhaustive.

135. Marcus Terentius Varro (116–27 BC) was known as Rome's greatest scholar. Cf. Jerome, Ep 33.1–2. Of his almost 500 books only 55 titles are known. He wrote on nearly every branch of inquiry: history, philosophy, music, medicine, architecture, literary history, religion, agriculture, and language. The achievements of the Augustans are scarcely conceivable without the foundation that Varro laid.

136. This threefold classification of Origen's writings seems to have been Jerome's idea. Cf. the preface to Jerome's translation of Origen's *Homilies on Ezekiel*, and Jerome's prologues to his commentaries *On Galatians*, *On Isaiah*, and *On Matthew*.

137. The *Scholia* or "selections" (*Excerpta*) are Origen's annotations on the books of Exodus, Leviticus, Numbers, Isaiah, Psalms 1–15, Ecclesiastes, and the Gospel of John. None of the *Scholia* have survived intact, though several fragments exist in the catena collections, patristic commentaries that were collected in antiquity. Rufinus integrated material from Origen's *Scholia* on Numbers into his translation of Origen's *Homilies on Numbers*.

138. Almost three hundred of Origen's homilies survive in both Greek and Latin translations. They constitute the oldest surviving collection of Christian sermons.

139. The "tomes" are also called "books" or "commentaries." Origen designed these as a more systematic and scientific analysis of specific books of scripture. Extant in large measure are those on John, Romans, Song of Songs, and Matthew. Fragments of others survive.

leisure to write a commentary proper, he usually dictated brief little annotations on the more obscure passages. The *Homilies* you could legitimately call "conversations": the man of matchless modesty assigned to the grand enterprise a familiar name. To teach people publicly is a difficult and, to be sure, a princely matter. But he moderates his speech in such a way that he seems to be having a conversation with the people. He did not write down these sermons himself, but allowed them to be taken down by stenographers, and yet they say that he did not permit this until he was sixty, as I said before.[140] He called the third class of works *Tomes* in Greek, which you could translate as "commentaries" or "books." Origen wrote them out himself, and since he wrote for the learned, he brought to light certain more hidden mysteries, unfurling all the sails of his genius, as Jerome says.[141]

Of the first class nothing remains, of the second a great deal survives, in the third there are the books of *On First Principles* and the *Commentary on the Gospel of Matthew*, although the ignorant have divided up this work into Homilies. In fact, there are some works that seem to belong to none of the three classes, such as his letters, and he wrote many of these to various people.[142] Nor do I know whether one may classify the five books of the *Stromata* as *Scholia*.[143] For in these he seems to mix together various things, from which comes their name, taken from embroidered rugs. He borrowed this title from Clement.[144] But in what class shall we put the *Hexapla* and *Tetrapla*? For when he had applied his mind to the writing of commentaries on the divine scriptures, he discovered in the very act of doing it that it could not be carried out as it ought without his acquiring expertise in Hebrew.[145] For from these sources the sacred books, particularly those of the Old Testament, first came down to us, and either disagreements among the translators, or the corrupt codices, or the obscure nature of the language forced him to return to them

---

140. Cf. Eusebius, HE 6.36.1.

141. Cf. Jerome's preface to his translation of Origen, *Homilies on Ezekiel*.

142. Only two of Origen's letters have survived intact, the letter to Gregory Thaumaturgus and to Julius Africanus. Eusebius (HE 6.36.3) testifies to having access to about one hundred of Origen's letters.

143. *Stromata* is no longer extant. It was a collection of higher level questions to pose and resolve for more advanced Christians. It was written before 231, and Eusebius had an autograph copy of it (HE 6.24.3). Jerome was probably referring to this work in Ep 70.4 where he said that Origen compared elements of Christian teaching with the doctrines of the various schools of philosophy. Jerome translates a lengthy excerpt from Origen's *Stromateis* in his own *Commentary on Galatians* 5.13.

144. Cf. Eusebius, HE 6.13.1.

145. Ibid., 6.16.1.

again and again. Lest our Adamantius should be maimed[146] in this connection, he endured the nuisance of learning a barbarous and foreign language contrary to the spirit of the age and to the habit of his people.[147]

Once he had learned Hebrew, he brought together into one book not only the Septuagint[148] but also the versions of others, namely the translations of Aquila of Pontus,[149] Theodotion,[150] and Symmachus.[151] The latter two men were Ebionites, and for this reason Jerome calls them "Judaizing heretics."[152] That sect maintained that Christ had been a mere man.[153] Their man Symmachus wrote a commentary on the Gospel of Matthew, attempting from that source to shore up his own impiety.[154] In addition to these, Origen, who thoroughly investigated everything, also added a fifth, sixth, and seventh version, and he arranged all of them in columns in such a way that each could be compared either with the others or with the Hebrew. He entitled this work *Exapla*. A second time he arranged separately the versions of Theodotion, Aquila, and Symmachus along with the Septuagint. Consequently, he calls this work the *Tetrapla* from the fourfold arrangement. Therefore, it seems that *Hexapla* should be read with the first vowel aspirated.[155] And yet the codices consistently have *Exapla* with smooth breathing on the

---

146. An allusion to Origen's self-mutilation?
147. Cf. Jerome, *De viris illustribus* 54.6.
148. The Septuagint was the Greek translation of the Hebrew Old Testament, produced in Alexandria, Egypt, beginning in the third century BC. This version was the Bible of the early church. In Origen's *Hexapla* the Septuagint occupied the fifth column.
149. Cf. Eusebius, HE 6.16.1. Aquila of Pontus was a Jewish translator active in the first quarter of the second century who produced a Greek version of the OT that was preserved in the third column of Origen's *Hexapla*. He reputedly was born a pagan, converted to Christianity, then to Judaism. His translation was noted for its extreme literalism.
150. Cf. Eusebius, HE 6.16.1. Theodotion was the author of a Greek version of the OT composed during the reign of Commodus (180–92). Irenaeus says he was a proselyte at Ephesus (*Adversus Haereses* 3.21.2). Jerome calls him an Ebionite (*De viris illustribus* 54). Epiphanius calls him a disciple of Marcion (*On Weights and Measures* 17). Theodotion's translation is essentially a revision of the Septuagint, harmonized with the Hebrew text. His version occupied the sixth column of Origen's *Hexapla*.
151. Cf. Eusebius, HE 6.16.1. Symmachus was the late-second century translator of the Greek version of the Hebrew Old Testament. Eusebius and Jerome considered him an Ebionite, but Epiphanius called him a Samaritan who went over to Judaism (*On Weights and Measures* 16). Symmachus's translation occupied the fourth column of Origen's *Hexapla*.
152. Cf. Jerome's preface to his *Commentary on Job*.
153. Cf. Eusebius, HE 6.17.1.
154. Cf. ibid.; Jerome, *De viris illustribus* 54.
155. That is, with rough breathing, so the word is pronounced *Hexapla*, not *Exapla*.

initial vowel, and that in my opinion is more appropriate. If you take Theodotion, Aquila, and Symmachus and add the Septuagint version to the fifth, sixth and seventh versions, there will be seven columns. In Greek *exaploo*[156] has the sense of *explano* in Latin: "I display" or "I make plain." And so, they were called *Exapla* not[157] because of the number of columns, but because something is displayed before our eyes, simply and without wrapping.

But now that we have briefly called to mind those writings that have not survived, I will set forth my opinion about those which have come down to us.[158] In that case, I request that the reader not immediately stir up a tragedy for me if I convey anything that disagrees with his taste and with the opinion that he has received. I will advance my opinion in public. Let it be taken into consideration before it is condemned. If upon examination it does not meet with satisfaction, the reader should allow my opinion to stand and be pleased with his own, and, in accordance with the advice of St. Paul, with friendship intact be content with his own judgment.[159]

Assessment of the *Homilies on Genesis*[160]

Rufinus, not Jerome, translated the *Homilies on Genesis*.[161] The preface has been curtailed, since neither Rufinus nor Jerome [LB 8:431] is accustomed to publish anything without a prologue. But Rufinus was burdened down by the deepest suspicion, namely that of being an Origenist. For under this des-

---

156. This Greek word, ἐξαπλόω with smooth breathing, means in the first instance "to unfold, stretch out, extend," and secondarily "to explain, express." Eusebius, HE 6.13.5, uses ἐξαπλόω to describe Origen's *Stromateis*, as a work where Origen "unfolds" much history. With rough breathing the word means "to multiply by six."

157. A reader of my manuscript has informed me that the lack of negation—"dicta sunt a numero columnarum"—in LB 8:430E is a mistake. The original printed version reads "dicta sunt non a numero columnarum." See *Origenis opera* (Basel: Froben, 1536), b1r.

158. Erasmus is here introducing his "assessments" of Origen's works. His words chiefly point forward to what he is about to say, but they also apply to his previously expressed opinions in the preface and dedications of individual works. Godin thinks that one cannot exclude from Erasmus's field of vision his fear of a future charge of "Origenism" (*Erasme lecteur d'Origène*, 604). He may be trying to disarm this charge in advance.

159. Cf. Rom 14:5. For a fuller discussion of this view, see Erasmus's *Adages* I, iii.7, *Quot homines, tot sententiae* where he quotes the same verse from Paul. It appears that in what follows Erasmus is chiefly registering his scholarly disagreements with his immediate editorial predecessors: the Aldine edition of Origen's works (Venice, 1503) and the edition of Jacques Merlin (Paris, 1512).

160. Origen wrote sixteen *Homilies on Genesis* which survive in a Latin translation by Rufinus. See the translation by R. Heine in *FOTC* 71 (Washington, D.C.: The Catholic University of America Press, 1981).

161. In the Merlin edition, these homilies were wrongly ascribed to Jerome.

ignation the heresy of the Arians tried to reappear.[162] And so, in place of the invidious name of Rufinus, the name of Jerome was gratuitously inserted. Doubtless these are the ways of booksellers, who remove things that might immediately alarm potential buyers at the first look and add things to entice them. For an author's reputation produces an extraordinary appetite for purchasing a work.[163] By a similar pretense common people impose their goods on the unwary, when for example they falsely say that some piece of cloth has been brought from England, when in fact they have never even seen England; or when they sell wine that originated near the walls of Louvain and try to pass it off as Burgundy.[164]

The style is very pure and flows along smoothly enough, though it is not absolutely pure. Would that he had added to this virtue the reliability that we demand of translators. But this freedom, or rather license, to add, remove and change proclaims that Rufinus is the translator. He confesses that he employed this freedom in his translations of Origen's *Homilies on Leviticus* and the *Commentary on the Epistle to the Romans*, and of Eusebius's *Ecclesiastical History*.[165] Furthermore, what work did Rufinus ever undertake that

---

162. Erasmus's report is true, that the Origenists were suspected of Arianism, but he is wrong to link Rufinus with them. The charge is based on Jerome's slanders of Rufinus. In reality Rufinus was orthodox and had even been persecuted and imprisoned by Arians while in Egypt, as Rufinus himself testifies in his *Apology to Anastasius* 2 (NPNF2 3:430). For an assessment of the controversy between Jerome and Rufinus, see J. N. D. Kelly, *Jerome: His Life, Writings, and Controversies* (New York: Harper and Row, 1975); Murphy, *Rufinus of Aquileia*; E. Clark, *The Origenist Controversy: The Cultural Construction of an Early Christian Debate* (Princeton, N.J.: Princeton University Press, 1992).

163. Erasmus's target here is apparently the Aldine edition of 1503. Cf. Schär, *Das Nachleben des Origenes im Zeitalter des Humanismus*, 290.

164. Belna, here translated as Burgundy, indicates a region that, unlike the surroundings of Louvain, was famous for its excellent wines.

165. Erasmus is here alluding to Rufinus's statements about his translation method found in the epilogue to his translation of Origen's *Commentary on the Epistle to the Romans* and in the prologue to his translation of Eusebius's *HE*. In the former passage, Rufinus admits that in his translations of Origen's *Homilies on Genesis, Exodus* and *Leviticus*, he has filled out Origen's text with material external to the original homilies, but he is almost certainly referring to *Origenian* material gathered from elsewhere, not his own compositions. Erasmus himself acknowledges this Origenian source below, but he nevertheless disapproves of this in principle as a translation method. Rufinus says that he did this because of the hortatory style of those specific homilies of Origen, which raised textual questions but then left them unanswered, a practice that frustrated his Latin readers. Thus Rufinus supplied from Origen's other writings the answers to some questions Origen had raised in those homilies. In the preface to his translation of Eusebius's *HE*, Rufinus states that because Eusebius's tenth book is devoted to discussions about particular bishops that add nothing to our knowledge of the facts, he has omitted these discussions as superfluous matter

he did not spoil in this manner?[166] Gennadius[167] testifies that anything of Origen that has been translated was translated by Rufinus, with the exception of the works that Jerome translated.[168] But in his *Catalogue of Writers*, when Jerome reviews by name what things of Origen he had translated, he makes no mention of this work, though, as he himself testifies, it was when he was a young man that Jerome translated certain works of Origen, while he published the work about ecclesiastical writers as one who was now more advanced in age. But what need is there of this evidence when Rufinus himself, in the epilogue that he added to his translation of Origen's *Commentary on the Epistle to the Romans*, professes that he was the translator of Origen's *Homilies on Genesis*, *on Exodus*, *on Leviticus*, likewise *on Joshua son of Nun*, and *on the Book of Judges*? I am not unaware that even in these works the name of Jerome has been inserted in place of Rufinus, but this was done very impudently, as I will forthwith show.

---

and placed any historical matter from Eusebius's tenth book into the ninth book of his translation. In order to bring the work up to date, Rufinus says that he has added a tenth and eleventh book on his own based on later historical traditions and on his own personal knowledge of events. Erasmus reproaches Rufinus for having granted himself license "to add, remove and change." For a more favorable assessment of Rufinus's method, see M. M. Wagner, *Rufinus the Translator: A Study of His Theory and His Practice as Illustrated in His Version of the Apologetica of St. Gregory Nazianzen* (Washington, D.C.: The Catholic University of America Press, 1945); and Humphries, "Rufinus's Eusebius," 143–64, who shows that Rufinus's translation procedure is not significantly different from Jerome's practice in his translation of Eusebius's *Chronicle*.

166. "Spoil" (*contaminare*) is a technical term and refers to the criticisms of Luscius of Lanuvium against the plays of Terence, which consisted of two principal accusations: (1) that Terence spoiled his Greek originals and (2) that he plagiarized them and committed theft. By "contamination," Luscius meant the spoiling of one Greek play by the introduction of material from another. By "theft," Luscius meant repeating material that had already been used in a Latin play. For Terence's response to these criticisms, see *Andria* 9–14; *Heautontimorumenos* 16–19; *Eunuchus* 19–34; *Adelphi* 6–14. Erasmus has adapted this technical term to his criticisms of Rufinus's translation technique.

167. Gennadius of Marseilles wrote a *De viris illustribus* that continues where Jerome's work with the same name leaves off. It is a catalogue of fifth century church writers. Gennadius lived at the time of Pope Gelasius (492–96). Some streams of older scholarship, which attributed to Augustine a theological principate, claimed that Gennadius's *De viris illustribus* is a tendentious work composed with specific anti-Augustinian views. Cf. A. Feder, "Der Semipelagianismus im Schriftstellerkatalog des Gennadius von Marseille," *Scholastic* 2 (1927): 481–514. More recent scholarship, exemplified by S. Pricoco, says that this charge of semi-Pelagianism "is absolutely without foundation" ("Gennadius of Marseilles," in EEC, 342). See my own brief discussion of Gennadius in Thomas P. Scheck, "Bishop John Fisher's Response to Martin Luther," *Franciscan Studies* 71 (2013): 498–504.

168. Cf. NPNF2 3:389.

Assessment of the *Homilies on Leviticus*[169]

In the epilogue that I just referred to,[170] Rufinus admits that he translated these homilies quite freely, that is to say, he added on his own many things that he says were missing. This unfortunate circumstance is quite tolerable, though he does not expressly indicate what he has removed or what he added, as he did in his translation of Eusebius's *Ecclesiastical History*, from which he removed the ninth book and in its place inserted his own narratives. But the person who reads the *Homilies on Leviticus* and the *Commentary on the Epistle to the Romans* is uncertain whether he is reading Origen or Rufinus. By this device a man who was desirous of glory reckoned that he had found a sure way by which he would be read frequently by all men who would otherwise be reluctant to read his books.[171]

Assessment of the *Homilies on Joshua, Son of Nun*[172]

Here the audacity of the booksellers waxed large. On the frontispiece of the whole work a large number of copies have replaced Rufinus's name with that of Jerome, having torn out the preface.[173] In its place they affixed a preface, but it is so lifeless and inept that it offers the most convincing proof to persuade us that this work was not translated by Jerome. Clever men figured that no one would be inclined to doubt it. Later on, the preface was inscribed with the words: "to Chromatius," for whom Jerome sometimes wrote.[174] But

---

169. Origen's sixteen *Homilies on Leviticus* were translated by Rufinus at the same time as the *Homilies on Genesis and Exodus*, between 403 and 405, for a certain Heraclius, for whom Rufinus also translated Origen's *Commentary on the Epistle to the Romans*. No preface is attached to them. See the translation by G. W. Barkley, FOTC 83 (Washington, D.C.: The Catholic University of America Press, 1990).

170. He means the epilogue to Rufinus's translation of Origen's *Commentary on the Epistle to the Romans*. See the translation by T. Scheck, FOTC 103 and 104 (Washington, D.C.: The Catholic University of America Press, 2001–2), 311–13 in FOTC 104.

171. Modern scholarship tends to limit the corruptions in Rufinus's translations of Origen to passages where Rufinus has Origen use the anachronistic language of post-Nicene Trinitarian orthodoxy.

172. Origen's twenty-six *Homilies on Joshua* were translated by Rufinus. See B. Bruce's translation, FOTC 105 (Washington, D.C.: The Catholic University of America Press, 2002).

173. Schär, *Das Nachleben des Origenes im Zeitalter des Humanismus*, 290, identifies Erasmus's target here as above all the Aldine (Aldus Manutius) edition of Origen's works (Venice, 1503). One of the prefaces in that edition may have been written by Jerome Aleander, the future cardinal.

174. Chromatius of Aquileia was a member of the clergy of Aquileia and a close collaborator of bishop Valerian in the synod of 381 that condemned so-called western Arianism. Bishop of Aquileia from 387, he was pastorally active in the controversies between Jerome and Rufinus and

consider with me, candid reader, how like Jerome it would be for him to address Chromatius as "his Chromatius." It says: "And you, O my ever venerable Chromatius." And yet, the entire thought of the preface is like this, that is, it is written in such a way that it could be applied to any work. The rhetoricians call this kind of preface "vulgar."[175]

I will not mention the fact that in his absurd garrulousness the impostor was amplifying this very thought with things that he had stolen from the writings of Jerome. And in the meantime he makes both Jerome and Chromatius equally foolish. He makes a fool of Chromatius when he has him "enjoin" and "instruct" without indicating what work he desires to see translated, from which author, and for what reasons. Chromatius simply orders the translator to give to Latin ears something from the wealth of the Greeks, as if Jerome had never done this before. The impostor makes Jerome into a fool by having him offer no reason why he has undertaken to translate this work of Origen. But does this not seem to be similar to Terence's joke in the passage where Pamphilus desires to get rid of his curious and garrulous slave by any pretext whatsoever and commands him to go to the port and find his host from Myconos? The slave asks in response whether he wants him to say anything to him. "Or do I just find him?"[176] In the same way Jerome could reply to Chromatius, "Do you have nothing to say about what I am to translate, from whom, whether it should be a learned or unlearned work, pious or impious? Or do I just translate?"

Although the preface is very long, [LB 8:432] he does not add a single word that is relevant to commending and understanding the work. For the moment I will say nothing about the grammatical mistakes and linguistic absurdities. He says that Origen delivered these brief orations *ex tempore*,[177] as if Origen, whom Athanasius more than once calls the most careful of all,[178] did not approach the pulpit prepared to speak by means of careful reflec-

---

in the matter of John Chrysostom. Before his death in 407 he witnessed the terrors of the Gothic invasion. Jerome dedicated his commentaries on Habakkuk and Jonah to him.

175. Or "ordinary, every day, commonplace, general, suited to the masses." Cf. Cicero, *De finibus* 3.1.3; *De Officiis* 1.16.52; Quintilian, *Inst.* 18.56.

176. Cf. Terence, *Hecyra* 436.

177. Rufinus says this generally of Origen's homilies in the preface to his translation of Origen's *Homilies on Joshua* and specifically of Origen's *Homilies on Leviticus* in the epilogue to his translation of Origen's *Commentary on the Epistle to the Romans*. Pamphilus, in *Apology for Origen* 9, also calls Origen's daily discussions *ex tempore*.

178. Erasmus may be referring to Athanasius's description of Origen as labor-loving (φιλόπονος) in *De decretis Nicaenae synodi* 27, but this is not certain.

tion;[179] or as if anything that is said before the people in order to be taken down by stenographers may be said to be *ex tempore*.[180] But how awkwardly has he here mentioned Bezalel,[181] as if dragging him in by the scruff of the neck, as they say.[182] By what lifeless comparisons does he interpret the things that were offered for the construction of the temple. And how prettily did he say the following: "The delivery of unpolished words blunts the force of the insights." The reason for this was: "An unpolished style of speaking makes the meaning less pleasing." He says: "*Repute* it to you yourself," instead of: "*Impute* it." How fittingly that in the writings of this "Jerome," the impostor makes Jerome ignorant of how to translate Greek into Latin! Jerome was not so completely dissatisfied with himself in this field of study but that he would rather lay claim to some authority for himself.

To this evidence I will add that in his *Catalogue of Writers*, Jerome does not mention this work.[183] Thus Rufinus, in the epilogue that I cited earlier,[184] professes that he is the translator of this work and of that on Judges, which is the book that follows Joshua. He adds something that I find amazing: he denies that in his translation of Origen's Homilies on Joshua he added anything or took anything away, but in good faith translated for Latin ears what he found in the Greek manuscripts.[185] This seemed impressive to many,[186] owing to the dull and fastidious sense of judgment of certain persons who attribute too much to titles and brief prefaces. Nonsense of this sort that comes

179. Erasmus describes Jean Vitrier's preaching this way in CWE 8, ep. 1211.

180. Erasmus's reproach of Rufinus's description of Origen's homilies as extemporaneous compositions seems unnecessarily censorious. Origen himself admitted that he spoke *ex tempore*. For example in his Homily on 1 Kings (1 Samuel) 28, at the very beginning of the homily, Origen asks the bishop who is present to point out to him which pericope, of the four that have been read publicly in the church, that he is supposed to expound.

181. Bezalel was a Judahite in charge of making the wilderness tabernacle and its equipment. He was descended from Caleb (cf. Ex 31:2, 35:30–35, 36:1–2, 37:1, 38:22; 1 Chr 2:20; 2 Chr 1:5). His skill as a versatile craftsman is attributed to the Spirit of God. Assisted by Oholiab and other workers, Bezalel received offerings of precious metals, woods, linen, and animal skins from the people, and with them created artistic designs out of various media for the adornment of the tabernacle. In the preface to his translation of Origen's *Homilies on Joshua*, Rufinus compares his dedicatee Chromatius with this Bezalel for the way he has enjoined and instructed him to bestow something for the building and construction of the divine tabernacle from the wealth and riches of the Greeks.

182. Cf. Plautus, Poenulus 3.5.45.

183. Cf. *De viris illustribus* 135.

184. That is, the epilogue to the translation of Origen's *Commentary on the Epistle to the Romans*.

185. Cf. Rufinus's epilogue to his translation of Origen's *Commentary on the Epistle to the Romans*.

186. Godin was unable to identify Erasmus's referent here but he may have Jacques Merlin in mind, who had a more favorable view of Rufinus than Erasmus does (*Erasme Lecteur d'Origène*, 608).

from impostors is forced down the throats of the learned, and those who are not sufficiently careful are deceived, and they become indignant with us who open the eyes of readers by warning them.[187]

Assessment of the *Commentary on Job*[188]

I will now give my opinion of the three books on Job, which is namely what the facts themselves make clear. The preface is by a loquacious, unlearned, and shameless creature. Or shall we understand it as evidence of his modesty that he did not add his own name and did not insert the name of anyone else? He suppressed his own name and the name of the man to whom he is writing, and he says only that once this preface has been read it will be clear who the translator of the work is. And yet by all means he wants this preface to be read before you engage the commentary. Yet the preface contains nothing that builds a road to understanding the work. He adds that the work had previously been translated into Latin (*Latine*) by others, or as he says it, "in Latin" (*in Latinum*), but "not into the Latin language" (*sermone Latino*). At this point, then, a second translator added the little flowers of his eloquence. But the one who crafted the second preface did not know the term *Latine*, which is absolutely nothing more than sheer and wretched stammering.

Moreover, it is obvious that the one who wrote the commentary, even if he is fluent in his own style of speaking, nevertheless it is clear that he did not learn his eloquence from the books of Cicero, but from ecclesiastical writers. Now what could be more ridiculous than that comparison between a physician and a translator by which he nevertheless seems marvelously pleased with himself.[189] I beseech you, reader, what race produced this man? What ignorance, what tediousness! And yet worthless ravings of this sort are forced upon the literate and the illiterate alike.

187. Godin remarks that there is no satisfying explanation for Erasmus's incoherence in this section (*Erasme Lecteur d'Origène*, 608).

188. The discussion that follows concerns a commentary on Job known today as *Anonymus in Iob*, now available in Steinhauser's critical edition, as noted in chapter 4. The work was transmitted erroneously under the name of Origen until Erasmus exposed it as inauthentic. It was printed in Merlin's edition of Origen's works (Paris, 1512) and reprinted among the spurious works of Origen in PG 17:371–522. Erasmus's assessment of this work is his longest "assessment," which indicates that the Origenian attribution was firmly anchored in the minds of Erasmus's contemporaries; cf. Godin, *Erasme lecteur d'Origène*, 608.

189. The comparison is given in the preface at PG 17:371. A similar comparison is used by Rufinus in the preface to his translation of Eusebius's HE.

Up to this point I have spoken about the preface. It is so inept that this above all else makes plain that the booksellers wanted to deceive us. Now I will speak about the content of the work. There are a few trivial grounds for conjecturing that this commentary was translated from Origen, though not by the author of this preface. The first is that, based upon Jerome's letter to Pammachius and Marcellinus, it is certain that Origen wrote on Job, although even among the Latins there were several who wrote on Job.[190] The second is that he testifies here that he has written on Genesis, a book on which Origen also wrote. But of course Origen was not the only one who wrote on Genesis. Comparison shows that this work has a somewhat Origenian flavor, for the author readily transcends the letter in order to make room for allegory. For example, Job is called εὐγενής, which Jerome had translated "great" (*magnus*).[191] This author reads, "He was of the best race," and he denies that Job was descended from the good, and he introduces us to many kinds of virtues from which Job was sprung, "from the greater ones," doubtless "from the best ones." But the term "best" (*optimi*) does not refer to character but to fortune. This is why the persons who are called aristocrats (*optimates*) are not those who have the most praiseworthy morals, but those who are of noble birth, wealth, and who stand forth in dignity. Granted, nothing prevents even some of these from being good men in the moral respect. The author has said things that could be seen to agree with Origen, but there is no one who does not see how baseless these sorts of inferences are.

Now consider the ways in which this work is discordant with Origen. [LB 8:433] The whole thing is full of vain-babbling [*battologiis*], that is, with repetitions of the same thought. Most of these redundancies are lifeless and superfluous. Fulgentius excelled in this manner of speaking, a man who was otherwise fluent.[192] This feature at least does not sound like Origen. Moreover, many times he repeats the passage that he is explaining, as though lay-

---

190. Erasmus seems to have conflated references in Ep 33 to Paula, where Jerome gives a list of Origen's writings (but without any mention of a work on Job), Ep 84 to Pammachius and Oceanus, where Jerome attempts to justify his early enthusiasm for Origen, and Ep 61.2 to Vigilantius, where Jerome reports that Hilary of Poitiers rendered into Latin Origen's *Homilies on Job*. This last statement is confirmed in *De viris illustribus* 100, where Jerome says that Hilary wrote a treatise, *On Job*, "which he translated freely from the Greek of Origen."

191. Cf. Job 1:3; cf. PG 17:379.

192. Fulgentius (467–532) was made bishop of Ruspe in 507. He defended Chalcedonian orthodoxy against the Arians and radical Augustinianism against the so-called semi-Pelagians in answer to a series of requests. According to his doctrine human nature was fundamentally corrupted by Adam's sin transmitted to his descendants, which makes man incapable of willing the good and saving himself by his own strength through free will.

ing a path for the subsequent additions. For example, he frequently repeats, "There was a man," when he is about to say something about the man.[193] I do not reproach this manner of teaching. Whenever Origen makes use of this style, he does so quite moderately and skillfully, without its being out of place or redundant.[194] But how much time does this man waste on this method, as he fabricates words for his character and as he invents apostrophes addressed to the devil![195]

But lest I drag on my discussion longer, as far as I am concerned each one should be allowed to keep to his own judgment on this matter. I judge that the author was a Latin, that he wrote in Latin, that the man was finely trained in the holy scriptures, and that he was suited to teach by an expansive way of speaking that was not in the common manner, but that he was an Arian.[196] This is clearly detected by the way he writes the following: "The devil makes three horns,"[197] he says, "as a type and figure of that sect of the three names, and of the heresy of the three Gods, which has filled the whole world with a measure of darkness, which sometimes worships the Father and the Son and the Holy Spirit as three, sometimes it adores One, just as they recall the language of the Greeks, 'Triad'[198] or 'homousion.'[199] Therefore that very cunning devil long ago pointed out that sect of the Trinity and their heresy and infidelity, and he sent three horns[200] against Job,"[201] etc.

His reference to the "sect of the three names" could apply to the Noetians[202] and the Sabellians,[203] who teach that the Godhead consists in a

---

193. Cf., e.g., PG 17:377–78.

194. Origen uses something like this technique in his *Homily on 1 Kings* 28.

195. An apostrophe (ἀποστροφή) is a rhetorical figure where the speaker turns from the judges and addresses the plaintiff. Cf. Quintilian, *Inst.* 3.24, 9.2.38.

196. Erasmus's critical powers are shown to be outstanding in this section. Modern scholars confirm Erasmus's judgment about the Arian authorship of *Anonymus in Iob*. See Quasten, *Patrology*, 4:103.

197. Job 1:17.

198. This is apparently a transliteration of τρίας, the Greek term for Trinity.

199. This is a Latinized spelling of *homoousios* (ὁμοούσιος) which can be translated "of the same substance, consubstantial, one in being."

200. *Cornu* (horn) is used very frequently in Latin (cf. Caesar, *Bellum Gallicum*) to refer to the wing of an army. In the present context it means the hordes of the Chaldeans.

201. PG 17:428.

202. The Noetians were a sect named after Noetus of Smyrna, who was the first to spread the Patripassian doctrine at the end of the second century, for which he was condemned by the presbyters of Smyrna. Patripassianism taught that the Father suffered on the cross.

203. Sabellianism was a sect named after Sabellius, who was condemned at Rome in 220 by Callistus as an exponent of patripassian monarchianism. His origins are uncertain. This sect

single person, but that this person is designated by three names. When he creates and establishes the universe, he is the Father. The same person had his name changed when he assumed flesh and suffered for the redemption of the human race, namely, he is now the Son. And again, the same person came upon the apostles and is now the Holy Spirit. But this sect never "filled the whole world." Moreover, the things that follow do not permit us to understand this passage of the Sabellians. For they did not profess three Gods, which no sect has ever taught. On the contrary the Arians raised this as a false objection to the orthodox, because the orthodox worshipped three Persons, each of whom they professed to be God. Now it appears that what he has added about "what is called in the language of the Greeks 'Triad' and 'homusion'" could only have been said by the Arians against the orthodox. For the Arians denied the Trinity in the deity and execrated the word *homusios*. They did not even tolerate the term *homoeusios*, because they denied that God's most simple nature is communicable and that there is anything "like" God among created things.[204]

Likewise he makes mention elsewhere of the Father, Son, and Holy Spirit, but from that passage as well you can discern that he is an Arian. For he bestows the name of God on the Father alone. He sets forth the essence of the faith in this manner when he says: "They do all things in vain," he says, "if they do not do them in faith; they act without reason unless in the recognition of the one unbegotten God, the Father, and in the confession of his one only-begotten Son, our Lord Jesus Christ, and in the illumination of the Holy Spirit, the glorious and venerable Paraclete,"[205] etc. You see that he assigns the name of God to the Father alone, and him alone he calls "unbegotten," because he alone had no beginning. For by this ambiguous word the Arians were simply trying to deceive. He calls the Son "Lord," and the Holy Spirit "venerable, glorious, and Paraclete." From these things I think it is sufficiently clear that he was an Arian. It follows from this that the author could not have been Origen. For the sect of the Arians arose after Origen's lifetime.[206]

---

extended the original patripassian doctrine to include the Holy Spirit: one sole God is manifested as Father in the Old Testament, as Son in the incarnation, and as Holy Spirit poured out upon the apostles at Pentecost. By this development he avoided Noetus's statement which had met intense opposition, that the Father himself had been incarnate and had suffered. Erasmus seems to have collapsed the two sects together into a single doctrine.

204. The Arians rejected both *homoousios*, "of the same substance," and *homoiousios*, "of a similar substance" or "of like substance."

205. PG 17:381.

206. Origen died in 254. The heresy of Arius was condemned at the Council of Nicaea in 325.

The style agrees with the *Commentary on Matthew*, which they call an incomplete work, and which bore the name of Chrysostom, although based on the same work we have declared that he was an Arian.[207] Those who wanted to force this work on the reader altered many things in it. Certain things in it deceived them on the basis of which the Arian author betrayed himself. My suspicion is that the author was the bishop Maximinus,[208] whose disputations with the blessed bishop Augustine are extant.[209] For even he preferred to waste the time of St. Augustine, who pressured him with acute dialectics and with an uninterrupted flow of words by which he prevailed over him. Above all it is the flavor of the work that indicates that the author was a Latin. For almost no one can translate Greek so nicely that the Latin discourse does not have the taste of its original to us. Sometimes he translated Greek words but in such a way that one recognizes a native Latin speaker, as for example when he teaches us about the nature and meaning of "adamantus."[210] There was need for a complete work, but he only explains the opening chapter, which he thinks was added by Moses, and Job's initial speech, but he does not seem to have pursued it any further. He reveals that at the conclusion of the third book. Nor [LB 8:434] do I see what the conclusion would have been, if he had wanted to investigate the details in a similar manner. The work is worth reading, and would that the church had many such bishops, excluding his impious opinion.[211]

---

207. Erasmus is referring to an incomplete work on Matthew, *Opus imperfectum in Matthaeum*, which is the most extensive existing commentary on Matthew in Latin from antiquity. The work is now available in English as *Incomplete Commentary on Matthew (Opus imperfectum)*, trans. James A. Kellerman, 2 vols. (Downers Grove, Ill.: Intervarsity Press, 2010). For a discussion see Quasten, *Patrology*, 4:101–5. For a long time this work was attributed to John Chrysostom and under his name it was enthusiastically admired in the medieval period, above all by Thomas Aquinas. The work is definitely Arian, as Erasmus surmises. The work is reprinted in PG 56. Simonetti (Quasten, *Patrology*, 4:102) says that this reprinted edition is "practically useless in those places where the text displays an Arian content" (since the Arian passages have been corrected by an orthodox editor).

208. Maximinus the Arian is the one Latin Arian author whose personality can be partly reconstructed. He was born ca. 360 in Rome and became bishop of an Arian community, possibly in Illyricum. He debated publicly with Augustine at Hippo in 427 or 428. A stenographic account of the debate survives (*Collatio Augustini cum Maximino*, PL 42:743–814). Erasmus's attribution of both *Opus imperfectum in Matthaeum* and *Anonymus in Iob* to Maximinus has been vindicated in modern times by Meslin, *Les Ariens d'Occident*, 226, as noted in chapter 4.

209. PL 8:677–744; PL 42:743–814.

210. Erasmus evidently means that the way the author has Latinized the Greek word, *adamas*, by *adamantus*, gives away that he is a native Latin speaker, since this form misspells the form of Origen's cognomen, Adamantius.

211. Simonetti's description of this work (Quasten, *Patrology*, 4:103) sheds some light on

Assessment of the *Commentary on the Three Psalms*[212]

I have not made up my mind about this work. It scarcely reproduces Origen's genius and diction, coming nearer to the diction of Chrysostom. For I surmise that the one who wrote it was a Latin, or if Rufinus translated it, in his manner he made the work of another his own when he translated it, that is to say, when he spoiled it. The man who writes the preface does not say that he translated these homilies *from Origen*. In the epilogue that he attached to the *Commentary on the Epistle to the Romans*, Rufinus admits that he translated these homilies literally [*simpliciter*] as they were found in the Greek. In that passage he does not identify the name of the author.[213] Now there are some things that are awkwardly expressed, others that are translated lifelessly, others that are unnatural and affected [*aliena et ascititia*].[214]

The following translation is awkward: "Do not provoke jealousy in [in] evil doers, do not offer to evil men an opportunity to do evil."[215] For according to scriptural usage, it would seem rather that the same sentence has been repeated. For the preposition "in" has been added because of a peculiarity of the Hebrew language. Thus in the very next verse the thought is repeated: "For they will quickly wither away like grass, and they will quickly fall like garden plants."[216] In what follows, he has heaped up many things from Deuteronomy and from Paul concerning παραζήλου that are unnatural. For μὴ παραζήλου is used as a passive verb, which could have been more appropriately translated: "Do not be provoked to envy," or "to jealousy, and do not admire evil men." For this is what ζηλοῦν denotes to the Greeks. And in fact the things that we admire are the things that we strive to imitate. "Do not be envious, do not admire the happiness of evil men, since it is in vain and will soon fade away. But they are truly happy who have fixed their hope in the Lord. This is the source of true riches, of delights that are true." St. Jerome translates μὴ παραζήλου as "do not contend with," defining contention as an exceedingly strong desire to emulate.

Erasmus's relatively positive impression: "The tone of the work is always grave and often exaggerated in keeping with the prevailing interests of a moral and didactic character."

212. Origen's *Homilies on Psalms 36–38* were translated by Rufinus. See H. Crouzel and L. Brésard, *Homélies sur les Psaumes 36 à 38*, Sources chrétiennes 411 [hereafter "SC"] (Paris: Cerf, 1995).

213. This is surely a carping criticism of Rufinus, whose words in context make it perfectly obvious that it is *Origen's Homilies on Psalms 36–38* he has translated.

214. In the essay on Origen's homiletical style below, Erasmus says that Origen did not possess these two traits.

215. Cf. Ps 37:1.   216. Cf. Ps 37:2.

The translation "not a race" is feeble, not a single nation called to faith, just as the law was given to the Jewish race, but others were called from all the other races. Scripture however speaks of "not a race" when it is referring to the most contemptible race, yet one that has experienced true religion. In the same way Paul speaks of "non-entities" when he is referring to those things that in the world's estimation were reckoned as nothing, things that are low-born, destitute, humble, and uneducated.[217] There are other things that resemble ground up corn meal, which I will not pursue lest I become wordy. It is adequate to have pointed out these things as examples.

Now the preface seems to have been stitched together out of lifeless and badly cohering short sentences. In the first place, I marvel at the man's effrontery when he declares that he has translated from Greek, but does not make known what author he has translated! Then he explains that he has so arranged these homilies that they form a single corpus, as if he himself, not the author, had done the arranging. But that is not the task of a translator. Then he calls this entire work a "discourse," lest anyone suspect that they were not homilies. For I surmise that either Rufinus, or maybe someone else, has translated rather freely from a continuous commentary, and that he divided up the work into homilies. In order to prevent anyone from detecting this, he suppressed the name of the author. In the end, he feared that Apronianus's sister might become frustrated with his work if she constantly finds it laborious to understand owing to the "roughness" [*asperitas*] of the problems.[218] He has said "roughness" instead of difficulty. And he says such things as if he himself is not accustomed to write what is not remarkably refined. Meanwhile I do not examine the way he has said in Latin "It will offer that [*quod*]" instead of "It will offer that [*ut*]," or about the fact that he has called it his own work, though he has professed that he is the work's translator, and then he speaks as though the clarity of the explanation is owing to him, and not instead to the author. He has added a very pretty thought when he says: "A human body could not be made up solely of nerves and bones, unless divine providence had interwoven with them the softness of flesh and the grace of fat." He seems to think that this ease of explanation is the flesh and fat of the work and that the difficult questions are the nerves and bones. Is there any limit to the stammering nature of these words and to the man's incompetence at expressing his meaning? I hardly think that Rufinus was so

---

217. 1 Cor 1:28; Rom. 4.17.

218. Apronianus is Rufinus's dedicatee for his translation of Origen's *Commentary on Psalms 36–38*. He was a Roman nobleman converted by Rufinus and Melania.

tongue-tied, who even if we grant that he lacked skill, was at least fluent by nature. But if someone protests that Rufinus was not a stranger to incompetence, I will not continue to fight back. Let us at least agree on the point that the spirit of this work does not reproduce Origen's fertility. [LB 8:435]

Assessment of the Four *Homilies on the Canticle of Canticles*[219]

St. Jerome admits that he translated two homilies of Origen on the Canticle of Canticles and in fact from a commentary that Origen wrote on the same Canticle.[220] He also says that he was afraid to undertake the work, because of the loftiness of the mysteries and the profundity of the subject matter, and also because of the great expense and work involved.[221] And in fact this commentary was listed among the works of Jerome, though it is neither Origen's nor Jerome's, but was composed by a Latin-speaking man, wonderfully learned and extremely articulate.[222] You can conclude that he was not Greek from the fact that in the preface he refers to Greeks as foreigners. He says: "Since among the Greeks those who seem wise and learned."[223] Likewise it is clear from his translation of love, charity, delight, and desire. I suspect that it was by him whose books are extant, *On the Calling of the Gentiles* and a commentary on certain Psalms. But since out of humility he was unwilling to add his own name, the booksellers prefixed the name Ambrose.[224] These are not homilies, as the booksellers have indicated, but a continuous though incomplete commentary. For it does not go beyond two chapters of the Canticle.

---

219. According to Eusebius, HE 6.32.2, Origen wrote five books of his *Commentary on the Canticle* in Athens about the year 240 and five books later at Caesarea in Palestine. Rufinus translated the prologue to the *Commentary* and the first three books of the commentary in Sicily about the year 410, but he did not attach a preface to the work, which makes Erasmus's confusion about the authorship more understandable. Two homilies on the Canticle had previously been translated by Jerome, who wrote a preface dedicated to Pope Damasus. See the translation by R. P. Lawson, ACW 26 (Westminster, Md.: Newman, 1957).

220. Cf. *De viris illustribus* 135.

221. See Jerome's preface to his translation of *Origen's Two Homilies on the Song of Songs*.

222. Erasmus's judgment is sound with respect to his identification of this work as a commentary and not homilies. However his critical powers have failed him when he claims that the work is not Origen's. In fact this commentary is Origen's as translated by Rufinus. Again Erasmus's excessive hostility toward Rufinus may explain his inability to recognize Rufinus as the translator.

223. Cf. prologue, 3.

224. Cf. PL 17:1073–1132.

Assessment of the *Vision of Isaiah*

In his *Catalogue of Ecclesiastical Writers*, St. Jerome admits that he translated this fragment from Origen's *Commentary on Isaiah*.[225] But I am surprised that there is no preface attached to it, since Jerome very often writes a preface when there is no need of a preface. Anyone who reads the prefaces that he has added to his individual books will admit that this is true, among which works are found his *Commentary on Isaiah*.[226] He does not even write a preface for his work *On Jeremiah*,[227] though the preface for *On Ezekiel* does make reference to a previous translation.[228] I suspect that the prefaces were removed by those to whom he had written, after Origen's name had become so terribly unpopular to the Romans. This is consistent with the fact that in these prefaces he enthusiastically praised Origen's talent, which he likewise does in the preface that he attached to his translation of Origen's *Commentary on Ezekiel*,[229] where he identifies Origen as "the second teacher of the churches after the apostles."[230] In that passage even the name of the man to whom Jerome is writing was removed. Not even Jerome's name was left in place. Yet there is no doubt that this preface was written by Jerome, because Rufinus makes this the basis of his objection to Jerome, that he called Didymus "his own Seer."[231] The Hebrews call prophets "seers,"[232] and Didymus had his eyesight taken from him.

---

225. Cf. *De viris illustribus* 135. This treatise is Jerome's Ep 18 to Damasus, sometimes entitled *De seraphim*. It dates to around 381 AD. Fremantle observes: "At the time when he wrote it he was much under the sway of Origen. But great as was his admiration for the master, he was not afraid to discard his exegesis when, as in the case of the seraphim, he believed it to be erroneous" (NPNF2 6:22). Jerome's translations are not accompanied by a preface. Also in his own *Commentary on Isaiah* 3.3, Jerome reports that while he was in Constantinople studying scripture under Bishop Gregory Nazianzen, he dictated a "brief and hastily composed treatise" on the vision recorded in Is 6:1–9 in which he wanted to make an experiment of his meager talent and obey his friends who commanded him. I have translated Jerome's Ep 18 in *St. Jerome, Commentary on Isaiah, Origen, Homilies 1–9 on Isaiah*, ACW 68 (Mahwah, N.J.: Newman Press, 2015).

226. Jerome's *Commentary on Isaiah* in eighteen books contains prefaces to each book. Jerome also translated nine homilies of Origen on Isaiah that he leaves unmentioned in his catalogue. See Alfons Fürst, "Jerome Keeping Silent: Origen and His Exegesis of Isaiah," in *Jerome of Stridon*, ed. Cain and Lössl, 141–52; and my discussion in *St. Jerome, Commentary on Isaiah, Origen, Homilies 1–9 on Isaiah*, 881–84.

227. Jerome died while working on this commentary.

228. Cf. Jerome's preface to his *Commentary on Ezekiel*.

229. I believe Erasmus means Origen's *Homilies on Ezekiel*.

230. Cf. Jerome's preface to Origen's *Homilies on Ezekiel*.

231. Rufinus's objection is found in *Apology* 2.12. Jerome praised Didymus as a man of brass in Ep 50.2. He boasts Didymus as his teacher in Ep 84.3. In the preface to Jerome's translation of Origen's *Homilies on Ezekiel*, Jerome calls Didymus "the seer."

232. Cf. 1 Sm 9:9.

Assessment of the Commentary on Matthew[233]

I am not going to say anything about the Commentary on Matthew because I plan to add a preface to this particular work.

Assessment of the Homilies on Luke[234]

There is no doubt that the thirty-nine Homilies on Luke were translated by Jerome, since he himself plainly admits this in the preface.[235] In the Catalogue, however, he mentions this work in such a way that it seems instead that he translated it from Didymus.[236] For when he had much earlier left behind a mention of Origen, after this he speaks as follows: "Didymus's Concerning the Holy Spirit, which I translated into Latin (in Latinum), one book, On Luke thirty-nine homilies, On the Psalms, from the tenth to the sixteenth, seven treatises. The Life of the Captive Monk," etc. There are two possible explanations of these words: either the work is Jerome's, or it was translated by him from Didymus. I do not know whether he did this by chance or out of zeal. There are no homilies of Origen that are as concise as these. Secondly, while in the rest of the homilies there are no errors to be found, here there are many things that are suspect and condemned.[237] Now this is a slight indication that this work was not worked on adequately enough, so that it originated from the young Origen.[238] And yet Jerome did not make any changes to it when he trans-

---

233. Origen composed this commentary at Caesarea in 246. Eight books (10–17) survive in Greek, which cover his comments on Mt 13:36–22:33. See PG 13:835–1600. Erasmus made a new translation of this work in 1527 (LB 8:439–84) which, however, only covers the material found in PG 13:835–1015 and corresponds to ANF 10:414–59. We also possess an anonymous Latin translation of the commentary, presumably from the sixth century, that spans Mt 16:13–27:63. It is called Commentariorum in Matth. Series. The remains have been edited in by Klosterman in Origenes Werke, 10–12, in GCS 38, 40, 41 (Berlin: 1935–55). Books 10 and 11 were edited and translated by Girod (SC 162).

234. Jerome translated Origen's thirty-nine Homilies on Luke. See the translation by Lienhard in FOTC 94.

235. Sider observes that Erasmus, in his New Testament Annotations, constantly expresses doubt about the authenticity of the Homilies on Luke without giving any rationale for his suspicions ("Erasmus and the Search for Authenticity," 241). Cf. LB 6:57F, 126C, 219C, 225E, 227D, 234E, 236B, 236F, 288D, 308E–F. It appears that here Erasmus gives the rationale.

236. Cf. De viris illustribus 135.

237. Erasmus says something similar in his Apology against Latomus (CWE 71:72–73): "There are very few passages in his [Origen's] surviving books which are suspect.... None of his poisonous doctrines are extant except in Jerome, who made it his business to see that the world knew about Origen's errors, but not about the sound points he made."

238. Jerome reports in the preface: "In these sermons Origen is like a boy playing at dice. The works of his full manhood, and the writings of his old age, are of another sort" (trans. Leinhard, 4).

lated it, but translated it just as it was found in the Greek. Thus he simultaneously excuses Origen and clears himself of responsibility. Pardon is owed to [youthful] age, nor can a translator be made responsible for anything that is not published as his own work but that renders the work of another in good faith. Now of course it is not difficult to conjecture why the names of those to whom Jerome wrote were deliberately removed.

Assessment of the *Homilies* on Various Books

Among these it is certain that some of them are not Origen's, but by a Latin man, the rest were impudently spoiled by Rufinus. [LB 8:436]

Assessment of the *Commentary on the Epistle to the Romans*[239]

Here we have a case where the booksellers laid aside all sense of shame. In the epilogue they inserted the name of Jerome in place of Rufinus, that is to say, they tried to force a piece of glass on the reader as if it were a jewel. And up to now, at least, they succeeded in deceiving the unwary.[240] For the preface was deemed to be Jerome's, but in the epilogue the shrew mice, as it were, betray themselves by a sign. It says: "After this, of course, a work is calling us that was long ago enjoined, but now is being pressed even more insistently by the blessed bishop Gaudentius, namely that of Clement, the Roman bishop and companion of the apostles, whose books are being translated into Latin by us, that I may give knowledge of them to his successors," etc.[241] They should have erased this passage if they wanted to convince us that Jerome was the translator of this work. For it is a fact known both from Gennadius[242] and from Rufinus's own preface that Rufinus, not Jerome, translated the books of the *Recognitions of Clement*.[243] Moreover Rufinus wrote

---

239. Origen composed his *Commentary on the Epistle to the Romans* in fifteen books. Rufinus translated about half the work into Latin in 406 in a coherent form that covers the entire text of the epistle (see trans. Scheck, 13).

240. Erasmus was the first editor of a printed edition of Origen's writings to correctly identify Rufinus as the translator of Origen's *Commentary on the Epistle to the Romans*. The previous editions by Theophilus Salodianus (Venice, 1506) and Jacques Merlin (Paris, 1512) both named Jerome as the translator. Erasmus describes the process that led to this detection in an annotation to Rom 3:5 added in 1535 to his *Annotations on Romans* (CWE 56:94–96).

241. Gaudentius was bishop of Brescia from 387 to 410 and warmly supported John Chrysostom when the latter had been condemned to exile. In the preface to his translation of the pseudo-Clementine *Recognitions*, Rufinus praised the intellectual gifts of Gaudentius.

242. Cf. Gennadius, *De viris illustribus* 17.

243. The *Recognitions of Clement* was an apocryphal work written ca. 250 AD, attributed to

other things as well for this Gaudentius. Therefore the booksellers have accomplished nothing at all by introducing Jerome's name, or rather, the act of inserting these things increases the suspicion of deceit. For higher up it reads as follows: "For they say to me: 'In what you write, since many things are attributed to your own work, put your name in the title and write, for instance: *The Books of Jerome's Commentary on the Epistle to the Romans.*'" At the end of the epilogue it reads as follows: "For lest it should be thought to be Jerome's, Clement will be written," etc. There is also the following weighty piece of evidence, that as a favor to Ursatius, at whose command he undertook this labor, Rufinus translated the *Rule of Basil*; and as a favor to Gaudentius, whose name he records here, he translated Clement.[244]

For the moment I will say nothing about the style.[245] Who has ever raised as an objection to Jerome that what he translated, he has truncated, expanded, altered, and made his own work out of the work of another?[246] This is the unique characteristic of Rufinus's rashness, whose sole object seems to have been to spoil all the works of brilliant authors by setting his hands on them. Is he not ashamed to admit in this epilogue that he has altered Origen's *Homilies on Genesis, on Exodus,* and especially *on Leviticus* in such a way that "what Origen spoke after the manner of the common people in his zeal to edify them," these works Rufinus has translated "in the form of a commentary"? He has in fact expressly made a distinction between "edification" and "explanation," as though explanation does not also have in view the edification of the hearers. Furthermore, what are the things he had to supply in these homilies? Questions, he says, that Origen struck up but

---

Clement of Rome (cf. ANF 8). Rufinus of Aquileia had translated the work on the assumption that it was authentic. In CWE 12, ep. 1790, a preface to a translation of some *Lucubrations* by Athanasius, Erasmus notes the recent edition of the *Recognitions* published in Basel (1526) by Johannes Bebel. Cf. P. S. Allen, *Opus Epistolarum Desiderii Erasmi Roterodami*, ep. 1790, 73 (the same work had been published by Jacques Lefèvre d'Étaples in 1504). Erasmus argued that the work was a forgery, basing his judgment on the trivial and fabulous character of the narrative. Cf. LB 6:653D, 1068C, 433E; Sider, "Erasmus and the Search for Authenticity," 238.

244. At the monastery of Pinetum, Rufinus translated a shorter edition, in 203 questions, of Basil's *Asceticon*, which he called the "Rule." It was the first spiritual text Rufinus brought to the attention of the west. Cf. Quasten, *Patrology*, 4:252. For this same Ursacius Rufinus translated Origen's *Homilies on Numbers*.

245. In his *Annotations on Romans* at 3.5 (CWE 56:94), Erasmus said that the style of this work seemed purer than in other translations of Rufinus.

246. Erasmus evidently does not believe Rufinus's charges in *Apology against Jerome* that Jerome indeed had done this. Ironically, in modern times Alfons Fürst has now proven the truth of Rufinus's charge, in his articles "Jerome Keeping Silent" and "Origen Losing His Text."

then abandoned. But such questions still exist in the homilies that Rufinus has translated. But he had to supply things. From what source did he supply them? From his own intellect? He was not equal to the task.

In my judgment he means from Origen's commentaries, where Origen treats in more detail what he had discoursed on when he spoke before the people, either because Origen did not want to burden his hearers with sermons that were too lengthy, or because he was unwilling to heap upon raw recruits and upon those who were insufficiently attentive things that were more concealed.[247] What I am speaking of, Rufinus himself admits in the preface to his books *On First Principles*. Or was it defective farther on in that work, where something could be added? Why then did he not supply material from Origen's *Scholia*? Why did he make a continuous commentary out of Origen's homilies, in which Origen expounds certain select passages? Each work is complete and satisfactory in its own genre in which the author supplied what he proposed and promised. Up to this point I have spoken about the epilogue.

Now in the preface he says the following: "For some of the books from this very work are missing from nearly all the libraries, of course the reason for this is uncertain," etc. What is he saying? Has he visited all the libraries of everyone? But he cautiously adds "nearly."[248] But if these books were not missing in some of the libraries, why did he choose to supply things on his own what could have been added from them? At the least he should have indicated these books, that we might know what comes from Origen and what comes from Rufinus. He adds something that is the most impudent thing of all: that he compressed the entire work to nearly half its original length. Who can endure this man who truncates, adds to, and alters the written works of such great men and the precious riches of the church according to his own desire? In the *Ecclesiastical History* [of Eusebius] he spoiled the ninth book by transferring into it things that seemed fitting from the tenth. The reason he did this, he says, is because it had very little to do with events that had been accomplished, but was occupied with discussions in praise of bishops.[249] But material that the extremely learned man Eusebius judged to be worth his

---

247. It is also the judgment of Daniélou that Rufinus has supplied the outside material from Origen's commentaries (*Origen*, xi).

248. Erasmus is the only critical scholar known to me who discusses the significance of this word in Rufinus's text. It is ignored in modern discussions, for example that by H. Chadwick, "Rufinus and the Tura Papyrus of Origen's Commentary on Romans," JTS 10 (1959): 10–42.

249. Cf. Rufinus's preface to his translation of Eusebius's HE (NPNF2 3:565).

trouble to write about would have been worthwhile for us to read about. But if Rufinus had anything to say about the events of his own lifetime, he should have documented this separately, in twenty books for all I care, without tampering with the text of Eusebius. But he was afraid for himself, and to that end, in the manner of a cuckoo, he substituted his own chicks for someone else's brood.[250] He behaved no differently when he translated the books *On First Principles*. He removed some things and in their place substituted other things.[251] Certain other things that were spoken rather obscurely, [LB 8:437] he translated more expansively based on Origen's other works. Nor does he indicate what passages he has removed or what passages he has shed light upon.

In former times playwrights used to complain that it was not right for plays to be spoiled.[252] How much less fitting is it to spoil the books of illustrious teachers of the church. Rufinus frequently forces upon us everything that he dictated, referring this to Origen. In my judgment even if Rufinus had worked hard, scratched his head from time to time, struck the lectern and chewed his fingernails, he would hardly have been capable of writing anything worthy of learned ears.[253] And this is the man that Gennadius praises without qualification! He is proclaimed to be "not the least portion among the doctors of the church," though Gennadius, when he commemorates Augustine and Jerome, who were very great pillars of the church, does not refrain from affronting them.[254]

Would that the Greek works of Origen had indeed survived, so that we could detect Rufinus's devices. Nevertheless we owe to him the fact that some fragments of Origen survive for us.[255] But we would owe him much more if his achievement had been adorned with reliability. From the foregoing I think it is sufficiently clear in the case of this commentary that it was through the deceit of the booksellers that Jerome's name was added to the

---

250. Cf. Pliny, *Naturalis Historia* 10.9.11, 25.   251. See Rufinus's preface to this work.

252. See note 166 above.

253. The portrait seems to be drawn from Jerome's caricature of Rufinus's habits in *Ep* 125.18 to Rusticus.

254. Gennadius's entry on Augustine (*De viris illustribus* 39) is not disrespectful. He calls Augustine a man "unblemished in the faith, pure in life," who "wrote works so many that they cannot all be gathered." Gennadius has no specific entry on Jerome, but his admiring entry on Rufinus (17) alludes anonymously to Jerome as a "detractor" of Rufinus's works who was incited to polemics against Rufinus out of jealousy.

255. It is hardly reasonable for Erasmus to describe Rufinus's translation achievement as comprising "some fragments of Origen." In fact Rufinus's translations of Origen occupy at least 1,835 columns of Migne, about 50 percent of the total that survive. See the table in chapter 2.

preface in place of Rufinus. They were trying to entice buyers by attaching to the work an alluring title. They did the same thing in the work on the Apostles' Creed. For they transmitted that book in Cyprian's name, but with many things altered in such a way that the facts themselves declare that this was not done by accident but intentionally.[256]

Assessment of the Things That Are Lost

Now to investigate further into Origen's many works that have been lost to us is to do nothing else but to exasperate the grief of the learned, something that promises to do no good. For Origen neglected no part of scripture on which he did not write either *Scholia*, *Homilies*, or *Commentaries*, or all three. In addition to the homilies, he wrote twelve books on Genesis.[257] Pamphilus cites from the preface of this work in his *Apology*.[258] For Origen was not accustomed to write a preface for his homilies. The same is true of his books on Job, as Jerome testifies in his epistle to Pammachius and Marcellinus. Moreover, Origen wrote on the Psalms, up to the twentieth, from which Jerome declares that he translated those from the tenth to the sixteenth.[259] Pamphilus refers to a work of Origen on the Proverbs of Solomon. Jerome, in the preface to his published translation of the thirty-nine *Homilies on Luke* relates that Origen commented on Matthew in thirty-six books,[260] five on Luke,[261] thirty-nine on the Gospel of John.[262] It is thought that he wrote on the latter book while he was still living in Alexandria.[263] Pamphilus refers to a work of Origen on the epistle of Paul to Titus,[264] likewise on the epistle to the Hebrews.[265] He cites from the third book of Origen's work on the epistle

---

256. In light of his intense hostility toward Rufinus, it is somewhat ironic that Erasmus mentions this work, *A Commentary on the Apostles' Creed*, which unbeknownst to Erasmus was in fact an original composition of Rufinus. In his *Explanation of the Creed* (CWE 70:263), Erasmus called the author of that work "a man as learned as he was pious," without knowing that he was speaking about Rufinus. Had Erasmus known that Rufinus was the author, he would have either had to change his assessment of the work or of Rufinus. See *Rufinus: A Commentary on the Apostles' Creed*, trans. J. N. D. Kelly, ACW 20 (Mahwah, N.J.: Paulist Press, 1955).

257. Cf. Eusebius, HE 6.24.2.   258. Cf. Pamphilus, *Apologia* 5–7.
259. *De viris illustribus* 135.   260. The modern text has twenty-six.
261. This agrees with the modern text.   262. The modern text has thirty-two.

263. This is Erasmus's only explicit allusion to this work of Origen, which he seems to have known about only from Eusebius's mention of it (HE 6.24.1). Godin notes that Erasmus remained strangely silent about this major work of Origen, especially in the preface to his *Paraphrase on the Gospel of John* (*Erasme lecteur d'Origène*, 626). The fact is that the work was not accessible in Erasmus's day.

264. Cf. Pamphilus, *Apologia* 33–35, 162–65.
265. Cf. ibid., 49, 95–97, 99.

to the Colossians.²⁶⁶ There are thirty books on the third part of Isaiah, up to the description of the four-footed creature in the desert.²⁶⁷ There are twenty-five books on Ezekiel.²⁶⁸ He published these in his sixtieth year. He left behind ten books entitled *Stromata*.²⁶⁹ Pamphilus cites from the third book of this work, and Jerome frequently makes mention of it.²⁷⁰

Concerning Origen's Method of Teaching and Speaking

What Horace wrote about the Greeks can be most justly applied to Adamantius: "To Origen the Spirit gave genius, to Origen He gave the ability to speak with a well-turned phrase, desirous of nothing but Christ."²⁷¹ He had a marvelous ability for extemporaneous speaking and great clarity of diction, even in obscure matters.²⁷² Nor is brevity absent, whenever the subject calls for it. Certainly everywhere his thought flows along, nor does he entangle himself with words that weigh down weary listeners.²⁷³ Nowhere is he carried away by tragic style, which Jerome attributed to Hilary, for which reason, Jerome says, less learned brothers avoid reading Hilary.²⁷⁴ Nor does he lengthen out his books by unnatural ornamentation sought from a long way off, which Jerome sometimes does. He does not strive to provoke laughter in his listeners by witty and sarcastic remarks, which Tertullian does very often. Jerome too, in imitation of Tertullian, does this more than enough. But by what one might call a constant cheerfulness of style, Origen does not allow sleep to creep up on his audience. Nor does he strive after the little flowery adornments of the orators and their subtle little maxims and exclamations.²⁷⁵ It is reported that from childhood Ambrose and Jerome were completely preoccupied with these things from the rhetorical school.

---

266. Cf. ibid., 119–20.
267. Cf. Eusebius, HE 6.32.1; Jerome, *Commentary on Isaiah*, pref. to bk. 1. Cf. Is 30:6 LXX.
268. Cf. Eusebius, HE 6.32.1.   269. Cf. ibid., 6.24.3; Jerome, *Ep* 70.
270. Cf. Jerome, *Ep* 70.4.
271. Cf. Horace, *Ars Poet* 323–24: "To the Greeks the Muse gave genius, to the Greeks the Muse gave / the ability to speak with a well-turned phrase, desirous of nothing but praise."
272. In the epilogue to his translation of Origen's *Commentary on the Epistle to the Romans*, Rufinus reports that Origen's homilies were given "extemporaneously in the lecture hall of the church."
273. Cf. Horace, *Satires* 1.10.9–10: "You need brevity, to let the thought run freely on / without becoming entangled in a mass of words that will weigh down weary listeners."
274. Jerome, *Ep* 58.10 (NPNF2 6:122).
275. *Epiphonemata* are exclamations or other striking expressions used to provide a resounding conclusion to an argument or an exposition of facts; see Quintilian, *Inst.* 8.5.11. In CWE 12, ep.

Origen takes no delight in delaying the reader with unusual words, like Tertullian. He does not waste time with frequent digressions, as Augustine often does in his discussions before the people. Nor is he superstitious about the structure of his oration by completing his thoughts with interrupted sections and periods, of which our Gregory[276] is not free.[277] It is not that Gregory strove after this, in my opinion, but that from boyhood he had grown accustomed to these things. [LB 8:438] With Origen there never occurs occurs ὁμοιόπτωτα[278] and ὁμοιοτέλευτα[279] in which Augustine took delight. He never cites testimonies from the Gentiles except when the subject matter itself demands it.[280] Although he had grasped with exactness every class of authors, just as he had grasped the entire study of the humanities, yet he never displays annoying ostentation which irritates us in the books of some of the scholastics, where "the Philosopher" is invoked on every third line, but seldom do they cite testimonies from the holy scriptures, and when they do, they do not do so very successfully.[281] But all the words of Origen are distinguished everywhere by thoughts from the sacred volumes. These are inserted like jewels in a mosaic, and so appropriately and at the right spot that the oration runs on no less well. You might say that they are not foreign but originate there. They are not sought from elsewhere, but they are his own, spontaneous, ready at hand.[282]

Origen does not interrupt the flow of his orations by citing passages

---

1800, his dedicatory epistle of an edition of Latin translations of Chrysostom's works, Erasmus used almost these exact same terms to described John Chrysostom's homiletical style.

276. "Our Gregory" refers to Pope Gregory the Great (590–604) who was regarded throughout the medieval period as the first amongst the masters. The epithet "our Gregory" imitates the admirers of Virgil who used to say "our Virgil." Cf. de Lubac, *Medieval Exegesis*, 2:118.

277. Erasmus describes Jean Vitrier's homilies similarly in CWE 8, ep. 1211.

278. The use of words with a similar inflection or in a like case.

279. Ending a clause or verse with words ending alike.

280. Cf. de Lubac: "Except in the *Contra Celsum*, he [Origen] almost never quotes secular authors. He was not a private instructor, a lecturer, but was above all a catechist and a preacher" (*History and Spirit*, 62).

281. As early as the *Methodus*, Erasmus complained of the excessive use of Aristotle and neglect of the Bible in contemporary theological works.

282. In his letter of dedication to Pope Adrian VI of the Psalms commentary of Arnobius the Younger (CWE 9, ep. 1304), Erasmus describes Arnobius's style similarly: "At no point does he cite the testimony of Holy Writ for mere display; but his whole style is skillfully put together like inlay or mosaic from scriptural elements, and often he weaves together several verses of the psalm he is expounding with such skill that the addition of a few words enables him to throw light even on what he does not expound."

in order to be more thorough.[283] For sometimes allusion is more pleasing than citation. Add the fact that the people in Origen's day were rather well acquainted with the words of scripture, since they were practiced in the reading of the divine books. For back then both male and female weavers had the sacred codices at home, which they held in their hands on feast days or whenever they had leisure.[284] Nor was there need of another language to understand these things, only the one that the illiterate public used.[285] Indeed, the very act of reading the passage brought a benefit, as they sat in the temples more docile to the one who was explaining the mysteries of scripture.[286] The facts themselves show that Origen held all of canonical scripture in his memory, as scarcely any of us is more readily familiar with his own fingers and toes.[287] So much so did his indomitable effort prevail, so much so did it exert an influence in respect to the things he had imbibed from earliest childhood. Horace thinks that pardon ought to be granted if sleep creeps in in a long work.[288] But to say nothing about his daily homilies to the people, Origen produced so many books that you would think he never slept or grew tired.[289] Every-

283. Literally "out of an ambitious diligence."
284. I am not sure why Erasmus picked out the term "weavers" here, or if Origen ever makes reference to them. In Jerome's Ep 46, he describes Christians living in the land of Christ's birth as people who were very familiar with scripture: "Wherever one turns the laborer at his plough sings alleluia, the toiling mower cheers himself with psalms, and the vine-dresser while he prunes his vine sings one of the lays of David. These are the songs of the country; these, in popular phrase, its love ditties: these the shepherd whistles; these the tiller uses to aid his toil." Erasmus modeled his Paraclesis in his 1516 New Testament on Jerome's text and adds: "I should prefer that all women, even of the lowest rank, should read the evangelists and the epistles of Paul, and I wish these writings were translated into all the languages of the human race, so that they could be read and studied, not just by the Irish and the Scots, but by the Turks as well, and the Saracens.... I would hope that the farmer might chant a holy text at his plow, the spinner [= weaver] sing it as she sits at her wheel, the traveler ease the tedium of his journey with tales from the scripture. Let all conversation between Christians draw from this source."
285. That is, Greek.
286. Erasmus seems to be reflecting the thought of Origen's Hom in Jos 20, where Origen describes the benefit that comes to the soul through the sheer act of hearing the scriptures read publicly at church, even when the passages are not completely understood. By hearing alone, the divine power is released and overthrows the power of the evil spirits that seek to harm Christian souls. For Erasmus, the editor of the first published Greek New Testament, this power was all the more manifest when the scripture was read in the original language.
287. This is said of Jean Vitrier (CWE 8, ep. 1211). It reflects Juvenal, Satires 7.232; Adagia II iv.91.
288. Ars poet 360.
289. Eusebius, HE 6.8.6, says that as a catechist Origen spent the greater part of his nights in studying the Bible. Epiphanius reported that Origen wrote six thousand books. Jerome reported the more reasonable figure of two thousand.

where he is eager and lively, everywhere he burns with enthusiasm. He loved the things he was speaking about, and we speak of things that we love with delight.[290] This is the source of Origen's perpetual enthusiasm and his constant vigor.

From the length of his homilies among the people it appears that he never composed a sermon that lasted more than an hour; frequently he finished them in less than half an hour. He was not unaware how great the fastidiousness of the laity is. Most of them could hardly be brought to church.[291] They were disinclined to listen to the priest discoursing on heavenly things in the temples, preferring instead to listen to mime actors telling worthless stories in the theater that are both obscene and harmful to the soul.[292] And so, he judged it to be a better plan to teach often rather than at length. In reproving conduct, everywhere he remembers Christian moderation. He never bursts into flame with dramatic exclamations, mindful that he is preaching homilies, which is a term of intimacy, not one used to describe the severity of a censor. Yet sometimes he does sting and has sufficient sharpness, but never bitterness. Frequently, when the rebuke is rather harsh, he numbers himself among those whom he is rebuking.[293] He does not display men's domestic filth or their secret sins, which some ignorant men tend to do, who compose their sermons out of secrets from the confessional, not without affronting sexes, conditions, or orders, scarcely failing to mention the people involved. Quite frequently Origen makes no use of scolding. The reason for this was that people rarely came to listen to the word of God. And those who were present were yawning as they listened to things that they should have been receiving with complete alertness of mind.[294] Origen judged rightly

---

290. Erasmus says this also of Jean Vitrier (CWE 8, ep. 1211); of Irenaeus of Lyons, *An Exposition of Psalm 38* (CWE 65:43); and of Augustine (CWE 15, ep. 2157).

291. In *Hom in Gn* 10.3, Origen reproaches his hearers for coming to church only on Sundays and not on other feast days as well.

292. Cf. Origen, *Hom in Lv* 11.7: "What shall we say about those who hasten to the spectacles with crowds of pagans and defile their sight and hearing with shameless words and deeds? It is not for us to judge about such as these. For they can think and see for themselves which part they have chosen for themselves" (trans. Barkley).

293. See Origen's *Hom in Ezek* 5.4; *Hom in Jdg* 7.2.

294. Generally Erasmus is right about Origen's infrequent use of harsh scolding, but Origen was capable of reproaching his listeners. Cf. Origen's *Hom in Gn* 10.1: "But I fear that the Church is still bearing sons in sadness and sorrow. Or does it not cause her sadness and sorrow when you do not gather to hear the word of God? And scarcely on feast days do you proceed to the Church, and you do this not so much from a desire for the word as from a fondness for the festival and to obtain, in a certain manner, common relaxation.... You spend most of this time,

from this that the advancement of or defection from piety was the most important thing.

When the reading is rather long and involved, like the things Moses reports concerning the kinds and rites of the sacrifices, concerning the investigation of leprosy, concerning the consecration of priests and Levites, he does not pursue the details, lest it become tedious to the audience.[295] Rather, with an unbelievable adroitness he sets forth some things in such a way that from the things he does say, the hearer understands the gist of the whole subject. When he has to treat a subject that is involved and complicated, and on this account unpleasant, he paves the way for the hearer with a wonderful introduction.[296] He sheds a little light that convinces the hearer that the things that seem to be impediments can be easily comprehended and, moreover, that they are actually very beneficial. Further, he shows that the things that seemed unpleasant and superfluous are in fact very pleasant. Frequently he highlights and explains the history itself in such a way, and he abridges it in such a way, that the hearer is easily able both to understand and to remember the complex events recorded in the books of Moses. Very often he does this for one who is inquiring and trying hard, sometimes for one who is nearly in despair. The result is that he stirs up the spirit of the hearer [LB 8:439] to the same zeal for inquiry, and he leads him on in suspense, so to speak, and attentive.[297] Sometimes Origen himself prays and seeks to be assisted by the prayers of the audience, and he offers hope to them that more sublime things can be discovered by them, if they focus their minds.[298]

He does not use any strange introductions but fitting and necessary ones, hastening to seize the audience into the midst of the subject matter.[299] He generally follows this order. He explains the history very clearly and

---

no rather almost all of it in mundane occupations; you pass some of it in the marketplace, some in business; one has time for the country, another for lawsuits, and no one or very few have time to hear the word of God. But why do I reproach you about occupations? Why do I complain about absences? Even when you are present and placed in the Church you are not attentive, but you waste your time on common everyday stories; you turn your backs on the word of God or to the divine readings" (trans. Heine). Cf. *Hom in Gn* 10.3; *Hom in Ex* 12.2, 13.3.

295. Cf. Origen, *Hom in Lv* 5.9, 8.6–7.
296. Of the many examples that could be given, cf. Origen's *Hom in Ezek* 11.3.
297. A classic example of this technique that was deeply admired by Erasmus is Origen's emotional telling of the Abraham/Isaac story (Gn 22) in his *Hom in Gn* 8.
298. Cf. Origen, *Hom in Ezek* 4.3; *Hom in Gn* 6.1; *Hom in Jer* 19.14.
299. Cf. Horace, *Ars poet* 148–49, of Homer: "He always presses on to the outcome and hurries the reader / into the middle of things as though they were quite familiar." *Satires of Horace and Persius*, trans. N. Rudd (Harmondsworth: Penguin, 2005), 194.

briefly, whenever the subject requires this. Then he stimulates his audience to discover the deepest meanings of the allegory. Lastly he treats the moral aspects.[300] In this respect he has followed Paul, who in the first part of his epistles discusses more sublime things. [LB 8:440] Once these things have been clarified, he descends to the instruction about morals and living.[301] But Origen does not seek his allegories from the philosophers or from the Talmud of the Hebrews,[302] or from the Kabbalah,[303] or from dreams out of his own head, but from the scriptures themselves, by comparing passages with passages. And if the allegory seems a bit strained to the audience at the first hearing, he softens it in advance with a little introduction.[304] He never dwells upon it longer than is necessary, avoiding tedium on all occasions. For in moral subject matter Chrysostom is almost excessive. And in addition to the fact that a style that is lively, distinct, and very lucid does not allow tedium to sneak in, such a style likewise avoids fastidiousness by its very brevity.

300. De Lubac describes Erasmus's remarks here as "most apt" (*Medieval Exegesis*, 1:145).

301. For instance, Rom 1–11 and 12–16 are often interpreted according to this division of doctrine and moral exhortation.

302. The Talmud consists of compilations of commentary on the Mishnah whose texts have become the core for Jewish legal and moral understanding.

303. The Kabbalah was a system of occult and mystical interpretation of the scriptures used by some Jewish rabbis and a few medieval Christians, at first handed down orally through chosen individuals, and later committed to writing. The Kabbalists assumed that every letter, word, number, and accent of scripture contained a hidden sense and that their system provided the key for ascertaining the hidden meanings. John Reuchlin, Erasmus's contemporary, had published a work on the Kabbalah entitled *De arte caballistica*.

304. While Erasmus was generally supportive of Origen's allegorical interpretations, he could also be critical of his excesses. In *Methodus*, he warns the reader against Origen's unnecessary allegorizing (cf. LB 5:126; trans. Conroy, 309).

APPENDIX: SIXTEENTH-CENTURY ASSESSMENTS OF ERASMUS

Recently a scholar has depicted Peter Canisius's (1521–97) reception of Erasmus as characterized, first of all, by the practice of plagiarizing Erasmus's writings extensively into his own works; then by his openly attacking Erasmus in terms that are ambivalent, confused, and bizarrely contradictory.[1] In contrast with this, it appears that there was no such ingratitude and ambivalence in John Colet's (1466–1519) assessment of Erasmus. In response to the publication of Erasmus's New Testament in 1516, John Colet, dean of St. Paul's Cathedral in London and father confessor of Thomas More, famously wrote: "The name of Erasmus shall never perish."[2] John

---

1. See H. Pabel, "Praise and Blame: Peter Canisius's Ambivalent Assessment of Erasmus," in *Reception of Erasmus*, ed. Enenkel, 129–59.

2. CWE 3, ep. 423. The fuller context is worth providing: "The copies of your new edition sell here like hot cakes and are read everywhere, and many approve your labors and marvel at them; some however disapprove and find fault, making the same criticisms that Maarten van Dorp makes in his letter to you. But these are theologians, of the kind you describe with as much truth as wit in your *Moria* and elsewhere, to be praised by whom is a discredit, and whose dispraise is praise. Personally I like your work and welcome your new edition, but in a way that rouses mingled feelings. At one time I am sorry that I never learned Greek, without some skill in which we can get nowhere; and then again I rejoice in the light which is shed by your genius like the sun. In fact, Erasmus, I am astonished at the fertility of your intellect—you conceive so much, have so much in gestation, and bring forth some perfectly finished offspring every day—especially as you have no certain abode, and lack the support of any fixed, substantial endowment.... I long to see the result of your work on the Epistle to the Romans. Do not hesitate, my dear Erasmus, but when you have given us the New Testament in better Latin, go on to elucidate it with your explanations, and let us have a really long commentary on the Gospels. Length from you will seem short. In those who love Holy Scripture the appetite can only grow, provided their digestion is sound, as they read what you have written. If you make the meaning clear, which no one will do better than you, you will confer a great benefit on us all, and make your name immortal. Immortal, did I say? The name of Erasmus shall never perish, but you will win for your name eternal glory, and as you toil in Jesus, you will win for yourself eternal life."

Colet himself had been described by Thomas More as "a man both as learned and as holy as any of our countrymen has been for the last several centuries."[3] Erasmus's revered status in the eyes of some of his other contemporaries is confirmed by testimonies from high-ranking ecclesiastical scholars from Italy, England, Germany, and Poland. The Italian bishop of Carpentras (in southern France), Jacob Sadoleto, to whom Erasmus dedicated his edition of the works of Basil, dubbed Erasmus "the father of us all in this century; the one who brought back sacred letters to their pristine beauty and splendor."[4] Sadoleto was elected as cardinal in 1537 by Pope Paul III and was one of Erasmus's staunchest defenders in the Roman Curia.[5] His sentiment was shared by the future saint and martyr, Thomas More, who although a layman was also regarded as one of pre-Reformation England's greatest Catholic apologists and theologians.[6] More wrote the following in defense of Erasmus: "I confess that I love Erasmus vehemently for practically no other reason than that for which all of Christendom cherishes him, namely that this one man's unceasing exertions have done more to advance all students of sound intellectual disciplines everywhere in both secular and sacred learning than virtually anyone else's exertions for the last several centuries."[7] More's defense of Erasmus calls attention to Erasmus's objective achievements in both the liberal arts and theological studies. In fact Thomas More wrote book-length treatises in defense of Erasmus that were cited in chapter 1 and will be quoted later in this appendix.[8]

Along similar lines, Fisher placed Erasmus in the front rank as the most zealous of the German champions of the Catholic church against Luther.[9] Fisher describes Erasmus as one who is "truly orthodox and renowned in scriptural exegesis," and adds: "Erasmus teaches irrefutably that every man must pursue the teaching of the Catholic Church."[10] More and Fisher were intimately acquainted with Erasmus's anti-Protestant apologetic writings (works that are seldom discussed in modern scholarship) and they felt that the Catholic church owed an enormous debt of grati-

3. *Letter to a Monk*, 1519 (CW 15:269–71).

4. September 17, 1530. P. S. Allen, *Opus Epistolarum Desiderii Erasmi Roterodami* IX, ep. 2385, 48–50: "quando tu quidem in sacris litteris ad antiquum decorem splendoremque revocandis et omnium nostrum et huius seculi es pater."

5. Cf. R. Douglas, *Jacobo Sadoleto 1477–1547: Humanist and Reformer* (Cambridge, Mass.: Harvard University Press, 1959), 21.

6. See Christopher J. Malloy, "Thomas More on Luther's *Sola Fide*: Just or Unjust?," *Angelicum* 90 (2013): 761–98.

7. Thomas More, *Letter to Edward Lee* (1519) (CW 15:159–61, with slight changes).

8. CW 15 contains More's apologies for Erasmus.

9. See my article "Bishop John Fisher's Response to Martin Luther," *Franciscan Studies* 71 (2013): 463–509.

10. T. Marie Dougherty, "St. John Fisher's *De Veritate Corporis et Sanguinis Christi in Eucharistia*, The Prefaces: Text and Translation with Introduction and Notes" (PhD diss., The Catholic University of America, 1969), 62–63. This correlates to *Ioannis Fischerii Opera Omnia* (Farnborough: Gregg Press, 1967), col. 748.

tude to Erasmus. These latter two testimonies in particular do not deserve to be neglected, since they stem from the only two canonized saints who personally knew Erasmus. Rudolf Padberg emphasizes this point and contrasts the attitude of More and Fisher with that which emerged in some sectors of the post-Tridentine Catholic church (among the Jesuits, Peter Canisius and Robert Bellarmine, for example). Of the former group Padberg writes: "They knew Erasmus, they defended him ... their assessment of Erasmus weighs more heavily than the assessment of the next generation and of the period of Church revolution, which saw itself compelled to turn all instruments of peace into weapons."[11] I certainly agree with Padberg on this point and hope that devout Catholics will allow the opinion of the canonized saints who knew Erasmus to carry more weight than the more widely publicized views of those who did not know him.[12]

From Germany there is the testimony of Christopher von Stadion (1478–1543), who became bishop of Augsburg in 1517, after studying at Tübingen, Freiburg, and Ferrara, where he received his doctorate.[13] In response to receiving Friedrich Nausea's eulogy of Erasmus (the *Monodia*) in October 1537, in which Nausea, the future bishop of Vienna, called for Erasmus's canonization—I will summarize the content of this oration later in this appendix—bishop Stadion wrote the following in reply:

> The praise and virtue of Erasmus is so great that no human voice is capable of proclaiming it in view of his merits. I confess that it is from him that I have received the greatest portion of my Christianity (if indeed I have any). It was he who pointed with his finger (so to speak) to the true way of piety and religion. Since the birth of Christ no man who has been born in the world deserves better from the Christian republic.[14]

This laudatory exclamation is matched by the view of the Polish cardinal Stanislaus Hosius (1504–79), who became known as the "hammer of the heretics" in Poland for his effectiveness in winning back Protestant territories for the church. Peter Canisius styled Hosius as "the most brilliant writer, the most eminent theologian and the best bishop of the times."[15] In his youth Hosius wanted to become a personal student of Erasmus, and also in the later years of his life it was his desire to visit Erasmus on his return from Italy, but he was prevented from doing so when he

---

11. Padberg, *Erasmus als Katechet*, 18–19.
12. To me it seems both strange and disappointing that most modern Catholic biographers of Fisher and More seem to feel nervous about their subject's positive assessment of Erasmus.
13. Cf. Allen, *Opus Epistolarum Desiderii Erasmi Roterodami* VII, ep. 2029.
14. Cf. Allen, *Opus Epistolarum Desiderii Erasmi Roterodami* VII, ep. 2029: "[Erasmi] laus ac virtus tanta est ut nulla humana voce pro meritis praedicari possit. A quo non minimam Christianitatis portionem (si saltem in me aliqua residet) me accepisse profiteor. Is fuit qui veram pietatis ac religionis viam digito (ut ita loquar) demonstraverit. A Christo nato non fuit natus in terris qui melius de re Christiana meritus fuerit."
15. Hipler, *Hosii Epistolae* I, 422; cited in "Stanislaus Hosius," *Catholic Encyclopedia* (New York: Encyclopedia Press, 1917).

fell prey to highway robbers.[16] Hosius believed that he was completely united with Erasmus in his reform aims and pastoral intentions. In 1551 at a synod of Polish clergy, he recommended Erasmus's *Enchiridion* and *De modo orandi Deum* (*On Praying to God*) for parish priests to read.[17] Hosius's own Catholic apologetic writings used Erasmus's *Hyperaspistes* directly, a reprint of which Hosius secured in Krakow.[18]

In Hosius's later work, *Confutatio of Johannes Brenz*, Erasmus is again commended and cited at some length.[19] Hosius appended an encomium in praise of Erasmus to a Polish edition of Erasmus's letter to Sigismund I.[20] Padberg has noted that although his predecessor had introduced a new catechism only shortly before, Bishop Hosius decided to introduce Erasmus's *Explanation of the Creed* (1533) for use in the diocese as a catechism.[21] Hosius's own catechetical handbook shows in many respects that he had inherited much from Erasmus's major catechism.[22] Hosius is thus an impressive Polish witness to the belief in Erasmus's ecclesiastical reliability. His own prominence as papal legate and one of the presidents at the final session of the Council of Trent provides evidence that suggests that that reform council could not have been as "anti-Erasmian" in spirit as it is often depicted. (I will say more of Erasmus's influence at the Council of Trent later in this appendix.) Finally, there is the impressive support for Erasmus's Christian mission by Beatus Rhenanus, his first Catholic biographer. This subject has been recently discussed.[23]

---

16. Cf. J. Lortz, *Kardinal Stanislaus Hosius. Beiträge zur Erkenntnis der Persönlichkeit und des Werkes* (Braunsberg: Herder, 1931), 13, 225; P. Bietenholz, "Concordia christiana: Erasmus' Thought and the Polish Reality," *Erasmus of Rotterdam Society Yearbook* 21 (2001): 66; Howard Louthan, "A Model for Christendom? Erasmus, Poland, and the Reformation," *Church History* 83, no. 1 (March 2014): 18–37.

17. Bietenholz, "Concordia christiana," 67. Bietenholz seems to want to downplay Hosius's active commendation of Erasmus's writings.

18. *Hyperaspistes* is Erasmus's two-volume response in which he refutes the errors of Martin Luther (CWE 76 and 77).

19. The citations come from Erasmus's anti-Protestant writings: *In pseudevangelicos* (1529), *Ad fratres Inferioris Germaniae* (1530), and *Hyperaspistes II* (1527). The former two works have recently appeared in their first English translation in the CWE 78. Cf. Bietenholz, "Concordia christiana," 67, and Pabel, "Praise and Blame," 129–59.

20. Cf. Allen, *Opus Epistolarum Desiderii Erasmi Roterodami*, ep. 1819; F. Flitner, *Erasmus im Urteil*, 85n167.

21. The Catechism in question is Erasmus's *Explanation of the Creed* (1533). It is found in English translation in Desiderius Erasmus, *Spiritualia and Pastoralia*, ed. John W. O'Malley, CWE 70 (Toronto: University of Toronto Press, 1998). I will say more about Erasmus's *Catechism* later in this appendix.

22. Padberg, *Erasmus als Katechet*, 152–53. Padberg also sadly notes that Joseph Lortz, in his monograph *Kardinal Stanislaus Hosius, Beiträge zur Erkenntnis der Persönlichkeit und des Werkes*, shows no awareness of Hosius's dependence on Erasmus. This seems to be symptomatic of Lortz and of the Lortzian school of ecclesiastical historiography: to denigrate and downplay Erasmus's works.

23. See K. Enenkel, "Beatus Rhenanus' Second Vita Erasmi (1540)," in *Reception of Erasmus*, ed. Enenkel, 25–40.

APPENDIX: SIXTEENTH-CENTURY ASSESSMENTS 191

Papal Support for Erasmus

In chapter 1, I briefly reported the first criticisms of Erasmus's curricular proposals made by Jacob Latomus of the University of Louvain. This dispute occurred early on in Erasmus's career (ca. 1519). A decade later, certain statements extracted from Erasmus's writings were censured by the University of Paris's theological faculty (the Sorbonne), led by Noël Béda.[24] Erasmus's writings thus had the same fate as those of Cardinal Cajetan, the greatest Dominican theologian of the sixteenth century, whose exegetical works on scripture were also censured by the Paris theological faculty.[25] There were a number of other victims of this sort of persecution, such as John Reuchlin, who was attacked by the Dominicans for promoting Hebrew studies, and Jacques Lefévre, who suffered at the hands of academic theologians for dissenting from medieval legends in his exegesis.[26]

In modern times the Catholic historian A. Renaudet, a professor at the Sorbonne, capitalized on these university-level censures of Erasmus in order to reproach Erasmus's Catholic orthodoxy generally and to depict him as a forerunner of the "modernists."[27] De Lubac and Bouyer lacked sympathy for Renaudet's attack on Erasmus's character and orthodoxy and the way it implicitly equated the voice of Erasmus's most reactionary critics at Paris and Louvain with the voice of Catholic orthodoxy itself, to the neglect of the papal office. Bouyer offered the following rebuttal:

To the continual approval shown Erasmus by the Popes, M. Renaudet opposes a condemnation by the faculties of theology and by several priests. We can pass over the fact that on the testimony of M. Renaudet's book it was the faculty of Paris alone that at this epoch condemned Erasmus, and this was done solely upon the perusal of a translation of his work M. Renaudet himself shows to have been erroneous. Besides this, there are the

---

24. See CWE 82; Rummel, *Erasmus and His Catholic Critics*, vol. 2, chap. 2. Bouyer remarks: "What should be noted however is that this unfortunate affair all turned on misconceptions. The texts judged by the Sorbonne were translations made by Berquin. Only when it was too late Erasmus discovered that they distorted and misrepresented his thought in a definitely Lutheran sense" (*Erasmus and His Times*, 133).

25. Cf. Thomas Aquinas Collins, OP, "The Cajetan Controversy," *American Ecclesiastical Review* 128, no. 2 (February 1953): 90–100; T. Collins, OP, "Cardinal Cajetan's Fundamental Biblical Principles," *CBQ* 17 (1955): 363–78; J. Wicks, "Catholic Old Testament Interpretation in the Reformation and Early Confessional Eras," in *Hebrew Bible / Old Testament, The History of Its Interpretation*, 2 vols., ed. Magne Saebo (Goettingen: Vandenhoeck & Ruprecht, 2008), 2:617–48.

26. See the respective essays in Rummel, ed., *Biblical Humanism and Scholasticism in the Age of Erasmus*.

27. A. Renaudet, *Études Érasmiennes 1521–1529* (Paris: Librairie E. Droz, 1939). Renaudet's views unfortunately were adopted and intensified by church historian Joseph Lortz. In addition to Bouyer's great book, the best refutation of this alleged "undogmatic" Erasmus is C. J. De Vogel, "Erasmus and His Attitude towards Church Dogma," in *Scrinium Erasmianum*, 2 vols., ed. J. Coppens (Leiden: Brill, 1969), 2:101–32. De Vogel had no difficulty disproving Lortz's accusations and even showing that Lortz was unfamiliar with Erasmus's writings.

condemnations brought against him by individual theologians. But they speak for no one but themselves. In any case, what sort of Catholicism is this, on what basis can one pass judgment on the position of the humanist while wholly discounting the authority of the pope in comparison with that of the theological faculties, admittedly of distinction, or even as compared with a crowd of mere controversialists?[28]

The questions raised here strike me as fundamentally important. What was the attitude toward Erasmus of the popes of his lifetime? Can their interventions on Erasmus's behalf and their defense of his orthodoxy be validly overlooked by those who wish to make determinations about Erasmus's ecclesiastical reliability? Is Erasmus to be faulted for following the advice of the popes, who commended his scholarship in public letters and advised him to continue his scholarly work, even in the face of the conservative criticisms he was simultaneously receiving from other quarters? Or should he have ignored the popes and listened to the advice of Noël Béda, who told him to put down his pen?

Pope Leo X

Pope Leo X (1513–21) has been described in these words: "The most vilified of all the Renaissance popes is also the one most completely vindicated. After Pastor's work, it can no longer be denied that the Holy See was occupied, in Cardinal Giovanni de' Medici, by a priest who was sincerely—if not always effectively—conscious of the obligations of the priesthood."[29] Pope Leo X commended Erasmus's scholarship in public letters which Erasmus published. Some of these letters were written at the very height of the controversy over Erasmus's *Praise of Folly*, while Erasmus was responding to critics of his satire such as Martin Dorp.[30] Others were sent after Erasmus's edition of Jerome's writings and the first edition of the New Testament had been published. Far from being offended by Erasmus's satire of bad popes in *Praise of Folly*—which Leo X knew did not apply to him in any case—or critical of Erasmus's patristic and scriptural studies, Leo X heartily endorses Erasmus's scholarship: "For our part, such is our general devotion and love toward sound learning and such our particular belief in your virtue and scholarship, we greatly desire that on some suitable occasion our liberality may find a way to serve your honor and your advantage, as our good will towards you demands and as your worth deserves."[31] These are words directly addressed to Erasmus from the pope.

28. *Erasmus and His Times*, 140. In his scathing invective against Erasmus, Joseph Sauer's article "Desiderius Erasmus" in the *Catholic Encyclopedia* let the following words slip out: "It is a remarkable fact that the attitude of the popes towards Erasmus was never inimical."
29. Bouyer, *Erasmus and His Times*, 42.
30. In the *Controversy with Alberto Pio* (CWE 84:58), Erasmus reported from reliable sources that Pope Leo X read through *Praise of Folly* and liked it. In reply, Alberto Pio admitted the truth of Erasmus's statement.
31. CWE 3, ep. 338 (July 1515).

A letter written at the same time from Pope Leo X to Henry VIII contains an even stronger recommendation of Erasmus's patristic scholarship:

> Towards learned men ... we feel a certain warm interest and a more than common inclination, which was born in us from childhood, strengthened by the principles of our upbringing, and increased by the maturer judgment of advancing years; and this, not only because we have now learnt by repeated experience that these men who devote themselves to good letters and the arts are of excellent character and unimpeachable integrity, but also because we know that such knowledge, and the literary gifts of the doctors of Holy Church, have been the source of very great advantage and adornment to our Christian polity. For these reasons we have a high regard in the Lord for our beloved son Erasmus Rotterdam, whom we consider to be among the leaders of such learning and such arts, a man known to us aforetime from personal acquaintance in a lower station of life, and since then far better known and most highly esteemed for the works of genius which he has published. This man has sent us from England, where he now resides, a letter full of dutiful sentiments, which is all the more welcome in that it brings with it evidence from him of your royal excellence and kingly spirit, a reminder than which nothing could give us greater pleasure in view of the high place which your Majesty holds in our good will. We have therefore thought fit to recommend him to your Majesty, not that at this time we have any definite request to make of you on his behalf, nor does he himself ask us for anything of the kind; but this is something we do of our own free will, to solicit on behalf of those who enjoy our sincere good wishes and the same good will and favor from others who are in a position to comply. It will therefore give us great satisfaction, should he ask anything of your Majesty's grace, favor and benevolence, if over and above the generosity which you may show him of your own mere motion, you should let it be known that this recommendation from us has added further weight.[32]

Since he had this kind of public support from the papal office, it is no wonder Erasmus felt emboldened to continue his scholarly work even in the face of conservative criticisms that would plague his entire scholarly career. The reader should be reminded that Leo X's letter to Henry VIII recommending Erasmus was written more than fifteen years before this king introduced the Anglican schism.

In light of subsequent developments that will be described later in this chapter, it is of great interest to observe that in the very letter from Erasmus that had inspired Pope Leo X to send his encouragement and blessing to Erasmus, Erasmus had reported that the bishop of Chieti, an Italian humanist scholar named Gianpietro Carafa who was also papal legate to England, had provided him enormous encouragement in his studies and even the revival of his own spirits. Erasmus tells Pope Leo X that Carafa's approval of his scholarship had recalled Erasmus to the post of duty.

> A man with such a gift of speech might persuade one to do anything; who would not be moved by the authority of such an upright and authoritative prelate, or inspired by the rare

32. CWE 3, ep. 339 (July 1515).

holiness of that excellent man? ... This great man attached such great importance to these labors of mine that, were I the most conceited of men, I still could not accept his opinion. And yet somehow or other that praise of his applied the spur to my weariness, supported my exhaustion, and refreshed my flagging energy.[33]

Erasmus is here describing the very same man who in 1559, as Pope Paul IV, would place all Erasmus's writings on the Index of Prohibited Books. Yet in the year 1515, when he was bishop of Chieti and papal legate to England, Carafa had so highly praised Erasmus's scholarly achievements that his words bordered on flattery. Carafa had energetically encouraged Erasmus to persevere in his most important scholarly work, knowing full well the hostile reception of Erasmus's scholarship by obscurantist critics of the Renaissance. It is no wonder that Paul IV's Index created such a scandal in the church when it was published in 1559.

In 1516 Erasmus published his edition of Jerome's works, as well as the New Testament, which had been dedicated to Pope Leo X. Erasmus then received a letter from Leo in January 1517 which contains the following words:

The uprightness of your life and character, your exceptional learning, and the outstanding merit of your virtues, which are not only strongly corroborated by the wide renown of your published works but also commended to us by the opinion of the most learned men, and not least by letters from the king of England and from his Catholic Majesty [Charles V], make us wish to encourage you with some singular and special favor. We have therefore gladly acceded to your request, and furthermore will display our concern for you more fully, when you give us the opportunity or chance brings it within our reach. For we judge it right that your sacred industry, which toils unceasingly for the common good, should be urged on by suitable rewards to yet greater undertakings.[34]

Finally, a crowning testimony of very great importance is Pope Leo X's formal expression of papal approval for the second edition of Erasmus's New Testament (which interestingly enough was regarded as the most provocative of the five editions published in Erasmus's lifetime.) This letter, deeply appreciated by Erasmus, was printed on the reverse of the title page of Froben's text and is dated September 10, 1518. Pope Leo X writes:

To our beloved son Erasmus of Rotterdam, Doctor of Divinity, from Pope Leo X. Our beloved son, greeting and apostolic benediction. We derived great pleasure from the studies of the New Testament which you published some time ago, not so much because they were dedicated to us as for the new and exceptional learning by which they were distinguished and which earned them a chorus of praise from the world of scholars. The news that you had lately revised them, and enriched and clarified them by the addition of numerous annotations gave us no little satisfaction; for we inferred from the first edition, which used to seem a most finished performance, what this new one would be, and how much it would benefit all who have at heart the progress of theology and of our orthodox faith. Go forward

33. In CWE 3, ep. 335 to Leo X (May 1515).
34. CWE 4, ep. 519 (January 26, 1517).

then in this same spirit: work for the public good, and do all you can to bring so religious an undertaking into the light of day, for you will receive from God himself a worthy reward for all your labors, from us the commendation you deserve, and from all Christ's faithful people lasting renown.[35]

In light of such encouragement from the highest living authority in Christendom, it is certainly understandable why Erasmus pressed forward with his scholarly mission over the next twenty years. He had been told by the popes (and by the young bishop Carafa) to do just that. When his New Testament was attacked by conservative critics, in his own defense Erasmus appealed to the papal support he had received. For example, in response to Edward Lee, Erasmus wrote: "Leo twice approved it, and even if his approval does not apply to every single part of the work, it certainly applies to my zeal and enterprise. I suppose no one will blame me if I put more trust in Leo's judgment than in Lee's."[36]

Pope Adrian VI

Pope Adrian VI, who was the last non-Italian pope prior to John Paul II, was elected to the papacy on January 9, 1522, and died September 14, 1523. He has been described as a pope who not only deplored and condemned heresy and the schism in the church produced by the early Lutheran movement, "but he also laid bare the deeper causes and with an unprecedented candor admitted the guilt of Curia and Church."[37] Adrian did this in his *Instruction to Chieregati*, 1522.[38] In epistle 1324 (December 1, 1522) Pope Adrian VI summoned Erasmus to write against Luther.[39] Erasmus referred to this papal letter as the *Breve aureum*, the "golden letter." He cites it frequently against his conservative Roman Catholic critics, because it gave such unmistakable evidence of the pope's goodwill toward him. Erasmus later revealed that Adrian offered him (doubtless orally through John Fabri) an honorific ecclesiastical promotion and a gift of money, both of which he declined.[40] The letter reached Erasmus in January 1523.

In this letter Pope Adrian VI says that he wishes to put Erasmus's mind at rest concerning the bad reports of him that he has heard were circulating in Rome. The pope admits that he has heard such reports, but says that he does not lend a ready ear to information that discredits learned men like Erasmus who are also noted for

---

35. CWE 6, ep. 864 (September 10, 1518).
36. *Response to Edward Lee* (CWE 72:74).
37. E. Iserloh, J. Glazik, H. Jedin, eds., *Reformation and Counter Reformation, History of the Church*, 10 vols. (New York: Seabury, 1980), 5:109. See also M. W. F. Stone, "Adrian of Utrecht and the University of Louvain: Theology and the Discussion of Moral Problems in the Late Fifteenth Century," Traditio 61 (2006): 247–87.
38. This document is available in English translation in John C. Olin, ed., *The Catholic Reformation: Savonarola to Ignatius Loyola* (New York: Fordham University Press, 1992), 118–27.
39. CWE 9.
40. CWE 9, ep. 1341A, 1681–83; cf. CWE 9, ep. 1345:19–20.

their holiness of life. Adrian attributes the bad reports to envy. Then he firmly challenges Erasmus to use his intellectual gifts in defense of the Catholic church and even invites Erasmus to come to Rome to live.

Do not expect, moreover, that you will ever be given a more apt opportunity of doing God a greater service or conferring a more fruitful benefit on your own nation or indeed on the whole of Christendom than you have now: you have only to take the heresies, as stupid and boorish as they are godless, not so much invented by Martin Luther as inherited from the heresiarchs of former times (who have often been condemned by the Catholic church and by the holy Fathers under the unquestionable inspiration of the Holy Spirit) and by him as it were newly unearthed from the depths of hell, which daily, sad to say, subvert the souls of so many of your brethren and fill the world with criminal confusion—these you must take and, following the example and the praiseworthy zeal of your own master Jerome and of Augustine and all the other Holy Fathers, you must confound them, abolish them, explode them by all the powers of reason and all the authoritative texts of Holy Scripture.[41]

Pope Adrian VI accuses Luther of reviving ancient heresies and he summons Erasmus to write against him and to refute him on the basis of scripture and the Fathers. Why would the pope think Luther is attempting to revive ancient heresies? Article thirty-six of *Exsurge Domine* condemns the following proposition as an "error of Martin Luther": "Free will after sin is a matter of title only; and as long as one does what is in him, one sins mortally."[42] This proposition is an exact rendering of a thesis Luther drew up for the Heidelberg Disputation in 1518.[43] In his assertion of the condemned article thirty-six, Luther defended this thesis by claiming that all the orthodox doctors of the church were opponents of divine grace because they defended free will.[44] He says:

Hence there can be no doubt that the teaching of Satan brought this phrase "free will" into the church in order to seduce men away from God's path into his own paths. . . . Have you got anything, miserable pope, to snarl against this? Hence it is also necessary to revoke this article. For I misspoke when I said that free will before grace exists in name only; rather I should have simply said "free will is a fiction among real things, a name with no reality." For no one has it within his control to intend anything, good or evil, but rather, as was rightly taught by the article of Wycliffe which was condemned at [the Council of] Constance, all things occur by absolute necessity.[45] That was what the poet meant when he said, "All things are settled by a fixed law."[46]

The citation comes from the Stoic astrologer Manilius.[47] In this text which is his official response to a papal document, Luther prefers the doctrine of ancient pagan

---

41. CWE 9, ep. 1324.   42. DS 776.
43. WA 1:35, 359; LW 31:48.
44. *Martin Luther's Assertion Article 36* (WA 7:147–48; CWE 76:309–10).
45. H. Grisar, *Luther*, 2:232n1, indicates that this passage was toned down after Luther's death in the Wittenberg edition (1546) and Jena edition (1557).
46. CWE 76:306, *Martin Luther's Assertion Article 36*; WA 7:145.
47. *Astronomica* 4.14.

APPENDIX: SIXTEENTH-CENTURY ASSESSMENTS   197

astrologers to that of the Church Fathers. Evidently this seemed to be sufficient evidence to the pope that Luther was replicating the views of the ancient heretics who had been refuted by the Fathers.[48] Moreover, as we have seen in the first chapter, Melanchthon's *Loci Communes* of 1521, which was penned as a defense of Luther's condemned doctrines, insists that since "all things that happen, happen necessarily according to divine predestination, our will (*voluntas*) has no liberty."[49] In the same work Melanchthon said that the Church Fathers who wrote in defense of the freedom of the will wrote without the Spirit of God.[50] Pope Adrian VI goes on to challenge Erasmus to take up his pen against these newly arisen heretics:

> Carnal men themselves and contemptuous of authority, their aim is to make all others resemble them. Can you then refuse to sharpen the weapon of your pen against the madness of these men, whom it is clear that God had already driven out from before his face and manifestly abandoned to a reprobate mind, that they might say and teach and do what is not right? By them the whole church of Christ is thrown into confusion, and countless souls are involved together with them in the guilt of eternal damnation. Arise therefore to bring aid to God's cause, and employ your eminent intellectual gifts to his glory, as you have done down to this day.[51]

According to this text the pope is convinced that up to the present day Erasmus has employed his intellectual gifts to God's glory. He urges Erasmus to employ them now to refute Luther.

Adrian's exhortation met with obedience from his spiritual son. Erasmus wrote a series of volumes against Luther's doctrines (*De libero arbitrio*, 1524; *Hyperaspistes* I–II, 1527/28), which inflicted grave damage on the Lutheran movement.[52] Proof of this is seen three months after the publication of Erasmus's *Hyperaspistes* II, when the Holy Roman Emperor Charles V wrote to Erasmus, having heard that Lutheranism was in decline as a result of Erasmus's anti-Lutheran writings. Charles says that Erasmus alone has "accomplished that which emperors, popes, princes, universities, and hosts of learned men failed to attain. Wherefore we are most pleased to see that undying praise among mortal men and eternal glory in heaven will ever be yours, and we sincerely congratulate you on your success."[53] To the very end of

---

48. John Fisher assessed Luther similarly. See my "Bishop John Fisher's Response to Martin Luther."

49. Cf. *Loci Communes* (1521), in *Melanchthon and Bucer*, ed. Wilhelm Pauck, Library of Christian Classics (Philadelphia: Westminster, 1969), 23–24; correlates to C. B. Bretschneider and H. E. Bindseil, eds., *Corpus Reformatorum: Philippi Melanthonis opera quae supersunt omnia*, 28 vols. (Halle and Brunswick, 1834–60), 21:86.

50. I am aware that Melanchthon later repudiated his own early views on this subject—see G. Graybill, *Evangelical Free Will: Phillipp Melanchthon's Doctrinal Journey on the Origins of Faith* (Oxford: Oxford University Press, 2010)—but I do not see how that is relevant to the point I am making in the present context, which is to explain why Pope Adrian VI thought the first Lutherans were reviving ancient heresies.

51. CWE 9, ep. 1324.   52. See CWE 76–78.
53. CWE 13, ep. 1920.

his pontificate, Pope Adrian VI remained firmly in Erasmus's corner and defended him against his conservative critics. M. Stone observes: "Adrian also took Erasmus' part in later years, when he [Erasmus] came into conflict with the theologians of Louvain. Even just before his death Adrian intervened on Erasmus's behalf with the Sorbonne."[54]

It is noteworthy that Adrian's successor, Pope Clement VII, likewise held steadfastly to his faith in Erasmus, "believing like Adrian VI that he was indispensable as an ally against Wittenberg."[55] Solid evidence of Pope Clement VII's support of Erasmus can be seen in epistle 1846, where the pope, writing to Alonso Manrique de Lara, verifies Erasmus's orthodoxy, praises Erasmus's writings and warns Erasmus's Spanish critics "to say nothing henceforth that is not to the honor of Erasmus, a man of eloquence, learning, and untiring zeal."[56] So it seems that although Erasmus had indeed been criticized by theologians of the Sorbonne and Louvain, and by monks in Spain, he had also been defended against these attacks by the pope himself, whose authority stood on a higher plane. These testimonials from holders of the papal office are of great importance. Bouyer and de Lubac are justified in calling attention to Erasmus's papal support.

Pope Paul III

On May 31, 1535, Pope Paul III (1534–49) informed Erasmus in a letter which Erasmus published (epistle 3021) of his intention to enlist Erasmus in the College of Cardinals for the future Council.[57] Paul III praised Erasmus in an extraordinary manner, not only for his firm doctrine and his eloquence, but for his rare piety and the uprightness of his conduct. Specifically, the pope commends Erasmus's writings in defense of the church, referring to Erasmus's works against Luther mentioned above and those written against other Protestants, such as his work "Against the Pseudo-Evangelicals," in which he opposed the doctrines of what came to be known as the "Reformed" movement.[58] Paul III writes: "We are well aware how much your excellent learning, to which is joined an equal eloquence, can assist us in eradicating a leaning towards these current errors from the minds of many."[59] The pope, moreover, exhorts Erasmus to join him in defense of the Catholic faith leading up to, and during, the next general Council (which finally came together in Trent in 1545, nine years after Erasmus's death, but still during Paul III's pontificate, which

---

54. "Adrian of Utrecht," 263n84.

55. Douglas, *Jacobo Sadoleto*, 46–47.

56. CWE 13, ep. 1846.

57. This is found in ep. 3021 from Paul III. That Paul III offered the cardinalate is also evidenced in Allen, *Opus Epistolarum Desiderii Erasmi Roterodami*, ep. 3007:5n; that Erasmus declined it is shown in the same text, ep. 3052.31–35.

58. See CWE 78.

59. Allen, *Opus Epistolarum Desiderii Erasmi Roterodami*, ep. 3021.12–14: "Nec vero ignoramus, quantum tua excellens doctrina pari coniuncta eloquentia nobis adiumento esse possit ad novos istic errores ex multorum animis abscindendos."

lasted until 1549). In epistle 3048 to Bartholomew Latomus (August 24, 1535), Erasmus describes the events that have transpired and how in spite of his ill health he has become a candidate for the cardinalate. He is gratified by the Supreme Pontiff's feelings towards him.[60]

Yet in spite of Erasmus's humble demurs and hesitations, Paul III began preparations for Erasmus's elevation to the cardinalate by awarding him the provostship of Deventer. This action was intended to supply in part the annual income necessary to obtain the office of cardinal.[61] Erasmus's contemporary Roman Catholic biographer Beatus Rhenanus, in his *Life of Erasmus*, writes:

> That Pope Paul III, as much because of his opinion and inclination for Erasmus's virtue and learning as for the result [it would have], was in fact prepared to favor him at every opportunity, this henceforth is clear because not only had the proposal been made that Erasmus be admitted into the college of cardinals, but the pope himself also offered Erasmus the provostship at Deventer in the diocese of Utrecht, which is said to grant an income of six hundred gulden. He offered it, did I say? On the contrary, he bestowed it, not only dispatching an apostolic letter concerning it, lest the weariness and expense of the undertaking diminish the value of the benefice, but also in an affectionate letter addressing your [Charles V's] sister Mary, the most illustrious queen of Hungary and your regent in Flanders, that in consideration of her filial devotion toward the Roman See and of her royal generosity toward deserving men, she take care that the occupancy of the aforementioned provostship be kept free from intruders for Erasmus. However, Erasmus, an autarch because he had determined to refuse a benefice, remained his own master, saying that he, who was about to die in a short time, had sufficient resources.[62]

Pope Paul III's letter to Erasmus awarding him the provostship at Deventer contains the words: "We are mindful of your uprightness and innocent character and your eminence in various kinds of studies, no less of your merits with respect to the Apostolic See, when you fought against the deserters of the faith with supreme force."[63] The latter words are a clear reference to Erasmus's anti-Protestant writings, which obviously were well known in Rome and much appreciated. At precisely this time Friedrich Nausea and John Cochlaeus likewise received benefices from Paul III. Oelrich comments on the timing of these elevations: "Thus from Rome's perspective Erasmus appears in a series with the champions of the anti-Protestant front in Germany. Even in respect to the intended Council the Holy See was thinking of elevating Erasmus to the dignity of a Cardinal, along with other outstanding

---

60. Ibid., ep. 3048. Translations of this letter can be found in J. Huizinga, *Erasmus and the Age of Reformation* (Princeton, N.J.: Princeton University Press, 1984), 251–53, and H. Hillerbrand, ed., *Erasmus and His Age: Selected Letters of Desiderius Erasmus*, trans. M. A. Haworth, SJ (New York: Harper, 1970), 285–87.

61. Cf. Allen, *Opus Epistolarum Desiderii Erasmi Roterodami*, ep. 3007:n15 and ep. 3033.

62. Cf. Olin, ed., *Christian Humanism*, 58.

63. Cf. Allen, *Opus Epistolarum Desiderii Erasmi Roterodami*, ep. 3033:1–4: "Memores probitatis et innocentiae tuae et in vario disciplinarum genere eminentiae, nec minus meritorum erga apostolicam sedem, cum adversus desertores fidei summa vi pugnasti."

representatives of the inner-Church reform movement—one thinks of Contarini, Sadoleto, Pole."[64] Erasmus died on the night of July 11/12, 1536. Paul III's appointment of new cardinals occurred in December 1536. In a letter to Reginald Pole dated Cracow, April 7, 1537, the Polish bishop Stanislaus Hosius testifies that this promotion would have included Erasmus "if a cruel death had not begrudged them [that is, Pole, Contarini, Sadoleto] this honor."[65] Thus it was only his premature death that prevented Erasmus from receiving the honor of the cardinalate.

The Council of Trent

In light of the above-cited testimony, it should not be surprising that there is a significant body of evidence that points to Erasmus's high reputation at the Council of Trent (1545–63) itself, and the influence of his religious thought upon the bishops and theologians who participated in that Council. Yet this evidence has scarcely been noticed or discussed in previous scholarship. I believe that this is partially due to an inexplicable prejudice against Erasmus that was mentioned by de Lubac in the citation at the beginning of this book, and that continues to plague Catholic ecclesiastical historiography, as I will mention below. To begin with, in the bishop of Vienna John Fabri's preparatory epistle to the papal nuncio and Cardinal Morone, Erasmus is listed, alongside John Fisher and Thomas More, among the recently deceased Catholic authors who fought bravely against Lutheranism and whose writings can provide much help for the coming council.[66] We have already noted that Pope Paul III, who summoned the Council, referred to Erasmus's anti-Protestant writings in his letter to Erasmus alluding to his intention to promote Erasmus to the cardinalate, and said that Erasmus's excellent learning would assist him in eradicating recent errors from the minds of many. Jedin reports additionally that the ecclesiastical theologians Cervini and Seripando adopted the Erasmian program of biblical renewal by striving to promote biblical studies.[67] They faulted those who only knew scripture from commentaries. This latter opinion is derived directly from Erasmus's *Methodus*, as I pointed out in chapter 1. In this

64. Oelrich, *Der späte Erasmus und die Reformation*, 23.
65. F. Dittrich, ed., *Regesten und Briefe des Kardinals Gasparo Contarini* (Braunsberg, 1881), no. 322 (96–97).
66. S. Merkle, ed., *Concilium Tridentinum, Diariorum, Actorum, Epistularum, Tractatuum nova collectio*, 13 vols. (Freiburg im Breisgau: Herder, 1901–2001), 4:55n7 [hereafter "CT"]. Cardinal Morone (1509–80) was bishop of Modena (1529) and a presiding cleric of the Council of Trent. A man of stainless character and impeccable orthodoxy, he would later be seized and imprisoned by Pope Paul IV (1555–59) under suspicion of heresy. He remained in prison for two years but was immediately freed and reinstated upon Paul IV's death.
67. Marcello Cervini was chosen to preside over the Council of Trent in 1545, along with Cardinals del Monte (afterward Pope Julius III) and Pole. Cervini became Pope Marcellus II (1555). Girolamo Seripando (1492–1563) was theologian and cardinal legate at the Council of Trent and one of the most influential of the council members.

context Jedin writes: "It is characteristic of the mental attitude of the members of the Council of that period that beside the books already available and which were adequate to the requirements, viz. the *Sentences* of Peter Lombard, the *Compendium* of St. Thomas and the *Breviloquium* of St. Bonaventure, mention was also made of Erasmus's *Enchiridion* and Rufinus's *Expositio in symbolum apostolorum* (wrongly attributed to Cyprian)."[68] Thus Erasmus's name appears alongside Lombard, Aquinas, Bonaventure, and, as it was believed, Cyprian, as a Catholic author whose writings need to be in the hands of all priests. Jedin's assessment of the pro-Erasmian spirit and letter of the Council of Trent contradicts the depiction by R. Douglas, who claims that this council drew its inspiration not from the Christian humanists or Catholic apologists but from medieval Paris and the monastic schools. It was allegedly a "triumph of militant monasticism."[69] It seems that Trent was a far more complex affair than that.

Revealingly, however, the great Jedin himself, who is considered the world's leading authority on the Council of Trent, frowned upon this inclusion of Erasmus's *Enchiridion* in such a list of authors whose books were to be placed in the hands of all future priests. Jedin had the effrontery to dismiss this suggestion in these words: "Not by the easy road of mediocrity, but by the steep path of holiness alone would the Church rise again."[70] Jedin apparently regards the Tridentine bishops who made the suggestion as being advocates of mediocrity, and opponents of holiness by which the church would rise again. I leave it for others to determine whether he is right about this.[71] Certainly no one who has read Erasmus's *Enchiridion* could say that this work is characterized by a spirit of mediocrity, though it seems doubtful that Jedin ever found the time to read Erasmus's work.

The *Roman Catechism*: An Erasmian Document

In addition to its Canons and Decrees, the most important document of the Council of Trent is the *Roman Catechism*, or *Catechism of the Council of Trent* (1566). A brief history of this catechism and a perusal of its content will demonstrate the

68. Jedin, A History of the Council of Trent, 2:100n1; cf. CT 5:117.
69. Douglas, Jacobo Sadoleto, 93.
70. Jedin, A History of the Council of Trent, 1:161.
71. Jedin expresses amazement that men like Thomas More, Jacques Lefèvre, John Colet, Pope Leo X, Pope Adrian VI, Bishop Christoph von Utenheim (whom Jedin describes as "one of the best bishops of the period"), Archbishop William Warham, Bishop John Fisher, and Duke George of Saxony were all "taken in" by Erasmus. Jedin marvels that all these men seemed to believe that Erasmus's reform ideas could bring real renewal to the church. It is further striking that in A History of the Council of Trent, 1:399, Jedin omits Erasmus's anti-Lutheran works from his catalogue of pre-Tridentine Catholic apologetic literature. Unless I am mistaken, this is evidence either that Jedin was simply not familiar with Erasmus's anti-Lutheran apologetic writings or that his scholarship was driven by a very deep prejudice against Erasmus, as was undoubtedly the case for Joseph Lortz. In fact my suspicion is that it was probably Lortz's blind hatred of Erasmus that spilled over and infected Jedin.

influence of Erasmus upon it. Friedrich Nausea (1490–1552), the reform-minded bishop of Vienna, was regarded by Pope Paul III as one of the most reliable defenders of the Catholic church in Germany.[72] Nausea is a powerful witness in the Roman Catholic episcopate to the belief in Erasmus's ecclesiastical reliability.[73] Nausea had personal contact with Erasmus from 1525 on and engaged with him in a lively and friendly correspondence until Erasmus's death in 1536. When Erasmus died on the night of July 11/12, 1536, Nausea expressed his grief by composing a *Monodia* (from the Greek μονῳδία, solitary lament), a work dedicated to King Ferdinand from Mainz on August 18, 1536, and printed by Gymnich at Cologne in the same year.[74] In this oration (which is not discussed or even mentioned by Gollob, Nausea's most recent biographer), after recounting Erasmus's virtues, Nausea expresses his hope that by a public decree of the church, Erasmus will soon belong to the number of canonized saints.[75]

72. Nausea (Grau) was born in Waischenfeld in Upper Franconia (hence he is called Blancicampanius). Educated at Leipzig and Pavia, where he took a doctorate in law, in 1524 he became secretary to Cardinal Lorenzo Campeggio, archbishop of Bologna and papal legate in Germany. Appointed cathedral preacher at Frankfurt in 1525, Nausea was forced out by a popular uprising in favor of the Lutheran Reformation. His strong resistance to the Reformation attracted the attention of Johannes Fabri, bishop of Vienna, who brought him to the notice of King Ferdinand. Nausea eventually succeeded Fabri as bishop in 1541.

73. See H. Gollob, *Bischof Friedrich Nausea (1496–1552): Probleme der Gegenreformation* (Nieuwkoop: B. De Graaf, 1967); CWE 11, ep. 1577; J. Metzner, *Friedrich Nausea aus Waischenfeld, Bischof von Wien* (Ratisbon, 1884); R. Bäumer, *Lexikon für Theologie und Kirche*, 10 vols., eds. J. Hofer and K. Rahner, 2nd ed. (Freiburg: Herder, 1957–65), 7:847.

74. *Friderici Nauseae Blancicampiani in magnum Erasmum Roterodamum nuper vita functum monodia* (Cologne, 1536); reprinted without pagination in LB 1 among the preliminary pieces (Epitaphia). Cf. CWE 11, ep. 1577; Flitner, *Erasmus im Urteil*, 22–23; Padberg, *Erasmus als Katechet*, 21; Mansfield, *Phoenix of His Age*, 8–11. The Greek word is found in Gn 4:10; cf. John Chrysostom, *Homily 23.5 on Romans*.

75. LB 1. I will paraphrase the content of Nausea's *Monodia* in this note. (At the time of writing, Nausea was court preacher in Vienna and about forty-six years old.) He celebrates the life and achievements of Erasmus of Rotterdam, giving thanks to God for Erasmus's theological mission, his moral example, and life work. Nausea deeply grieves over the passing of "the great Desiderius Erasmus of Rotterdam of happy and praised memory, the most brilliant ornament of the Catholic Church." His personal friendship with Erasmus obligates him to open the eyes of the world to see what they have lost by this death. He writes that Erasmus was a German, who possessed in large measure the characteristics of his Batavian homeland: peacefulness, common decency, sincerity, and upright morals. Erasmus was a unique and infallible archetype and witness of these qualities in himself. He was so simple and sincere that he was incapable of pretense. His faith was clear to see and incorrupt. Nausea says that Erasmus's erudition surpassed belief, yet it was linked with a remarkable humility and innocence of character. His divinely inspired wisdom was coupled with an equally stupendous eloquence, so that both his life and his reputation were preserved intact and free from all reproach. He was never accused of moral blemishes nor did he ever become the subject of sinister rumors. And rare is the man whose virtues and morals are not tainted by vices. A huge number of admirers, including popes, the emperor, kings, cardinals, and rulers had praised him as blessed and recognized him as a kind of demigod in his learning and eloquence, as if he had descended straight from heaven and had not been born on earth. Nausea says that Erasmus's productive capacity was

Padberg has shown through careful analysis that Nausea's own major catechetical work, *Catechismus Catholicus* (1543), is modeled on Erasmus's *Explanation of the Creed* (1533).[76] Bishop Nausea's catechism was dedicated to Pope Paul III in 1543 and was itself used as the basis of the *Roman Catechism*. In fact, the *Roman Catechism* has been described as "the principal redaction" of Nausea's *Catechism*.[77] Padberg correctly surmises from this relationship that the *Roman Catechism*, "in its first-rate structure, in its concentration on the most important doctrinal formulas, in its exemplary intellectual freedom, agrees completely with the structure and the thought of Erasmus's."[78] This shows that Erasmus's 1533 catechetical writing exerted a formative influence on both pre-Tridentine and Tridentine catechetical literature. Therefore, scholars who claim that the Council of Trent signifies the repudiation of Erasmian theology, catechesis, and reform are flouting the facts.

It is noteworthy that the *Roman Catechism* cites no scholastic writers within its pages. Primacy is given to the common faith of the church as witnessed in the writings of the Church Fathers. According to my calculations, the Fathers are cited in the *Roman Catechism* with the following frequency: Augustine (90), Ambrose (23), John Chrysostom (19), Jerome (17), Pseudo-Dionysius (12), Cyprian (9), Gregory the Great (8), John Damascene (7), Hilary (5), Cyril of Alexandria (4), Eusebius (3), Irenaeus (2), Gregory Nazianzen (2). There is no mention whatsoever of Peter Lombard, Thomas Aquinas, or Duns Scotus. R. Bradley has recently claimed that it was

---

truly miraculous and the exquisitely learned library of books he left behind is sufficient proof of this. His writings obtained such great authority and reliability among everyone that today they are famous and celebrated throughout the world. All men of wisdom and intelligence who desire knowledge of theological matters have Erasmus's writings in their hands, and they turn these pages night and day. Anyone who needs abundant material for speaking eloquently, for wise counsel, for deliberation, or for refuting the heretics goes to Erasmus's writings. Nausea alludes to Pope Paul III's intention of awarding Erasmus with the dignity of the cardinalate. He calls upon kings and rulers, leaders and common people, all who go by the name Christian, to honor and esteem the great Erasmus with that dignity that would display him to the people as a model of holy living and holy dying, namely canonization. For even during his lifetime, Erasmus was venerated by many as a saint. Precious was his death, and holy had been the life that preceded. One cannot die badly whose good life has come first. Erasmus's death proclaimed many powerful indications of his sanctity. Now that he is deceased, we should confer upon him the recognition of his sanctity, which we did not deny to him while he lived. Before his death it was not permissible to call him "blessed"; but now, exclaims Nausea, we must assume that the pope and cardinals will soon officially declare his sanctity, which is no longer doubtful to many. Because Erasmus lived as an example to the world of poverty, chastity, and self-sacrifice, Nausea expresses the hope that by a public decree of the church, Erasmus will soon belong to the number of canonized saints.

76. Padberg, *Erasmus als Katechet*, 151–53, shows the remarkable parallels which pertain to both structure and content. Erasmus's catechism is available in CWE 70.

77. Cf. Gollob, *Bischof Friedrich Nausea (1496–1552)*, 95: "Nauseas Arbeit ist die Grundlage jenes und dieser Katechismus romanus ist gleichsam die Hauptredaktion nach demselben." See also R. I. Bradley, *The Roman Catechism in the Catechetical Tradition of the Church: The Structure of the Roman Catechism as Illustrative of the "Classic Catechesis"* (Lanham, Md.: University Press of America, 1990), 95–96.

78. Padberg, *Erasmus als Katechet*, 155–56.

the influence of Erasmus's approach to catechesis and theology that explains why no scholastic authors are cited by name in the pages of the *Roman Catechism*. Bradley interprets the significance of this as follows: "The last thing, in the Council's judgment—and in the concurring judgment of Pius V and Borromeo—that the Catholic faithful needed or were looking for in this work was 'theology' in the scholastic sense—or rather, in the 'scholastic' sense as the Erasmians would define it. In this respect the Erasmian influence in the Council, and through the Council on the Catechism, was a positive good."[79] I agree with Bradley that the exclusion of partisan scholastic quarrels and questions from the realm of fundamental church dogma is an "Erasmian" theological principle and should be assessed as a "positive good." The obvious primacy granted to the Church Fathers over against the scholastics in the *Roman Catechism* seems to be a fruit of Erasmus's effort to renew Catholic theology and catechesis on the basis of scripture and the Fathers. However, I do not see how the complete absence of citation of scholastic theologians from the *Roman Catechism* can fairly be described as an "Erasmian influence," since Erasmus never supported the complete banishment of the schoolmen from theology and catechesis. He believed that they had preserved and even advanced Catholic dogma during those centuries. Indeed, in his own *Explanation of the Creed* he engages them regularly and incorporates their theological developments into the catechetical discussion.[80]

I do not know for certain why the editors of the *Roman Catechism* chose to refrain from citing scholastic theologians as authorities. What is certain is that Bradley himself is intensely hostile to Erasmus in his book. He erroneously claims, for example, that Erasmus in his *Methodus* has "only disdain" for the scholastics.[81] Bradley could have more justifiably concluded that of the editors of the *Roman Catechism*, who unlike Erasmus do not cite the scholastics with appreciation. Moreover, Bradley says that Erasmus "decries Scholasticism as pagan and dialectical, but he replaces it with stoicism and rhetoric."[82] These are the kind of retrograde judgments typical of Catholic scholarship in the first half of the twentieth century but which seem to be impossible to kill. To me it seems very clear that Bradley is in the dark about Erasmus and lacks accurate information regarding his actual approach to catechesis and theology.

Although there are definitely similarities, I believe there are also real differences between Erasmus's *Catechism* and the *Roman Catechism*. The *Roman Catechism* cites Pseudo-Dionysius at least twelve times to "prove" the antiquity of Catholic sacramental customs. This is a non-Erasmian feature, since Erasmus did not accept the authenticity of that work but regarded it as a forgery of later centuries.[83] Therefore

79. Bradley, *The Roman Catechism*, 149.
80. For instance, Erasmus discusses Thomas Aquinas's commentary on the Apostles' Creed (cf. CWE 70:307).
81. Bradley, *The Roman Catechism*, 89.
82. Ibid.
83. Erasmus was censured for his opinion by the theology faculty of the University of Paris. See

he would have regarded the writings of "Dionysius the Areopagite" as being without value for Catholic apologetics, if they are being used to prove historical points about the practices of the most ancient Christian church. On this point Erasmus's non-use of Pseudo-Dionysius anticipates the modern *Catechism of the Catholic Church* which does not cite from the writings of Pseudo-Dionysius at all and has completely revised its explanations of the historical development of Catholic sacraments, especially when it is compared with the *Roman Catechism*.[84]

In the light of the complete lack of citations from medieval theologians, including Thomas Aquinas, it seems quite misleading and partisan for Dominican theologians to describe the *Roman Catechism* as a "Thomist document." Bradley defends such a misnomer on the following grounds: "That appellation is correct if by 'Thomist' we mean adherence, not to a particular school in the Church, but to the teaching common to all the schools as taught by the 'Common Doctor' of the Church: St. Thomas Aquinas."[85] But according to this definition, all Catholic dogma should be labeled Thomist; the Nicene Creed should be called a Thomist confession and the New Testament should be labeled a Thomist collection of writings. It seems better to refrain entirely from using partisan labels to describe the Tridentine catechism; but if one is demanded, it appears to me that a stronger case can be made for describing the *Roman Catechism* as an "Erasmian document," since his own *Catechism* has been shown to have been a formative influence upon it both directly and indirectly. In any case it appears to me that the time is ripe for further research into the question of Erasmus's formative influence upon the Catholic dogmatic tradition in the sixteenth century. A comparison between the canons on justification and the theological positions articulated in Erasmus's anti-Protestant writings would be a good starting point.

Pope Paul IV's Index of Prohibited Books

In a major and important study of Erasmus's legacy, A. Flitner writes: "The Council of Trent brings to the legacy of Erasmus simultaneously fulfillment and condemnation: fulfillment, when an internal reform of the Church took place, proceeding from within, stemming from Rome, just as Erasmus himself wanted it to happen; condemnation, in the assessment that the Council passed on the most

---

CWE 82:242, topic 31. The censure reads: "It is not to the truly learned but rather to the temerarious and the pursuers of novelty that the person who wrote *The Ecclesiastical Hierarchies* does not seem to be Dionysius the Areopagite." According to P. Casarella, "On the 'Reading Method' in Rorem's Pseudo-Dionysius," *The Thomist* 59, no. 4 (1995): 633–44, there are 1,700 citations of Pseudo-Dionysius in Aquinas; cited by Riordan, *Divine Light*, 63n94. A number of modern scholars have observed that for Thomas Aquinas the authority of [Pseudo-]Dionysius ranks higher even than that of Augustine himself. Cf. de Gandillac, *Oeuvres completes*, 18.

84. On Dionysius the Areopagite, see Moreschini and Norelli, *Early Christian Greek and Latin Literature*, 2:665–73.

85. Bradley, *The Roman Catechism*, 149.

important writings of Erasmus."[86] The first half of this statement strikes me as exactly correct: the Council of Trent represents the fulfillment of Erasmus's hopes for an internal reform of the Catholic church proceeding from Rome. However, in my opinion Flitner's second statement pertaining to the Council's alleged condemnation of Erasmus's most important writings seems to need some qualification (unless we regard *Praise of Folly* and *The Colloquies* as Erasmus's most important writings), since the Council of Trent restored to the church's use purified versions of most of the writings of Erasmus that had been condemned by Pope Paul IV (Carafa) outside the sessions of the Council. When read against the immediate backdrop of Paul IV's action, the Council of Trent represents more a rehabilitation of Erasmus than his repudiation.

I have already noted above that as bishop of Chieti and papal legate to England in 1515, Gianpietro Carafa had been one of Erasmus of Rotterdam's stoutest supporters.[87] Indeed, Carafa's praise for Erasmus's scholarship was so exalted that Erasmus told Pope Leo X that he could not accept it at face value, though he admitted to receiving much encouragement and inspiration from having the learned Carafa's backing. When this same Carafa became Pope Paul IV forty years later in 1555, at the age of seventy-nine, he would become Erasmus's deadliest enemy. In 1557, during what McNally calls "the unfortunate recess (1552–62) of the Council,"[88] Pope Paul IV (born Gianpietro Carafa) created the Index of Prohibited Books through the Congregation of the Inquisition. The Index was a list of books that Catholics were forbidden to read on pain of excommunication because the books were considered imprudent, scandalous, dangerous, or contrary to faith or morals. During the time of the Index—which only ended under Pope Paul VI in 1966 because it was considered to be contrary to the teaching of Vatican II concerning freedom of inquiry—all books by Protestant writers or their forerunners were condemned, such as Hus, Wycliffe, Luther, Melanchthon, Zwingli, Oecolampadius, Hubmaier, Menno Simons, Tyndale, Bucer, Capito, Calvin, Beza, and Cranmer.[89] In addition, the Index prohibited the reading of Talmudic and rabbinical literature as well as the Koran. It also forbade all vernacular translations of the Bible.

A number of texts by Catholic writers in good standing or who died in good standing were also prohibited, particularly those who were suspected of being secret adherents of Protestant doctrines, even when there was no factual basis to this suspicion. In the year 1559, twenty-three years after Erasmus's death, in this first general Roman Index, Pope Paul IV forbade the entire body of Erasmus's writings, regardless of content. Paul IV singled out Erasmus's name in the first classification

---

86. Flitner, *Erasmus im Urteil seiner Nachwelt*, 33.
87. See Erasmus's letter to Pope Leo X (CWE 3, ep. 335; May 1515), which is cited above.
88. McNally, "Trent and Vernacular Bibles," 226.
89. On the Index, see the *New Catholic Encyclopedia*, 15 vols., ed. D. Dee and D. Sheridan, 2nd ed. (Detroit: Gale, 2003): 7:389–91.

under this heading: "the first or last names of those of whom it has been recognized that they have erred more than the rest and as it were 'ex professo' [intentionally], and therefore all their writings are absolutely forbidden, and it doesn't matter what they are about."[90] According to this declaration Erasmus had erred "on purpose." The name of Erasmus alone contains the additional incriminating charge: "with all his commentaries, annotations, Scholia, dialogues, letters, assessments, translations, books and writings, even when these contain absolutely nothing contrary to or concerning religion."[91] No such addition is found even by the names of Luther and Calvin. Paul IV's ban of Erasmus in all of its severity was republished by Pope Sixtus V in 1590. In 1596, however, Pope Clement VIII restored the Index of Pius IV (see below).

How does one begin to make sense of this most aberrant action of the pope? By "aberrant," I mean both that the action contradicts Carafa's own high praise and defense of Erasmus in his earlier career as bishop of Chieti, and that it departs radically from the support given to Erasmus by Paul IV's papal predecessors. Research into the history of Paul IV's papacy leads one to conclude, in the first place, that his treatment of Erasmus was not much different than his treatment of a significant number of good Catholics, even men of the highest standing in the church. Erasmus was not the only Catholic to be listed as a "heretic of the first class" in Paul IV's Index. Also listed there were: Jacques Lefèvre, Wilibald Pirckheimer, Beatus Rhenanus, George Cassander, Ulrich Zasius, and John von Staupitz.[92] These men

---

90. Cf. J. M. De Bujanda, ed., *Index des Livres Interdits, Volume VIII: Index de Rome, 1557, 1559, 1564* (Sherbrooke: Droz, 1990), 429–33; H. Reusch, *Der Index der verbotenen Bücher*, 2 vols. (Bonn: Scientia Verlag Aalen, 1883), 1:347.

91. Reusch, *Der Index der verbotenen Bücher*, 1:347; Padberg, *Erasmus als Katechet*, 9.

92. On Lefèvre, see G. Bedouelle, "Attacks on the Biblical Humanism of Jacques Lefèvre D'Etaples," in *Biblical Humanism*, ed. Rummel, 140. Willibald Pirckheimer (1470–1530) was a leading German humanist and Greek scholar from Nürnberg, who served on the city council in 1505–23. He published a series of Latin translations of Greek works. Pirckheimer was initially sympathetic to Luther, and attacked John Eck in a bitter satire, *Eccius dedolatus*. He was included in the bull of excommunication of Luther in 1520, but was absolved in 1521 after formally denouncing Luther's teaching. He became a firm opponent of Protestantism and published treatises against Oecolampadius, defending the Catholic doctrine of the eucharist (cf. Reusch, *Der Index der verbotenen Bücher*, 1:347). Beatus Rhenanus (1485–1547) of Selestat was a scholarly collaborator of Erasmus in Basel and Erasmus's first biographer. He published the first edition of Tertullian's writings in 1521 (cf. Reusch, *Der Index der verbotenen Bücher*, 1:356–57). George Cassander (1513–66) was a humanist and liturgist who died in good standing in the Church (cf. Reusch, *Der Index der verbotenen Bücher*, 1:361). Ulrich Zasius (1461–1535) was professor of law at the University of Freiburg im Breisgau. Reusch, *Der Index der verbotenen Bücher*, 1:364, indicates that Zasius died a Catholic and had stood firmly against the Protestants. One of his works was erroneously taken to be a Lutheran writing. John von Staupitz (d. 1524) was vicar-general of the Augustinian Observants in Wittenberg and Martin Luther's spiritual director. He was condemned by Paul IV merely for his association with Luther. See Jared Wicks, "Johann von Staupitz under Pauline Inspiration," in *A Companion to Paul in the Reformation*, ed. R. Ward Holder (Leiden: Brill, 2009), 319–35.

and others, out of sheer ignorance, were viewed by Paul IV or his advisers as crypto-Protestants.[93] Moreover, by some oversight, the name of Theodore Beza, Calvin's successor in Geneva, does not appear on this Index, although it had appeared on earlier indices.[94] Was it Paul IV's intent thereby to exculpate Beza from all suspicion of heresy? That would probably be an erroneous inference to draw. Ironically, or rather, tragically, Pope Paul IV even placed the product of his own work as Cardinal Carafa on the Index: the report of the 1537 reform commission, *Consilium de emendanda Ecclesia*.[95] The chief writer of this document was Cardinal Contarini, president of a commission of cardinals appointed by Pope Paul III to diagnose the disease that was infecting the church. Thanks to Paul IV, it was banned. One would have to conclude that Erasmus's writings had some impressive company on Paul IV's Index.

Secondly, we observe that Paul IV's Roman Index also forbade all publications issued in the preceding forty years without the name of the author or publisher. Regardless of content, it forbade all products of sixty-one printers specified by name, fourteen of whom were from Basel alone. The great majority of editions of the Bible and of the Fathers fell under the prohibition.[96] This sort of global condemnation of the entire production of printing presses, irrespective of content of the works prohibited, indicates that the operative principle in Paul IV's mind was guilt by association. The presence of real error or heresy in such works was not even taken into consideration. Jorgensen remarks: "The Roman Index of Paul IV shows the extent to which he thought the Catholic Church should censor literature. The cultural repression tragically put him in opposition to much of what was meant by the word Renaissance."[97]

Thirdly, we observe that Paul IV's first papal Index completely condemns all vernacular translations of scripture: "No Bible translated into the vernacular, German, French, Spanish, Italian, English, or Flemish, may in any manner be printed or read or possessed without permission in writing from the Holy Office of the Roman Inquisition."[98] This universal ban of Bibles embraced both Catholic and Protestant translations of scripture.

Paul IV's measures specifically against Erasmus can only be assessed as aberrant and anomalous when judged against the preceding spirit and letter of his papal predecessors, of the first two sessions of the Council of Trent, and of his own earlier

---

93. Reusch, *Der Index der verbotenen Bücher*, 1:269.

94. Ibid., 1:269, 279.

95. This remarkable document is available in translation in C. Olin, ed., *Catholic Reform: From Cardinal Ximenes to the Council of Trent, 1495–1563* (New York: Fordham University Press, 1990), 65–79.

96. H. Jedin, ed., *Reformation and Counter Reformation (History of the Church)* (New York: Seabury, 1980), 5:486–87.

97. K. J. Jorgensen, "The Theatines," in *Religious Orders of the Catholic Reformation in Honor of John C. Olin on His Seventy-Fifth Birthday*, ed. R. L. DeMolen (New York: Fordham University Press, 1994), 6.

98. Quoted in McNally, "The Council of Trent and Vernacular Bibles," 226.

views. It appears that Carafa was susceptible to radical changes of heart and mind which had very dramatic consequences. Even Erasmus's modern Catholic nemesis H. Jedin had the integrity to disapprove of Paul IV's papal action and to indicate the church of Rome's response to this prohibition of Erasmus: "The scholarly defenders of the dogmas and institutions of the Church leaned on the shoulders of Erasmus, so that when Paul IV prohibited his editions of the Bible and the Fathers ... Rome itself was greatly embarrassed."[99] Many scholars saw themselves deprived of their scholarly tools. Jedin reports that Seripando, archbishop of Salerno, had to have a new edition of the Bible ordered in Rome, because all that he had in his possession fell under the Index.[100] Seripando described Paul IV's severity as "inhuman."[101] From Germany the future saint Peter Canisius wrote of Paul IV's measure: "Even the best Catholics disapprove of such rigor."[102] Both Canisius and the Jesuit theologian Lainez endeavored with all their strength to see this Index revised.[103] John C. Olin described Paul IV as "fierce and frantic."[104] It is probably impossible to measure the amount of damage inflicted upon the reputation of the Catholic church as a result of Paul IV's action. The blanket condemnation of all vernacular translations of the Bible in particular continues to be a point of great embarrassment to Catholic scholars and apologists today, at least to those who are willing to own up to this papal action.[105]

It is interesting to compare Paul IV's action against Erasmus with the general tenor and other specific actions of his papacy. He can hardly be described as a pope who has won universal approval. Louis Bouyer observed that this pope became more and more hardened in his reactionary tendencies and was characterized by immoderation. "The new pope grew suspicious of all the saints of the counter-reform, one after the other—of St. Ignatius as well as of St. Philip Neri."[106] Paul IV fanatically prosecuted Cardinal Giovanni Morone, who had been one of the presiding clerics of the earlier sessions of the Council of Trent, whom he threw into prison for two years under suspicion of (Protestant) heresy.[107] He also deprived

99. Jedin, *A History of the Council of Trent*, 1:162.
100. Jedin, *Geschichte des Konzils von Trient, Dritte Tagungsperiode und Abschluss* (Freiburg: Herder, 1975), IV.1:19.
101. Cf. Pastor, *The History of the Popes*, 24:260.
102. Cf. Jedin, ed., *Reformation and Counter Reformation*, 5:486–87.
103. Cf. Flitner, *Erasmus im Urteil seiner Nachwelt*, 39n26.
104. *Six Essays on Erasmus*, 59.
105. Cf. McNally, "The Council of Trent and Vernacular Bibles," 226. It strikes me as misleading for the Catholic apologist, Karl Keating, in *Catholicism and Fundamentalism: The Attack on "Romanism" by "Bible Christians"* (San Francisco, Calif.: Ignatius, 1988), 95, to say that no "authentic Bible" has ever been placed on the Index of Prohibited Books. Keating is either assuming that vernacular translations of scripture do not count as "authentic Bibles" or he is in serious error and is overlooking Paul IV's and subsequent indices.
106. *Erasmus and His Times*, 55.
107. See Pastor, *The History of the Popes*, 14:289–318.

Cardinal Reginald Pole of his office of papal legate to England, intending to prosecute him in Rome as a heretic. In the midst of these tribulations Pole fell ill and died during the summer of 1558, feeling deeply betrayed.[108] Cardinal Morone, on the other hand, was lucky enough after Paul IV's death to be released from prison and rehabilitated.

Paul IV has left behind a grim memoir of his thoughts about these living cardinals in an "extraordinary interview" with the ambassador of Venice.

On this occasion he talked himself into one of his paroxysms, inveighing against "that accursed school and apostate household of the Cardinal of England" [Reginald Pole]. Then he went on: "Why do you suppose we deprived him of the legation? You will indeed see the end of it; we mean to proceed, and shall use our hands. Cardinal Pole is the master, and Cardinal Morone, whom we have in the Castle, is the disciple, although the disciple has become worse than the master. Priuli is upon a par with these, and so was Flaminio who, were he alive now, would have to be burned." And then, after a good deal more of this, he made the most terrible statement of all: "If our own father were a heretic, we would carry the faggots to burn him."[109]

Pole's modern biographer, Schenk, reproaches the way Carafa's unlimited belief in himself as the Vicar of Christ led him to identify all his own interests and fancies with the concerns of the church. "Small wonder that he ended up by serving, not Christ, but only his petty self."[110] G. R. Elton characterized Paul IV as "to all intents insane during his pontificate."[111] His temperament was hot-blooded and volcanic, leading to unpredictable and irrational behavior. His reputation for nepotism marred his papacy, as did his draconian severity in ecclesiastical reform and in other matters pertaining to his administration of Rome. Pastor describes his papacy as a "reign of terror" in which incredible accusations were made and proceedings taken against bishops and cardinals "which are as incomprehensible as they were baseless."[112] In my judgment his treatment of Erasmus was among these actions "as incomprehensible as they were baseless." In any case it seems that Paul IV's condemnation of Erasmus was not much different than his repudiation of other good Catholics who had served the church well during their lifetimes.[113]

---

108. See Thomas F. Mayer, *Reginald Pole: Prince and Prophet* (Cambridge: Cambridge University Press, 2000), 302–20.
109. Cf. W. Schenk, *Reginald Pole: Cardinal of England* (London: Longmans, 1950), 136.
110. Ibid., 134.
111. *Reformation Europe 1517–1559* (New York: Harper, 1963), 207; quoted in Mayer, *Reginald Pole*, 302.
112. Pastor, *The History of the Popes*, 14:287.
113. Diarmaid MacCulloch, *Reformation: Europe's House Divided 1490–1700* (London: Penguin, 2003), 277–78, writes: "Erasmus was not the only bête noire for Paul IV. He was a good hater, and his hatreds ranged from the trivial to the profoundly politically important. He hated nudity in art, and famously commissioned a forest of figleaves for the sensuous religious painting and sculpture of Renaissance Rome, including Michelangelo's forty-year-old frescos on the Sistine Chapel ceiling. He hated Jews, and confined the Jewish communities of the Papal States for the first time in ghettos and

APPENDIX: SIXTEENTH-CENTURY ASSESSMENTS 211

Paul IV's death in August 1559 was greeted by popular rejoicing. Before he actually died a mob began to attack the Palace of the Inquisition and destroyed the building and many of its records. The statue of himself that Paul had erected on the Capitoline was also attacked by a mob, which threw the head into the Tiber.[114] My view is that if it was Erasmus's destiny to have one pope in history turn violently against him and try to render grave harm to his legacy as a Catholic theologian, this is the pope I would have chosen.

Erasmus's Rehabilitation at the Council of Trent

The widespread dissatisfaction among Catholic leaders with Paul IV's Index led the fathers of the reconvened Council of Trent, under the direction of Pope Pius IV (1559–65), to establish a commission to undertake its revision. The president of that commission was Anton Brus von Müglitz, archbishop of Prague and bishop of Vienna (1558–63).[115] Brus stood firmly in Erasmus's corner and against what he regarded as his unjust treatment by Paul IV. He boldly argued that all restrictions should be removed from Erasmus's writings in recognition of his services to the church and to Christian scholarship.[116] Unfortunately, Brus's charitable assessment of Erasmus was not unanimously supported by all committee members. On February 3, 1563, Archbishop Brus reported in a letter to the Emperor Ferdinand (1558–64) that for the past year a revision of Paul IV's Index had been underway

in which, whether as the result of a mistake or for other reasons, even such men who lived piously and as Catholics, are placed among the heretics, and many books are forbidden which are useful for the world and which in no way deal with religion and faith. We have deleted the names of those whom we know lived or are still living within the bosom of the Church and who submitted their writings to the judgment of the Church, for example, Jo. Campensis, Ant. Flaminius, Henr. Glareanus, George Agricola ... Leon. Fuchs. Conr. Gesner, etc. We are now engaged with the writings of Erasmus. Many of these have been reproached, *Praise of Folly*, *The Colloquies*, some apologetic writings and many letters; others

---

made them wear distinctive yellow hats. He hated the independent spirits of the Jesuits, and once they had lost the temporizing skills of their founder Ignatius on his death in 1556, Pope Paul forced them to surrender much of their freedom of decision-making and began remodeling them into a more conventional religious Order. He also hated the senior clergy who had fostered the *Spirituali* and who, after their 1540s debacle, had tried to preserve something from the wreck."

114. Cf. L. von Ranke, *History of the Popes: Their Church and State*, rev. ed. (New York: Cooperative Publication Society, 1901), 1:211; V. Hudon, "Paul IV," in *The Oxford Encyclopedia of the Reformation*, ed. H. J. Hillerbrand (New York: Oxford, 1996), 3:229–30.

115. Cf. Jedin, *Geschichte des Konzils von Trient*, IV.1:234. Archbishop Brus is nowhere mentioned in Mansfield's *Phoenix of His Age*. This seems negligent in light of his importance and relevance to the subject matter of Mansfield's book. In 1560 this same Anton von Müglitz allowed a painted epitaph to be set up at the burial place of Bishop Friedrich Nausea on the pillar near the altar to St. Katherine in St. Stephen's Cathedral [Stephansdom] in Vienna, Austria. See Gollob, *Bischof Friedrich Nausea*, 133.

116. Cf. Jedin, *Geschichte des Konzils von Trient*, IV.2:234.

are being so over-anxiously corrected that Erasmus would not recognize them as his own, should he return to the world.[117]

Archbishop Brus assumes what is obvious: that Pope Paul IV had simply erred in his catalogue of heretics. Brus goes on to report that he and some of his colleagues are united in supporting the release of Erasmus's writings

because he [Erasmus] always submitted himself to the judgment of the Church, because Leo X commissioned him to continue his literary activity, because he died as a Catholic and often fought against the heretics laudably and victoriously, because he made the writings of the Church Fathers accessible again in good editions, because he reanimated scholarship that had been neglected, in such a way that other nations envy us because of him.[118]

In Archbishop Brus we seem to have an ecclesiastic who shared the attitude toward Erasmus espoused by Thomas More, John Fisher, Jacob Sadoleto, Friedrich Nausea, Paul III, Hosius, and so many others. Brus emphasizes that Erasmus had always been obedient to papal authority, both in his continuance of his scholarly activity on the New Testament and in his submission of his writings to the judgment of the church.

Thomas More had supplied a number of these arguments in defense of Erasmus in 1519 in his *Letter to Edward Lee*. Lee had claimed that Erasmus ought not to have made his New Testament translation at all and ought not to have published the discrepancies between the Greek texts and the Latin. More says in response that Lee and his supporters are reported to be unequivocally unfair to Erasmus, whether they are motivated by plain human jealousy or whether, as More thinks is more likely, Satan has incited them, secretly instigating his demons to deter Erasmus from the virtuous labors which he was performing for the good of the entire world. Of Erasmus's critics More says:

With a pretense of holiness they claim to be furthering Christ's work, but they are actually hindering Christ's work as they create work with their irksome slanders for the man who is really pursuing Christ's work and divert him from writing about sacred scripture, out of which, as if out of an inexhaustible storehouse, he used to bring something new almost daily for the advancement of scholarship, to writing apologies which are not so much useful to us as compulsory for him.[119]

In the opinion of Thomas More, at least, Erasmus's Catholic critics are servants of the devil, though they pretend to be concerned with God's work. More claims that not only do all learned men both in Louvain and in England disagree with Edward Lee on each of the points on which he attacks Erasmus, but the pope [Leo X],

---

117. I have translated from the German translation cited in Reusch, *Der Index der verbotenen Bücher*, 1:320; cf. Flitner, *Erasmus im Urteil seiner Nachwelt*, 43. The original letter, which I have not been able to obtain, is found in F. W. von Bucholtz, *Geschichte der Regierung Ferdinands I*, 9 vols. (Vienna, 1831–38), 9:685.

118. Reusch, *Der Index der verbotenen Bücher*, 1:32; cf. Flitner, *Erasmus im Urteil seiner Nachleben*, 43, and Jedin, *Geschichte des Konzils von Trient*, IV.2:234.

119. Thomas More, letter to Edward Lee (CW 15:165–67).

APPENDIX: SIXTEENTH-CENTURY ASSESSMENTS 213

best and greatest of primates, who ought to take precedence over all learned men's votes, disagrees with Erasmus's critics.

For at his pious urging Erasmus obediently undertook that task, which with God's help he has now performed twice with success, and thereby he has twice earned the pope's special thanks and approval, as his solemn missives acknowledge. Therefore, given that this book contains the teaching of Christ, if I trusted the vicar of Christ to assess it, who has twice now declared the book useful, if I trusted the pope, I repeat, even though you oppose him and write that the book is pernicious, I judge that I have done nothing rash or unjust to you, even if your own book were completely unknown to me.[120]

More takes it for granted that the papal approval of Erasmus's work during Erasmus's lifetime takes precedence over isolated and partisan criticisms of him.

Similarly, in his *Confutation of Tyndale's Answer*, Thomas More explicitly commends Erasmus for his writings against the heretics. William Tyndale had complained that More was partial toward "his darling" Erasmus and prejudiced against his opponent Tyndale. More responds in what has become a famous text:

I have not contended with Erasmus my darling, because I found no such malicious intent with Erasmus my darling, as I find with Tyndale. For had I found with Erasmus my darling the cunning intent and purpose that I find in Tyndale: Erasmus my darling should be no more my darling. But I find in Erasmus my darling that he detests and abhors the errors and heresies that Tyndale plainly teaches and abides by and therefore Erasmus my darling shall be my dear darling still. And surely if Tyndale had either never taught them, or yet had the grace to revoke them: then should Tyndale be my dear darling too. But while he holds such heresies still I cannot take for my darling him that the devil takes for his darling.[121]

More is reflecting here directly upon Erasmus's anti-Protestant works and cites them to prove Erasmus's repudiation of the Protestant heresies that Tyndale has espoused. G. Marc'Hadour notes that the tenfold repetition of *darling* conveys the same affection for Erasmus as More had conveyed in his defenses of Erasmus penned in 1517. Moreover: "The shrillness and stridency of the taunt reflect the same tone as More's vindication of Origen and of Aquinas when Tyndale provoked his indignation by slighting these giants: thus More's longest and harshest work placed Erasmus in the best imaginable company."[122] Such arguments used in Erasmus's defense were made by Roman Catholics in different decades of the sixteenth century. They apply chiefly to his annotated New Testament, which conservative obscurantists repeatedly attacked, and to his anti-Protestant works, in which works More believed that Erasmus had greatly served the Catholic church and placed it in his debt. I do not know with certainty whether Archbishop Brus knew of Thomas More's defenses of Erasmus, but clearly his own defense of Erasmus is congruent with More's.

Archbishop Brus goes on to say, however, that the majority of his committee

---

120. CW 15:167–69.
121. Adapted into modern English from CW 8.1:177.
122. Cf. Marc'Hadour, "Thomas More in Emulation and Defense of Erasmus," 211–12.

members are of another opinion. For them it was sufficient to remove Erasmus's name from the first category of Paul IV's Index.[123] The majority said that it is a favor to Erasmus if after the cleansing of some of his works and the reproach of others, his memory is not allowed to perish.[124] Brus concludes: "Thus the few of us, who wish to preserve the works of a spirit who has so meritoriously served the Christian community, are being outvoted."[125] He then requests of the emperor to be allowed to step down from the commission. "My standpoint is different from that of those in Spain and Italy who don't want to have anything to do with 'heretics.'"[126] Moreover, through his tasks as imperial orator he is often prevented from attending the meetings. The emperor answered the archbishop by saying that he wants Brus, as the only German, to remain on the commission, and "to bring it about that no longer, as has happened up to now, even splendid works and the authors of such works, should be condemned."[127] What emerges from this exchange is that there was tension between the Spanish, Italian, and German members of the commission. It is also evident that the emperor himself was a strong supporter of Erasmus, whom he viewed as an author of "splendid works" that he does not want to see unjustly condemned. It is well known that Pope Paul IV had been a fierce opponent of Charles V, having relinquished the neutrality of his papal predecessor.

I find the following story revealing about the character of these times; it may also help to explain the suspicion of Erasmus that was found on Brus's committee. In 1537 Cardinal Jacob Sadoleto wrote a courteous appeal to the Lutheran theologian Philipp Melanchthon in a manner that was polite, irenic, and free from verbal abuse.[128] Sadoleto was denounced by many of his own side as little better than a traitor and a heretic for using this moderate tone with a "heretic." In the midst of the controversy, Cardinal Morone wrote a letter of sympathy to Cardinal Sadoleto in which he said the following: "There are in these parts many reputed defenders of the Catholic faith who think that our religion consists in nothing but hatred of the Lutherans ... and they are so wedded to this point of view that, without ever looking into the matter itself, they take in bad part not only all negotiations with the Lutherans, but every single word spoken about them which is not abusive."[129] Morone advises Sadoleto to treat his critics with silent contempt, and he states his

---

123. Brus also succeeded in having Henry Glareanus, Ulrich Zasius, Leonard Fuchs, and Conrad Gesner removed from the Index. Cf. Jedin, *Geschichte des Konzils von Trient*, IV.2:234.

124. Cf. Reusch, *Der Index der verbotenen Bücher*, 1:320; cf. Flitner, *Erasmus im Urteil seiner Nachleben*, 43.

125. Cited in German translation in Flitner, *Erasmus im Urteil seiner Nachleben*, 43. My colleague Michael Waldstein assisted me in the translation of this text.

126. Reusch, *Der Index der verbotenen Bücher*, 1:320–21.

127. Ibid., 1:321.

128. For a discussion of this episode, see R. M. Douglas, *Jacobo Sadoleto, 1477–1547: Humanist and Reformer* (Cambridge, Mass.: Harvard University Press, 1959), 116–22.

129. Letter to Sadoleto, *Archiv für Reformationsgeschichte* 1 (1904): 80–81, cited in the article, "Morone, Cardinal," in the *Catholic Encyclopedia*.

own conviction that to show charity to heretics was a better way than to overwhelm them with abusive language, adding: "if only this course had been adopted from the first, there would probably be less difficulty than there is in bringing about the union of the Church."

Brus, it seems, was cut from the same cloth as Sadoleto and Morone, but he sat on a committee composed of Catholics of a different stripe. Erasmus of Rotterdam's writings, like Sadoleto's, were well known for being courteous and free from verbal abuse in his polemics with Protestants and with his own Catholic critics. I believe that it was partially for this irenicism, especially in his dealing with Protestants, that he was detested by ultra-conservatives within the Catholic fold, who measured loyalty to the Catholic church by the degree of abusiveness in one's writings. These are my own speculations about some of the grounds for Paul IV's animosity against Erasmus.

Although Brus, the chairman of the Index commission, wanted all of Erasmus's writings to be freely permitted to Catholics, Erasmus's works were instead placed in the second class of the Index of Pius IV in 1564. In this classification were found the names not of heretical authors but of individual books, "which are being reproached because they contain a doctrine which is not sound or is suspicious or can be morally offensive to the faithful, even though the authors of these books never fell away from the Church."[130] For such books it was required that university censors purge from the works certain passages which in the opinion of the censor could cause scandal in the new post-Reformation religious environment. In this list, the name of Desiderius Erasmus is found just after Dante, whose writings were also forbidden. This *Index expurgatorius* was published in the Tridentine Index (also known as the Index of Pius IV).[131] Archbishop Brus's defense of Erasmus prevailed insofar as Erasmus and a host of others were indeed removed from the first category of heretics of Paul IV's Index, but Brus was defeated in his effort to have all of Erasmus's writings released.

In light of the total repudiation of Erasmus's works in Paul IV's Index, it is remarkable that only five of Erasmus's works (and an Italian translation of a sixth) actually remained completely forbidden. Forbidden were his satire, *Praise of Folly*, and his humorous dialogues, *The Colloquies*, which were intended to teach Latin to grade-school boys. Also forbidden were his books *The Tongue*, on the forbidden eating of meats, *Institution of Christian Matrimony*, and an Italian translation of the *Paraphrase on St. Matthew*.[132] All the other theological and religious writings of Erasmus were eli-

---

130. Reusch, *Der Index der verbotenen Bücher*, 1:325.

131. Ibid., 1:347n1, explains that the name *Erasmus Roterodamus* is listed in the first class of the Tridentine Index with a note: *Vide supra in litera D* (see above under the letter "D"). Under "D" it reads: "Desiderius Erasmus in the Second Class." This ambiguity has given rise to the misconception that Erasmus remained in the first class in the Tridentine Index, when in fact committee action had officially removed him from that classication.

132. Cf. Mansfield, *Phoenix of His Age*, 27.

gible for republication once the text had been reviewed by university censors. There is no doubt that the Council of Trent's action represents a bold and public correction of the extremely unjust policies of Paul IV. It was aimed to give Erasmus his due. Out of a corpus that comprises ten folio volumes and over 115 individual titles, only five works would now remained completely banned, and two of those five (*Praise of Folly* and *The Colloquies*) were of the genre of humorous and playful religious fiction. Though Erasmus had the company of Dante on the Index of Forbidden Books, whose name stood directly above his own, it seems that Erasmus's fate was different from Dante's. Most Catholics I have spoken with are not even aware that Dante was once a forbidden author. Erasmus's reputation, on the other hand, was permanently damaged by the action of Paul IV, especially as the personal memory of Erasmus's piety and devotion to the church faded. In subsequent decades at least two important saints of the Counter-Reformation, Peter Canisius and Robert Bellarmine, would take the side of Erasmus's worst critics and treat him virtually as a heretic.[133]

Tragically (in my judgment), Pope Paul IV's legislation completely banning the use of vernacular Bibles was officially promulgated by the Council of Trent in 1564, which stated that common experience proves that vernacular scripture reading by the laity "does more harm than good."[134] The Tridentine council mitigated Paul's IV's stance very slightly by allowing local bishops (rather than the Roman Inquisition) to decide whether to permit Catholics, on a case by case basis, to obtain and read scripture in the vernacular, but this was only to be allowed to individual Catholics who obtained permission *in writing* from their bishop. Even members of religious orders were not allowed to obtain vernacular translations without permission. Book sellers who sold vernacular Bibles to people who did not have permission slips from the Roman Inquisition would forfeit the price of the book to the bishop's treasury, "which is to be applied by the bishop to pious purposes."[135] According to McNally, this rule set the tone for the unbiblical atmosphere of post-Tridentine lay Catholicism.[136] The Catholic church would have to wait four long centuries before the papal office would officially encourage Catholics to make use of vernacular translations of scripture. The first to do so was Pope Benedict XV in 1920 in the encyclical *Paraclitus Spiritus*. Today the Catholic church's papal magisterium firmly supports the dissemination of vernacular translations of scripture.[137]

---

133. See Pabel, "Praise and Blame: Peter Canisius's Ambivalent Assessment of Erasmus," in *Reception of Erasmus*, ed. Enenkel, 129–59.

134. See Rule IV of the "Ten Rules Concerning Prohibited Books Drawn up by the Fathers Chosen by the Council of Trent and Approved by Pope Pius," in *Canons and Decrees of the Council of Trent*, trans. Schroeder, 279.

135. Ibid.

136. Cf. McNally, "The Council of Trent and Vernacular Bibles," 227.

137. See the document, "Post-Synodal Apostolic Exhortation *Verbum Domini* of the Holy Father Benedict XVI to the Bishops, Clergy, Consecrated Persons and the Lay Faithful on the Word of God in the Life and Mission of the Church" (Vatican City: Libreria Editrice Vaticana, 2010).

SELECTED BIBLIOGRAPHY

Primary Sources
Editions of Origen's Works (by editor/translator)

Balthasar, H. Urs von, ed. *Origen: Spirit and Fire. A Thematic Anthology of His Writings.* Translated by R. J. Daly. Washington, D.C.: The Catholic University of America Press, 1984.

Barkley, G. W., trans. Origen. *Homilies on Leviticus, 1–16.* FOTC 83. Washington, D.C.: The Catholic University of America Press, 1990.

Borret. M., trans. Origène. *Homélies sur Ezéchiel.* SC 352. Paris: Cerf, 1989.

Bruce. B., trans. Origen. *Homilies on Joshua.* Edited by C. White. FOTC 105. Washington, D.C.: The Catholic University of America Press, 2002.

Chadwick, H., trans. *Alexandrian Christianity: Selected Translations of Clement and Origen.* Edited by H. Chadwick and J. E. L. Oulton. LCC 2. Philadelphia: Westminster, 1954.

Crouzel, H., and L. Brésard, eds. and trans. Origène. *Homélies sur les Psaumes 36 à 38.* Texte critique établi par E. Prinzivalli. SC 411. Paris: Cerf, 1995.

Dively Lauro, E., trans. Origen. *Homilies on Judges.* FOTC 119. Washington, D.C.: The Catholic University of America Press, 2009.

Heine, R., ed. and trans. *The Commentaries of Origen and St Jerome on St Paul's Epistle to the Ephesians.* Oxford: Oxford University Press, 2002.

———, ed. Origen. *Commentary on the Gospel according to John, Books 1–10.* FOTC 80. Washington, D.C.: The Catholic University of America Press, 1989.

———, ed. Origen. *Commentary on the Gospel according to John, Books 13–32.* FOTC 89. Washington, D.C.: The Catholic University of America Press, 1993.

———, ed. and trans. Origen. *Homilies on Genesis and Exodus.* FOTC 71. Washington, D.C.: The Catholic University of America Press, 1981.

Lawson, R. P., ed. and trans. Origen. *The Song of Songs, Commentary and Homilies.* ACW 26. Westminster, Md.: Newman, 1957.

Lienhard, J., trans. Origen. *Homilies on Luke, Fragments on Luke.* FOTC 94. Washington, D.C.: The Catholic University of America Press, 1996.

Scheck, T. P., trans. Origen. *Commentary on the Epistle to the Romans.* 2 vols. FOTC 103 and 104. Washington, D.C.: The Catholic University of America Press, 2001–2.

———, trans. Origen. *Homilies on Ezekiel*. ACW 62. Mahwah, N.J.: Newman Press, 2009.
———, trans. Origen. *Homilies on Numbers*. Downers Grove, Ill.: Intervarsity Press, 2010.
———, trans. *Pamphilus' Apology for Origen*. FOTC 120. Washington, D.C.: The Catholic University of America Press, 2010.
Smith, J. C., trans. Origen. *Homilies on Jeremiah, Homily on 1 Kings 28*. FOTC 97. Washington, D.C.: The Catholic University of America Press, 1998.

Editions of Desiderius Erasmus's Works (by editor/translator)

Adams, Robert M., ed. *Desiderius Erasmus, The Praise of Folly and Other Writings*. New York: Norton, 1989.
Allen, P. S., H. M. Allen, and H. W. Garrod, eds. *Opus epistolarum Desiderii Erasmi Roterodami*. 12 vols. Oxford: Oxford University Press, 1906–58.
Brady, J., and J. Olin. Desiderius Erasmus, *Patristic Scholarship: The Edition of St. Jerome*. CWE 61. Toronto: University of Toronto Press, 1992.
Dolan, John P., ed. *The Essential Erasmus*. New York: Mentor, 1964.
Leclerc, Jean. *Desiderii Erasmi Roterodami Opera Omnia*. 10 vols. Leiden, 1703–6; reprinted in Hildesheim: Olms, 1961–62.
Olin, John C., ed. *Christian Humanism and the Reformation: Selected Writings of Erasmus with His Life by Beatus Rhenanus and a Biographical Sketch by the Editor*. 3rd ed. New York: Fordham University Press, 1987.
Rupp, G., and A. N. Marlow. Desiderius Erasmus. *Diatribe on the Free Will*. In *Luther and Erasmus: Free Will and Salvation*. LCC. Philadelphia: Westminster, 1969.
Trinkaus, C., ed. Desiderius Erasmus, *Controversies: De libero arbitrio. Hyperaspistes I*. CWE 76. Translated by Peter Macardle and Clarence H. Miller. Toronto: University of Toronto Press, 1999.
———, ed. Desiderius Erasmus, *Controversies: Hyperaspistes II*. CWE 77. Translated by C. Miller. Toronto: University of Toronto Press, 2000.
Welzig, W., ed. *Erasmus von Rotterdam: Ausgewählte Schriften*. 8 vols. Darmstadt: Wissenschaftliche Buchgesellschaft, 1990.

Other Works Cited

Backus, I. "Erasmus and the Antitrinitarians." *Erasmus of Rotterdam Society Yearbook* 11 (1991): 53–66.
———, ed. *The Reception of the Church Fathers in the West: From the Carolingians to the Maurists*. 2 vols. Leiden: Brill, 1997.
Bejczy, I. *Erasmus and the Middle Ages: The Historical Consciousness of a Christian Humanist*. Leiden: Brill, 2001.
Bietenholz, P. G. "*Concordia christiana*: Erasmus' Thought and the Polish Reality." *Erasmus of Rotterdam Society Yearbook* 21 (2001): 44–70.
———. *Encounters with a Radical Erasmus: Erasmus' Work as a Source of Radical Thought in Early Modern Europe*. Toronto: University of Toronto Press, 2009.
———. "Ludwig Baer, Erasmus, and the Tradition of the *Ars bene moriendi*." *Revue de littérature comparée* 52 (1978): 155–70.

Blowers, Paul M. et al., eds. *Dominico Eloquio—In Lordly Eloquence: Essays on Patristic Exegesis in Honor of Robert Louis Wilken*. Grand Rapids, Mich.: Eerdmans, 2002.
Boeft, Jan den. "Erasmus and the Church Fathers." In I. Backus, ed., *The Reception of the Church Fathers in the West: From the Carolingians to the Maurists*, 2 vols., 2:537–72. Leiden: Brill, 1997.
Bouyer, L. *Erasmus and His Times*. Translated by Francis X. Murphy. London: Newman Press, 1959.
———. "Erasmus in Relation to the Medieval Biblical Tradition." In *The Cambridge History of the Bible: The West from the Fathers to the Reformation*, edited by G. Lampe, 3 vols., 2:492–505. Cambridge: Cambridge University Press, 1969.
Boyle, Marjorie O'Rourke. "Erasmus and the 'Modernist' Question: Was He a Semi-Pelagian?" *Archiv für Reformationsgeschichte* 74 (1984): 59–77.
———. *Erasmus on Language and Method in Theology*. Toronto: University of Toronto Press, 1977.
Bradley, R. *The Roman Catechism in the Catechetical Tradition of the Church: The Structure of the Roman Catechism as Illustrative of the "Classic Catechesis."* New York: University Press of America, 1990.
Cain, A., and J. Lössl, eds. *Jerome of Stridon: His Life, Writings and Legacy*. Aldershot: Ashgate, 2009.
Chantraine, G. *Erasme et Luther: libre et serf arbitre*. Paris: Lethielleux, 1981.
———. *Mystère et Philosophie du Christ selon Erasmus*. Gembloux: Duculot, 1971.
———. "The Ratio Verae Theologiae (1518)." In *Essays on the Works of Erasmus*, edited by R. L. DeMolen, 179–85. New Haven, Conn.: Yale University Press, 1978.
Christ-Von Wedel, Christine. *Erasmus of Rotterdam: Advocate of a New Christianity*. Toronto: University of Toronto Press, 2013.
Clark, E. *The Origenist Controversy: The Cultural Construction of an Early Christian Debate*. Princeton, N.J.: Princeton University Press, 1992.
Cochlaeus, John. *The Deeds and Writings of Martin Luther*. In *Luther's Lives: Two Contemporary Accounts of Martin Luther*. Edited by E. Vandiver, translated by Elizabeth Vandiver, Ralph Keen, and Thomas D. Frazel. Manchester: Manchester University Press, 2002.
Cohen, J. "The Mystery of Israel's Salvation: Romans 11:25–26 in Patristic and Medieval Exegesis." *Harvard Theological Review* 98, no. 3 (2005): 247–81.
Collins, Thomas Aquinas. "The Cajetan Controversy." *American Ecclesiastical Review* 128, no. 2 (February 1953): 90–100.
———. "Cardinal Cajetan's Fundamental Biblical Principles." *CBQ* 17 (1955): 363–78.
Congar, Yves, OP. *A History of Theology*. Translated and edited by Hunter Guthrie, SJ. New York: Doubleday, 1968. [Based on the article "Théologie" in *Dictionnaire de Théologie Catholique* XV (Paris: Editions Letouzcy & Ané, 1946).]
———. *True and False Reform in the Church*. Translated by Paul Philibert. Collegeville, Minn.: Liturgical Press, 2011. [A translation of *Vraie et fausse réforme dans l'Église*, revised edition. Paris: Les Éditions du Cerf, 1968.]
Conroy, D. M., trans. "The Ecumenical Theology of Erasmus of Rotterdam: A Study of the *Ratio Verae Theologiae*." PhD diss., University of Pittsburgh, 1974.
Coppens, Joseph, ed. *Scrinium Erasmianum*. 2 vols. Leiden: Brill, 1969.

Courcelle, P. *Late Latin Writers and Their Greek Sources*. Translated by H. E. Wedeck. Cambridge, Mass.: Harvard University Press, 1969.

Crouzel, H. "A Letter from Origen to 'Friends in Alexandria.'" In *The Heritage of the Early Church: Essays in Honor of George Vasilievich Florovsky*, edited by D. Neiman and M. Schatkin, translated by J. D. Gauthier, 135–50. Rome: Pontificio Istituo Orientale, 1973.

———. *Origen: The Life and Thought of the First Great Theologian*. Translated by A. S. Worrall. Edinburgh: T&T Clark, 1989.

———. "Theological Construction and Research: Origen on Free-Will." In *Scripture, Tradition and Reason: A Study in the Criteria of Christian Doctrine. Essays in Honor of R. P. C. Hanson*, edited by R. Bauckham and B. Drewery, 239–65. Edinburgh: T&T Clark, 1988.

Daniélou, J. *Origen*. Translated by W. Mitchell. New York: Sheed and Ward, 1955.

DeMolen, Richard L., ed. *Erasmus of Rotterdam: A Quincentennial Symposium*. New York: Twayne, 1971.

———. *Essays on the Works of Erasmus*. New Haven, Conn.: Yale University Press, 1978.

———. "First Fruits: The Place of *Antibarbarorum Liber* and *De Contemptu Mundi* in the Formulation of Erasmus' *Philosophia Christi*." In *Colloque Érasmien de Liége: Commémoration du 450e Anniversaire de la Mort d'Érasme*, edited by Jean-Pierre Massaut, 177–96. Bibliothèque de la Faculté de philosophie et lettres de l'Université de Liège, fasc. 247.

———. "The Interior Erasmus." In *Leaders of the Reformation*, edited by R. L. DeMolen, 11–42. Selinsgrove, Penn.: Susquehanna University Press, 1984.

———. *The Spirituality of Erasmus of Rotterdam*. Nieuwkoop: De Graaf Publishers, 1987.

Denzinger, Heinrich. *Compendium of Creeds, Definitions, and Declarations on Matters of Faith and Morals*. Edited by Peter Hünermann, R. Fastiggi, and Anne Englund Nash. 43rd ed. San Francisco, Calif.: Ignatius, 2010.

De Vocht, H. *History of the Foundation and Rise of the Collegium Trilingue Lovaniense*. Louvain: Librairie Universitaire, 1951–53.

———, ed. *Jerome de Busleyden, founder of the Louvain Collegium Trilingue, his life and writings, edited for the first time in their entirety from the original manuscript*. Humanistica Lovaniensia 9. Turnhout: Brepols, 1950.

———. *Monumenta Humanistica Lovaniensia: Texts and Studies about Louvain Humanists in the First Half of the Sixteenth Century*. Louvain: Louvain University Press, 1934.

De Vogel, C. J. "Erasmus and His Attitude towards Church Dogma." In *Scrinium Erasmianum*, edited by J. Coppens, 2:101–32. 2 vols. Leiden: Brill, 1969.

Dolfen, C. *Die Stellung des Erasmus zur scholastischen Methode*. Osnabrück: Meinders & Elstermann, 1936.

Dorival, G., and A. Le Boulluec., eds. *Origeniana Sexta: Origène et la Bible/Origen and the Bible*. Leuven: Leuven University Press, 1995.

Douglas, R. M. *Jacobo Sadoleto, 1477–1547: Humanist and Reformer*. Cambridge, Mass.: Harvard University Press, 1959.

Enenkel, Karl A. E., ed. *The Reception of Erasmus in the Early Modern Period*. Leiden: Brill, 2013.

Epiphanius. *The Panarion of Epiphanius of Salamis*. 2 vols. Translated by Frank Williams. Leiden: Brill, 1994.

Eusebius. *The Ecclesiastical History*. 2 vols. Translated by K. Lake (vol. 1) and J. E. L. Oulton (vol. 2). Cambridge, Mass.: Harvard University Press (Loeb), 1980.

———. *Eusebius Werke: Die Kirchengeschichte (Die griechischen christlichen Schriftsteller der ersten drei Jahrhunderte)*. Edited by E. Schwartz and T. Mommsen. Berlin: Akademie, 1999.

———. *The History of the Church from Christ to Constantine*. Edited by Andrew Louth, translated by G. A. Williamson. London: Penguin Books, 1989.

Eusebius Pamphili. *Ecclesiastical History*. 2 vols. FOTC 19 and 29. Translated by R. J. Deferrari. Washington, D.C.: The Catholic University of America Press, 1955.

Flitner, A. *Erasmus im Urteil seiner Nachwelt: Das literarische Erasmus-Bild von Beatus Rhenanus bis zu Jean Leclerc*. Tübingen: Max Niemeyer, 1952.

Fürst, Alfons. "Jerome Keeping Silent: Origen and His Exegesis of Isaiah." In *Jerome of Stridon: His Life, Writings and Legacy*, edited by A. Cain and J. Lössl, 141–52. Aldershot: Ashgate, 2009.

———. "Origen Losing His Text: The Fate of Origen as a Writer in Jerome's Latin Translation of the Homilies on Isaiah." In *Origeniana Decima: Origen as Writer: Papers of the 10th International Origen Congress*, edited by S. Kaczmarek, H. Pietras, and A. Dziadowiec, 689–701. Louvain: Peeters, 2011.

———. *Von Origenes und Hieronymus zu Augustinus: Studien zur antiken Theologiegeschichte*. Berlin: De Gruyter, 2011.

Godin, A. "De Vitrier à Origène. Recherches sur la patristique érasmienne." In *Actes du Colloque international réuni à Mons du 26 au 29 octobre 1967 à l'occasion du cinquième centenaire de la naissance d'Érasme*. Mons: Centre universitaire de l'Etat, 1968.

———. "The Enchiridion Militis Christiani: The Modes of an Origenian Appropriation." Translated by H. Gibaud. *Erasmus of Rotterdam Society Yearbook* 2 (1982): 47–79.

———. *Erasme lecteur d'Origène*. Geneva: Libraire Droz, 1982.

———. "Fonction d'Origène dans la pratique exégètique d'Erasme: Les Annotations sur l´Épitre aux Romains." In *Histoire de l'Exégèse au XVIe siècle*, edited by O. Fatio and P. Fraenkel, 17–44. Geneva: Libraire Droz, 1978.

Hale Williams, Megan. *The Monk and the Book: Jerome and the Making of Christian Scholarship*. Chicago: University of Chicago Press, 2006.

Halkin, L. *Erasmus: A Critical Biography*. Translated by John Tonkin. Oxford: Blackwell, 1993.

Hartmann, L. N. "St. Jerome as an Exegete." In *A Monument to St. Jerome*, edited by F. X. Murphy, 37–81. New York: Sheed and Ward, 1952.

Heine, R. *Origen: Scholarship in the Service of the Church*. Oxford: Oxford University Press, 2010.

Humphries, M. "Rufinus's Eusebius: Translation, Continuation, and Edition in the Latin Ecclesiastical History." *JECS* 16, no. 2 (Summer 2008): 143–64.

Iserloh, E., J. Glazik, and H. Jedin. *Reformation and Counter Reformation*, volume 5 of *History of the Church*, edited by H. Jedin. New York: Seabury, 1980.

Jarrott, C. A. L. "Erasmus' Biblical Humanism." *Studies in the Renaissance* 17 (1970): 119–52.

Jedin, H. "Changes Undergone by the Image of Luther in Catholic Works on Ecclesiastical History." In *Martin Luther: 450th Anniversary of the Reformation*, 80–94, edited by Helmut Gollwitzer. Bad Godesberg: Internationes, 1967.

———. *Geschichte des Konzils von Trient IV/2, Dritte Tagungsperiode und Abschluss*. Freiburg: Herder, 1975.

———. *A History of the Council of Trent*. 2 vols. St. Louis, Mo.: Herder, 1961.

———. "Das konziliare Reformprogramm Friedrich Nauseas." *Historisches Jahrbuch der Görres-Gesellschaft* 77 (1958): 229–53.

Jerome. *On Illustrious Men* [*De viris illustribus*]. FOTC 100. Translated by T. Halton. Washington, D.C.: The Catholic University of America Press, 1999.

Kelly, J. N. D. *Jerome: His Life, Writings, and Controversies*. New York: Harper & Row, 1975.

Lackner, W. "Erasmus von Rotterdam als Editor und Übersetzer des Johannes Chrysostomos." *Jahrbuch der Oesterreichischen Byzantinistik* 37 (1987): 293–311.

Lienhard, J.. "Origen and the Crisis of the Old Testament in the Early Church." *Pro Ecclesia* 9, no. 3 (2000): 355–66.

Lortz, Joseph. "Erasmus—kirchengeschichtlich." In *Aus Theologie und Philosophie: Festschrift für Fritz Tillmann zu seinem 75. Geburtstag*, edited by Theodor Steinbüchel und Theodor Müncker, 271–326. Düsseldorf: Patmos, 1950.

———. *The Reformation: A Problem for Today*. Translated by John C. Dwyer, SJ. Westminster, Md.: The Newman Press, 1964.

———. *The Reformation in Germany*. 2 vols. Translated by Ronald Walls. New York: Herder and Herder, 1968.

Louthan, Howard. "A Model for Christendom? Erasmus, Poland, and the Reformation." *Church History* 83, no. 1 (March 2014): 18–37.

Lubac, Henri de. *Exégèse Médiévale: Les Quatre Sense de L'Ecriture*. 4 vols. Paris: Aubier, 1964.

———. *History and Spirit: The Understanding of Scripture according to Origen*. Translated by Anne Englund Nash with Greek and Latin translation by Juvenal Merriell of the Oratory. San Francisco, Calif.: Ignatius, 2007. [French original: *Histoire et esprit: L'Intelligence de l'Ecriture d'après Origène*, Paris: Montaigne, 1950.]

———. *Medieval Exegesis, volume 1. The Four Senses of Scripture*. Translated by M. Sebanc. Grand Rapids, Mich.: Eerdmans, 1998.

———. *Medieval Exegesis, volume 2. The Four Senses of Scripture*. Translated by E. M. Macierowski. Grand Rapids, Mich.: Eerdmans, 2000.

———. *Medieval Exegesis, volume 3. The Four Senses of Scripture*. Translated by E. M. Macierowski. Grand Rapids, Mich.: Eerdmans, 2009.

———. *Theology in History. Part One: The Light of Christ. Part Two: Disputed Questions and Resistance to Nazism*. Translated by A. E. Nash. San Francisco, Calif.: Ignatius, 1996.

Lukens, M. B. "Joseph Lortz and a Catholic Accomodation with National Socialism." In *Betrayal: German Churches and the Holocaust*, edited by R. P. Ericksen & S. Heschel, 149–68. Minneapolis, Minn.: Fortress, 1999.

Luther, Martin. *Bondage of the Will*. Translated by P. S. Watson in collaboration with B. Drewery. Volume 33 of *Luther's Works, American Edition*, edited by J. Pelikan and H. T. Lehmann. Philadelphia: Muhlenberg, 1955–86.

———. *De servo arbitrio*. In *Luther and Erasmus: Free Will and Salvation*, translated by P. S. Watson with B. Drewery. LCC. Philadelphia: Westminster, 1969.

Maguire, J. B. "Erasmus' Biographical Masterpiece: Hieronymi Stridonensis Vita." *Renaissance Quarterly* 26 (1973): 265–73.

Mansfield, B. *Phoenix of His Age: Interpretations of Erasmus c 1550–1750*. Toronto: University of Toronto Press, 1979.

Marc'Hadour, Germain. "Erasmus: First and Best Biographer of Thomas More." *Erasmus of Rotterdam Society Yearbook* 7 (1987): 1–30.

———. "Thomas More in Emulation and Defense of Erasmus." In *Erasmus of Rotterdam: The Man and the Scholar*, edited by J. Sperna Weiland and W. Th. M. Frijhoff, 203–14. Leiden: Brill, 1988.

Margerie, Bertrand de. *An Introduction to the History of Exegesis, volume II: The Latin Fathers*. Petersham, Mass.: St. Bede, 1995.

Martens, Peter. *Origen and Scripture: The Contours of the Exegetical Life*. Oxford: Oxford University Press, 2012.

Massaut, Jean-Pierre, ed. *Colloque Érasmien de Liége: Commémoration du 450e Anniversaire de la Mort d'Érasme*. Paris: Société d'Édition Les Belles Lettres, 1987.

———. "Érasme et Saint Thomas." In *Colloquia Erasmiana Turonensia*, edited by J.-C. Margolin, 2:581–611. 2 vols. Paris: Vrin, 1972.

McConica, J. *Erasmus*. Oxford: Oxford University Press, 1991.

McGuckin, J., ed. *The Westminster Handbook to Origen*. Louisville, Ky.: Westminster John Knox Press. 2004.

McNally, R. E. "The Council of Trent and Vernacular Bibles." *Theological Studies* 27 (1966): 204–27.

McSorley, H. *Luther: Right or Wrong? An Ecumenical-Theological Study of Luther's Major Work, The Bondage of the Will*. Minneapolis, Minn.: Augsburg Publishing House, 1969.

Merkle, S., ed. *Concilium Tridentinum, Diariorum, Actorum, Epistularum, Tractatuum nova collection*. 13 vols. Freiburg im Breisgau: Herder, 1901–2001.

Meslin, M. *Les Ariens d'Occident*. Paris: Éditions du Seuil, 1967.

More, Thomas. *The Complete Works of St. Thomas More, volume 15. In Defense of Humanism: Letter to Martin Dorp, Letter to the University of Oxford, Letter to Edward Lee, Letter to a Monk, with a New Text and Translation of Historia Richardi Tertii*. Edited by Daniel Kinney. New Haven, Conn.: Yale University Press, 1986.

———. *The Complete Works of St. Thomas More, volume 7. Letter to Bugenhagen, Supplication of Souls, Letter against Frith*. Edited by F. Manley, G. Marc'hadour, R. Marius, and C. H. Miller. New Haven, Conn.: Yale University Press, 1990.

———. *Responsio Ad Lutherum*. Translated by Sister Gertrude Joseph Donnelly. Washington D.C.: The Catholic University of America Press, 1962.

Murphy, F. X., ed. *A Monument to Saint Jerome*. New York: Sheed & Ward, 1952.

———. *Rufinus of Aquileia (345–411): His Life and Works*. Washington, D.C.: The Catholic University of America Press, 1945.

———. "Saint Jerome." *New Catholic Encyclopedia*, 2nd ed., 15 vols., 7:756–59. Farmington Hills, Mich.: Gale, 2002.

Nautin, P. *Origène, sa vie et son oeuvre*. Paris: Beauchesne, 1977.

Oelrich, Karl Heinz. *Der späte Erasmus und die Reformation*. Münster: Aschendorf, 1961.

Olin, John C. *The Catholic Reformation: From Savonarola to St. Ignatius of Loyola*. New York: Fordham University Press, 1992.

———. "Erasmus and Saint Jerome: The Close Bond and its Significance." *Erasmus of Rotterdam Society Yearbook* 7 (1987): 33–53.

———, ed. *Erasmus, Christian Humanism and the Reformation: Selected Writings of Erasmus.* 3rd ed. New York: Fordham University Press, 1987.

———, ed. *Luther, Erasmus and the Reformation: A Catholic-Protestant Reappraisal.* New York: Fordham University Press, 1969.

———. *Six Essays on Erasmus.* New York: Fordham University Press, 1979.

O'Malley, John, SJ. "Erasmus and Luther, Continuity and Discontinuity as Key to Their Conflict." *Sixteenth Century Journal* 5, no. 2 (1974): 47–65.

———. "Erasmus and Vatican II: Interpreting the Council." In *Christianesimo nella Storia: Saggi in onore di Giuseppe Alberigo*, edited by A. Melloni, D. Menozzi, G. Ruggieri, and M. Toschi. Mulino: Società editrice il Mulino, 1996.

———. *What Happened at Vatican II?* Cambridge, Mass.: Harvard University Press, 2008.

Oulton, J. "Rufinus's Translation of the Church History of Eusebius." *JTS* 30 (1929): 150–74.

Pabel, H. *Herculean Labours: Erasmus and the Editing of St. Jerome's Letters in the Renaissance.* Leiden: Brill, 2008.

Padberg, R. *Erasmus als Katechet.* Freiburg im Breisgau: Herder, 1956.

———. "Glaubenstheologie und Glaubensverkündigung bei Erasmus von Rotterdam, dargestellt auf der Grundlage der Paraphrase zum Römerbrief." In *Verkündigung und Glaube: Festgabe für Franz X. Arnold*, edited by T. Filthaut and J. A. Jungmann, 58–77. Freiburg: Herder, 1958.

———. "*Reformatio Catholica*: Die Theologische Konzeption der Erasmischen Erneuerung." In *Volk Gottes: Zum Kirchenverständnis der Katholischen, Evangelischen und Anglikanischen Theologie, Festgabe für Josef Höfer*, edited by R. Bäumer and H. Dolch, 293–305. Freiburg: Herder, 1967.

Pastor, Ludwig. *The History of the Popes from the Close of the Middle Ages.* 40 vols. St. Louis, Mo.: Herder, 1891–.

Peters, Robert. "Erasmus and the Fathers: Their Practical Value." *Church History* 36, no. 3 (1967): 254–61.

Quasten, Johannes. *Patrology.* 4 vols. Allen, Tex.: Christian Classics, 1975.

Reese, A. "'So Outstanding an Athlete of Christ': Erasmus and the Significance of Jerome's Asceticism." *Erasmus of Rotterdam Society Yearbook* 18 (1998): 104–17.

Renaudet, A. *Études Érasmiennes 1521–1529.* Paris: E. Droz, 1939.

Reusch, F. H. *Der Index der verbotenen Bücher.* 2 vols. Darmstadt: Scientia Verlag Aalen, 1967.

Rex, R. *The Theology of John Fisher.* Cambridge: Cambridge University Press, 1991.

Rix, H. D. *Martin Luther: The Man and the Image.* New York: Irvington, 1983.

Rummel, E., ed. *Biblical Humanism and Scholasticism in the Age of Erasmus.* Leiden: Brill, 2008.

———. *Erasmus and His Catholic Critics.* 2 vols. Nieuwkoop: De Graaf, 1989.

Sauer, J. "Erasmus, Desiderius." *The Catholic Encyclopedia.* 16 volumes. New York: Encyclopedia Press, 1917.

Schär, M. *Das Nachleben des Origenes im Zeitalter des Humanismus.* Basel: Helbing and Lichtenhahn, 1979.

SELECTED BIBLIOGRAPHY

Schätti, Karl. *Erasmus von Rotterdam und die Römische Kurie*. Basel: Helbing and Lichtenhahn, 1954.
Scheck, Thomas P. "Bishop John Fisher's Response to Martin Luther." *Franciscan Studies* 71 (2013): 463–509.
———. "Erasmus's Edition of Origen." In *Tradition and the Rule of Faith: Festschrift for Joseph T. Lienhard*, edited by R. Rombs and E. Hwang, 308–36. Washington, D.C.: The Catholic University of America Press, 2010.
———. "The Influence of Origen on Erasmus." In *The Oxford Handbook of Origen*, edited by Ronald E. Heine and Karen Jo Torjesen. Oxford: Oxford University Press, 2016.
———. "Justification by Faith Alone in Origen's Commentary on Romans and its Reception During the Reformation Era." In *Origeniana Octava: Origen and the Alexandrian Tradition, Papers of the 8th International Origen Congress, Pisa, 27–31 August 2001*, edited by L. Perrone, 2:1277–88. 2 vols. Louvain: Peeters, 2003.
———. *Origen and the History of Justification: The Legacy of Origen's Commentary on Romans*. Notre Dame, Ind.: University of Notre Dame Press, 2008.
———. "Origen's Interpretation of Romans." In *Handbook on St. Paul in the Middle Ages*, edited by S. Cartwright, 15–49. Leiden: Brill, 2010.
———. "Pelagius's Interpretation of Romans." In *Handbook on St. Paul in the Middle Ages*, edited by S. Cartwright, 79–113. Leiden: Brill, 2010.
Schulze, M. "Martin Luther and the Church Fathers." In I. Backus, *The Reception of the Church Fathers in the West: From the Carolingians to the Maurists*, 2 vols., 2:573–626. Leiden: Brill, 1997.
Sider, R. "Early Commentators in Erasmus's Annotations on Romans." In Paul M. Blowers et al., eds., *Dominico Eloquio—In Lordly Eloquence: Essays on Patristic Exegesis in Honor of Robert Louis Wilken*, 118–43. Grand Rapids, Mich.: Eerdmans, 2002.
———. "Erasmus and Ancient Christian Writers: The Search for Authenticity." In *Nova & Vetera: Patristic Studies in Honor of Thomas Patrick Halton*, edited by J. Petruccione, 235–54. Washington, D.C.: The Catholic University of America Press, 1998.
———. "The Just and the Holy in Erasmus' New Testament Scholarship." *Erasmus of Rotterdam Society Yearbook* 11 (1991): 1–26.
Siecienski, A. E. "(Re)defining the Boundaries of Orthodoxy." In *Tradition and the Rule of Faith: Festschrift for Joseph T. Lienhard*, edited by R. Rombs and E. Hwang, 286–307. Washington, D.C.: The Catholic University of America Press, 2010.
Steinhauser, K. B. *Anonymi in Iob Commentarius*. CSEL XCVI. Vienna: Verlag der Österreichischen Akademie der Wissenschaften, 2006.
Steinmann, Jean. *Saint Jerome and His Times*. Translated by R. Matthews. Notre Dame, Ind.: Fides Publishers, 1959.
Stewart-Sykes, A. "Origen, Demetrius, and the Alexandrian Presbyters." *St. Vladimir's Theological Quarterly* 48, no. 4 (2004): 415–29.
Surtz, E. *The Praise of Wisdom: A Commentary on the Religious and Moral Problems and Backgrounds of St. Thomas More's Utopia*. Chicago: Loyola University Press, 1957.
———. *The Works and Days of John Fisher*. Cambridge, Mass.: Harvard University Press, 1967.
Sutcliffe, Edmund F., SJ. "Jerome." In *The Cambridge History of the Bible*, volume 2: The

West from the Fathers to the Reformation, edited by G. Lampe, 80–101. Cambridge: Cambridge University Press, 1969.

Tracy, J. D. "Erasmus and the Arians: Remarks on the *Consensus Ecclesiae*." *The Catholic Historical Review* 67, no. 1 (1981): 1–10.

Trigg, J. *Origen: The Bible and Philosophy in the Third-Century Church*. Atlanta, Ga.: John Knox Press. 1983.

Vandiver, E., ed. *Luther's Lives: Two contemporary accounts of Martin Luther*. Translated by Elizabeth Vandiver, Ralph Keen, and Thomas D. Frazel. Manchester: Manchester University Press, 2002.

Verfaillie, C. *La doctrine de la justification dans Origène d'après son commentaire de l'Épître aux Romains*. PhD diss., Université de Strasbourg, 1926.

Verger, Jacques. "L'exégèse de l'Université." In *Le Moyen Age et la Bible*, edited by P. Riché and G. Lobrichon, 199–232. Paris: Beauchesne, 1984.

Visser, Arnoud. "Reading Augustine through Erasmus' Eyes: Humanist Scholarship and Paratextual Guidance in the Wake of the Reformation." *Erasmus of Rotterdam Society Yearbook* 28 (2008): 67–90.

Von Ranke, L. *History of the Popes: Their Church and State*, revised edition. 13 vols. New York: The Cooperative Publication Society, 1901.

Wagner, M. M. *Rufinus the Translator: A Study of His Theory and His Practice as Illustrated in His Version of the Apologetica of St. Gregory Nazianzen*. Washington, D.C.: The Catholic University of America Press, 1945.

Westcott, B. F. "Origenes." In *A Dictionary of Christian Biography*, edited by W. Smith and H. Wace, 4 vols., 4:96–142. London: John Murray, 1887.

Wicks, J. "Catholic Old Testament Interpretation in the Reformation and Early Confessional Eras." In *Hebrew Bible / Old Testament, The History of Its Interpretation, Volume II: From the Renaissance to the Enlightenment*, edited by Magne Saebo, 617–48. Goettingen: Vandenhoeck and Ruprecht, 2008.

Wind, E. "The Revival of Origen." In *Studies in Art and Literature for Belle Da Costa Greene*, edited by D. Miner, 412–24. Princeton, N.J.: Princeton University Press, 1954.

INDEX

Abelard, Peter, 72, 87
Achilles, 93
Adamant, 140, 145
Adamantius, 96, 110, 118, 138, 145, 150, 158, 169, 180
Adamantius, Dialogue of, 48, 51, 52
Adrian, 4
Adrian VI, pope, xxiii, xxvii, 181, 195–98, 201
Aegidius, 4
Aeterni Patris, 28
Alaric, 114
Albert "the Great," xxviii, 4, 14
Aldus Manutius, 92–94, 111, 162
Aleander, Jerome, xix, 92, 93, 96, 112, 132, 162
Alexander of Hales, 4
Alexander of Jerusalem, bishop, 47, 125, 145, 147, 148
Alexandria, Synod of, 90, 150
Amabilis, 77
Ambrose of Alexandria, 144, 145, 153, 154
Ambrose of Milan, xix, 3, 4, 10, 13, 20, 24, 35, 36, 47, 61, 71–80, 101, 103, 104, 118, 129, 146, 155, 172, 180, 203
Ambrosiaster, 27, 100, 101, 144
Ambrosius, Ferarius, 63
Amico, John F., 113
Amidon, P., 84
Ammonius, 144, 155
Anastasius, pope, 90, 160
Anna van Borssele, 1, 148
Annotations, 5, 12, 26, 27, 36, 41, 100, 106, 133, 174, 175, 176, 194, 207, 213

Anonymus in Iob, 95, 132, 165, 167, 169
Anthony, St., xii
Antibarbari, 28, 120, 121
Apollinaris, 79, 140
Apollonius, Rhodius, 139
Apostrophe, 167
Apronianus, 171
Aquila, 131, 158, 159
Aquinas, see Thomas Aquinas
Arianism, 43n1, 51–53, 78, 95, 132–34, 160, 166–69
Aristarchus, 122, 143
Aristophanes of Byzantium, 143
Aristotle/Aristotelian, xxv, 3, 5, 13–15, 19, 21, 22, 26, 28, 37, 40, 41, 89, 96, 107, 135, 181
Arius, 104, 126, 127, 134, 151, 168
Arnobius the Younger, xix, 24, 181
Assertion of Article Thirty Six, 103, 196
Atarbius, 81
Athanasius, xii, xiii, xix, 10, 22, 24, 47, 53, 73, 91, 132, 133, 163, 176
Athenodorus, 152
Auer, A., xxvi
Augustine, xii, xix, 3, 10, 11–16, 20, 22, 24, 27, 28, 32, 59, 68–76, 88, 90, 100, 101, 105, 107, 109, 110, 118, 129, 132, 135, 146, 149, 155, 161, 166, 169, 178, 181, 183, 196, 203, 205
Augustinian Hermits, xii, 92
Auxentius of Durostorum, 132
Averroes, 13, 107
Aymon, 4
Ayres, L., 52–53

227

228 INDEX

Backus, I., xix, xxxiv, 24, 87, 133
Bade, Josse, 95
Baer, Ludwig, 29, 127
Bainton, R., 62
Balthasar, Hans Urs von, xxxiv, 47
Balthasar von Hubmaier, 32, 41, 128, 206
Bammel, C. P. Hammond, 47–49, 52, 53, 69, 94
Baranina, 79
Bardenhewer, O., xxxiv, 24
Barnabites, xii
Basil the Great, xii, xiii, xix, 10, 22, 24, 47, 83, 84, 101, 133, 138, 146, 176, 188
Batmanson, John, xix
Beda, Noël, xi, xix, 34, 39, 96, 97, 107, 108, 110, 191, 192
Bedouelle, G., 207
Bejczy, I., 17, 27, 107
Bellarmine, 133, 189, 216
Benedict, St., xii
Benedict XV, pope, xxxii, 216
Benedict XVI, pope, xxxv, 49, 50, 216
Bernard, St., 14, 16
Beyer Moser, M., 53
Beza, Theodore, 206, 208
Biel, Gabriel, 4, 7, 35
Boeft, Jan den, xix, xx, 24, 112, 113, 138, 139
Bonaventure, 4, 14–16, 28, 87, 201
Boreas, 139
Borromeo, 204
Boudet, Michael, 96, 97
Boussart, Dean, 32
Bouyer, Louis, xviii, xxii, xxiv, xxv, 6, 7, 23, 24, 55, 56, 74, 191, 192, 198, 209
Boyle, M. O'Rourke, 6, 7
Bradley, R., 203–5
Brady, James F., xx, 117
Brattston, D., 65
Brenz, Johannes, 190
Bricot, 4
Brown, Raymond, 6
Brus, Anton von Müglitz, archbishop, 211–16
Bucer, 206
Buchheit, V., 52
Bultmann, R., 113
Busleiden brothers, 30, 119

Cain, A., 78, 79, 80, 116, 173
Cajetan, 32, 191

Calvin, J., 17, 206, 207, 208
Campeggio, 202
Canisius, Peter, 187, 189, 209, 216
Capito, W., 17, 127, 128, 206
Cappadocians, 53, 71, 79, 83, 84, 85, 102, 138
Carafa, Gianpietro, xxxv, 193–95, 206–10. *See also* Paul IV
Carmelites, xii
Carondelet, Jean, 104
Carrensis, 4
Cartwright, S., 72, 87, 107
Casarella, P., 15, 205
Cassander, George, 207
Cassian, John, 50, 76
Cassiodorus, 50, 86
Catechesis, catechist, xi, xx, xxxv, 44, 49, 121–24, 140, 144–47, 150, 153, 181, 182, 203, 204
Catechism of the Council of Trent, 74, 201–5. *See also* Roman Catechism
Catechumen, 44, 144, 146, 147, 155
Cervini, Marcello, 11, 200. *See also* Marcellus II
Chadwick, H., 54, 146, 177
Chantraine, Georges, xv, xxii, 2, 6, 9, 11, 12
Charles V, Holy Roman Emperor, 194, 197, 199, 214
Chieregati, Instruction to, 195
Christian philosophy, 73, 74, 141, 144
Christ-Von Wedel, Christine, 25, 26
Chromatius of Aquileia, bishop, 77, 114, 162–64
Chrysippus, 13
Chrysostom, John, xii, xix, 10, 13, 19, 21, 22, 24, 27, 47, 78, 81, 101, 102, 103, 133, 135, 138, 153, 163, 169, 170, 175, 181, 185, 202, 203
Cicero, 16, 22, 28, 96, 163, 165
Cleanthes, 13
Clement VII, pope, 198
Clement VIII, pope 207
Clement of Alexandria, 13, 146, 147, 157
Clement of Rome, 175, 176
Cochlaeus, John, 199
Colet, John, xxxv, 113, 119, 123, 136–37, 148, 154, 187, 188, 201
Collins, T. A., 191
Colloquies, 206, 211, 215, 216
Concilium de Emendanda Ecclesia (1537), 124, 208

INDEX 229

Congar, Yves, xvii, xxxi, 3, 39–42
Conroy, D., 6–13, 16, 19–30, 60, 104, 119, 185
Constance, Council of, 196
Contarini, 200, 208
Courcelle, P., 78, 85, 86
Courtebourne, 99
Couturier, 32. *See also* Petrus Sutor
Crane, M., 96
Cranmer, T., 206
Croesus, 85
Cromwell, Thomas, 28
Crouzel, H., xxxiv, 43, 46, 59, 68, 113, 120, 138, 139, 148, 149, 152, 153, 155, 170
Cyprian, xii, xix, 3, 4, 10, 13, 24, 109, 110, 141, 151, 179, 201, 203
Cyril of Alexandria, 10, 203

Daley, B., 68
Damascene, John, 22, 203
Damasus, pope, 77, 79, 80, 172, 173
Daniélou, J., xxxiv, 49, 70, 120, 150, 177
Dante, xviii, xxvii, 215, 216
De Lubac, Henri, xii, xv, xvi, xviii, xix, xx, xxii, xxxi, xxxii, xxxiv, 1, 2, 6, 32–34, 51, 54–68, 71–73, 81, 82, 86–91, 98, 110, 181, 185, 191, 198, 200
De Vocht, H., 30
De Vogel, C. J., xvii, xxvi, xxxv, 74, 191
Decius, 46, 120, 147
Demetrius, bishop of Alexandria, 44, 45, 124–26, 144–48, 150, 153
DeMolen, R., xiii, xxii, 8, 9, 208
Denifle, H., 3, 87
Deventer, provostship of, 199
Dibelius, M., 113
Di Bernardino, A., 15
Didymus, 47, 53, 78, 80, 91, 173, 174
Diogenes Laertius, 155
Dirks, 34
Divino afflante spiritu, 32, 34
Dolan, John, 100, 123
Dolfen, Christian, 26, 39
Dominican, xii, 28, 41, 191, 205
Donation of Constantine, 25
Donatus, 143
Dorp, Martin, xix, xx, xxiv, xxvii, xxviii, 18, 19, 20, 30, 34, 73, 121, 122, 187, 192
Dougherty, 18, 188
Douglas, R., 188, 198, 201, 214

Duns Scotus, John. *See* Scotus
Dupré, Louis, xxvi
Durand, 4
Dürer, A., xviii

Ebionite, 158
Eck, John, 73, 207
Edwards, M., 155
Egidius, 4, 107
Egmondanus, 34
Elton, G., 210
Emsted, John, xxv
Enchiridion, 24, 63, 99, 100, 104, 120, 190, 201
Enenkel, K., xvii, xxxiii, 117, 187, 190, 216
Epicurus, 155
Epiphanius, 81, 83, 125, 140, 149, 158, 182
Erechtheus, 139
Eusebius of Caesarea, bishop, 43–46, 53, 55, 64, 78, 79, 83, 84, 91, 113–20, 125–26, 129–31, 138–65, 172, 177–82, 203
Eusebius of Cremona, 77
Eustochium, 77, 156
Exsuperius, bishop of Toulouse, 77
Exsurge Domine, 196

Fabri, John, 195, 200, 202
Farge, J., 39, 71, 88, 96
Farkasfalvy, D., xxxii, 15
Faustus of Riez, xix, 24
Favaroni, Augustinus, 87
Feder, A., 161
Ferdinand, king, 202, 211, 212
Ficino, Marsilio, 88–89
Fifth Ecumenical Council (553), xi, xxxii, 47, 68, 83, 90, 98, 118, 129
Fifth Lateran Council (1512), 92
Firmilian of Caesarea in Cappadocia, 47, 151
Fisher, John, xixn14, xxvii, xxviii, xxxv, 17–19, 24, 25, 27, 29, 30, 33, 34, 38, 113, 136, 161, 188, 189, 197, 200, 201, 212
Flaminio, 210, 211
Flitner, A., 190, 202, 205, 206, 209, 212, 214
Florovsky, G., 64
Fox, Richard, 30
Franciscans, xii, 28, 99, 127, 135
Francis of Assisi, 99, 120
Fremantle, W., 97, 173
Froben, xxix, 22, 102, 110, 111, 113, 159, 194

INDEX

Fuchs, Leonard, 214
Fulgentius, 166
Fürst, A., 78, 83, 116, 173, 176

Gabriel. *See* Biel, Gabriel
Gaudentius, 175, 176
Gelasius, pope, 97, 98, 161
Gennadius, 50, 161, 175, 178
George, duke of Saxony, 139, 201
Gerson, Jean, 4, 14, 26, 27
Gesner, Conrad, 214
Giles of Viterbo, 92, 94, 106
Giovanni de'Medici, 192. *See also* Leo X
Glossa Ordinaria, 87
Godin, A., 27, 63, 99, 111, 113, 118, 120, 127, 132, 135, 143, 149–51, 154, 159, 164, 165, 179
Gollob, H., 202, 203, 211
Graybill, G., 38, 197
Gregory Nazianzen, xiii, xix, 10, 24, 47, 78, 79, 83, 84, 101, 138–39, 146, 173, 203
Gregory of Nyssa, 53
Gregory Thaumaturgus, 44, 47, 83, 114, 152, 157
Gregory the Great, pope, 59, 72, 118, 181, 203
Grisar, H., 196
Grammarian, 2, 65, 79, 121, 122, 143

Halkin, L., xxii, xxiv, 1, 6, 7, 100
Hammond, C. P. *See* Bammel
Harnack, A., 81
Haymo, xxv
Heidelberg Disputation, 196
Heine, R., 62, 63, 65
Heisey, D., 29
Heliogabalus, 152
Henry VIII, king, xxviii, 35, 193, 194
Heraclas, 144, 153
Heraclides, 46, 55, 144
Hercules, 128
Hero, 144
Herodotus, 96
Hexapla, 47, 78, 80, 82, 130, 131, 157–59
Hesiod, 50, 143
Hilary, xix, 3, 4, 10, 16, 24, 47, 61, 71, 74, 75, 76, 78, 101, 104, 166, 180, 203
Hippolytus, 45, 145, 149, 153
Holbein, Hans, xviii
Holcot, 4, 13

Homer, 50, 54, 76, 93, 96, 102, 143, 184
Horace, 129, 134, 153, 180, 182, 184
Hort, F., 52
Hosius, Stanislaus, 189, 190, 200, 212
Hubmaier. *See* Balthasar von Hubmaier
Huizinga, J., xviii, xx, 6, 34, 199
Huet, D., 63, 98
Humphries, M., 115, 116, 152, 161
Hunter, D., 80
Huss, John, 31, 41, 206
Hyperaspistes, xviii, xxvi, 74, 75, 100, 101, 103, 107, 127, 128, 190, 197

Ignatius of Antioch, 44
Ignatius of Loyola, 124, 195, 209, 211
Immaculate Conception, 5
Index expurgatorius, 215
Index of Prohibited Books, xviii, 18, 194, 205–16
Irenaeus, xii, xix, 24, 57, 109, 142, 145, 149, 158, 183, 203
Iserloh, E., 195
Isidore, 4

Jaki, Stanley, xviii
Jason, 23
Jedin, Hubert, xxxi, 39, 41, 195, 200, 201, 208–14
Jerome, xii, xviii, xix, xx, xxviii, xxix, xxxi, xxxii, 3, 4, 6, 10, 11, 13, 14, 16, 20, 22, 24, 27, 30–37, 45–51, 63, 65, 71–86, 91–119, 125, 129–34, 138–66, 170–82, 192, 194, 196, 203
Jesuits, xii, 24, 189, 209, 211
Joachim, Perionius, 63
Johannine Comma, 132–33
John XXIII, pope, xxi
John of Jerusalem, bishop, 47, 81
Johnson, L., xxxii
Jonas, Justus, 120, 127, 135
Jorgensen, K., 208
Jungmann, J., 146
Justinian, emperor, 68, 83
Justin Martyr, 57

Kabbalah, 136, 137, 185
Karlstadt, 128
Keating, K., 209
Keen, R., 36
Kellerman, J., 169

INDEX

Kelly, J., 50
Kleinhans, R., 123
Koch, A., 154
Komonchak, J., xxii
Koran, 206
Kötter, F., 123
Kselman, J., 6
Kurz, W., xxxii

Lainez, 209
Latomus, Bartholomew, 199
Latomus, Jacob, xi, xix, xxxiv, 3–8, 13, 20, 25, 30–34, 36, 101, 106, 108, 174, 191
Lee, Edward, xix, xxiv, xxvii, 49, 188, 195, 212
Lefèvre d'Etaples, Jacques, 1, 32, 176, 191, 201, 207
Leo X, pope, xxi, xxxiii, 5, 192–95, 201, 206, 212, 213
Leo XIII, pope, 28
Leonides/Leonidas, 43, 44, 119, 140–42
Lienhard, J., xxxiv, 61–62, 126, 174
Livy, 96, 129
Loci Communes, 35–37, 67, 197
Lombard. *See* Peter Lombard
Longland, John, 22
Lorenzo de Medici, 89, 90
Lortz, Joseph, xvi, xvii–xix, xxviii, 74, 124, 190, 191, 201
Louthan, Howard, 190
Luscius of Lanuvium, 161
Luther, Martin, xi, xii, xvi, xvii, xxiii–xxvi, xxx, xxxi, 1, 17, 25, 26, 28, 32–38, 40, 41, 66, 67, 73–75, 87, 92, 93, 95, 100–103, 106, 108, 127, 128, 132, 133, 151, 161, 188, 190, 191, 195–202, 206, 207, 214

Macardle, P., xxvi, 33
MacCulloch, Diarmaid, 210
Madruzzo, 11
Malloy, C., 25, 188
Mammaea, Julia, 46, 152
Mangan, J. J., xxv
Manilius, 196
Manrique, Alonso de Lara, 198
Mansfield, B., 6, 133, 202, 211, 215
Marcella, 77
Marcellinus, 166, 179
Marcellus II, pope, 11, 200. *See also* Cervini
Marcellus of Ancyra, 53

Marc'Hadour, G., 213
Marcion, 59, 151, 153, 154, 158
Margeri, de, B., 61
Martens, P., 59, 60
Martyrdom, martyr, xxviii, 43–48, 54–57, 78, 85, 105, 114, 119–22, 140–45, 151, 188
Mary, queen of Hungary, 199
Massaut, J-P., 27
Masson. *See* Latomus, Jacob
Maurice of Armagh, 4
Maximinus, 132, 169
Mayor, Thomas F., 210
McConica, J., xxiv, 100
McCool, G., xviii, xxii, 28
McCue, J., 16
McGuckin, J., 43, 45, 58, 80, 111
McNally, R., xxi, 7, 8, 11, 33, 136, 206, 208, 209, 216
Melanchthon, Philipp, xi, xxx, xxxi, 1, 35–38, 66, 67, 75, 108, 127, 197, 206, 214
Melania, 81, 171
Menander, 76, 96
Menno Simons, 206
Merlin, Jacques, 88, 92, 95–98, 104, 105, 107, 111, 112, 129, 132, 155, 159, 164, 165, 175
Meslin, M., 132, 169
Methodius, 52, 55
Miller, Clarence E., xxvi
Minervius, 77
Minos, 50
Mishnah, 185
Mommsen, T., 113, 116
Montanus, 151
Monte, del, cardinal, 200
Monti, D., 16
More, Thomas, xvii, xviii, xix, xxiii, xxiv, xxv, xxvii, xxviii, xxxv, 17–21, 24–25, 30, 34, 38, 73, 89, 113, 121, 122, 187–89, 200, 201, 212, 213
Moreschini, C., 205
Moria. See Praise of Folly
Morone, G., cardinal, 200, 209–10, 214–15
Murphy, F. X., xviii, 50, 81, 82, 116, 160
Myconos, 163

Nausea, Friedrich, xiii, xxxiv, 189, 199, 202, 203, 211–12
Nautin, P., 113, 114, 140, 152
Neri, Philip, 209

Newman, John Henry, xiii, xxxv
Nicaea, Council of (325), xi, 43, 52, 53, 106, 168
Nicholas of Cusa, 7
Nicholas of Diesbach, 112
Nichols, Aidan, 40
Nicolas of Lyra, 4
Nodes, D., 89–92
Noetians, 167
Norelli, E. 205
Notker the Stammerer, 86–87

Ockham, William of, 4, 26, 28, 35, 107
Oecolampadius, J., 17, 18, 32, 41, 127, 128, 206, 207
Oelrich, K., 199, 200
Olin, John C., xx, xxi, xxii, xxviii, 92, 99, 117, 124, 136, 195, 199, 208, 209
O'Malley, J., xvi, 24, 39, 40, 92, 124, 190
Opus imperfectum in Matthaeum, 169
Oreithyuia, 139
Oulton, J., 115, 116, 125, 131, 148
Ovid, 16, 129, 139, 153

Pabel, H., 187, 190, 216
Padberg, R., 123, 124, 189, 190, 202, 203, 207
Palladius, 50, 145
Pammachius, 77, 166, 179
Pamphilus, character in Terence's play, 163
Pamphilus of Caesarea, martyr, 44, 45, 47, 48, 51, 54, 55, 78, 81, 85, 90, 91, 95, 114, 115, 163, 179, 180
Pantaenus, 145
Pastor, Ludwig, 192, 209, 210
Patripassianism, 167
Pauck, W., 36, 37, 67, 197
Paul III, pope, 25, 124, 188, 198–203, 208, 212
Paul IV, pope, xxxv, 194, 200, 205–16. See also Carafa, Gianpietro
Paul VI, pope, 206
Paula, 47, 77, 78, 156, 166
Paulinian, 81
Paulinus, 79
Pelagian/Pelagius, xxvi, 101, 107, 161, 166
Pericles, 117
Persona, Christopher, 54, 88
Peter Lombard, 4, 13, 14, 18–20, 34, 73, 87, 106, 201, 203
Phaedrus, 139

Philip, Roman emperor, 153
Philo, 58, 61
Philocalia, 138
Pico della Mirandola, xxxii, 4, 69, 71, 72, 75, 88–92, 97, 98, 129
Pierre d'Ailly, 4, 26, 35
Piety, pious, xxii, 8, 29, 91, 110, 112, 119, 122, 127, 140, 141, 142, 144, 150, 163, 179, 184, 189, 198, 211, 213, 216
Pio, Alberto, xvii, xix, xx, xxi, xxi, xxiii, 14, 40, 132, 133, 192
Pirckheimer, W., 139, 207
Pius IV, pope, xxi, 207, 211, 215, 216
Pius V, pope, 204
Pius XII, pope, 32, 34
Plato, Platonism, 54, 89, 96, 105, 139, 140, 155
Plumer, E., 75–76
Plutarch, historian, 22, 50, 117
Plutarch, martyr of Alexandria, 144
Pole, R., 200, 210
Poncher, Stephen, 30, 119
Porphyry, 79, 140, 155
Potamiena, 145
Praise of Folly, xxiv, xxv, xxv, xxvii, xxviii, 187, 192, 206, 211, 215, 216
Pricoco, S., 161
Priuli, 210
Pseudo-Chrysostom, 169
Pseudo-Clement, 175
Pseudo-Dionysius, 14, 15, 22, 40, 203–5
Pusino, I., 92

Quasten, J., xxxiv, 24, 132, 167, 169, 176
Quintilian, 163, 167, 180

Ramelli, I., 53
Ranke, Leopold von, 211
Ratzinger, Joseph, xxii, xxxiv. See also Benedict XVI
Reedijk, C., 127
Renaudet, A., xviii, 6, 41, 74, 191
Reuchlin, John, 113, 136, 137, 185, 191
Reusch, H., 207, 208, 212, 214, 215
Rex, R., 27, 29
Rhenanus, Beatus, xvii, xxxiii, xxxiv, 99, 110, 111, 113, 117, 151, 190, 199, 207
Riordan, W., 15, 205
Roman Catechism, xvi, 74, 201–5. See also Catechism of the Council of Trent.

INDEX   233

Rombs, R., 67
Rousselle, A., 140
Rufinus of Aquileia, xxxii, 45–55, 69, 71, 78, 80–86, 90–98, 111–16, 123–25, 130–32, 139–80, 201
Rummel, E., xxvii, 23, 31–33, 39, 92, 106, 109, 110, 133, 191, 207
Runia, D., 58
Rusticus, 178
Rydstrom-Poulsen, A., 87

Sabellians, 167, 168
Sadoleto, Jacob, 188, 198, 200, 201, 212, 214–15
Sauer, Joseph, xvi, xxiv, xxv, 74, 192
Savonarola, 91
Schär, M., 88–98, 131, 160, 162
Schenk, W., 210
Scholasticism, xvii, xxii, xxv, xxvi, xxx, xxxv, 2–8, 12–42, 73, 74, 113, 135, 143, 161, 181, 191, 203, 204
Scott, M., 46, 69, 109
Scotus, John Duns, xxv, 4, 5, 7, 13–19, 26–29, 35, 107, 203
Scylla, xviii, 22, 23
Sedulius Scottus, 87
Serenus, 144
Seripando, 200, 209
Servius, 143
Severus, Alexander, 46, 152
Severus, Septimus, 43, 140, 141, 147, 152
Sider, R., 5, 111, 174, 176
Siecienski, A. E., xxxiv, 110
Sigismund I, 190
Simon de Lueres, 94
Sixtus IV, pope, 88
Sixtus V, pope, 207
Smith, Dominic Baker, 39
Society of Jesus. *See* Jesuits
Somaschi, xii
Souter, A., 33
Spinoza, B., 40
Spiritus Parclitus, xxxii, 216
Spoil, 161, 170, 175–78
Stadion, Christopher von, 189
Staupitz, John von, 207
Steinhauser, K., 132, 165
Stone, M., 195, 198
Strabo, Walafrid, 87
Suidas, 141

Surtz, E., xxviii, 19, 29, 33
Sutor, Petrus, 32, 33, 34
Symmachus, 131, 158, 159
Symplegades, 22, 23
Syrtes, 22, 23
Syrus, 152

Talmud, 136, 137, 185, 206
Tartaretus, 4, 13
Terence, 20, 76, 96, 143, 161, 163
Tertullian, 3, 10, 102, 104, 108, 113, 115, 126, 127, 142, 145, 151, 180, 181, 207
Tetrapla, 157, 158
Theatines, xii, 208
Theoctistus of Caesarea, bishop, 45, 47, 125, 147, 148
Theodorus, 152
Theodotion, 131, 158, 159
Theophilus, bishop of Alexandria, 81
Theophilus Salodianus, 94–95, 175
Theophylact, 27, 101, 103
Theseus, 50
Thomas à Kempis, 8
Thomas Aquinas, xviii, xxii, xxv, xxvi, xxviii, 4, 5, 12–18, 26–29, 35, 40, 41, 56, 69, 72, 87, 102, 107, 169, 191, 201, 203, 204, 205, 213
Thucydides, 26
Tillemont, 59
Trent, Council of, xx, xxi, xxiii, xxvi, xxxii, xxxv, 1, 7, 11, 16, 33, 34, 39, 74, 92, 123, 136, 190, 198, 200–211, 216
Trigg, J., 113
Trilingual College at Louvain, 30, 119
Turin, University of, 1
Turnus, 140
Tyndale, W., 206, 213

Ursatius, 176
Utopia, xxv, 19

Valentinus, 144, 145, 153
Valla, Lorenzo, 25–27
Varro, Marcus, 122, 129, 156
Vatican Council II, xxi, xxii, xxxii, xxxv, 28, 40, 206
Verbum Domini, 216
Verfaillie, C., 87
Vergara, Alfonso, 127
Vernacular translations of Scripture, xviii,

Vernacular translations of Scripture (cont.) xxi, 7, 11, 33, 41, 135, 136, 206, 208, 209, 216
Vincentius, 77, 130
Virgil, 16, 76, 96, 129, 134, 140, 143, 153, 181
Vitrier, Jean, 99, 100, 113, 120, 127, 135, 141, 150, 164, 181, 182, 183
Vives, Juan Luis, 30
Voderholzer, R., xix, xxxiv
Vredeveld, H., 128, 154
Vulgate Bible, 2, 11, 26, 29, 32, 33, 34, 38, 133

Wagner, M., 116, 161
Waldstein, Michael, 214
Warham, William, 201
Wengert, T., 67, 75

Westcott, B., 95
Wicks, J., 191, 207
Wiles, M., 65, 66
William of Paris, 4, 35
William of St. Thierry, 13, 72, 87
Williams, Megan Hale, 50, 78, 80, 84
Wind, E., 92–94
Winkler, 6
Worms, Diet of, 92, 93, 124, 127
Wyclif, 32, 41, 196, 206

Yarnold, E., 146

Zasius, Ulrich, 207
Zephyrinus, pope, 153
Zuniga, 132
Zwingli, Ulrich, xxxiii, 17, 41, 127, 128, 206

Erasmus's Life of Origen: A New Annotated Translation of the Prefaces to Erasmus of Rotterdam's Edition of Origen's Writings (1536) was designed in Quadraat and composed by Kachergis Book Design of Pittsboro, North Carolina. It was printed on 60-pound House Natural Smooth and bound by Sheridan Books of Chelsea, Michigan.